The Quiet Warrior

CLASSICS OF NAVAL LITERATURE

JACK SWEETMAN, SERIES EDITOR

This series makes available new editions of classic works of naval history, biography, and fiction. Each volume is complete and unabridged and includes an authoritative introduction written specifically for Classics of Naval Literature. A list of titles published or currently in preparation appears at the end of this volume.

The Quiet Warrior

A BIOGRAPHY OF
ADMIRAL RAYMOND A. SPRUANCE

By THOMAS B. BUELL

With an introduction and notes by
John B. Lundstrom

NAVAL INSTITUTE PRESS
Annapolis, Maryland

This book was originally published in
1974 by Little, Brown and Company,
Boston, Massachusetts

Copyright © 1987 on the introduction and notes
by the U.S. Naval Institute
Annapolis, Maryland

Second printing, 1988

The photographs in this book, unless otherwise stated, are from the Naval
Historical Collection, Naval War College, Newport, Rhode Island.

The author is grateful to the following for permission to quote previously
published material:

The United States Naval Institute for the article "Admiral, R.N., 1776,"
by A. W. Moffat, published in the *U.S. Naval Institute Proceedings,* February,
1972. Copyright © 1972 by the U.S. Naval Institute.

Rear Admiral Samuel Eliot Morison for the following quotations from
History of United States Naval Operations in World War II: Volume VII, pp.
119–120, description of passage to Tarawa. Copyright 1951 by Samuel Eliot
Morison; Volume XIV, pp. 51–52, text of Japanese propaganda broadcast.
Copyright © 1960 by Samuel Eliot Morison; and from *The Two-Ocean War:*
page 162, assessment of Spruance; page 334, assessment of Spruance. Copyright © 1963 by Samuel Eliot Morison.

Vice Admiral Morton L. Deyo, USN (Ret.), for his letter to Admiral
Morison quoted in *The Two-Ocean War,* pp. 11–12.

W. W. Norton & Company, Inc. for the letter from Secretary of the Navy
Claude Swanson to Eleanor Roosevelt, quoted on page 514 of *Eleanor and
Franklin* by Joseph P. Lash. Copyright © 1971 by Joseph P. Lash.

The Viking Press Inc. for the paragraph on statesmanship on page 239 of
Studies in War and Peace by Michael Howard. Copyright © 1969 by Michael
Howard.

Library of Congress Cataloging-in-Publication Data
Buell, Thomas B.
    The quiet warrior.
(Classics of naval literature)
    Bibliography: p.
    Includes index.
    1. Spruance, Raymond Ames, 1886–1969.   2. Admirals—
United States—Biography.   3. United States. Navy—
Biography.   4. World War, 1939–1945—Naval operations,
American.   5. World War, 1939–1945—Campaigns—Pacific
Ocean. I. Title. II. Series.
V63.S68B8   1987   940.54'5'0924 [B]   87-15177
ISBN 0-87021-562-0

Printed in the United States of America

CONTENTS

INTRODUCTION

WHAT are the essential features that combine to create a truly effective biography? Certainly it is easy to detect their absence. Some purported biographers merely recite in broad fashion the primary events surrounding the life of their subject and sprinkle a few entertaining anecdotes into the narrative. They offer no deep insights into the individual's personality or his way of thinking. In creating the setting in which their hero or villain lived, worked, prospered, or declined, they are apt to become so engrossed with collateral events and stage setting that they lose sight of their subject.

The principal goal of a biography is to help the reader understand what a person was actually like, how he viewed life and how he reacted to the challenges that it posed. Thus, it is not only vital to have a grasp of what he did, but also to know *why* he did it. Only in that way is it possible to measure the man, to assess his strengths and weaknesses, and, most important, to gauge his impact upon events and his fellow men.

At first glance, Admiral Raymond Ames Spruance would seem an ideal subject for a naval biography, particularly a superficial one. All the major events of his naval career took place at such a lofty level that the whole Pacific Fleet, even many civilians at home, knew in a general way what he did in World War II. Hundreds of documents and many books describe what the forces under his command were able to accomplish.

What was Spruance's role in the victory over Japan? First of all, he emerged as the key leader in the most famous carrier action of history, the Battle of Midway in June 1942. Then, after a year's tour of duty as chief of staff to Admiral Chester W. Nimitz, commander in chief of the Pacific Fleet (CINCPAC), Spruance was given the Fifth Fleet. This became the principal Pacific Fleet amphibious command, charged with conducting the invasions of the Gilberts, the Marshalls, the Marianas, Iwo Jima, and the climactic assault on Okinawa. Spruance directed the vital thrust through the Central Pacific towards the Japanese home islands. Along with Nimitz and Admiral William F. Halsey, he stood in the first rank of naval leaders in the Pacific war.

As an individual, however, Spruance presents extraordinary problems for a biographer. He was a very private person, unemotional and undemonstrative in public. To a great degree he was unconcerned about his image, caring little for "glory" in the conventional sense. His gods were logic and reason. The character of Mr. Spock in the popular science-fiction series *Star Trek* could easily have been patterned after Spruance. The admiral competed not with others but with his own impossibly high self-expectations, and that is the way he judged his successes and failures. A man who relied on deeds rather than words to make his mark, Spruance seemed oblivious to what posterity would think of him. He did not like to speak publicly, nor did he do much writing if he could avoid it. He authored no wordy, self-justifying memoirs. His achievements, intellect, and integrity were responsible for the great respect accorded him by his peers.

For a number of reasons, Thomas B. Buell's *The Quiet Warrior* is able to surmount these difficulties and get to the heart of the man. As a naval officer Buell shared many of the same experiences, albeit two generations later, that shaped the young Spruance. Like Spruance, he attended the U.S. Naval Academy, learned the ropes at sea and ashore, gradually accepting more responsibilities. Both men knew the joys and perils of commanding destroyers. Finally, both profited from a close association with the U.S. Naval War College. The similarities in their backgrounds gave Buell an insight into the challenges Spruance faced in his earlier career and how he applied the lessons he learned to his commands during the war years.

Buell had the great good fortune of meeting the man whose biography he would write. Also, he had access to Spruance's letters to some of his close associates and to other historians. However, because Spruance did not often record what he thought or felt, it became vital that Buell assess the man by determining his impact upon others, particularly those who were near to him—his family and his staff. Mrs. Margaret Dean Spruance, the admiral's wife, and Margaret Spruance Bogart, his daughter, offered Buell an intimate look at the private Spruance through the eyes of those closest to him. Equally important was the testimony of several officers who served on his staff. Two especially valuable witnesses were his longtime friend and chief of staff, Rear Admiral Charles J. ("Carl") Moore, and his flag lieutenant, Captain Robert J. Oliver. The outcome of Buell's research and insight is a masterpiece of American biography, a work whose evocation of its elusive subject can be favorably compared to Rear Admiral Samuel Eliot Morison's classic *John Paul Jones: A Sailor's Biography*.

Perhaps the most important, though certainly not the fairest, way of judging an historical study is to assess its influence upon subsequent works dealing with the same subject. In other words, how does one book affect those that follow? By that criterion alone, *The Quiet Warrior* commands respect. It has come to be accepted as the authentic portrait of Raymond Spruance. Ever since its publication in 1974, virtually all historians who have dealt with Spruance in any significant way have cited this book. Whether or not these authors have chosen to adopt Buell's conclusions, they could not afford to overlook them.

What is particularly interesting to this writer is the manner in which other authors have reacted to the sections in Buell's book that deal with Spruance's two most controversial command decisions. Both concern his conduct of carrier operations, the first in the Battle of Midway, in June 1942, and the second almost precisely two years later in the Battle of the Philippine Sea. Coming up through the ranks as a surface-ship commander from destroyers to battleships, Spruance was largely unfamiliar with the intricacies of naval aviation, and carrier operations in particular. Whether or not this lack of specialized experience was detrimental to his handling of a carrier task force in battle is debatable. Certain aviators thought so, however, and smarted at serving under a non-aviator, who, they felt, did not really understand carriers and their capabilities.

The reports of Spruance's role in the victory at Midway, and how this role has come to be viewed by others, offer an instructive example as to the manner in which "history" is written and illuminate some of the pitfalls that ensnare unwary historians, who have either misread the evidence themselves or depended upon others who have. Historical myths once planted are almost impossible to eradicate. Spruance's actions at Midway have engendered a small, but tenacious, myth, which Buell's book does its utmost to dispel, though not altogether successfully.

To follow the growth of this myth, some background information is necessary.[1] In late May 1942 as the Pacific Fleet readied itself to do battle with the Japanese Combined Fleet near the tiny Central Pacific island of Midway, its main carrier commander, Vice Admiral Halsey, fell ill. Placed in overall command of the three U.S. carriers available was Rear Admiral Frank Jack Fletcher, a non-aviator who earlier that month had won the Battle of the Coral Sea, the first carrier-versus-carrier confrontation in history. To exercise direct control over Task Force 16 with two of the three carriers—the *Enterprise* (CV 6) and the *Hornet* (CV 8)—Halsey nominated his cruiser force commander, Rear Admiral Raymond Spruance. Admiral Nimitz accepted his choice. Spruance thereupon shifted his flag to the *Enterprise,* where, with the exception of his own flag lieutenant, Lieutenant Robert J. Oliver, he inherited Halsey's aviation staff under Captain Miles R. Browning, a most outspoken, prickly, and irascible individual.[2] Perhaps the aviators expected the quiet Spruance to sit back and let the more experienced aviation staff run the carriers. Such was not to be the case.

The morning of 4 June the American carriers waited in ambush northeast of Midway. Their primary targets were the four or five Japanese flattops radio intelligence indicated were leading the enemy ad-

1. The literature on the Battle of Midway is growing. Since the original publication in 1974 of *The Quiet Warrior,* the following books have appeared that relate to the battle: the late Gordon Prange's *Miracle at Midway* (New York, 1982), which is largely based on the fine 1971 Ph.D. dissertation, "Decision at Midway" (University of Maryland) by Robert E. Barde; H.P. Willmott's *Barrier and the Javelin* (Annapolis, 1983), which suffers from being based mainly on secondary sources; and the editor's *The First Team* (Annapolis, 1984), covering carrier operations in detail, with special emphasis on fighter operations. Herman Wouk's excellent fictional treatment of Midway in his novel *War and Remembrance* (New York, 1978) benefited strongly from insights imparted to him by Buell.

2. For the unhappy career of Miles Browning, see Commander Harold L. Buell, USN (Ret.) (no relation to Thomas Buell), "Death of a Captain," U.S. Naval Institute *Proceedings* (April 1986), pp. 92–96.

vance. They expected the first Japanese move to be a dawn air strike against Midway. While Fletcher conducted an air search, Spruance made ready to attack with nearly the full power of his two carrier air groups. He needed only a firm position report of the enemy flattops to send his strike planes toward their targets. Finally, almost two hours after dawn, a patrol plane report placed two of the Japanese carriers 175 miles southwest of Task Force 16. Fletcher, who also intercepted the message, ordered Spruance to launch his attack as soon as the enemy carriers were "definitely located."[3] At this point, matters become controversial.

According to most accounts, Spruance was worried about the range of his carrier aircraft, particularly his torpedo planes. Supposedly he thought that because the reported enemy position could be inaccurate, his planes might have to use up time and fuel searching for the enemy, reducing their effective range. Because of his worry over these factors, Spruance is said to have made the highly conservative decision to wait *three hours* until his force, steaming at 25 knots, could decrease the distance between itself and the enemy to 100 miles. Then he would launch his strike. (What the Japanese would be doing for those three hours is not considered in these accounts.)

At this juncture, Miles Browning is alleged to have intervened to persuade his neophyte carrier boss to dispatch his strike in one rather than three hours—that is, at a range of 150 rather than 100 miles. Browning's motives, according to this version, were first, not to keep his carriers exposed to attack in their most vulnerable condition, with fueled and armed planes on deck, and second, to catch the Japanese precisely in that situation after they had landed their Midway attack groups. Spruance is said to have bowed to the superior logic of his chief of staff and rescinded his orders in order to launch when Browning recommended. Most of Task Force 16's planes did find the enemy, and in combination with aircraft from the *Yorktown* (CV 5), sank three of the four enemy carriers, a stunning victory.

Browning later received the lion's share of praise for victory at Midway, at least among the aviation community. Indeed, he was decorated with the Distinguished Service Medal, the citation for which included the following passage:

3. Order recorded in the Task Force 16 War Diary, June 4, 1942, in the Operational Archives, Naval Historical Center, Washington, D.C.

By his judicious planning and brilliant execution [he] was largely responsible for the rout of the enemy Japanese fleet in the Battle of Midway.

One naval historian has called Browning's action the "shrewdest decision" in the history of carrier warfare.[4]

In researching Spruance's role in the victory at Midway, Buell came up with a totally different version of the decision to launch the strike. He talked at length with Captain Oliver, who was present during the deliberations. On the basis of Oliver's clear recollections, Buell concluded that Browning never talked Spruance out of delaying the launch, because the admiral did not propose to delay it. Both Spruance and Browning wanted to strike the Japanese carriers as quickly as possible. Spruance simply ordered Browning to "launch the attack," and Browning, after some calculations, suggested that the planes take off about an hour later, when Task Force 16 would have closed to about 150 miles of the target.

The reasons behind Browning's suggestion can easily be deduced. The prevailing wind was from the southeast. To conduct flight operations, the *Enterprise* and the *Hornet* would have to turn into the wind and steam away from the Japanese at 25 knots for as long as it took to launch the 132 aircraft of the strike groups and combat air patrol. Browning knew that by the time so many planes took off, formed up, and departed, nearly an hour would have passed, and the range to the enemy would have opened to 175 miles. That is what happened. It had been necessary to close to 150 miles before launching to ensure that the aircraft would not have to fly farther than 175 miles, the accepted maximum effective radius of action, to reach their target. This was Browning's contribution.

Interestingly, one postwar study, conducted by the Naval War College when Spruance was its president, actually commended the admiral for not launching immediately the contact report was received.[5] After the time it took to launch them, his aircraft would have been at their extreme range, 200 miles. Spruance was willing to wait 45 minutes to put his planes 25 miles closer to the enemy and give them a greater margin of fuel to search for the enemy if need be. (Fletcher's air task group commander at Coral Sea, Rear Admiral Aubrey W. Fitch, had

---

4. Excerpt of Browning's Distinguished Service Medal citation and quotation from Clark G. Reynolds, *The Fast Carriers* (New York, 1968), p. 29.

5. U.S. Naval War College, *The Battle of Midway* (Newport, 1948), pp. 122–23.

launched his 7 May strike at 200 miles, which he felt was within the capability of the aircraft, and so it was.)

Buell marshalled strong, virtually overwhelming evidence for his case. In two instances his version was accepted—by this writer in his book *The First Team* (Annapolis, 1984) and by Ronald H. Spector in *Eagle Against the Sun* (New York, 1985). One highly popular recent account of Midway seems to try to have it both ways! In the late Gordon Prange's *Miracle at Midway* (New York, 1982), which cites *The Quiet Warrior* in its bibliography, Spruance is quoted as telling Browning to "launch everything you have at the earliest possible moment and strike the enemy carriers." (p. 239) The next page reverts to the old story, in which Spruance intended to delay the launch until he had closed to within 100 miles of the target and was dissuaded by Browning. This account is confused, to say the least.

In discussing the two versions of the Spruance-Browning incident, references to specific times have been deliberately omitted until now. With Buell's findings as a guide to an original document relating to the battle, it becomes possible to explain how this myth arose.

Virtually all published accounts of the battle use Midway local time (in Greenwich Civil Time, Zone plus 12) as their chronological framework. This would put the key times of the mythical version as:

0603   Spruance received the sighting report placing the enemy carriers 175 miles southwest.

0900   Spruance's intended launch time, when his carriers, after steaming three hours at 25 knots, would have closed to within 100 miles of the enemy.

0700   The launch time advocated by Browning, two hours earlier than Spruance proposed, and the time the strike was actually launched at the enemy 155 miles away.

In examining the original documentation of the Midway operations, one quickly discovers that the U.S. carrier task forces did not operate on Midway local time (Zone plus 12), but on Zone plus 10 or *two hours ahead* of Midway local time. It was a sort of daylight-saving time. Dawn on 4 June according to Midway local time was 0415, while on board the carriers it was reckoned as 0615. All of Task Force 16's documents are recorded in time Zone plus 10. When survivors of the battle are asked to recall specific events, they invariably do so in the context of the time they actually used, that is, Zone plus 10. Nevertheless, in 1943 a navy combat narrative on Midway, which has become the standard source of all subsequent historical narratives, converted all times to Midway local time (Zone plus 12),[6] thus creating the resultant confusion.

Convert the three times listed above in Zone plus 12 time, 0603, 0900, and 0700, back to Zone plus 10 (two hours later), and they will be 0803, 1100, and 0900. The discrepancy in the time zones used and the necessity of converting the times constantly back and forth to establish the actual hour an action occurred could easily cause a serious mix-up, perhaps even create a myth.

That is precisely what happened to Samuel Eliot Morison, in whose history the myth first appears.[7] In researching his volume on Midway, he relied heavily on the Naval War College analysis (set in Zone plus 12), but he did examine some original sources. One that he saw was the Task Force 16 War Diary compiled by Spruance's staff. It was kept in Zone plus 10 time, or two hours later than the times with which he was familiar. He read this entry for 4 June:

Time (Z + 10)

0838   CTF-16 [Spruance] informed *Enterprise* and *Hornet* that present intention was to launch attack groups about 0900, search attack procedure, each group to attack one carrier. Force will continue to close [after launch] to about 100 miles.[8]

Here are all the key elements of the myth refuted in *The Quiet Warrior:* Spruance wanting to wait until 0900 (Zone plus 12 time) to launch when his carriers would have closed to within 100 miles of the target. Convert the times in the War Diary entry to Midway local time by subtracting two hours, as Morison should have done, and a new picture emerges. There was to be no three-hour delay. Spruance intended to launch his strike at 0700 Midway time and would *thereafter* continue to steam toward the enemy until he was within 100 miles of them. That

6. Office of Naval Intelligence, ONI Combat Narrative, *The Battle of Midway* (Washington, 1943).

7. Samuel E. Morison, *History of U.S. Naval Operations in World War II*, vol. 4, *Coral Sea, Midway, and Submarine Actions May 1942–August 1942* (Boston, 1950), p. 113.

8. Task Force 16 War Diary, June 4, 1942.

information was tacked on to enable the pilots to find their carriers when they returned from the mission.

Morison, thinking he had discovered the reason for Browning's fame at Midway, was the one who created the fiction of Spruance's supposed desire to delay the launch. It did not arise from Browning's wartime reputation or from any recollections by participants. When specifically asked by Buell where he found the source of what has been here dubbed the myth, Morison was unable to remember.

Browning's credit for victory at Midway probably arose among naval aviators who thought that, because he was a pilot and Spruance was not, he must have been responsible for Task Force 16's success in the air. The pilots on board the *Enterprise* certainly did not go along with that. They had serious complaints about Browning's actions at Midway, and this is examined in detail for the first time in *The Quiet Warrior*. Browning's leadership was sorely tested and found to have serious flaws. His conduct there helps to explain his later problems as Halsey's chief of staff in the South Pacific and his eventual disgrace while captain of the second *Hornet* (CV 12).

In *The Quiet Warrior*, Buell exonerates Spruance of the blunder of planning to wait three hours to launch his attack. Not all historians have agreed with this assessment. Another aspect of Midway for which Spruance has been criticized, mainly by aviators, was his decision on the night of 4 June not to rush in headlong pursuit of the Japanese, who were withdrawing after the loss of their carriers. The pilots thought he should have headed west to enable them to attack the Japanese battleships and cruisers the next morning. As Buell rightly observed, Spruance feared running into more powerful forces at night, when his carriers would have done him no good. Japanese sources have confirmed Spruance's apprehensions. Yet some still felt Spruance threw away an opportunity for complete victory at Midway, as if four carriers sunk was not enough.

In treating Spruance's decisions leading up to the second controversial carrier action, the Battle of the Philippine Sea (19–20 June 1944), Buell concluded that the admiral's reasoning might indeed have been flawed. Spruance's Fifth Fleet was conducting the invasion of Saipan in the Marianas. While the battle raged ashore, Japanese carrier forces approached from the southwest with the intention of drawing the American carriers into a decisive, long-range battle. Spruance suspected that the Japanese might be seeking to lure his carriers away from Saipan in order to attack the transport force, loaded with troops and vital supplies. He refused to give his carrier commander, Vice Admiral Marc A. Mitscher, permission to steam to the west and attack the Japanese flattops. Instead he preferred to keep the carriers just west of Saipan and risk absorbing a long-range air attack so that they would be in position to deal with any Japanese force that might be approaching from another direction. On 19 June, the Japanese launched an all-out air strike on the American carriers, only to suffer a tremendous defeat at the hands of Mitscher's fighter pilots. In an action that became known as the Marianas Turkey Shoot, almost all of the enemy aircraft were destroyed without inflicting significant damage on the Americans.

Only after the Japanese attack had been repulsed did Spruance, convinced now that no Japanese "end runs" were bound for Saipan, release Mitscher's carriers to head west after the withdrawing Japanese. Late on the afternoon of 20 June Mitscher dispatched a strike at maximum range just before sundown. His aviators sank one carrier and damaged two others—submarines had sunk two big carriers the day before—but they suffered heavy losses in aircraft while trying to find and land on their flattops after dark. Mitscher and the aviation community believed that Spruance had wasted a magnificent opportunity to smash the Japanese carrier force once and for all, and in daylight.

Like most other historians of the action, Buell decided that Spruance should have gone after the Japanese carriers on 18 June, when they were first detected approaching the Marianas. Buell thought that in this instance Spruance depended too much on what he believed the enemy commander would or would not do and concluded that the Japanese posed a greater danger to the transports than to Mitscher's carriers. Another student of the battle, William T. Y'Blood, concurred with Mitscher's and Buell's assessments in his book *Red Sun Setting* (Annapolis, 1981). Of Spruance's decision to hold Mitscher back, Y'Blood commented (page 210):

> If Spruance had been more conversant with the aviation capability of his fleet perhaps he would have headed west for the "decisive" action.

It has occurred to this writer that Spruance was probably "conversant with the aviation capability of his fleet" and knew that its far superior fighters, radar, and antiaircraft guns could handle the Japanese air attacks. It appears as though he could not believe that the Japanese commander would be so bold as to challenge the American carriers to a slugfest, even at long range, and that the Japanese must have something else up their sleeve. They did not, and they paid for it.

It is ironic that in the two carrier battles he fought, Spruance hurt the Japanese in two different ways. At Midway all four Japanese carriers were sunk, but most of their aviators were saved. In the Philippine Sea, six of nine carriers survived, but almost all of the aviators died. Either way, the result was the same: the Imperial Japanese Navy suffered crippling defeats. The constant was that every time Admiral Raymond A. Spruance commanded an operation against the Japanese, they lost.[9]

Thomas Bingham Buell, the author of *The Quiet Warrior,* was born in Detroit in 1936 and spent his boyhood on a farm in northern Michigan. Having at an early age set his sights on becoming a career naval officer, in 1954 he obtained an appointment to the U.S. Naval Academy. At Annapolis his favorite course was naval history. He discovered how much he liked doing historical research and writing. After graduation in 1958, he found in the Naval Institute *Proceedings* an outlet and forum where he could publish articles and exchange ideas. He is especially grateful to the Institute for its encouragement of junior officers as writers. Another source of intellectual satisfaction for Buell has been the Naval War College, where he was first a student and then on the staff. The high point of his naval career and the fulfillment of a childhood dream came in 1973 when he took command of the *Joseph Hewes* (FF 1078), an Atlantic Fleet destroyer escort, later designated a frigate. Commander Buell retired from the navy in 1979. Today he lives in the Minneapolis area and is employed by Honeywell International.

One historian whose works Buell has read closely is Samuel Eliot Morison. Despite inadvertently creating the Spruance-Browning launch myth at Midway, Morison throughout his massive *History of United States Naval Operations in World War II* treated Spruance with the utmost respect and admiration. This viewpoint was transmitted to Buell, who became deeply interested in the admiral. Because of his growing experience in writing naval history, he was able to transform his interest into a superb biography, whose excellence was recognized

9. Two other books published since 1974 that relate in part to Admiral Spruance's career are the biographies of his great contemporaries by E.B. Potter: *Nimitz* (Annapolis, 1976) and *Bull Halsey* (Annapolis, 1986). An excellent overview of the Pacific War is Ronald H. Spector's *Eagle Against the Sun* (New York, 1985).

by the Alfred Thayer Mahan Prize in naval history. In 1980 he completed a second fine study of a famous naval officer, *Master of Sea Power: A Biography of Fleet Admiral Ernest J. King.* In it he deals with someone much different from Spruance in temperament, if nothing else, but he shows the same ability to draw out the essence of his subject and to render understandable his viewpoints and actions. Like *The Quiet Warrior,* it is also a classic of naval literature.

JOHN B. LUNDSTROM

The Quiet Warrior

The Quiet War

To Marilyn, David, and Melora

The opinions or assertions contained herein are those of the author and are not to be construed as official or reflecting the views of the Navy Department or the Naval War College.

CONTENTS

Part III: After the War

ILLUSTRATIONS

Maps and Charts

INTRODUCTION

RAYMOND AMES SPRUANCE was a professional naval officer, a warrior who commanded the greatest and most powerful fleet in the history of the world. His battleground was the Pacific Ocean, where he fought the sweeping naval campaigns of World War II. He began the war as an unknown rear admiral in command of four Pacific Fleet cruisers. By an act of fate, he was given command of two of the three aircraft carriers that won the Battle of Midway, the epic American victory that finally stopped the offensive momentum of the Japanese navy.

Greater responsibilities followed. His Fifth Fleet became enormous: hundreds of ships, thousands of aircraft, hundreds of thousands of sailors, Marines, soldiers, and airmen. His naval campaigns were fought over millions of square miles of ocean. His objectives were separated by vast distances. Spruance first seized the Gilbert and the Marshall Islands, two thousand miles from the main American base at Pearl Harbor. From the Marshalls his fleet leaped to the Mariana Islands, a thousand miles to the northwest, thence to Iwo Jima six hundred miles even further north. Spruance's final campaign was the invasion of Okinawa, an undertaking equal in magnitude to the Normandy invasion. Okinawa was adjacent to Japan—the American invaders were almost seven thousand miles from home.

Spruance remained almost unknown to the American public at war's end. He was shy and reticent and avoided publicity. History, he felt, would judge his performance in war on the basis of what he did, not what he said. Historians have since studied his battles and have made their judgments. "Spruance's leading characteristics were attention to detail, poise, and power of intelligent decision," wrote Samuel Eliot Morison. "He envied no man, regarded no one as rival, won the respect of all with whom he came in contact, and went ahead in his quiet way winning victories for his country."

Spruance's chief throughout the war was Fleet Admiral Chester W. Nimitz. "It is given to few Americans," said Nimitz, "to serve their country so effectively and at such high levels as did this man." Fleet Admiral Ernest J. King, the wartime Chief of Naval Operations, considered that Spruance was the most intelligent flag officer in the United States Navy.

Similar opinions have been shared by an inner circle of those in the military and the government who either knew of Spruance or about him. Still, not everyone has approved of his performance. There have been critics—writers and naval officers—who have held that Spruance did not appreciate the use of aviation, or that his caution prevented even greater victories at Midway and the Philippine Sea. But they are a minority.

The Navy has honored Raymond Spruance by giving his name to a new class of destroyers and to a new academic building at the Naval War College. He is now a mystical figure in the hierarchy of naval heroes.

The Navy, and naval historians, never understood Spruance during his lifetime. When he died in December 1969 at the age of eighty-three, he had become a legend with an aura of intellectual infallibility. The man, however, remained a mystery; he had a shadowy, elusive quality that persisted throughout his naval career and afterward. His private life, his feelings about war and about the naval profession, his motivations and his prejudices, his hopes and his fears, his very way of thinking—all were unknown, except perhaps to his family and closest friends.

His self-appraisals are startling. "When I look at myself objectively," he wrote just before his death, "I think that what success I may have achieved through life is largely due to the fact that I am a good

Artist's conception of USS *Spruance* (DD963), first of a new class of 30 destroyers. The *Spruance* was launched in November 1973. (Courtesy of Litton Industries)

judge of men, I am lazy, and I never have done things myself that I could get some one to do for me. I can thank heredity for a sound constitution, and myself for taking care of that constitution."

He was similarly unpretentious about his renowned intellect. "Some people believe that when I am quiet," he once said, "that I am thinking some deep and important thoughts, when the fact is that I am thinking of nothing at all. My mind is blank."

I first became aware of Raymond Spruance when I was a midshipman at the Naval Academy in the mid-1950's. Having a particular interest in naval history, I read versions of Spruance's exploits during my studies of World War II, especially in the works of Samuel Eliot Morison. Through Morison I received my initial impression of Spruance: a great yet modest naval officer with a superb mind, who had won important victories in the Pacific.

I met Spruance in the summer of 1963. At the time I was a Navy lieutenant, a student at the Naval Postgraduate School at Monterey, California. Hoping to write an article for a professional journal, I had phoned the admiral to seek his advice. He agreed to visit with me at his home. It was an impetuous act on my part. I did not know the admiral; I knew only that he lived in retirement at nearby Pebble Beach. In retrospect, I realize now that I was simply curious to meet him.

My vision of Spruance over the years had become larger than life. It was shattered when I met a spare man in his late seventies, of medium height, wearing old wash khakis and work shoes, who in no way fit my concept of an heroic admiral. He first showed me his garden and greenhouse—sources of obvious pride—and then we adjourned to his living room. Spruance sat in a rocking chair and told me to ask my questions.

I had prepared three broad, philosophical questions which I had hoped could be expanded into a lengthy discussion. To my surprise, Spruance answered them all in less than a minute. I was momentarily flustered. The interview appeared to be over before it had really begun, but I didn't want to leave. I had always been inquisitive about the personality and character and motivations of wartime leaders in high command, so I decided to see if Spruance would be willing to talk about the war in the Pacific.

The admiral was responsive, and our conversation lasted about an hour. His keen mind and decisiveness became vividly apparent. Beneath his calm exterior there emanated an aura of power and purpose that was awesome. His deceptive appearance had given me a false first impression. Now, clearly, he was indeed a fighting admiral who had led mighty fleets to victory in epic battles. My visit had become a profoundly moving experience. I have never before nor since met a man with such strength of character.

I never saw Admiral Spruance again.

I returned to sea and over the years continued my naval career in destroyers. In the summer of 1970 I came ashore as a student at the Naval War College in Newport, Rhode Island.

There is a legend that the college had been clairvoyant before World War II. Nimitz, for example, once said that we were able to beat Japan because the War College earlier had predicted almost everything that would happen through its war gaming studies. I decided to investigate whether that legend was true by using Spruance as the model. I chose Spruance because of my natural interest in him and because he had served three tours of duty at the college before the war. I hoped to discover how well the college had prepared him and his brother officers for World War II. The results of my study are contained in a monograph published by the college in 1971. It became the genesis for this biography of Admiral Spruance.

Professional curiosity was my greatest motivation in writing this book. So very little is known about our World War II admirals—and about Spruance, a master at making war on a scale and complexity that never again will be repeated, we have known the least of all. The longer that I studied Spruance, the more fascinated I became.

In this biography, I have attempted to rediscover Admiral Raymond A. Spruance, what he did, and why. Through him, through his successes and failures, and through his strengths and weaknesses, it is my hope that perhaps we shall better understand the professional warriors who serve in the Armed Forces of the United States.

Thomas B. Buell
Newport, Rhode Island
September 1973

CHRONOLOGY

3 July 1886	Raymond Ames Spruance born to Alexander and Annie Spruance, Baltimore, Maryland
2 July 1903	Spruance sworn as Midshipman, United States Navy
12 September 1906	Spruance graduates from Naval Academy
16 December 1907	Cruise of the Great White Fleet begins
13 September 1908	Promoted to Ensign
13 September 1911	Promoted to Lieutenant (junior grade)
10 March 1913	First command, USS *Bainbridge*
2 October 1913	Promoted to Lieutenant
30 December 1914	Raymond Spruance marries Margaret Dean
6 April 1917	United States enters World War I
31 August 1917	Promoted to Lieutenant Commander
21 September 1918	Promoted to Commander
11 November 1918	World War I ends
14 April 1919	Second command, USS *Aaron Ward*
2 May 1920	Third command, USS *Percival*

9 June 1924	Fourth command, USS *Dale*
3 November 1925	Fifth command, USS *Osborne*
6 July 1932	Promoted to Captain
30 April 1938	Sixth command, USS *Mississippi*
14 December 1940	Promoted to Rear Admiral
10 September 1941	Commander, Cruiser Division 5
7 December 1941	Japan attacks Pearl Harbor
4–6 June 1942	Battle of Midway
18 June 1942– 4 August 1943	Chief of Staff to Admiral Nimitz
19 June 1943	Promoted to Vice Admiral
5 August 1943– 8 November 1945	Commander, Central Pacific Force, and Commander, Fifth Fleet
20 November 1943	Assault on the Gilberts
31 January 1944	Assault on the Marshalls
21 February 1944	Promoted to Admiral
15 June 1944	Assault on the Marianas
19–20 June 1944	Battle of the Philippine Sea
19 February 1945	Assault on Iwo Jima
1 April 1945	Assault on Okinawa
2 September 1945	World War II ends
1 March 1946– 30 June 1948	President, Naval War College
1 July 1948	Spruance retires from the Navy
7 February 1952– 1 April 1955	Ambassador to the Philippines
13 December 1969	The death of Raymond A. Spruance

I

Before the War

Chapter 1

HERITAGE

RAYMOND AMES SPRUANCE was forged by his mother's fiery intellect and tempered by his father's serenity.

Spruance's mother, Annie Ames Hiss, had descended from nine generations of enterprising Massachusetts Yankees. The Ames family dominated her ancestry, which boasted scholars, clergy, patriots, pioneers, and pilgrims. Her mother was Annie Ames; her father was William Hiss, the scion of a wealthy, aristocratic Baltimore family.

A precocious child who had inherited the Ames intellect, Annie was loved and admired and spoiled. But the superficial education accorded nineteenth-century women thwarted Annie's aspirations, and when she was sixteen her grandfather wisely sent her to visit a relative—a consul in Genoa—who had a daughter Annie's age. There she spent two exhilarating years, absorbing European culture and broadening her horizons. She returned with an intellectual sophistication that she was eager to share with friends and family. But no one in Baltimore could satisfy her expectations.

Nor did Annie look forward to marriage and the raising of a family. Children required work, even with hired help, and Annie was physically lazy. Besides, marriage meant menial tasks that would stultify her mind.

Beset with dilemmas, she visited a friend in Indianapolis and there met a shy, quiet, gentle young man named Alexander Spruance. Alexander was a displaced descendent of five undistinguished generations of farmers, merchants, and slave owners who had lived in and near Smyrna, Delaware, just south of Wilmington. He proposed marriage and Annie accepted. They married in a Methodist Episcopal church in Baltimore on a late Thursday afternoon in April 1885. Then they returned to Indianapolis.

It was a marriage of convenience for Annie. She wanted to live in Indianapolis because she believed it was an enlightened community that would appreciate her talents. In Alexander, she had found a complaisant husband who would provide for her comfort and welfare. She saw that her married status would facilitate her entry into Indianapolis society.

Her first years of marriage were the happiest of her life. She thrived as president of a large woman's club, a forum for presenting her excellent papers and for meeting distinguished visitors. The literary world welcomed her when she became an editor with the publishing firm of Bobbs-Merrill, allowing her to associate with famous authors such as Booth Tarkington. It was all she had hoped for.

Then children came to complicate her life. Annie probably did not want children. Nevertheless, she became pregnant and returned to her family in Baltimore to deliver a son on 3 July 1886. She named her son Raymond Ames Spruance in allegiance to her Ames heritage and in memory of an illustrious ancestor, Bishop Edward Raymond Ames. Eighty years later Spruance stood with his daughter before a picture of the bishop. "If there is any good blood in us," he said, "that's where it comes from."

Spruance was a lonely child. Annie preferred her intellectual pursuits to child rearing, and Alexander was aloof and remote. The Spruance home was without love or warmth or spontaneous laughter. Seeking companionship, Raymond gravitated to the bustling family of Tom and Emily Dean, who lived across the street. There he found the affection and attention he craved but could not get at home. He especially enjoyed long carriage rides with Emily Dean. The two often visited Emily's relatives, including the home of a little girl named Margaret Dean. Margaret's family later recalled Raymond's visits, but Margaret was three years younger than Raymond, too young to remember the little boy with the sad eyes. She would marry him years later.

Annie spent the winters in Indianapolis but returned with Raymond to the East every summer to visit her family. The Hisses had moved to South Orange, New Jersey, and there Annie bore two more sons. The first was Billy—large, boisterous, and undisciplined, three years younger than Raymond. When Raymond was six, she delivered Philip, a sickly infant who was given little chance to live. The child survived, but at eight months he was frail, helpless, and clearly mentally retarded. Annie, although indifferent to her first two children, became intensely devoted to her defective son and swore to care for him.

Unwilling to abandon Philip, and unable to handle all three boys at once, she relinquished Raymond to the care of her parents and her sisters Sallie, Bessie, and Louie. His aunts—then girls in their teens and early twenties—adored Raymond. His four uncles would provide male companionship, and his grandparents would see to his education and character guidance. The bargain was struck. Annie returned to Indianapolis with Philip and Billy, and Raymond remained with his new family. The youngster was well pleased with the arrangement.

Spruance later recalled those years as the happiest of his boyhood. The Hiss home was a mansion on spacious grounds, and the family enjoyed the luxuries of wealth. His grandmother resembled his mother, being unusually intelligent but critical and domineering. His three aunts served as buffers, lavishing attention and substituting as father, mother, confidant, and friend. Spruance requited their love and later provided for their welfare until the end of their lives. They never married.

When Spruance began school he was shy and withdrawn among his classmates. A contemporary remembered that Spruance "was neither a leader nor an active participant in the boisterous running and shouting games that took place in the dusty schoolyard before school or at recess times. He always came to school with a neighbor boy who was a classmate and somewhat more robust, so that it sometimes seemed to me that Raymond rather avoided independence of action."

When Spruance became a famous naval leader, the same classmate recalled "wondering when or how such a great change had occurred in his personality—or were the elements of his greatness there all the time just temporarily blanketed by shyness?"

Spruance breezed through his schoolwork with high grades. He completed his lessons during the day, then left school empty-handed

Raymond Ames Spruance clutching his treasured
"London Maggie," 1888

while schoolmates carried books for homework. His teachers assumed
he was shirking and demanded that he too take books home. Spruance
acquiesced, but he never opened them.

He occasionally wrote to his mother. As a high school freshman he
was "getting along all right in school. I like latin best, algebra next and
don't like german at all." Annie had sent money for his clothes and had
instructed Grandmother Hiss to give him the extra for his personal use.
"I have $1.65 from two chickens and a doz. eggs," he asserted. "I have
no need for any money as my chicken [sic] bring me in sufficient
income. I want to thank you for it." He concluded the letter by
summarizing the books he was reading: *Captain Bonneville's Adventures*

Annie Hiss Spruance, 1884

by Irving; *Silas Marner, Ivanhoe,* and *The Talisman.* "The time is passing
very quickly to me and I hope it is doing so with you. How is Philip?
How are You and Papa? I enjoyed your letter very much. Write me
soon again. Raymond."

The stilted letter probably was written as a familial duty ("I have
been intending to answer your letter but I have been putting it off"). It
is typical of any boy who hates writing to distant relatives. But this and
similar letters are revealing. There is no suggestion of any love or
affection by Raymond for his parents. He refused their money and was
determined to earn his own. Clearly, he was alienated from Alexander
and Annie and was seeking his independence.

Raymond seldom saw his parents, except when his mother made her summer sojourns to Baltimore for brief reunions. Alexander did take Raymond to West Point, when Raymond was ten, to see if the boy was interested in the military. But Raymond was apathetic. Taking orders and marching in formation held no appeal to him then—or ever.

Spruance's blissful life suddenly ended when he became a teenager. Grandfather Hiss went bankrupt. The mansion and the servants vanished. Spruance was stunned that his grandfather's financial security had crumbled overnight, and the transition was psychologically devastating to him. Spruance vowed never to repeat the experience. For the next seventy years he was driven by an obsessive quest for financial security. In the end he had accumulated an estate worth a million dollars.

The now destitute Hiss family could no longer care for Raymond, and he reluctantly returned to Indianapolis. "It was absolute hell," he later said. Philip was too retarded to walk and too heavy for Annie to lift, and Billy was an incorrigible brat. By now Alexander was also bankrupt and had become a half-blind recluse. Annie, as an editor at Bobbs-Merrill, was the sole family provider.

Spruance's misery was intensified by the fact that he was a stranger to Indianapolis, and by his shyness, which prevented him from making new friends at high school and in his neighborhood. He made candy at home, and he wrote poetry. The school newspaper published his poems, to his mother's delight and to his own eventual embarrassment. He continued to earn money by raising chickens. His chief recreation was hiking—sometimes as many as fifty miles. And he accompanied his mother to numberless Methodist services, which he detested.

He thought about the future and wrote Aunt Louie, "When I leave here I am going to sell the chickens to Mamma. She won't be able to get along without the eggs. I am not going to give them away, because I paid for them all myself in the beginning and, while they have more than paid for themselves, that is my business, for I had to take the risk of them all dying."

Spruance turned sixteen several weeks after his 1902 high school graduation, and he returned to the Hiss family in South Orange. Unable to pay college tuition, Annie decided that he should go to the Naval Academy. It promised an advanced education and an honorable profession at no cost to the family. Annie sought help from Booth Tarkington and Harry New (the Republican Party national chairman) in her zeal to get her son a congressional appointment. In the interim, Spruance attended Stevens Institute in Hoboken. Having been reared and pampered by women, he sought through physical toughening to assert his masculinity and his independence. He would plunge into bitter winter weather without warm clothing, and to his grandmother's worried scoldings he would respond, "I won't be molly-coddled!" Throughout his life he continued to brave cold winds and cold waters, and to take pride in forcing his body to endure hardship and physical discomfort.

One day in May 1903, the newspaper announced that the local New Jersey congressman would sponsor a competitive examination the following day in order to select his Naval Academy appointee. Having heard nothing from his mother, Spruance took the exam. When he returned to the Hisses he found a telegram from Annie: she had secured an Indiana congressional appointment. His excited aunts phoned the New Jersey examining board to withdraw his name. The board objected. Two members hurried to the Hiss home, arguing that Spruance's examination score was so outstanding that they wanted him to represent New Jersey. Spruance concurred, because he had won the New Jersey appointment by his own efforts. "No!" his aunts insisted. "You must accept the Indiana appointment that your mother has worked so desperately hard to get for you." He relented and assented to go to the Naval Academy as a representative of Indiana, the state which had meant so little to him.

The Navy at the turn of the century was enjoying a renaissance, having been moribund for three decades following the Civil War. It had been a grim period in naval history. Congressional appropriations had been paltry. Ships had moldered and few had been replaced. Officers and midshipmen had been discharged and promotions had ceased. The Naval Academy had suffered from decrepit buildings, vacillating policies, and low morale.

One event and two great men resurrected the Navy toward the end of the nineteenth century. The event was the Spanish-American War. The men were Alfred Thayer Mahan and Theodore Roosevelt.

The war changed the Navy's mission from coastal defense and commerce protection to one of projecting American power throughout the world. Mahan was the prophet of the influence of sea power and an

Midshipman Spruance, 1906

advocate of American imperialism. Roosevelt was his disciple. Roosevelt wanted to implement Mahan's doctrine with big, new, powerful ships, and plenty of them. He needed many more naval officers than were then available, and the Naval Academy had to provide them. In the last decade of the nineteenth century the Navy had been small, and the Academy had supplied the Navy's needs for junior officers with an average of 43 graduates a year. Attrition had been severe, three nongraduates for every four survivors. The first five classes of the twentieth century slowly increased to an average of 60 graduates per year. When Roosevelt became President in 1901, the size of the incoming class doubled. Spruance's class was three and a half times larger than the classes that had preceded it a few years earlier. He began his Academy career with 266 classmates; some 209 would graduate.

The Academy had been established at Annapolis, Maryland, in 1845 at the site of an old Army installation, Fort Severn, at the mouth of the Severn River in Chesapeake Bay. Over the years its buildings had been constructed helter-skelter, subject to the vagaries of Congress and the Navy Department. By 1898 the buildings formed an ugly, unsanitary hodgepodge. The influential Board of Visitors demanded that they be replaced, and the Navy Department persuaded a reluctant Congress to authorize a sweeping construction program. The distinguished architect Ernest Flagg designed magnificent buildings, and work began as the Navy entered the twentieth century. The clamor and confusion of construction workers and machinery did not abate for many years.

Spruance was sworn into the Navy as a midshipman on 2 July 1903, one day before his seventeenth birthday. Annapolis summers are hot and humid. Spruance and his new plebe classmates sweltered as they went to their rooms in an ancient multistoried wooden barrack and began to adapt to a military routine. The simple things came first. The former civilians learned to square away their rooms, to wear a uniform, to spit-shine their shoes, to strap on their leggings, to stand at attention, and to respond to orders with "Aye, aye, sir," never "Yes, sir." The transformation had begun.

The Class of 1907 had much in common. They were white gentiles from predominantly upper-class and upper-middle-class families. Congress controlled nearly all the Academy appointments; although some appointments were awarded on merit (as with Spruance in New Jersey), most were acquired through political influence. The new plebes also were alike in that they had passed rigorous mental and physical tests, implying common characteristics and potential.

Young men sought an Academy appointment for various reasons. Some were Navy "juniors" (sons of naval officers) emulating their fathers' profession. The traditions of the Navy's earlier heroes and their glorious exploits impressed many young men, to whom a naval career promised adventure and honor. Some plebes (such as Spruance) were from respected families who could not afford a university education. For others, the Navy conferred a desirable social status that was otherwise unobtainable. And from a pragmatic standpoint, a naval career ensured modest financial security to all.

Regardless of background, Spruance's generation cherished patriotism. Most midshipmen were motivated to serve their country, although few had any conception of a naval officer's professional duties. Admiral Dewey and the Navy's triumphs in the Spanish-American War must have reinforced the nationalism of impressionable young men of Spruance's age, so the Naval Academy did not lack applicants.

The naval officer's raison d'être was the ship, a complex assembly of machinery which the midshipmen—as future officers—had to understand and master. Therefore they studied things physical, mechanical, and electrical. Steam, steel, explosives, ballistics, and navigation were their pragmatic considerations. Discipline and obedience, both essential to survival in a frail ship upon the perilous seas, were imbued as well. Ships and their equipment were operated under rigid procedures; deviation invited disaster. Subordinates questioned neither regulations nor orders. Above all, the Academy inculcated absolute loyalty to country and service.

The Academy's mission was clear: to provide uniformly conditioned graduates who conformed to the Navy's image of the ideal junior naval officer.

The Naval Academy would instruct Spruance in the same way it had taught generations of midshipmen before him, regardless of new buildings and a new President determined to invigorate the Navy. The Navy cherished its traditions and customs, and change came slowly. A half century after Spruance had graduated, the Academy was essentially the same.

At seventeen Raymond Spruance was a slender, handsome youth. His body was lean and wiry. It lacked athletic coordination but possessed vitality and endurance. His shy, quiet demeanor was unchanged from boyhood. During his Academy years few would know him well, even though the classes of that era were particularly close. Yet the friends he did make remained intimate and loyal to him throughout his life.

Plebe Summer was a grueling transition from civilian ways. During it the midshipmen had to learn basic military and seamanship skills to prepare for the academic year. Spruance suffered from the heat, as he always had and always would. Reveille sounded at 0600, followed by strenuous, continuous drills and exercises during the day. By taps at 2200 the weary midshipmen collapsed into bed. Marching was a daily torment. The ancient rifles were heavy, and the smaller midshipmen in the back ranks staggered as the weight increased with the heat and time of day. The colorful drillmaster, Lieutenant (later Admiral) Thomas C. Hart, pitied the "sandblowers" and offered to substitute lightweight wooden guns, a proposal they indignantly rejected.

Spruance hated every minute of it. He came to know a classmate, a short, pugnacious midshipman from Montana named Johnny Hoover, who hated everything about Plebe Summer as well. They became close friends.

The upperclassmen arrived from cruise in late summer, paused briefly to don civvies and buy train tickets, then disappeared for a month's leave. When they returned, Spruance discovered his inferior status within the Academy pecking order and was introduced to hazing.

Hazing was controversial and as old as the Academy itself. (It was also customary in most other civilian and military schools of the period.) Proponents claimed that it infused discipline and obedience and weeded out midshipmen who were psychologically unsuited for the naval profession. Better to screen the unfit before graduation, went the argument, than later, when weak officers folded in an emergency at sea or in the demands of war. Left unsaid was the fact that hazing also was an initiation rite for entry into the upper class.

Spruance detested hazing when he was on the receiving end and refused to haze plebes when he was an upperclassman. But he was an exception. Most midshipmen and naval officers accepted the practice— even though it violated federal law. The Congress in 1874 had decreed that guilty midshipmen were to be tried by court-martial and dismissed from the naval service. The Naval Academy did not enforce the law.

If Spruance ever had believed that Annapolis was a citadel of honor and virtue, he was disillusioned when the academic year began. The Academy officers violated federal law and the Academy *Regulations* by tacitly allowing hazing. Similarly, many upperclassmen regarded the Academy *Regulations* as rules to circumvent rather than to obey. Punishment often was confinement in an old sailing hulk, the *Santee*. It was a point of sardonic pride to have been a member of the "Santee Squad," immortalized by a group photo in the 1907 *Lucky Bag*, the Academy yearbook. The squad posed defiantly and unrepentantly with smirks, caps askew, and indolent posture. Spruance was not among them.

The severity of punishment added an element of danger that motivated the more daring to create even more clever and ingenious ways to beat the system. An idealistic contemporary of Spruance reflected sadly, "All of these things that I'd thought of as perfection in the way of midshipmen, I soon found were not so. My effort was to do everything perfectly the whole time I was a plebe, and eventually I found out that it just didn't pay. You couldn't do things that way."

The Naval Academy had no academic accreditation, and civilian universities considered it as a trade school. The quality of its instruction dismayed Spruance. It had two defects: a narrow curriculum and unqualified instructors. The curriculum was predominantly technical, leavened with a smattering of the humanities: Spanish, French, and a weak Department of English and Law. There were no electives. The midshipmen memorized details which were regurgitated during written examinations, then forgotten to make room for ingesting the next mass of new data. Most midshipmen failed to understand concepts and principles, and by the time Spruance and his classmates entered the fleet the machinery they had studied was obsolescent. Lacking knowledge of engineering fundamentals, many graduates were handicapped when they tried to understand the new machinery and equipment for which they were responsible.

Many instructors were naval officers, fresh from the fleet and lacking academic credentials because of their own deficient Academy education. They taught by rote, knowing only one way to solve the problems that were repeated annually, even though several other methods could achieve the correct answer. Spruance once solved a problem using an original procedure. He was briskly reprimanded by the instructor because he had failed to use the Academy method.

Spruance was a keen student with an inquisitive mind eager for new knowledge. His concept of education was to seek an understanding of principles which applied to a broad range of problems, encouraging the student to exercise sound reasoning and independent thinking. The Academy simply trained the memory. Still, as much as he disliked many Academy courses, he received excellent grades and assimilated the practical skills necessary to serve as a junior naval officer. And grades were important, because they determined class standing and the order of seniority for one's entire career.

Naval warships in the early twentieth century were driven by steam, but the Naval Academy did not forsake the virtues of teaching midshipmen the art of seamanship under sail. Spruance first practiced on spars and rigging located inside a drill hall, then clambered aloft on the three-masted square-rigged steel ships *Chesapeake* and *Severn*. He learned to respect the sea and the wind and their effect upon a ship; the handling of sails, sheets, and halyards emphasized teamwork and obedience. The rigors of heavy weather, hard work, and primitive living conditions developed fortitude. He gained self-confidence by working aloft and conquering any natural fear of height. The first sight of a tall mast can be overwhelming, especially when one knows that one will have to scramble up the shrouds, wriggle outboard on the yards, then grapple with heavy sails while clinging perilously in space with nothing below but a swaying footrope. Spruance was determined not to "squeeze the tar," a derisive term for timid souls who gripped the tar-coated rigging for fear of falling. He and his classmates displayed their ultimate triumph over natural fear by spiking their hats on the lightning rods atop the mast trucks, the end of the bowsprit, and the end of the spanker boom.[1]

Spruance first went to sea in the summer midshipmen cruise of 1904 aboard USS *Hartford*, Admiral Farragut's Civil War flagship. She combined steam and sail, and the midshipmen on the main yard frequently were sickened by the boiler stack gases. Spruance served as a topsail yardman where the air was clear.

To his chagrin, however, he discovered he was susceptible to seasickness. One myth holds that seasickness can be suppressed by will power. In fact, only modern medicine helps. At its worst, seasickness makes a

---

1. The Naval Academy long ago discontinued sailing cruises. However, the Coast Guard Academy and a number of foreign navies have retained this practice.

candidate for the naval service wonder if the life at sea is the life for him. Spruance was "a faithful supporter of the lee rail on all summer cruises," the *Lucky Bag* reported. "His dialogues with the wild sea waves were serious serials with semi-hourly installments." Spruance stayed sick in heavy weather throughout his career.

He was much relieved when *Hartford* entered calm anchorages in pleasant New England seaports. The people were friendly and the girls easily charmed. The hotels and inns were oases of food for famished midshipmen with enormous appetites whetted by salt air and hard work. Good New England lobster stew ashore was a godsend, for the shipboard food was vile. Meat was casually dropped on deck, the bread had brown weevils that "would run out and take a look at you and then run back in again," and the stench of rotten potatoes was gagging inside a hot ship without ventilation.

Following his first sea cruise, Spruance took his first leave in the late summer of 1904, with his parents in Indianapolis. After weeks at sea he was hard and slim, and his bronzed face and arms were a handsome contrast to his starched white uniform. A friend of his mother arranged a dinner dance in his honor, doubtless over his objections. Although proud of his uniform and status, he surely was self-conscious and extremely reluctant to display himself publicly.

The young ladies who had been invited were atwitter at the prospect of meeting Midshipman Spruance, whom they naïvely regarded as a naval officer. The star attraction was ill at ease all evening, and his future wife, meeting him for the first time, thought he was handsome but stuffy. Afterward she reported to her family that Raymond had stood the entire evening—probably to avoid wrinkling his splendid white uniform. Margaret Dean did not see him again for seven years.

Another year of instruction and a second summer cruise passed uneventfully. Following a month of leave, the Class of 1907 gathered for the hallowed Class Supper in Washington, D.C., in the fall of 1905. It was their last happy time together. They ate well, drank too much, sang "Anchors Aweigh" (originally the 1907 Class March), and basked in fellowship. The dinner was, in fact, the consecration of their class unity.

It was an important night to Spruance. He permanently retained his personal program of the great banquet, the last page containing signatures of twenty-two of his table companions and classmates. It is not difficult to visualize them, that emotion-charged night, pledging eternal friendship and allegiance to the Class of 1907.

Disaster struck that fall. It began with a fight between two midshipmen, the customary way to settle feuds. The clandestine fights resembled duels and were governed by elaborate rules. Although illegal, they were allowed, just as hazing was allowed. In early November, Midshipman James R. Branch, Jr., died as a result of blows received while fighting Midshipman Minor Meriwether, Jr.

Branch's death became a scandal that aroused congressional investigations, newspaper notoriety, and public wrath. All and any hazing, however minor, became associated with fighting and was furiously condemned.

The Navy responded by sanctimoniously prosecuting its midshipmen under the antihazing law it had ignored for twenty-eight years. The midshipmen grew demoralized as one after another was discharged from the naval service. But reason finally prevailed. Nearly all the midshipmen had indulged in one form of hazing or another. If the purge continued few would remain at the Academy, so lesser punishments were awarded in lieu of wholesale dismissals. Spruance most likely was one of the few midshipmen who escaped involvement. Curiously enough, there is no record of public censure by the Navy of the Academy officials who had failed to enforce the law prior to that fatal day in November 1905.

Life returned to a semblance of normality. Wounds healed but scars remained. President Roosevelt was anxious to man his new battleships, so Spruance and eighty-six classmates, the upper third of the class, remained at the Academy during the summer of 1906 to complete their studies for an early graduation that September. The other two-thirds (the "wooden ones") set sail for another East Coast summer cruise. The class never again assembled as one body.

Spruance graduated on 12 September 1906, standing twenty-fifth in a class of 209. The 1907 *Lucky Bag* recorded that he had acquired the nickname "Sprew" and that he was a "shy young thing with a rather sober, earnest face and the innocent disposition of an ingenue. . . . Would never hurt anything or anybody except in the line of duty."

Spruance hated the Naval Academy and vowed never to return. He deplored its academic standards and disliked its military routine, although he did regard it as a "fine place" to discipline and train future naval officers and to eliminate unsuitable candidates. His unhappiness as a midshipman could have been redirected at the Navy. But there is an old saying among midshipmen not to judge the Navy by one's experiences at the Academy. Keep an open mind and withhold final judgment until you graduate and have served in the fleet. There you shall find the real Navy.

Chapter 2

THE APPRENTICE

SPRUANCE left Annapolis as a twenty-year-old passed midshipman. He would serve two years in this capacity, could not marry, would earn $950 per annum, and would gain practical sea experience while proving himself worthy to become a naval officer. If he did well and passed a written examination, he would eventually be commissioned Ensign, United States Navy.

The 1906 United States Navy was a jumble of dissimilar ships handicapped for want of men. It was equal in tonnage to other major navies, but its 1160-man officer corps was only half the strength of comparable naval powers. The older ships had been stripped to provide the new battleships with crews for the 1907 world cruise of the Great White Fleet.

Nevertheless, the Navy had progressed and was now rated the world's second most powerful, ranking behind Great Britain and before France, Japan, and Germany in that order. Power was measured in quantity and quality of ships. The Navy's 276 ships in commission and 37 more being built or authorized impressed the naval experts. For a number of reasons, Roosevelt concentrated on building battleships, despite the need for smaller warships and auxiliaries.

Perceptive naval officers realized that American ships did not match the technological superiority of the Royal Navy, whose revolutionary

HMS *Dreadnaught* boasted armament, armor, and an engineering plant surpassing those of any ship afloat. In contrast, American ships were cluttered with guns of many sizes, protected by armor of many configurations, propelled by engineering plants of many designs, and built by many shipyards of varying competence. *Dreadnaught* had wreaked instant obsolescence upon all other navies.

The Navy's most important asset was its men. Here even more trouble brewed. Officer promotion was based upon longevity rather than performance, and senior officers were too old. Admirals first flew their flags about a year and a half before mandatory retirement at age sixty-two, hardly long enough to learn their job. Captains averaged nearly fifty-eight and often were physically unfit for the rigors of command at sea. Promotion was sluggish, and Congress would not authorize remedial legislation. The Secretary of the Navy voiced a dire future if Congress did not soon act. He predicted that members of Spruance's class would take twenty-five years for promotion to lieutenant.

Enlisted manning was correspondingly grim. The Navy was understrength by 4,000 men, having on board about 32,000 souls. Although a sailor's life had many drawbacks (such as civilian hostility), plenty of young men applied for enlistment. But the Navy was choosy and could not fill its quotas. Desertion depleted the ranks. One out of ten sailors went over the hill in 1906, and 3700 were AWOL when Spruance graduated. The Navy was baffled as to why sailors deserted but seemed uninterested in finding a cure.

Spruance's first duty was aboard the battleship USS *Iowa,* a nine-year-old, 11,400-ton veteran of the Spanish-American War. With white hull and yellow ochre superstructure, she mounted guns of all calibers, which once had fired in anger, although not too accurately. Her coal-burning boilers and triple-expansion reciprocating engines drove her through the water at 16½ knots when her bottom was clean.[1]

She was moderately habitable, as naval ships go. Steam heat warmed her in winter, but her interior was torrid in summer. The officers and midshipmen had comfortable staterooms but wore uncomfortable high-collared blue or white uniforms. Sailors wore either blue or white bell-

---

1. For the USS *Iowa,* see U.S. Navy, *Dictionary of American Naval Fighting Ships* [hereafter DANAFS], vol. 3 (Washington, 1968), pp. 453–54.

bottom uniforms. Only the wretched coal passers in the hellish fire-rooms were exempt from the battleship's spit and polish.

The sailors slept in hammocks and washed themselves and their clothes in buckets to conserve scarce fresh water. Black and Asian stewards served the officers' needs by preparing their food, tidying rooms, cleaning heads, and shining shoes. Ranks and ratings ate in separate messes, miniature communities unto themselves, so that Spruance and his three or four midshipman shipmates were segregated from the other officers. The cockroaches did not discriminate and availed themselves of samples from all the messes.

Iowa followed an unvarying daily routine, codified in the Plan of the Day, which established when one would rise, eat, work, play, and sleep. Spruance stood watches, supervised enlisted men, and learned the practical aspects of operating a man-o'-war.

Iowa's operating schedule was as fixed as her internal routine. Everyone knew a year in advance precisely where the ship would be and what she would be doing—mostly humdrum steaming along the Atlantic coast. Her useful life was ending; although less than a decade old, she was obsolete and required men and fuel that were needed elsewhere. In June 1907 she entered the Norfolk Navy Yard and was decommissioned. Spruance transferred to USS *Minnesota,* a big new battleship, one of the sixteen of the Great White Fleet that would tour the world to display American naval power.[2]

The cruise of the White Fleet was not the success portrayed in most naval histories. It was the American debut into the society of great world navies, a muscle-flexing spectacle conceived to awe, impress, and sometimes intimidate other countries. The American officers and men proclaimed their desire for friendship, but if their uneasy foreign hosts hesitated to reciprocate, perhaps it was because the sixteen white battleships riding at anchor were difficult to equate with benign intentions.

The ships provoked political crises with foreign governments sensitive to every nuance of naval diplomacy. Senior American naval officers fretted about coal availability in foreign ports; sailors' conduct ashore;

2. USS *Minnesota* (BB 22), displacement 16,000 tons, main battery four 12-inch guns, eight 8-inch guns, commissioned 9 March 1907. She served most of her career with the Atlantic Fleet. The *Minnesota* was decommissioned 1 December 1921 and scrapped three years later. DANAFS, vol. 4 (Washington, 1969), pp. 374–75.

whether they would be welcomed abroad; and whether their ships' boilers would even get them to their destinations. The social demands were debilitating. Transits between ports were devoted to recovering from heavy drinking, rich food, and late hours—and girding for the next round of receptions, concerts, banquets, parades, tours, and sporting events. Training lapsed, and thoughtful naval officers questioned the priorities that set protocol above operational readiness.

The Navy's system of promotion became an international embarrassment. The American officers were senior in age but inferior in rank, experience, and endurance to their foreign naval counterparts. Gout-ridden Rear Admiral Robley D. Evans could not complete the cruise, and his relief, Rear Admiral Charles M. Thomas, died shortly after taking command.

These problems did not concern Spruance. He was young, robust, and thrived on foreign hospitality. He attended elegant balls and danced with beautiful women. There were waltzes in Rio, two-steps in Monterey, polkas in San Francisco, and lancers in Melbourne. The midshipmen were inundated with invitations to parties, honorary memberships to private clubs, and complimentary train passes. Days in port were crammed with dawn-to-dusk activities among exotic people, smells, sounds, and sights. It was heady stuff for an unsophisticated midshipman.

The White Fleet had left Hampton Roads, Virginia, in December 1907. Ten months later, it approached Japan, one of the most important port calls of the cruise. The Americans were apprehensive because Japan was antagonistic and suspicious. Its navy had stationed dark-colored warships astride the island approaches, and the glistening white American hulls made easy targets. The Japanese not long before had demonstrated their excellent shooting skills against Russia, and nervous Americans regretted the time lost partying ashore while their guns lay idle. But they could not turn back and pressed on toward an uncertain and perhaps dangerous reception.

When a typhoon lashed the fleet off Luzon, Spruance was too seasick to worry about Japanese intentions. *Minnesota*'s interior became a shambles of gear cast adrift, slopping seawater, and tormented men. With ventilation secured, the stink of vomit in fetid air exacerbated Spruance's agony. Finally, thankfully, the wind abated and the sea calmed, and the disheveled crews cleaned themselves and their ships. The scattered fleet made rendezvous and shaped course for Yokohama through drizzle and fog. Tension increased as the Americans' attention shifted from the weather to the Japanese.

Seafarers delight when entering a strange foreign port. They sniff the land breezes laden with unfamiliar smells, and they search for features ashore that may reveal the city's character. Water-borne debris at the harbor's approaches provides subtle clues about what lies ahead. Spruance, always curious, always inquisitive, had recovered from his seasickness and was now absorbed in what these smells and sights and sounds were promising. He went to quarters in his gold-buttoned blue uniform and watched Japanese warships appear and fall in alongside, one for each American ship. Anchors dropped and accommodation ladders were rigged. The Americans anxiously waited for the Japanese to appear and to pay formal calls.

All went well. After an initial period of mutual nervousness, the tension disappeared. The familiar routine of social events began and Americans were enthusiastically welcomed and entertained. Spruance mingled with his hosts on streets and in trains and saw the immortal Admiral Togo at an afternoon garden party. In those October days of 1908 the foundations for Spruance's life-long respect and admiration for the Japanese nation were established.

Many months of sailing and adventure remained before the fleet returned to Hampton Roads in February 1909. Spruance loved the experience, spoke of it often in later years, and filled a scrapbook with nostalgic memorabilia, the only scrapbook he ever kept.

His unpleasant memories of the Naval Academy were behind. The cruise of the Great White Fleet had convinced him to make the Navy his career.

Command at sea is the ultimate goal of ambitious naval line officers, but only a chosen few obtain it. An officer proves worthy for command by performing well as a subordinate officer aboard a variety of ships in a variety of duties. His commanding officers train and supervise him, then report to the Navy Department on his fitness for promotion and his readiness for higher responsibility.

An officer aspiring to command seeks three kinds of experience. First, he must learn how to lead men. Second, he must become a competent mariner, primarily through standing innumerable watches at sea as an officer of the deck (OOD). Third, he must understand the internal organization and operation of the ship as well as its design, construction, equipment, and machinery.

Successful command was essential for promotion to senior rank in those years. Because sea duty was the only way to prepare for command, Spruance and most naval officers stayed at sea as long as possible. Secretary of the Navy Josephus Daniels codified this precept in 1912 by establishing a set amount of sea duty as a prerequisite to promotion. Spruance regarded shore duty as pleasant interludes that had no effect on his career, so relaxation took precedence over work when he was ashore.

Having chosen a naval career, Ensign Spruance set about to prepare himself for command at sea. Then he made a decision that began a chain of events that for years diverted him from this goal. He decided to become an engineering specialist.

Naval technology was abounding both with new inventions and with refinements of existing concepts. Armor had become lighter and stronger, guns had longer ranges and more accuracy, boilers were more efficient, and propulsion machinery was more powerful. But the greatest revolution was in electricity. That electric motors now moved heavy loads such as turrets and winches and ammunition hoists was important; the most exciting developments, however, were the gyro-compass and the wireless radio. Gyros allowed more accurate navigation and vastly improved gunnery fire control. Radio had proven itself during the White Fleet cruise; Washington had communicated with its ships at sea a half world away.

An ambitious naval officer with a flair for engineering subjects would be farsighted if he learned as much as possible about the naval technology of the future. Spruance applied for postgraduate training and was ordered to advance instruction in electricity at the General Electric Company in Schenectady. He left *Minnesota* in April 1909 with good but noncommittal fitness reports and two and half years of invaluable sea duty under his belt.

A year at General Electric meant both study and the practical application of what he had learned. He helped a company engineer adjust ammunition hoists on a new battleship and was rewarded with a grateful letter of appreciation that added luster to his service record. He also supervised the installation of radio equipment on submarines, having been tutored by the resident inspector of machinery at Schenectady,

Lieutenant Commander Luke McNamee, the pioneer in naval radio systems. McNamee was the first man to report that Spruance had special talents in electricity.

Spruance returned to sea in 1910 for duty aboard the battleship *Connecticut*.[3] She was commanded by Captain W. R. "Bill" Rush, a legendary martinet. An able seaman who ran a taut but unhappy ship, Rush was also harsh, demanding, and intemperate. The story goes that if a subordinate greeted him "Good morning," Rush often would snarl that it was not a good morning unless he said it was.

Spruance soon clashed with the irascible captain. Perhaps deceived by Spruance's apparent mildness, Rush time and again hectored the shy, young officer. Spruance rebelled with a hitherto unrecognized moral courage. He refused to be intimidated. Recognizing Spruance's emerging stubbornness and strength of character, Rush praised him in fitness reports. Yet he contrarily continued to harass and badger Spruance and to make his life miserable.

Spruance did not see the glowing fitness reports. He was aware only of Rush's grinding oppression. When the ship was in the New York Navy Yard in mid-April 1911, Spruance took a short leave to visit his aunts in East Orange. There he pondered about his future aboard *Connecticut* and perhaps discussed it with Bessie and Louie. He decided to resort to a traditional remedy: he requested a transfer. Rush returned the request with a conciliatory memorandum.

"Mr. Spruance is informed," wrote Rush, "that, if he submitted this application for detachment in the belief that his performance of duty is not satisfactory, he is hereby informed that his performance of duty is generally very satisfactory and that the Commanding Officer has no wish to have him leave the ship.

"Ensign Spruance's request is approved, however, in accordance with his wishes expressed therein, and the papers are placed in his hands for final decision. If he wishes to remain on *Connecticut* he can withdraw his request, if he wishes to go he can return request to Captain's Office and it will be forwarded *with regret.*"

3. USS *Connecticut* (BB 18), displacement 16,000 tons, main battery four 12-inch guns, eight 8-inch guns, commmissioned 29 September 1904. The *Connecticut* was Atlantic Fleet flagship for the "Great White Fleet's" around-the-world cruise, 1907–1909. She was decommissioned on 1 March 1923 and scrapped that year. DANAFS, vol. 2 (Washington, 1963), p. 166.

Spruance was unmoved and forwarded the request. The Bureau of Navigation[4] replied that it had been noted, placed on file, and would receive consideration (a procedure unchanged and unchangeable). No orders came, and Spruance remained on *Connecticut*.

Rush bore down even harder on Spruance. The next and most serious clash came several weeks later.

Connecticut was flagship for the Commander in Chief, Atlantic Fleet, and honors and ceremonies were frequent. The Marine detachment normally performed these functions in crisp, military fashion, but they were temporarily transferred from the ship. Sailors were substituted and Spruance became "Commander of the Guard." It was not a satisfactory solution, for sailors are reluctant to imitate Marines. The sailors performed listlessly, frequently failed to muster, and Rush was not happy.

Finally in exasperation Spruance put six men on report for failure to muster. Rush dismissed the charges, enraging Spruance by violating the cardinal principle that a commanding officer must support his subordinate officers. In that the two preferred writing to speaking, Spruance penned a protest to his commanding officer.

"On June 2, 1911, the Captain sent a memorandum to the Executive Officer," wrote Spruance, "directing him to inform the Commander of the Guard that, in the case of six men of the Guard who had been put on the report for failing to fall in promptly when the Guard of the Day had been called, the Commander of the Guard was the guilty person, and that any similar occurrence in the future would not be overlooked.

"The Commander of the Guard respectfully requests to be informed as to wherein he was derelict in his duty, in order that he may guard against any repetition of the offense. He was given no opportunity to present his side of the case before this memorandum was sent to the Executive Officer, nor has any opportunity been since given at the mast.

"The Commander of the Guard desires to assure the Captain that he investigated the cases of these men before putting them on the report . . . [therefore he] deemed it advisable to put the delinquents upon the report.

---

4. Predecessor to the Bureau of Naval Personnel, responsible for the assignment, training, and education of officers and men.

"If it is the purpose of the Captain to hold the Commander of the Guard personally responsible for the conduct of every man in the Guard, and to refuse to consider any reports made against them, the Commander of the Guard respectfully requests to be informed of this, both in order to know what course to pursue in the future and to be able the better to maintain discipline in the Guard."

Rush replied the next day that "The proper course of the Commander of the Guard to persue [sic] is to make certain that whatever proper orders he issues should be carried out." He later wrote on Spruance's fitness report, "Guard duty in Command of the Seaman Guard for four months during absence of Marines. Excellent. 4.0."

In the course of a naval career one works for good officers and poor officers and serves in good ships and poor ships. If fate places a Navy man under an officer or in a ship that makes him unhappy, it won't last forever. Perhaps the next ship will be an improvement, or maybe the disliked officer will be relieved by someone better. Spruance's turn came in late October 1911 when he was ordered to USS *Cincinnati* at Mare Island Navy Yard in California.

Spruance left *Connecticut* in New York the day he received his orders and struck out across country by train. He planned a brief stop in Indianapolis to visit his parents, whom he had not seen for many years.

That autumn Spruance fell in love.

It happened in Indianapolis when he strolled past a tennis court and saw Margaret Dean. "I fell in love with her then," he later said, "and I've never been able to get over it." He decided impulsively that he would marry her. He wired the Bureau of Navigation requesting a leave extension, it was approved, and the courtship began.

Margaret was twenty-three, the youngest daughter of a prosperous businessman who headed a happy, closely knit family of six children. Margaret was a lovely, popular young woman—effervescent, warm, fun-loving, and emotional. Although intelligent, she was not a good student. Mathematics was forever a mystery to her. She had recently attended Lake Erie College, a small school, where she had excelled in history and had been elected president of her senior class.

Spruance formally called upon Margaret at her home in order to meet her family, the customary first step in a proper courtship. Spruance had changed from the self-conscious midshipman of seven years before. Now he was a mature, handsome gentleman, an attractive and exciting contrast to the untraveled, unsophisticated Indianapolis youths whom Margaret had been dating. But her new suitor's most important virtue was that he was interested in her.

They had little time, only a week. The two spent every day together, and they got to know each other as well as could be expected in seven days. The night before he left he took Margaret to the theater, and then he was gone. He had neither proposed marriage nor made any promises for the future, but Margaret was certain that one day he would return to her.

Spruance resumed his journey westward and joined the *Cincinnati* at Mare Island in late 1911. She was a creaking old lady, and Spruance as engineer officer dived below decks to squeeze as many miles as possible from her obsolete engines and leaking boilers. *Cincinnati* responded to his coaxing by steaming for a year and a half across the Pacific and up and down the coast of China.[5]

During this period, the Great Powers were greedily establishing spheres of influence in a chaotic China, and the Taft administration was trying to implement "dollar diplomacy" in the Far East. *Cincinnati* joined the Asiatic Squadron, whose mission was to protect American business enterprises in China while simultaneously providing a show of force to preserve the Open Door policy. Far removed from the disciplining influence of the Navy Department, wives, and sweethearts, the squadron was a hard-working, hard-playing, nonregulation force.

By now the Navy had changed to a fitness report form that suggested a shift toward promotion by merit rather than longevity. "Reports on fitness form the basis for assignments to duty," said the new policy directive. "They are decisive of the service careers of the individual officers, as also for the efficiency of the entire Navy, which demands the right man in every place. The preparation of these reports is therefore one of the most important and responsible duties of senior officers."

A young officer is influenced by his seniors. If they are good, the subordinate will admire and respect them, and, consciously or uncon-

---

5. USS *Cincinnati* (C 7), cruiser, displacement 3,183 tons, main battery one 6-inch gun, 10 five-inch guns, commissioned 16 June 1894. She saw service in the Spanish-American War, 1898, and was placed out of commission from 1907 to March 1911. For the next six years the *Cincinnati* patrolled Asiatic waters, then spent World War I in the Caribbean. She was decommissioned for good on 20 April 1919 and sold in 1921. DANAFS, vol. 2 (Washington, 1963), p. 119.

sciously, will pattern his own behavior after their examples. Outstanding senior officers will impart their experience, skills, and wisdom to receptive subordinates. Conversely, an incompetent senior can ruin a fine young officer with good potential.

Spruance was blessed with outstanding senior officers who recognized and nurtured Spruance's talents. His two commanding officers, Samuel S. Robison and Jehu Valentine Chase, later became admirals, as did the executive officer, Cyrus W. Cole. Spruance performed well and established a reputation as a sober, earnest, and entirely competent naval officer. He was promoted to lieutenant (junior grade) and seemed content to continue on engineering duty for the indeterminate future.

Spruance was ordered to his first command, the destroyer *Bainbridge*, in early 1913.[6] The Asiatic destroyer force at that time was a disgrace. Spruance's engineer officer, Charles J. (Carl) Moore, described it vividly.

"Those destroyers had been the most completely ragtime, non-reg bunch of ships that you've ever seen in your life," said Moore. "The officers were dissolute, drunken, crooked, the darndest bunch of people you've ever seen, and demoralized completely by life in the Asiatic Station. . . . The idea of sending Spruance there was to try to straighten out this bunch of tough eggs and get the destroyers back on their feet."

Spruance took command of two ensigns, forty-five enlisted men, and a small, tired ship in Olangapo, Philippines. *Bainbridge* was a rusty, cramped 440-ton destroyer that once was capable of twenty-eight knots. Armed with light guns and torpedo tubes, she was the Navy's original destroyer, built to protect ponderous capital ships from small, fast torpedo boats, then in vogue as a threat to the fleet.

Bainbridge rarely got underway and was doomed to long days and weeks of swinging on the hook in hot, rainy Philippine anchorages. Spruance's greatest problem on his destroyer would be to overcome the boredom and apathy that accompanies enforced idleness on an uncomfortable ship, doing nothing and going nowhere. His wardroom officers were two rollicking ensigns, Ralph G. (Hax) Haxton, the executive officer, and Carl Moore, the engineer. On Spruance's earlier ships there

6. USS *Bainbridge* (DD 1), the Navy's first torpedo-boat destroyer, displacement 420 tons, armament two 3-inch guns, two 18-inch torpedo tubes, commissioned in Reserve Fleet 24 August 1902, full commissioning 12 February 1903. She saw hard duty with the Asiatic Fleet, mostly in the Philippines, and fought World War I in the Mediterranean and the Atlantic. DANAFS, vol. 1 (Washington, 1959), pp. 85–86.

had been a great age difference between the captain and his officers, and the captain had lived in splendid isolation. *Bainbridge* was entirely different. Spruance was a twenty-six-year-old skipper—only a few years older than his ensigns—and they would live in close company.

But at first their quiet, youthful captain was a stranger. He expected them to perform well and to run a good ship. That was just fine with Hax and Carl. He won the allegiance of his enlisted men by his interest in their work and by his personal supervision of their mess. Good food promotes good morale. They reciprocated by turning to with a will.

Haxton and Moore sized up Spruance as a fine commanding officer but too austere, so they conspired to "make him human." The ensigns were enjoying a free and easy life ashore with the daughters of local service families. The two persuaded a reluctant Spruance to join them. He was bashful among the girls, who compounded his embarrassment by calling him "Spriscilla Sprudence." More amused than affronted, he tolerated their teasing and began to enjoy his excursions ashore.

The three officers became close friends. Spruance watched the ship while the other two frolicked ashore, but all three gathered for the evening meal, unwilling that any one eat alone. Dinner became a charming ritual. First Hax and Carl broke out their violins and serenaded their skipper. After music, Hax would summon their Chinese steward. "Sam," he would say, "pass the shaker to the skipper." The abstemious Spruance would sniff the cocktail shaker, solemnly intone, "Thank God, rum has no hold on me," and return it to Sam. The steward then poured drinks for the musicians, for liquor aboard ship was not yet unlawful.

Then the three would sit at table and begin with soup. Invariably and deliberately, Moore would jiggle the miniature table and slop the soup. Silly, yes, but it helped them to preserve good spirits in the dismal, oppressive Philippine climate.

Spruance became closer to his enlisted men by joining their daily swimming party. The Navy wanted everyone to swim, and Spruance, who swam with power and endurance, decided to teach his crew. Before dinner one evening, he reported to Hax and Carl that Sam the steward had been making heavy weather of learning to swim that afternoon. Gasping "I tired," he had simply quit stroking and slid beneath the waves, nearly drowning before he was rescued.

Spruance sometimes attempted to redirect his ensigns' attention from frivolous things to matters of importance, such as government and

Lieutenant Spruance, c. 1914.

foreign affairs. He lectured often that a single-tax system on landowners was the best means of raising revenue, but his young companions
rarely understood his logic and were an unreceptive audience.

Months passed. Occasionally *Bainbridge* got underway with Spruance
conning from atop his miniature bridge. On high-speed runs the
rushing wind refreshed the topside crew, but the snipes (engineers)
below deck were enervated by the heat and the noise of the roaring
boilers and engines. Most of life, however, was spent interminably at
anchor, idly scanning windows and doors ashore through a long glass,

visiting adjacent ships for drinks and meals, and enduring the heat and the rain.

One foul night during a thunderstorm, Spruance attended a class reunion aboard a nearby monitor. Next morning Moore discovered his captain in deep, drugged sleep on his bunk, still wearing rain gear and uniform. When he awoke, the ensigns ragged him with wicked relish. Spruance was mortified that they had found a flaw in his armor: he could not handle liquor. During his early years he occasionally would drink too much, get sick, then not drink again for long periods. He was an anomaly in a hard-drinking Navy.

Spruance was extraordinarily reticent about his personal life. His two friends knew nothing about Margaret. Only once did Spruance mention Margaret in conversation—when he told Hax that he had sent her some beautiful embroidered cloth and would send the remainder if she wrote him a letter. Other than that, not a word.

Spruance relinquished command of *Bainbridge* in May 1914, having been promoted to lieutenant. He returned to the United States to resume courting Margaret Dean.

Chapter 3

MARRIAGE

R AYMOND is coming home!" Margaret was away on a visit when she received the thrilling news. She hastily returned to Indianapolis to wait for him. Spruance had written no more than three times during their separation. Predictably, he had given no warning of his return, and Margaret was caught by surprise.

In late July 1914, the courtship resumed after a two-and-a-half-year hiatus. Spruance wooed Margaret by telling her about the disadvantages of Navy life. Promotion was slow because Congress obstinately refused to increase the size of the officer corps despite years of Navy Department prodding and cajolery. He warned Margaret that a Navy family would always be poor and nomadic. Margaret suspected he was leading up to a marriage proposal. Within two weeks, the proposal was formally offered and gladly accepted.

Margaret's father was appalled, because he regarded the Navy as an unsavory profession. He had served in the Navy during the Civil War and once had considered it as a career. The story goes that he discussed this venture with an old salt whom the years had not treated kindly. "Look at me, lad," the ancient croaked. "Is this what you want to be thirty years from now?" Young Edward Dean promptly returned to Indianapolis. Thoroughly prejudiced, he feared his youngest daughter would become a glorified tramp.

Spruance sought to win Mr. Dean's approval through plain talk. Money would be scarce, he said, because he was helping to support both his parents and his aunts. Little would remain for a new wife. Although worried by Spruance's proposed starvation budget, Dean admired the responsible young man's honesty and character.

Spruance was the focus of intense curiosity to the Dean family, to whom he was like a visitor from another world. Their first impression was of a reserved, sophisticated naval officer, who had adventured in mysterious lands remote from parochial Indianapolis. Suddenly he had appeared to sweep lovely Margaret away with him into a perilous life. Yet he seemed gentle and kind, with an engaging sense of humor. They felt that Margaret was fortunate to have such an admirable suitor in view of the irresponsible local boys she had dated over the years. So the Dean family accepted him, and he was happy in their midst.

Still disinclined, Edward Dean consented to the marriage and the engagement was announced. It would be in December—so Margaret could have one last Christmas at home, she later joked. Spruance headed east while Margaret remained in Indianapolis to plan her wedding.

War had begun in Europe when Spruance reported as naval inspector of electrical machinery at the great private shipyard in Newport News, Virginia. His orders, as with all orders of that period, contained the curious statement, "This employment on shore duty is required by the public interest." He found a suitable apartment for his future bride and proudly wrote Margaret that it was thirty-five feet wide, including the walls.

When Spruance returned to Indianapolis in December, local interest in the wedding was at high pitch. Margaret would be the first Dean daughter to marry, and to marry a naval officer was cause for the entire community and relatives from afar to be present. The swarming wedding party jammed into the Dean home for the ceremony, and they later agreed that the bride was beautiful, the blue-uniformed groom handsome, and the ceremony dignified and impressive. The best man was a classmate, Jonas Ingram, a boisterous, hard-drinking former athlete. His behavior during the reception revived Edward Dean's reservations about naval morality, but Margaret was married and there was no turning back. After a ten-day honeymoon in South Carolina, the couple established their first residence in Newport News.

The two were happy together. Spruance was proud of his new

bride, and he invited his friends to meet Margaret and to see his new apartment. "Well, Margaret Spruance, I sure am glad to meet you," said one visitor. "We all wondered who was going to marry old Frozen Face."

Spruance was attentive to Margaret. Having come from a close and protective family, she frequently was homesick. She needed his company in the dreary, unfamiliar little town, and Spruance did not want her to be alone for long periods. One day he found Margaret weeping. She had smelled the cigar smoke from a man passing in the street, it had evoked memories of her father's cigars, and she had been overcome by a longing for her family. Spruance looked upon her, mocking gently, and asked if it would help if he took up cigar smoking.

Every naval officer family employed a housekeeper-cook, so Margaret had to interview and hire someone suitable. (Regardless of how poor any officer's family was, they *always* had a cook, up to World War II. Margaret herself did not cook until Spruance retired in 1948.) A black woman named Isabel Lightfoot seemed promising, but what to pay her? Isabel suggested four dollars a week. Naïve Margaret thought it a bargain and agreed. Much later Margaret discovered that she had offended the resident Southern ladies, who paid their cooks only three dollars a week. The shocking news had flashed throughout Newport News that the Northern stranger had upset the going wage system.

But Isabel was worth her pay, and the Spruances could now properly entertain their dinner guests.

In many ways their marriage was a gamble, for Spruance was a stranger when Margaret married him. A courtship of several weeks and a handful of letters during a three-year separation do not reveal much about a man who is naturally taciturn. With the stimulus of Margaret's love and warmth, however, Spruance's personality began to emerge.

Margaret discovered that her husband was a passionate man of deep feelings. He was sensitive, high-strung, and innately shy, and his emotions were easily stimulated. He suppressed and disguised his emotions because he felt it was unmanly to display his feelings. If his feelings were aroused, he became silent and impassive. Throughout their long marriage, Margaret continually was amazed that Spruance could be outwardly so serene while inwardly so turbulent. "His

The newlyweds: Raymond and Margaret Spruance, Newport News,
Virginia, 1915

self-control was an enigma to me," she once said. "Raymond was a stoic."

His suppressed emotions created internal tension that often became unbearable. He exercised intensely, mostly endurance walking and swimming, in order to relieve his tension and to restore his equilibrium. Exercise was also essential for physical fitness. He esteemed toughness and stamina and good health, carefully regulating his diet and daily routine so that his body was attuned for maximum efficiency.

Margaret was athletically active and shared his enthusiasm for exercise, and they rarely were sick. Spruance received mandatory periodic physical examinations from Navy doctors (Carl Moore suspected he was a latent hypochondriac), but otherwise he avoided them. Margaret did not consult doctors for any illness until she had a bad cold at seventy.

Other personality traits emerged. His high-minded integrity, honesty, and morality were uncompromising. He was strong-willed and stubborn, and when he felt he was right, he would insist that things be done his way. Margaret soon was persuaded that he rarely was wrong. He was unselfish and industrious, but he would neither work overtime nor bring work home. He was insatiably curious about the world and loved to explore things and places while he walked, or to pursue abstract ideas in men's minds—and in books.

He was an avid reader but had no personal library, other than books given him after retirement by publishers and admirers. Public libraries provided biographies and histories, which he preferred in early years, but he was not familiar with commonly accepted great works of literature. He chose books indiscriminately, perhaps selecting one whose subject had attracted his momentary interest. Other times he simply read whatever was readily available to occupy his idle hours.

Early on, Margaret found he owned two well-thumbed books that reflected his beliefs on religion, politics, and economics. One was the Bible, which he knew intimately, read often, and kept by his bed. But he read it for its beauty and not its doctrine. He was an agnostic and could not accept Christianity by faith alone. He needed proof, and there was none to his satisfaction.

Margaret was a Presbyterian and attended church regularly in their early days of marriage. Sundays would begin with his asking, "Well, I suppose you want me to go to church?" She did, and he would accompany her to please her—he would do almost anything to please her. But he was a sarcastic companion. "Why," he once asked Margaret, "do we

have to go to church every Sunday morning to listen to all that tripe?"
Decades later, however, his closest friends included Roman Catholic
cardinals and bishops, and one spoke of Spruance posthumously as a
"Christ-like man."

Spruance did have religious convictions, but Margaret never understood what they were. Probably Spruance didn't either; he sought but
could not find. When he commanded *Mississippi* twenty-five years later, he had long philosophical conversations with a young theosophist
lieutenant. On one occasion the lieutenant, conning *Mississippi* through
complicated maneuvers in company with other battleships, was much
distracted by his captain. "Tell me about reincarnation, evolution, and
karma," urged Spruance to his OOD, who was trying to maneuver the
huge battleship at high speed. Spruance appreciated the lieutenant's
answers and included in his fitness report that he was able to talk
intelligently on a wide range of subjects.

The other book that Spruance held dear was *Progress and Poverty* by
Henry George, an American economist and land reformer who popular-
ized the "single tax" idea. George had a large following that was
attracted by his patriotic and humanitarian appeals. Soon after his
marriage, Spruance tried to interest Margaret in the book's social and
economic tenets, repeating the lectures that he had forced upon the
Bainbridge ensigns. George held, and Spruance believed, that large
landowners inhibited economic progress and inflicted poverty upon the
working classes. His solution was to impose a single tax on all land
rental incomes and to abolish all other taxes.

But it was all too confusing to Margaret. Lacking mathematical
aptitude, she had no interest in her husband's discourses on George's
complex economic theories. She begged Spruance not to discuss or
explain them. Nevertheless, *Progress and Poverty* continued to be the
foundation of Spruance's reactionary political beliefs.

For example, Spruance believed that "the quality of the American
voter under universal suffrage is not too high." In his view, unscrupu-
lous politicians—who deprecated their electorate's judgment and intelligence—were elected by exploiting their voters' ignoble instincts.
Thus universal suffrage fostered incompetent elected public officials,
who reflected the poor judgment of their electorate. Spruance advocated a system whereby a limited number of "high-grade" Americans,
selected on the basis of their wisdom and integrity, would be allowed to
vote. But that would never happen, he reasoned. "So long as the Bill of

Rights remains in effect," he once wrote, "the American people will in the long run get about the kind of government they want and deserve."

Spruance also decried social welfare programs because, in his mind, they helped the "low-grade" elements of society to propagate, thereby debasing the character of the American nation. Moreover, Spruance had fixed theories on racial characteristics and heredity, and he unquestionably assumed that some races were inherently superior to others, a common belief of many Americans of his generation.

Decades later, when Spruance's military and diplomatic career had become history, Spruance was generally regarded as a man endowed with extraordinary intelligence and proven wisdom. Whether he was an intellectual is debatable. Intellectuals are commonly associated with the pursuit of the liberal arts and the physical sciences, with advanced academic degrees, and with learned writing and speaking. As a distinguished author recently observed, "In common parlance an intellectual is a man soaked in the advanced critical ideas of the liberal-academic establishment; and even an opponent of these ideas . . . has them all at his fingertips."

Using these standards alone, Spruance would not be regarded as an intellectual. His formal education ended at the Naval Academy, and he read few, if any, of the classic works in science, literature, and philosophy. He disliked writing, and what little he wrote was not for publication. He also disliked public speaking, and what few speeches he did make were soon forgotten.

Nevertheless, Spruance was an intellectual in the purest sense of the word. He was a person with superior mental power. He was deeply interested in fields of knowledge outside the technicalities of the naval profession. He once told some university students, "I think it is most desirable for you to retain and to stimulate your intellectual curiosity in other fields where you may have a natural interest." He explained that those with a liberal education in art, literature, and music had an advantage over people—such as himself—with only a technical education. "A knowledge and appreciation of these subjects enriches their lives," he said, "and makes them more interesting individuals to their friends and acquaintances."

Finally, Spruance was a classic intellectual in the sense that he was extremely rational and relied upon his intellect rather than his emotions or feelings. He later regarded the war against Japan as an intellectual exercise that posed a complex yet interesting series of problems that

Lieutenant Commander Spruance, his son Edward, and his grandmother
Annie Ames Hiss, Brooklyn, 1918

challenged and stimulated his mind. Those problems had to be solved using logic and reason that was unaffected by the violent passions of war.

When Margaret became pregnant, Spruance was delighted. Mrs. Dean was on hand when Margaret delivered a son in October 1915, named Edward Dean after Margaret's father.

The elder Dean later visited the Spruances and was reassured to see that Margaret had established a proper home and was happy and content. Spruance took his father-in-law aboard the new battleship *Pennsylvania* for sea trials, following her construction at the Newport News shipyard.[1] The brief cruise rekindled Dean's love of the sea, and he was impressed with the respect and admiration accorded Spruance by other officers. When Margaret greeted her father after his exposure to the seagoing Navy, he was beaming. He finally blessed and approved the marriage without reservation.

Spruance was a proud father of a fine son, but rearing the baby was entirely Margaret's responsibility. Margaret asked him to care for Edward only once, while she visited Norfolk. Returning, she found a flustered father unable to cope with a squalling baby. And shortly after Edward's birth, she asked Spruance to push the baby carriage as they strolled down the street. It was a painful task, and his face registered his distress. A perceptive neighbor admonished Margaret that she had "crucified" her husband. So Margaret got no help. Those first few months presaged his strained relationship with his children in their early years.

Spruance had been electrical officer on *Pennsylvania* for a year when the United States declared war upon the Central Powers. The fleet assembled in Yorktown, Virginia, and naval visionaries dreamed of a clash of battle lines with the High Seas Fleet of Germany. Because

1. USS *Pennsylvania* (BB 38), displacement 31,400 tons, main battery twelve 14-inch guns, commissioned 12 June 1916. For most of her long and useful service the *Pennsylvania* was a fleet flagship, first for the Atlantic Fleet during World War I, the Battle Fleet between the wars, and the Pacific Fleet in 1941. On 7 December 1941 during the attack on Pearl Harbor she sustained minor damage while in dry dock. During World War II she earned eight battle stars, including the Battle of Surigao Strait, 24–25 October 1944. Decommissioned 29 August 1946, the *Pennsylvania* was used as a target hulk for atomic bomb tests at Bikini Atoll and was finally sunk on 10 February 1948 off Kwajalein. DANAFS, vol. 5 (Washington, 1970), pp. 250–54.

Pennsylvania was a great, new battleship, Spruance could anticipate that he would see action in European waters.

But *Pennsylvania* wasn't going anywhere. Although the Allies controlled the seas wherever the mighty battleships roamed, the dreadnaughts concentrated in anchorages or on patrol stations in the North Sea, waiting for the Germans who never again would come out to fight. Indeed, Great Britain had all the battleships she needed. Destroyers were the crucial ships. German submarines were sinking scores of merchant ships and emasculating logistical support to Great Britain. Destroyers alone could gain control of the mid-Atlantic sea-lanes from the German submarines. But the United States owned few destroyers, because Roosevelt had set the precedent to build battleships almost exclusively.

Margaret had moved with Edward to a Hampton, Virginia, boarding-house to be nearby when *Pennsylvania* was in port. Other officers' wives lived there also, so Margaret was introduced to the camaraderie of the community of Navy families with husbands at sea.

One fall day in 1917, a *Pennsylvania* paymaster, whose family were neighbors, warned Margaret that Spruance had just received orders for shore duty and was determined to go to Washington to protest. Margaret was puzzled. Her husband would be ashore with her again and that would be grand. Besides, she couldn't leave Edward to accompany Spruance to Washington. The paymaster patiently explained that line officers wanted to be on ships at sea during war. Therefore her husband was distraught at the prospect of leaving *Pennsylvania* for shore duty, just as the war was approaching a climax.

As predicted, an angry Spruance next day announced to Margaret they were going to Washington. Innocently: "Oh, are we? What are you going there for?" Grimly: "Because I am not going ashore!" Later: "Every door has been slammed in my face. I'm going ashore."

Spruance unwittingly had become a technical specialist by consistently requesting engineering duty and by earning a reputation as an electrical expert. The Navy had plenty of "generalist" line officers for ships at sea, and Spruance had acquired scarce talents that were needed ashore. Now he regretted his decision to learn a technical specialty because it prevented him from getting the sea duty so necessary for promotion. Even a temporary promotion to lieutenant commander[2]

2. War had finally jolted Congress into expanding the officer corps.

could not assuage his torment when he came ashore to Brooklyn Navy Yard while his shipmates sailed overseas.

But he plunged into his work and soon was deeply absorbed. The Navy was rapidly developing new gunnery fire control systems, and Spruance became responsible for their installation and testing. He had unlimited travel authority that took him to East Coast ports, following the ships and working them on the run. Eventually he went to Europe to work on American and British ships overseas. At war's end he returned to the Brooklyn Navy Yard and became even more deeply involved in the development of gunnery fire control systems. He was particularly proud of a device he himself had invented that saved the government many thousands of dollars. Margaret never understood just what the invention was, nor was it mentioned in his service record.

Spruance never again sought electrical engineering duty. He wanted sea duty in the war zone. At war's end he was precipitately ordered as executive officer of the troop transport *Agamemnon,* a confiscated German liner pressed into service along with anything afloat that could carry soldiers.[3] Once the luxurious *Kaiser Wilhelm II,* she soon became the "Rolling Billy" in recognition of her behavior in the open sea.

Spruance and his commanding officer were the only Regular Navy officers aboard. With a wardroom of young reservists they set about (along with all other available ships) to help bring home two million impatient, clamoring doughboys. Their passengers were jolly, turbulent, and restive, yet Spruance managed every passage smoothly and efficiently. He served in *Agamemnon* for four months, made three trans-Atlantic crossings, and earned a letter of commendation for her cleanliness and smartness. It was a worthy achievement considering the ravages normally inflicted upon a troop transport by her human cargo.

The need for more officers had not abated. Promotions now were rapid, and thirty-two-year-old Spruance became a temporary commander in late 1918 after only a year as a lieutenant commander. Then the war was over.

3. USS *Agamemnon,* displacement 25,530 tons, speed 23.5 knots. Launched in 1902 as the German liner *Kaiser Wilhelm II,* she was seized by the United States in 1917 and commissioned 21 August 1917 with that highly ironical name. On 5 September 1917 she became the USS *Agamemnon.* Between October 1917 and mid-1919 she made 19 voyages carrying troops to Europe. On 22 August 1919 she was turned over to the War Department. DANAFS, vol. 1 (Washington, 1959), p. 15.

Margaret had missed her husband during his prolonged wartime field trips, but her father had comforted her that Raymond's sacrifice was not wasted. Perpetual peace was assured, he said, and little Edward never would have to go to war.

But if perpetual peace, why a navy? And if a navy would not be needed, why a naval career? These questions had to be addressed and answered by young Commander Spruance. There were lean years ahead.

If he indulged in a self-assessment, Spruance could be satisfied with his personal well-being. His five-foot, nine-and-a-half-inch frame carried a sinewy hundred-fifty-two-pound body, and his wife's feminine eye could appreciate his handsome features, ruddy complexion, and thick dark brown hair. Doctors had certified his excellent vision and robust health. His mental faculties were superb.

But should he devote his energy and talents to the Navy? America was stampeding into demobilization, and naval disarmament treaties soon would scrap ships and forbid construction. Operating funds were measly, and ships were idle for want of fuel. Dismayed by these ominous trends, many naval officers resigned their commissions to seek their fortunes in the civilian world.

Spruance decided to remain in the Navy, although in later years he would become dispirited with the Navy's peacetime doldrums and once contemplated resigning from the service because of the low pay. His work was frequently discouraging, as well. "I have had various disappointments in duty assignments—too many to write you about," he once wrote his son, "but I always took what I was handed and did the best I could with them. I was always ready and anxious to get to sea, and I always got the best sea job I could and tried to remain at sea as long as I could."

In the last years before World War II, two couples who were intimate friends ate dinner together in San Francisco. Bill and Fan Halsey and Raymond and Margaret Spruance were in a mellow mood, and, as their conversation drifted to their early years, Halsey became reflective. He and Spruance were both senior officers in their fifties, and Halsey asked, "Spruance, if you had your life to live all over again, what would you want to be?"

Spruance replied, "A successful naval officer."

"So would I," said Halsey.

Chapter 4

PEACE

A MERICA'S convulsive effort to build destroyers to fight German submarines came too late to help win the war, but its momentum continued during the months after the Armistice. It produced two hundred new destroyers, but the shrunken Navy had few men and even less money to operate them. The sleek new ships either deteriorated at their moorings with caretaker crews or were placed in mothballs.

Spruance was ordered in 1920 to command one of the many destroyers then under construction, the USS *Aaron Ward,* a flush-deck four-piper constructed by the master shipbuilders of Maine's Bath Iron Works.[1] He and the *Aaron Ward's* first crew became her brains, her blood, and her spirit, for through them the ship was transformed from an inert mass of dirty, rusty steel into a living personality. They were her soul, and as plankowners they always would retain a special affec-

---

1. USS *Aaron Ward* (DD 132), displacement 1,154 tons, main battery four 4-inch guns, twelve 21-inch torpedo tubes, commissioned 21 April 1919, decommissioned between 1922–1930 and 1937. Renamed HMS *Castleton,* she was one of the 50 destroyers given to Britain in September 1940 in exchange for bases in the Atlantic. As part of the Royal Navy, she saw extensive duty protecting convoys in the North Atlantic until finally reduced to reserve status, 13 March 1945. DANAFS, vol. 1 (Washington, 1959), pp. 2–3.

tion for their ship. The ship's admission into the Navy—the commissioning ceremony—followed an ageless ritual of military pageantry and patriotic symbolism. The new destroyer was fast and graceful. On her sea trials she sped at 35 knots, despite an errant screwdriver that, unknown to Spruance, was jammed in her low-pressure turbine.

Margaret moved to Jamestown, Rhode Island, across Narragansett Bay from the ship's home port of Newport. After a European cruise, *Aaron Ward* transferred to the Pacific Fleet in San Diego. Margaret, again pregnant, returned to Indianapolis to deliver her second child, a daughter, Margaret.

The Pacific Destroyer Force was a dashing outfit whose élan surmounted the handicaps of demobilization. The Force was led by two vigorous commanders, Rear Admiral Henry A. Wiley and his successor, Captain William V. Pratt.[2] Spruance worked directly under two superb destroyermen, Captain Frank Taylor Evans[3] (son of "Fighting Bob"), the squadron commander, and Commander William F. Halsey, the division commander. Spruance's good luck with his superior officers continued.

Spruance and *Aaron Ward* joined an elite six-destroyer division that reflected Bill Halsey's aggressive, exhilarating, skillful leadership. One contemporary described Halsey, Spruance, and the other commanding officers as supermen possessing incredible shiphandling abilities, because they drove their 1200-ton greyhounds at flank speed through intricate, audacious maneuvers that left observers aghast. Devout destroyermen beamed with approval (and sometimes envy) upon the division of graceful destroyers: bones in their teeth, rooster tails churning astern, pirouetting in unison with signal flags snapping in the breeze, plunging into steep seas and shaking green water from their forecastles—six commanding officers understanding one another perfectly, a brotherhood of proud and confident fighters and seamen.

The division presumably perfected these skills for war, and if war was too remote to contemplate, then for the zest of action and the satisfaction of being the best. The Battleship Force neither forgot nor forgave a torpedo attack by Halsey's destroyers during a training exercise using dummy warheads. Halsey's force sped toward four majestic

2. Pratt became the Chief of Naval Operations in the early thirties.
3. Captain Evans's correct name is Franck Taylor Evans. For more on the Pacific Fleet destroyers, see the fine biography by Gerald Wheeler, *Admiral William Veazie Pratt, U.S. Navy: A Sailor's Life* (Washington, 1974), pp. 158–65.

battleships steaming in column, veered to lay smoke, launched torpedoes at close range, then dived into the smoke screen before the startled eyes of the astounded battleship officers. Having many times maneuvered at high speeds and close intervals inside smoke screens, the destroyer commanding officers were confident they would avoid collisions. Havoc burst as the torpedoes struck home, causing more than a million dollars' damage solely by their impact. The expense of that training exercise was difficult to justify.

Spruance was calm and composed during these hair-raising adventures. Never perturbed. Never a raised voice. He commanded *Aaron Ward* as he would command all his ships—with dignity, tolerance, justice, professional competence, and quiet confidence. The respect and loyalty he showed to his officers and crew was reciprocated, and his ships were clean, efficient, and effective. Spruance was both a master mariner and an accomplished leader of men.

He saw *Aaron Ward* through two emergencies. Once he bashed and badly damaged the stern of Halsey's destroyer while steaming in column; Halsey had lost power and Spruance's OOD had not realized Halsey was dead in the water. Another, more serious emergency erupted when a sister ship, USS *Woolsey,* was rammed at night by a merchantman off South America. Spruance calmly directed rescue efforts that saved nearly all the *Woolsey* men.[4] It was ironical that the division was banged up or sunk not during dangerous maneuvers, but rather while routinely steaming.

It was during this period that Halsey and Spruance established an intimate friendship—a friendship based upon mutual admiration and respect despite their contrasting personalities. Halsey was Spruance's reporting senior during the two years that Spruance commanded first *Aaron Ward* and later *Percival.* He extolled Spruance in fitness reports for his skill as a destroyerman as well as for his character and brains. Spruance, in turn, admired Halsey's seamanship, his daring, and his fighting spirit.

The division officers and their ladies were amiable and gregarious, and their way of life was new and different to the Spruances. Heavy drinking dominated their weekend gatherings; often Spruance and Margaret were the only ones sober enough to eat the food at picnics and

---

4. One survivor was Emmet P. Forrestel, later his operations officer in World War II.

beach parties. But once in a while Spruance unwisely joined in their drinking. One Sunday morning he awoke with a hangover and a realization that his cherished Panama hat was missing. He had worn it the day before at a beach party and later that night when the group had caroused at a popular Coronado tavern. He asked Margaret to retrieve it, and at the tavern it was returned with an explanation that it had been found atop a palm tree. Margaret innocently mentioned this to Halsey, who teased Spruance unmercifully. In that liquor had disagreed with him in so many ways, he again vowed to be more abstemious. Thereafter he drank sparingly, when he drank at all.

Spruance and Margaret, although restrained, comfortably fitted into the social activities of the merry group. The Spruance-Halsey family friendship prospered during pleasant hours ashore. Margaret became fond of the charming and lovable "Billy," and he would drop in unannounced at any hour. Late one chilly evening Spruance and Margaret were enjoying their glowing fireplace when Halsey unexpectedly called. Spruance rummaged through his cupboard for something alcoholic and offered the remnants of a bottle of cognac. Halsey demurred. "Not at this time of night, Spruance," he chided. "You still haven't learned how to drink."

Spruance made lifelong friends among the roisterous wardrooms of Destroyer Division 32, and he renewed his friendship with Johnny Hoover, his pal from Annapolis days. Hoover was a dapper, dour man for whom Spruance had affection and respect. He was a difficult person, yet Margaret tolerated and understood his acerbity. The two couples maintained a close friendship, and Spruance made good use of Hoover during World War II.

The summer of 1921 brought Spruance a summons to shore duty at the Bureau of Engineering in Washington. It was a dire prospect, leaving convivial San Diego and its satisfying sea duty for a desk in muggy Washington. Spruance dreaded Washington weather. Sadly he drew a one-month "dead horse,"[5] packed his bags and family, and headed east in obedience with his orders. The only note of cheer was that the Navy was finally paying the travel expenses for Margaret and the children, as well as all other Navy dependents.

Spruance arrived in Washington in a broiling July, reported for

5. Advance pay to defray travel expenses.

duty, and started house-hunting. Rents were exorbitant, he had little money, and Margaret became desperate to find a home. "I've got to go back to sea duty," groaned Spruance in despair. "I just can't afford shore duty."[6] Margaret's family was vacationing in Rhode Island, and she wrote them of her plight. They helped with a small check, and finally Spruance found an unfurnished house on unimproved 41st Street in northwest Washington for one hundred dollars a month.

Spruance owned no furniture, so he felt himself fortunate to buy a complete set of used furniture from a naval officer with orders to Asian duty. It was worn and shabby ("Trash," Margaret later recalled), but they refurbished it as best they could and feathered their nest. Margaret impetuously bought some expensive imported French fabric, and she and Spruance wielded needles and tufted their settee. They were strangers to Washington and had no social activities, so their afternoons and evenings were devoted to home improvement. Spruance's sole hobby—furniture restoration—began as a result.

His work at the Bureau of Engineering went well. The chief of the bureau was Rear Admiral J. K. Robison, one of the Navy's finest engineers. Spruance shortly became head of the Electrical Division and was responsible for the development, testing, procurement, installation, and maintenance of all shipboard electrical equipment in the United States Fleet—an awesome task. Robison was delighted with Spruance's performance.

Money worries continued to nag. Spruance needed a car and somehow found the money to buy a Hupmobile. But the only new clothes that Margaret bought the first year were a pair of white gloves for President Coolidge's reception at the White House for the Washington military community. The Spruances zipped through the reception line and passed the President so rapidly that Margaret felt the gloves had been a waste of good money.

Spruance had not been long in Washington when his father died, and he went to Indianapolis for the funeral. His father's death filled Spruance with remorse. He reproached himself for his years of indifference to his father. While in Indianapolis Spruance visited boyhood friends who had become prosperous businessmen, and their affluence accentuated his own lack of money and the Navy's dismal future. He

6. An ill-considered act of Congress decreed that the pay of officers on shore duty would be less than those on sea duty.

visited Edward Dean and told him he was seriously considering leaving the Navy in order to enter business. Dean immediately wrote Margaret not to allow Raymond to resign from the naval service. His son-in-law was too honest, wrote Dean, and he never would survive in the unprincipled business world.

Spruance returned to Washington, dejected by his father's death and his need for money. He was guilt-ridden over his inability to provide Margaret with a better standard of living, but he would not halt his financial aid to his mother and aunts. Margaret tried to console and encourage her husband. The gulf between him and his father wasn't his fault, she insisted. She assured him she was happy as a Navy wife. They had the essentials—a home, a cook, and a car—and two fine children, and Margaret did not resent his sending money to his relatives.

Spruance remained in the Navy.

Spruance's luck improved. He was permanently promoted to commander in early 1922 and was ordered to command the destroyer *Dale* in the spring of 1924.[7] Then, just before Spruance took command, Margaret's father died and bequeathed her $50,000. After careful analysis, Spruance bought Margaret high-quality stocks and bonds, which he managed wisely and well during the next forty years. The inheritance improved their standard of living while growing to provide Margaret a personal estate of $400,000.

Spruance's astute management of his own meager naval salary was even more dramatic. While supporting his immediate family and helping his relatives, he eventually amassed a personal fortune of $600,000. Spruance, however, would not spend money on himself. He would not buy new clothes despite Margaret's demands that he renovate his wardrobe. He owned but one admiral's uniform cap, bought when the eagle's head on the cap device faced left. Secretary of the Navy Frank Knox early in the war decided that the eagle should properly face to starboard, and naval officers bought new devices facing in the authorized direction. But not Spruance. In a letter to Margaret during the war he grumbled that a new cap cost forty dollars, so he intended to

7. USS *Dale* (DD 290), displacement 1,190 tons, main battery four 4-inch guns, four 21-inch torpedo tubes, commissioned 16 February 1920, decommissioned 1 May 1930, and sold in 1931. DANAFS, vol. 2 (Washington, 1963), p. 233.

shine up old faithful and continue wearing it. The weathered eagle looked over his port shoulder throughout the war.

Spruance lived the Protestant Ethic: gaining wealth was virtuous, but personal indulgence was sinful. His daughter summed up his annoying parsimony by saying that he'd tear a Kleenex in half to avoid extravagance. Yet he was generous with his family and provided for their every need, particularly the education of his children and grandchildren. Why nothing for himself? Doubtless the shock of his grandparents' bankruptcy and the early struggle to provide for his family were contributory. In any event, his acquisition of wealth was motivated by a need for security—emotional as well as financial—and not by avarice or self-indulgence.

Spruance was eager to command *Dale* in the summer of 1924, for it would mean blessed relief from Washington shore duty. But shortly before he took command, Margaret sensed something was amiss when Spruance came home in a solemn, silent mood.

"What has gone wrong?" she asked.

Her husband replied with funereal voice that his orders had been changed. He would have to report as Assistant Chief of Staff to Commander Naval Forces, Europe, Vice Admiral Philip Andrews, an imperious man feared and disliked by his subordinates. Spruance would replace a close friend, whom Andrews recently had fired.

"This is the end," Spruance said. "I know I'll never get along with that man." The only bright spot was that Andrews's staff was permanently based in Europe, so Margaret and the two children would live overseas to be near Spruance.

Spruance was allowed to command *Dale* long enough to take her from Norfolk to Cherbourg. He stopped in Newport to fuel, then sailed eastward. The weather was dismal—cold, fog, and wind—and *Dale* passed uncomfortably close to Brenton Reef Lightship in Rhode Island Sound. The weather continued to match Spruance's mood: foul. On arrival in Cherbourg he was relieved. He had been commanding officer for twenty days.

With justified foreboding, Spruance reported to Vice Admiral Andrews in his flagship *Pittsburgh* at Cherbourg. Andrews represented the United States Navy in Europe, which meant that he and his staff and ships were required to visit foreign ports and inland cities to entertain

Vice Admiral Philip Andrews and Commander Spruance, Europe, 1925

and be entertained by military and civilian dignitaries of those countries. Major navies have "shown the flag" for centuries as an overt diplomatic act to win friends or influence people on foreign shores. Andrews's mission with his diminutive flotilla therefore continued a hallowed naval task and tradition. Spruance's duty would not be strenuous and could well be a pleasant cruise.

Except for Andrews. His reputation had not been exaggerated, for he bickered interminably and made petulant demands. Since Spruance hadn't wanted the job, he was damned if he would tolerate Andrews's petty arguments. One Andrews diatribe ended abruptly when Spruance exclaimed, "I'm not going to argue with you anymore, Admiral." Then he walked out. Another time, Andrews insisted on taking *Pittsburgh* into an attractive Spanish port, although Spruance warned that the anchorage was too shallow. Andrews stubbornly persisted; he was determined to drop anchor and go ashore. Spruance, exasperated, declared he would put his objections in writing. If *Pittsburgh* grounded, the record would show it was because Andrews had disregarded Spruance's advice.

Andrews canceled the port call and wrote on Spruance's fitness report, "A very capable conscientious officer of great natural ability—industrious and hard working—of agreeable personality."

Andrews was eccentric, in addition to his more disagreeable traits. He feared germs and barked, "Take coughing distance!" if Spruance came too close. (Spruance parodied Andrews's phrase to Margaret, thinking it a great joke.) He also was a devout prohibitionist, compelling the staff surreptitiously to gather for clandestine pre-dinner cocktails in their hotel rooms. Spruance would post a lookout to warn of the old man's approach, and the officers and their wives, feeling like mischievous children, hoped that their grumpy admiral would not find them sneaking drinks.

Andrews, however, could be inconsistent in enforcing prohibition. One of his friends was an alcoholic who, when invited to a formal dinner party, drank himself into a foolish spectacle. Andrews chuckled to Spruance next morning that his friend had been the life of the party. Spruance shook his head.

The admiral and his wife, a childless couple, were captivated by young Margaret,[8] then an appealing five-year-old, and the Spruances

8. For clarity, Spruance's wife will hereafter be referred to as "Margaret," and his daughter as "young Margaret."

soon became their touring companions throughout Europe. Spruance would grandly navigate from the front seat, while young Margaret entertained her elders seated in the back. The admiral rarely paused while traveling, causing discomfort to the other adults, who had hunger and other needs to attend to. They solved the problem by coaxing young Margaret to appeal, "I'm very hungry. Can't we stop?" Andrews would invariably order the caravan to halt.

The tempestuous relationship between Andrews and Spruance thus subsided into quiescence. Life became blissful—delightful excursions to European cities and countryside, as well as dinners, parties, and receptions midst royalty, the rich, and the famous. Spruance was not fluent in French, but he knew enough to use it to advantage in these gatherings.

Margaret wanted to settle down with the children and finally rented an apartment in Cannes, then hired an Italian cook and a French governess. With Edward enrolled in a French public day school, Margaret could leave from time to time to travel with her husband. The idyll ended when young Margaret contracted colitis. Her case was bungled by an English doctor, and her distraught parents helplessly watched her almost die. It was a very close thing.

In time Andrews returned to the States, and Spruance relieved Halsey in command of the destroyer *Osborne,* then in European waters.[9] Halsey had presided over a cheerful wardroom of jovial young officers. He advised them not to be misled by their new skipper's sobriety. Spruance would be a good fellow and a good captain. And then Halsey's uproarious laughter was gone. Good-natured profanity no longer was heard in the wardroom. The new captain was different, indeed. The officers quickly noted, for example, that Spruance addressed them by their last names, whereas Halsey had always addressed them by their first names.

As usual, Spruance spoke softly and economically and displayed his superior shiphandling skills. Spruance operated with "a quiet bridge," denoting a ship commanded with cool efficiency and not given to loud voices in times of stress. It is not easy to achieve, but Spruance's bridges

9. USS *Osborne* (DD 295), displacement 1,190 tons, main battery four 4-inch guns, twelve 21-inch torpedo tubes, commissioned in May 1920, decommissioned 1 May 1930, and sold the next year. DANAFS, vol. 5 (Washington, 1970), p. 180.

always were quiet. Crises large and small were dispatched without fuss. Once while *Osborne* was anchored in six fathoms in Bizerte harbor, French North Africa, a rattled torpedo officer confronted Spruance. "Captain," he said, "we just dropped a depth charge over the stern!" "Well, pick it up and put it back," responded Spruance. The lieutenant was astonished by Spruance's equanimity. "Yes, sir," he blurted, then fled from his captain's cabin. Without alerting the French (who could have provoked an embarrassing international incident), the crew safely recovered the depth charge.

By coincidence, both Spruance and Halsey had commanded both *Dale* and *Osborne* in the two-year period 1924–1926. Their subordinate officers discussed the two skippers during bull sessions and compared their contrasting characteristics. Halsey was bold, gregarious, theatrical, and profane. His compulsive actions were based upon instinct, and he was considered aggressive.

Spruance, on the other hand, was deliberate and cautious. He was a private person. His personal life and past experiences were a mystery; he never reminisced. Although puritanical, he was tolerant. His subtle humor, occasionally tinged with irony, was not always recognized unless one watched his dancing steel-gray eyes. Spruance rarely smiled. Rather his eyes smiled and always betrayed him when he was laughing inside.

Halsey was loved and Spruance was respected, but they had much in common. They were considerate of their men. Both were courageous, highly skilled professional naval officers with perseverance and endurance. Yet no one could safely predict how they (or any other naval officer) would perform in war. The qualities that make a good peacetime officer are not always the same qualities that make an effective officer in time of war.

Spruance had heard rumors he would attend the Naval War College in the summer of 1926 when he returned *Osborne* to the States. He sent his family ahead with instructions to establish residence in Newport. When Margaret arrived in Boston she was met by Vice Admiral Andrews, who said that Spruance would be going to Washington. Margaret was stunned. She had leased an apartment in Newport and knew that Spruance wanted duty there. Andrews pulled strings, and the War College orders were confirmed. Margaret, much relieved, waited for her husband to arrive.

The Naval War College existed to provide naval officers with advanced education in the art of naval warfare. It had tumultuous antecedents.[10]

Captains Stephen B. Luce and Alfred Thayer Mahan in the early 1880's were disturbed that naval officers concentrated on the technical details of ship operations. Although expert seamen, officers knew little about making war, which involved the broad and sometimes esoteric fields of strategy and tactics. The art of war could not be expressed with formulas and equations that were familiar to technically trained naval officers. Rather, war required an intellect that could reason, innovate, create, and think abstractly. Luce and Mahan battled to unshackle the minds of naval officers. Their reward was the Naval War College, established in 1885 over the opposition of those who believed that the naval officer need not concern himself with anything that lay beyond the boundaries of his ship.

Mahan was the Navy's most brilliant and prolific theoretician, and he became the college president in 1889. He had many enemies—senior naval officers who argued that higher education for naval officers was unnecessary, that sea-going experience was enough. Mahan was an intellectual whose profession was anti-intellectual. When he wanted to remain ashore to complete his writings, he was told that a naval officer's duty was on a ship at sea and not writing a book on dry land.

Eventually the Navy grudgingly accepted the college, and by the mid-twenties its eleven-month term was recognized to be of real benefit to a naval career. Mahan had become the apostle of seapower, and his famous books were carefully studied by War College students.

In the pre-dawn darkness of a summer morning, Margaret was wakened by a knocking on her Newport apartment door. She opened it to find her husband and a snarling, lunging schnauzer. Having recovered from her shock, she demanded an explanation about the dog. Spruance proudly explained he had bought the dog as a puppy in the Mediterranean. Wasn't he a handsome animal? "Peter" was the first of two fiery schnauzers whom Spruance loved, Margaret distrusted, and friends feared.

10. For the background of the U.S. Naval War College, see Ronald H. Spector, *Professors of War: The Naval War College and the Development of the Naval Profession* (Newport, 1977).

Spruance had seen the War College many times from afar, for the ships of the fleet passed by it often. It was an imposing three-story granite building that squatted upon a bluff on Coaster's Harbor Island, overlooking Narragansett Bay to seaward. Once Mahan, his staff, and their families had lived in the building, called Luce Hall. Now it provided offices for the staff and students, but the fireplaces remained. It had a distinctly unwarlike atmosphere. A casual visitor would see only middle-aged men in civilian clothes, reading and writing in quiet, austere surroundings.

Spruance was one of seventy students, forty-five in the senior class of captains and commanders, and twenty-five in the junior class. The majority expected to rest from sea duty, with plenty of time for reading and recreation. The students were mostly naval line officers, with a sprinkling of staff corps, Marine, and Army officers. As with War College classes immemorial, they fitted no narrow pattern of character or professional competence.[11] Some worked hard and some were lazy. Some wanted to be there, others were there against their wishes. There were "comers" who needed War College training to help them achieve flag rank. Others were "stashed" at Newport because they were temporarily without a permanent billet. And finally, some were there because the Bureau of Navigation felt they were inferior officers and hoped that in a year they either would choose, or be forced, to retire.

There was a great gap in the age, seniority, and thinking of the two classes. The juniors were considered too young to absorb the profound teaching and wisdom of their seniors. The lieutenants in turn felt that many of the senior officers refused to learn anything new or different. In some cases both opinions proved correct. The classes rarely mixed except for several war games and special studies.

The War College President was Rear Admiral William V. Pratt, assisted by a carefully selected staff of twenty officers. Pratt was ambitious, enlightened, imaginative, and extremely competent. The War College presidency was but one step in his successful quest to become the Chief of Naval Operations.

Spruance's course of instruction included naval warfare problems and war games; the study of strategy and naval history; a pilot course in

11. Five became distinguished flag officers: Raymond A. Spruance, Royal E. Ingersoll (Commander in Chief Atlantic Fleet in World War II), Edward C. Kalbfus, Frank H. Brumby, and a future Chief of Naval Operations, Forrest P. Sherman.

logistics; international law, taught by the prestigious George Grafton Wilson of Harvard; lectures by experts in government, economics, and international relations, and lots of reading. Pratt, undoubtedly the college's outstanding president between the two world wars, dictated every facet of the curriculum.

War games had begun at the turn of the century and were the essence of the War College education. The first step in "gaming" was to solve theoretical naval warfare problems using a reasoning process called the "Estimate of the Situation." It consisted of four parts: Deriving the Mission; The Decision; The Plan; and The Written Order. The "Estimate" had originated with the Germans, and the War College since 1910 had refined its procedures with each new president.

The students tested their solutions by playing war games, two opposing fleets fighting abstract sea battles upon a 200-inch by 308-inch wooden board located on the upper deck of Luce Hall. Miniature ships, an inch long, represented the actual ships of the world's navies. The rules were complex and the games were slow and protracted. The games later were transferred to the floor of a large room, but the principles were unchanged.

The benefits of war gaming were many: familiarity with possible future enemies; training in the techniques of developing sound war plans; and increased knowledge in the strategy and tactics of war at sea. Colors were assigned to various fleets of the world, and the two fleets that most often were opponents on the War College game board were Blue versus Orange: the United States versus Japan.

The War College and the Navy believed that Japan was America's most probable future enemy. By studying the Japanese national character, students tried to predict how Japan would wage war against the United States. The feeling was that the Japanese possessed high morale and effective military skills, were well disciplined, and were fanatically loyal to an autocratic government. (The students were wistful that Americans should be less disciplined than the Japanese.) Japanese were patient, they believed, and would endure great hardships. But it was also a general belief that Japanese fatalism made them unadaptable to new ideas, and that they had less mechanical aptitude than Americans. The students viewed Americans as individualists who would resist going to war. But when war came, they held, Americans would fight well, united by patriotism and an indomitable spirit and will to win.

The students' study of the Russo-Japanese War impressed them with one certainty in the Japanese character: Japan would start a future war by launching a surprise attack before issuing a formal declaration.

The Navy visualized that war as a prolonged naval campaign fought across millions of square miles of Pacific Ocean. The Japanese would slowly retreat toward their home islands, all the while gathering strength, shortening their supply lines, and fighting a delaying action that would weaken the Americans by steady attrition. When the Americans became exhausted and overextended in the western Pacific, the Japanese would concentrate their forces and attack for a decisive fleet action. Then the war would be decided by the huge guns of the battleships. If the Japanese battleships won, the war would be stalemated and the Americans would seek a negotiated peace. If the American battleships triumphed, Japan would be blockaded and forced to surrender.

The students viewed war in simple terms. Their game scenarios assumed that total war had begun with Japan and that the objective of both adversaries was the destruction of the other's fleet. The college never considered whether the United States government might have different ideas from the Navy about a war with Japan. Foreign policy and international relations were the domain of the politicians, and war with Japan was the concern of the Army and Navy.

Unfortunately, the college staff and students deceived themselves as to how that war would be fought. They glorified the battleship and were indifferent to newer tactics and weapons that might complicate a future war. For example, the Navy would need island bases to support an advance across the Pacific, but the college did not study the kind of amphibious warfare needed to capture those islands. Fortunately, the Marines did.

A fleet advancing across thousands of miles of ocean against a dangerous enemy needed logistical support. Pratt started a course in logistics, but it was jettisoned when he left. Logistics was too dull and tedious to interest naval officers. Ambitious officers served in warships and were unconcerned with the details of providing fuel, food, and ammunition to a distant fleet.

Submarines were considered too vulnerable and unwieldy to maneuver with the fleet. They were used mostly as scouts. Light cruisers were the only proper commerce raiders, said the students, and submarines would menace neither fleets nor merchantmen in a future war.

Carrier aviation was in its infancy when Spruance was a student. The War College regarded naval airpower as a supplement—but never a replacement—to the battleship. Aviators and surface officers were in opposite camps, and the latter dominated the War College up to the beginning of World War II. The fleet and not the college developed the strategy and tactics for air warfare in the Pacific.

Despite its shortcomings, the Naval War College helped Spruance to prepare for war. He enjoyed the academic atmosphere and his association with other ambitious officers. The college motivated him to study military history, strategy, tactics, and international relations; it focused his attention on Japan as his future enemy; and it exposed him to the enlightened thinking of Admiral Pratt. Spruance became an avid student of the art of naval warfare and earned a service reputation as a sound professional thinker. He would return for two tours of staff duty during the 1930's.

Spruance was intellectually stimulated by naval warfare problems, in the same way that a mathematician is stimulated by complicated calculus problems. He evaluated hundreds of student solutions as a War College staff officer, and his faculty for analyzing and solving problems became instinctive. When later confronted with the crises and complexities of the Pacific war, he could resolve them systematically and effectively.

He would treat the war in the Pacific with the same emotional detachment that he treated war games in Newport. "I believe that making war is a game that requires cold and careful calculation," he remarked after World War II. "Each operation is different and has to be analyzed and studied in order to prepare the most suitable plans for it. That is what makes the planning of operations in war such an interesting job."

But the war was many years in the future, and in 1926 Spruance and his classmates seemed to be anachronisms, studying war in a world that sought eternal peace. Many Americans wondered why the United States even needed a navy, and one influential critic deprecated "the peculiar psychology of the Navy, which frequently seems to retire from the realm of logic into a dim religious world where Neptune is God, Mahan his prophet, and the U.S. Navy the only true Church." Meanwhile, Spruance, in the remoteness and solitude of Luce Hall and his own mind, thought about abstract war and played abstract war games with toy ships upon a wooden board.

Following his graduation from the War College in the summer of 1927, Spruance was assigned to the Office of Naval Intelligence (ONI) in Washington, D.C. ONI was a division within the Office of the Chief of Naval Operations and mustered fewer than twenty naval officers.[12] Its director was a captain, Spruance as the only commander was the assistant director, and the remaining officers were lieutenant commanders and lieutenants. Intelligence data was collected largely by naval attachés (totaling fifteen to twenty in number) in selected embassies in Europe, Asia, and South America. ONI functioned to gather, collate, and compile the data, then distribute what was thought important to ships and shore establishments in a "Monthly Information Bulletin."[13]

Spruance and Margaret found a home with far less trauma than before. Her inheritance allowed them to rent a comfortable, well-built house, a triplex on Klingle Road in northwest Washington. Many Navy friends lived nearby, and social gatherings were frequent. Although Navy families moved often, they tended to congregate in major seaports or in Washington. One was never apart from old shipmates for long periods, and familiar faces were everywhere. The Navy was small, and everyone knew everyone else. They formed a close, intimate community with common interests and enduring friendships. When World War II began, the Navy's leaders all had belonged to the same club for many years.

Edward and Margaret, eleven and seven, had become little devils who delighted in ringing doorbells, then running and hiding. ("We were beastly!" recalled young Margaret.) They enraged the next-door neighbor, a choleric State Department officer who cursed and waved a menacing cane. He eventually complained to the Navy Department through official channels, and he and Spruance nearly came to blows. The neighbor finally broke his lease and left.

The children's behavior belied Spruance's discipline. He demanded obedience and did not tolerate childish faults. If they dawdled to their mother's gentle requests, Spruance would snap an order that galvanized them into immediate action. He helped with homework but became

12. By 1940, ONI had quadrupled in size. Three months after Pearl Harbor, it had over three hundred officers on its rolls.

13. The Office of Naval Intelligence between the wars is well covered in Jeffrey M. Dorwart's *Conflict of Duty: The U.S. Navy's Intelligence Dilemma 1919–1945* (Annapolis, 1983).

Young Margaret

impatient if they were slow to grasp his explanations. This once reduced young Margaret to tears, and she fled to her mother for solace.

Margaret tore into her husband. "You are absolutely no help if you
can't control your feelings," she scolded. "You simply can't act this way
when you are with these children, because you aren't helping them at
all. You are going to ruin Margaret as far as her coming to you for help,
and that is the last thing in the world you want to do." His behavior
improved.

He could be just as impatient with his wife by expecting her to
understand him without repeated explanation. ("I told you once.")
Margaret insisted that he change his ways, and her efforts bore fruit in

Edward

mid-1943 when Spruance was a vice admiral preparing for the attack on Tarawa. "I remember your frequent advice," he wrote, "to keep my temper, hold my tongue and let people have their say, before speaking my mind. I hope I am improving in that respect."

He expected much of Edward. Both father and son wore a coat and tie to dinner in even the hottest Washington weather. (Young Margaret recalled years later that the admiral changed in the last ten years of his life and wore a coat and tie only when going out.) Edward loved Saturday matinees but was required to cut the grass and weed the yard to qualify for the privilege. Spruance insisted on high scholastic marks, and Edward, trying to please, studied hard and not unwillingly—

except for mathematics. "Dad's natural mathematical ability," Edward once wrote, "ran headlong into my inability in that field."

As far as Edward was concerned, his father was austere, remote, and inflexible. They rarely did things together, except for walks or an occasional sail. (Spruance had given him a twenty-two-foot catboat which Edward treasured, and as a teenager in Newport he practically lived in it.) He could not confide in his father and later sadly reminisced, "I can not remember a harsh word ever being exchanged between him and my mother. Neither can I remember any display of affection toward me. . . . I always respected and was fond of him. He was a 'father presence' as I imagine it to be in some German families, always in control, always unruffled, busy with his career . . . we lived in two separate worlds that occasionally overlapped."

The children were awed by the many foreign naval attachés that visited their father's house, cultivating and being cultivated for tidbits of useful intelligence information over cocktails and conversation. They were even more impressed that their father served cocktails, in violation of Prohibition. He bought from a bootlegger and kept a good supply of liquor in the pantry. It could loosen tongues. Keeping illegal liquor could be risky, however, for a keg exploded in his closet when he later became executive officer of the *Mississippi* in Long Beach.

Spruance followed a premeditated plan to gain firsthand knowledge of the Japanese through Captain Tsueno Sakano, a Japanese naval attaché. They first exchanged calls; later Margaret helped Mrs. Sakano find a suitable school for their son. The Sakanos' gratitude blossomed into friendship, and they frequently exchanged visits. The two men's conversations were cordial yet cautious, because each knew that the other sought naval intelligence. Margaret was amused by their subtle sparring. It is not unlikely that they exchanged some information, a common practice between military attachés and their opposite numbers. Through Sakano, Spruance gained entrée into the Japanese embassy's social circle, and he and Margaret met many other Japanese naval officers and their families.

When the Sakanos returned to Japan in the early 1930's, Spruance and Margaret saw them off in Los Angeles, where Spruance was serving as executive officer of the *Mississippi*. Sakano became a vice admiral, but he opposed war with the United States and was ostracized in his own country. He lost everything and was destitute at war's end. Spruance resumed their friendship in 1946, and Sakano entertained young Margaret and her husband when they were stationed in Japan in the early 1950's.

Spruance's respect and admiration for the Japanese people was certainly nurtured through his association with Sakano and other Japanese during his duty in ONI. Whether he fully understood the complex Japanese culture is problematical, because Spruance was biased by the intense racialism in America at the time. Furthermore, Sakano's behavior was misleading. Although he liked Spruance, he nevertheless was ingratiating. He did not represent the Japanese military archetype that Spruance would fight during World War II. Spruance felt he could read the Japanese mind, but his decisions in one of his greatest Pacific battles of the war would be based upon wrong assumptions about another Japanese admiral's thinking.

While at ONI, Spruance requested sea duty as executive officer of a battleship. There were 16 battleships in the fleet and 410 commanders theoretically eligible to be their "execs." For those aspiring to flag rank, successful command of a battleship (or cruiser) was essential, but a tour as executive officer was a prerequisite to command. In effect, those who were ordered as battleship or cruiser executive officers were identified as potential admirals. Spruance therefore was delighted to receive orders as exec of the battleship *Mississippi* in late 1929.[14]

The United States Navy was in doldrums. After a spate of new construction under Coolidge, no keels would be laid under Hoover. The Washington Conference of 1921 had reduced the number of the Navy's larger ships, and American cruisers were inferior in numbers to Great Britain's and Japan's. The few "treaty cruisers" built in the late twenties were handicapped by design defects imposed under treaty limitations. The destroyers were deteriorating and no replacements were planned. The battleships, however, had been modernized one or

14. USS *Mississippi* (BB 41), displacement 32,000 tons, main battery twelve 14-inch guns, commissioned 18 December 1916. The *Mississippi* was probably Spruance's favorite ship. In December 1941 at the outbreak of the Pacific War, she was in the Atlantic, but returned the next year to the Pacific, where from 1943 through August 1945 she earned eight battle stars. Mostly the *Mississippi* provided gunfire support for amphibious invasions, but at the Battle of Surigao Strait (24–25 October 1944), she had her only chance to slug it out with Japanese battleships. After the war she served as a test platform for new weapons, and on 28 January 1953 was the first ship to fire a Terrier missile. She was finally decommissioned 17 September 1956 and sold for scrap. DANAFS, vol. 4 (Washington, 1969), pp. 388–89.

two at a time, contingent upon what little money a tightfisted Congress would appropriate. All naval ships now burned oil, and the filthy task of coaling ship was eliminated.

Little money was available for operations and training. Every drop of fuel was conserved and every projectile and powder case was hoarded for exclusive use in the fleet's battle-efficiency competition in engineering, communications, gunnery, and damage control. The Office of Fleet Training compiled and published exercise reports listing the score of every ship, every gun, and every turret. Outstanding gun crews won prize money and wore the "E" for excellence on their sleeves. Careers were made or broken on the relative standings among ships, and competition became an end in itself.

"Thus, while everyone worked hard, we began going in circles," wrote a contemporary naval officer. "The Fleet became more and more tied to bases, operating out of Long Beach—San Diego on a tight fuel budget, chained to the increasingly artificial, detailed mandates of the Office of Fleet Training whose word was law. The pencil became sharper than the sword, everyone tried to beat the target practice rules and too many forgot there was a war getting closer. Paper work wrapped its deadly tentacles around cabin and wardroom. . . . Glaring defects in guns, ammunition, torpedoes, battle tactics, went unnoticed so long as the competition rules made due allowances and gave everyone similar conditions."

The carriers *Saratoga* and *Lexington* had joined the fleet, and they and their expanding aircraft squadrons were draining manpower from the understrength surface forces. Some 84,000 enlisted men and 5,500 line officers were inadequate to man the ships of the fleet, even though the fleet was shrinking. Congress would not authorize more officers, and Naval Academy classes in the early 1930's required special congressional authority to commission graduates in excess of the number authorized by law.

Spruance and his messmates were poor because Congress had not authorized a pay increase for twenty years (and would not until World War II). Yet the cost of living had doubled. Worse yet, the pay tables were unfair; lieutenants sometimes drew more pay than admirals. Margaret's inheritance helped, but those without independent means were in trouble.

The Navy declared it had three missions. The first was to train for war and to provide a nucleus for expansion in case of a national emergency. The second was to protect American interests in China and Latin America, where insurrections and rebellions flourished. The last was showing the flag.

There is an old Navy saying that the exec runs the ship and the captain runs the exec. The job of the executive officer is the same regardless of the ship. He is second in command and is responsible for the ship's administration. *Mississippi* was a smart ship with a reputation for good performance and high morale, although she was cursed throughout her lifetime with disastrous turret explosions. She was a well-oiled machine. Spruance had to keep her ticking, occasionally tuning and refining her performance here and there.

The daily routine in port was invariable. Early each morning Spruance would briskly stride to the fleet landing from his apartment and ride the officers' launch to *Mississippi* at anchor in San Pedro harbor. The crew would be about, following a 0600 reveille, swabbing decks and shining brightwork. The liberty party and the officers on shore leave were aboard by 0800 and eating breakfast.

Quarters for muster sounded at 0900, the men fell in at divisions, and the department heads assembled with Spruance. He read the orders for the day, the officers posted, repeated the orders to their men, inspected them for appearance and smartness, and the daily work began.

The enlisted men of the *Mississippi* represented the hard core of professionals upon whom the wartime Navy would expand. During the Great Depression the applicants for enlistment were many and the vacancies few. Those who were selected were intelligent, educated, and competent. Civilian jobs were scarce, so most men reenlisted and made the Navy their career.

Young officers were expected to work alongside their men, although this practice varied widely. On many ships a smudged and dirty officer's uniform was a symbol of pride, for it testified that the wearer had shared the discomforts of his men. On other ships the officers were discouraged from soiling their hands.

The rationale for working closely with enlisted men was that it reminded the officer, "There, but for the grace of God, go I." There was, indeed, a wide disparity between their social statuses. Officers were married gentlemen, accepted by the upper classes of society. Sailors were largely bachelors, the ship was their home, and they were treated with indifference and contempt by many civilian communities. Loan sharks and gyp artists, whores and bar owners, all were out for the sailor's money.

On the bottom of the naval social spectrum were the steward mates, both Filipinos and blacks. They were restricted to messmen duties and were segregated from the white crewmen. Secretary of the Navy Claude Swanson justified the Navy's racial discrimination to Eleanor Roosevelt in response to her inquiry about the status of blacks in the Navy. "One of the chief reasons why the present restrictive policy exists," wrote Swanson, "is that in the event colored men be enlisted in a branch other than the messman branch, they would after training be subject to advancement to petty officers. In such a position they would be placed in charge of and have under them white men, all of which would result in a lack of team work, would create dissatisfaction, and would seriously handicap ship efficiency."

Spruance's feelings on blacks in the Navy were expressed in a 1966 letter to the Director of Naval History, written while Spruance was awaiting surgery. "It has been interesting, while sitting around the Army Hospital," he wrote, "to observe the considerable number of Negroes on duty in the Hospital. I would not desire to have a ship manned with them."

The policy of racial discrimination in the Armed Forces was abolished by President Truman following World War II. Many discriminatory practices lingered, nevertheless. The Navy today is committed to eliminating whatever intraservice discrimination may remain, largely through intensive education and indoctrination programs.

The men drilled in the morning. After lunch they scrubbed, swabbed, swept, buffed, shined, and polished so that *Mississippi* sparkled and glistened and glowed. On Thursday afternoons the captain, accompanied by Spruance, inspected the machinery spaces. Friday was Field Day, and the lower decks were attacked with renewed vigor for any sign of dirt. Spruance searched behind urinals for verdigris, on overheads for dust, and in the galley for rust. Despite *Mississippi*'s cleanliness, her cockroaches and bedbugs (those ancient naval nemeses) could not be eradicated.

On Saturday morning the crew unrolled their blues, rolled their neckerchiefs, spit-shined their shoes to a mirrorlike finish, donned snowy caps, and presented themselves for captain's inspection. Liberty call sounded at noon, and the liberty party went ashore. Holiday routine began and *Mississippi* slumbered through the weekend.

Spruance was a remote, authoritarian figure to the officers and men of *Mississippi*. If one obeyed the well-understood rules, all was well. Those who strayed felt the wrath of Spruance's sense of naval justice and morality. An indiscreet ensign once escorted a young woman, identified as his wife, to a dinner sponsored by the Long Beach Chamber of Commerce at the Pacific Coast Club. Some civilians discovered she was not his wife and complained to either Spruance or the captain. The ensign left the ship in disgrace and resigned his naval commission. The wardroom officers suspected that Spruance had initiated the harsh disciplinary action.

Yet Spruance was not unfriendly, and he often encouraged young officers toward a naval career. He would pace the quarterdeck at night with the watch officers, talking with them about many things. One ambitious ensign, first in his Academy class, wanted to be a naval aviator. Spruance argued that the battleship was the backbone of the Navy and that aviation was best suited for carefree, irresponsible types. Spruance liked the young officer and feared he would be wasted in naval aviation. "Stay with the ships," Spruance urged. The ensign disregarded the advice and became a successful aviator, then an admiral. Years later Spruance grudgingly admitted that the ensign had "probably" made the right decision.

Spruance as executive officer was president of the wardroom mess, for in the larger ships the captain ate alone in a private mess. The exec established the wardroom decorum, based upon the traditional customs for proper wardroom behavior. Throughout the Navy, officers normally dressed for dinner, sat in descending order of seniority, and behaved like gentlemen. Meals were served by stewards, and the tables were set with china and linen. Formal dinners frequently were held with wives and civilian guests. Officers had a proper rig for every occasion, choosing from evening dress, mess jacket, boat cloak, cocked hat, and epaulets.

Officers and enlisted men mingled for ship's parties ashore or afloat. Inter-ship athletic competitions in sailing, rowing, football, baseball, boxing, wrestling, and track were enthusiastically followed by all ranks and ratings. Intra-ship boxing and wrestling "smokers" on the fantail were universally popular when the ship was underway.

The social lives ashore of the *Mississippi* officers and wives were structured yet agreeable. The ship followed a regular schedule and was frequently in home port. During summer recreational cruises many wives followed the ship to meet their husbands at the more attractive ports of call on the Pacific coast. Everyone obeyed the rules of service etiquette. Naval custom required the wardroom officers and their wives to make formal calls upon Spruance and Margaret and to leave calling cards. The wives of senior officers felt responsible for indoctrinating the wives of junior officers into the ways of the Navy. Friendships flourished, and parties, teas, dinners, and receptions were frequent. Civilian clubs and organizations welcomed naval membership.

All in all, there were many compensations for service in the peacetime Navy.

Chapter 5

PRELUDE TO WAR

SPRUANCE returned to the Naval War College in the fall of 1931 as Officer in Charge of the Correspondence Courses Department. The department had been active for a good many years and was an important supplement to the resident course of instruction. Many officers enrolled in the correspondence course; few completed it. It was long and tough. Spruance's most difficult task would be to motivate students to complete their assignments within a reasonable time.

The department had two basic courses, Strategy and Tactics (S&T) and International Law. Approximately six hundred officers were enrolled, but Spruance wanted even more participation. He sent personal letters to the executive officers of large ships, soliciting their help in telling junior officers what he had to offer. He also gave the course synopsis to the graduating resident students, asking them to pass the word when they returned to the fleet.

The Depression had reduced the size of Spruance's staff, so he personally corrected all the S&T solutions. It was hard, mentally fatiguing work. He tried to make the course a success, but he felt that most students didn't seem to care. Their indifferent response to his efforts was a personal disappointment.

Home no longer was the place of comfort it once had been. His mother, Annie, had moved in. She had been independent for years and

Annie Hiss Spruance, 1935

wanted to remain that way, but now she was alone and in her sixties. Her son insisted that she live with him despite her objections. She was an annoying old woman who upset the family routine. Her sharp tongue and irascible temper made the children cringe. Although Margaret tolerated her mother-in-law's invasion of her home, she would not join Spruance and Annie at the breakfast table.

Mother and son enjoyed an intellectual rapport, and Spruance discussed more varied subjects and at greater length with his mother than he ever did with his wife. Annie was popular with Spruance's friends because she was witty and amusing, and she frequently accompanied Spruance and Margaret to cocktail parties. She indignantly refused offers of tea and insisted upon gin, for Annie enjoyed a drink. Spruance teased her by ceremoniously measuring the liquid level in the port bottle to see how much she had nipped during the day.

Captain Spruance, Naval War College, 1935

And there were other domestic problems. Their house was ugly and the cellar usually flooded, so Spruance had no place to refurbish furniture. "I'm going to need a rowboat down there," he once reported. "It's just like Venice."

Edward and young Margaret were teenagers. Strict when they were young, Spruance now was permissive. Teenage friends congregated in the Spruance home, and they adored Annie because she was interested in them. "I envy you all because you have opportunities for education," Annie often said. "When I wanted to go to college, ladies were not allowed."

College was also on Spruance's mind. Edward was a senior in high school and his future was a lively subject. Responding to his father's urging over the years, he was an excellent student and was qualified for any college or university. Spruance repeatedly emphasized the need for a good education, and he promised Edward he would send him to the college or university of his son's choice. He felt that Edward was unsuited for the Naval Academy because of his weakness in mathematics and because his individualism would not conform to naval discipline. Although Spruance described the advantages and disadvantages of a naval career, he and Margaret hoped that Edward would chose Princeton and major in liberal arts. The decision was Edward's.

Edward chose the Naval Academy, but his reasoning never was clear. Edward claimed years later that he went there because that was what his father wanted. Yet Margaret insists that her husband never pressured Edward to attend the Academy, although he was happy with Edward's decision. Perhaps Edward thought it would please his father; he had always tried to meet his father's expectations. For whatever reasons, Edward became a midshipman and endured four woeful years at Annapolis.

Spruance never communicated well with his children, perhaps contributing to the misunderstanding over Edward's Annapolis decision. Any outward affection was for Margaret alone. One evening the children spied a couple walking in the gathering dusk with arms entwined. "Edward," giggled his sister, "will you look at those lovers?" The children were surprised and embarrassed to discover the couple were their parents.

Spruance's first display of love for his children emerged unexpectedly when young Margaret left for college. To her shock and surprise, her father embraced her. His eyes filled with tears. "I'm going to miss you," he said. His daughter was flustered at her father's unprecedented emotion. "My gosh!" thought young Margaret. "He really *is* going to miss me."

The selection board for captain met in 1931 to consider Spruance and forty-three others for promotion. Approximately 60 percent of the eligible commanders would be selected. Those passed over would be forced to retire. Spruance and Margaret discussed the most probable selectees.

"Well," she remarked, "you don't have anything to worry about."

"Oh, indeed I have," he replied.

Then Spruance told his wife about a letter of reprimand he had received five years before.

When Spruance had commanded *Osborne* in 1926, a dishonest commissary steward had stolen provisions and falsified records, then had fled the *Osborne* shortly before Spruance had been relieved. An investigation revealed that the steward had embezzled thirty-nine hundred dollars. The Secretary of the Navy blamed Spruance by a letter of reprimand, charging that his lack of supervision had enabled the commissary steward to misuse government funds. The letter was harsh and damning and could have ended Spruance's career. He felt it was unfair and challenged its accusations.

Spruance defended himself vigorously with a letter of rebuttal. The Board of Investigation, he wrote, had not faulted his supervision of the *Osborne* commissary department. In Spruance's view, the fault lay with the commissary officer, the man responsible for supervising the commissary steward. Shortly after taking command, Spruance had discovered that the commissary officer was a careless bookkeeper and had admonished him to keep more accurate records. He had assumed that the warning would be sufficient. But the officer had not improved, argued Spruance, and his negligence and inattention had allowed the commissary steward to embezzle the government's money.

Spruance concluded his refutation by saying that he was not disclaiming his responsibility as a commanding officer. But he was questioning whether that responsibility included his detailed supervision of a supposedly competent and experienced commissary officer. "In the case in question," he wrote, "I cannot but feel that I had a reasonable justification for believing that the commissary officer, who had no press of other duties and who had been specially cautioned as to the necessity for care in making up his records, would perform the elementary duty of keeping a record of the bills outstanding and paid. Had he done this, the dishonesty of the commissary steward would have been discovered when it first occurred in March, 1926."

He later wrote a letter to the Chief of the Bureau of Navigation inviting attention to his letter of rebuttal, thereby alerting the selection board as well. Otherwise Spruance had continued to do his best, hoping that his record of performance would offset the reprimand. The fate of his career would be decided when the captain selection board met.

This incident illustrates a potential risk in Spruance's style of leadership. He trusted his subordinates. Having told them what he wanted done, he allowed them to do the job in their own way with a minimum of interference and supervision from him. They were grateful for Spruance's faith and support and responded with intense loyalty, inspired to use their initiative and not to fail Spruance.

This system works when one has able subordinates. It can fail if a subordinate is incompetent and lets down his commander. But Spruance felt that the benefits of trusting his people justified the risk of an occasional betrayal of that trust. His leadership philosophy never changed.

There were many able commanders competing with Spruance for promotion. The letter of reprimand—justified or not—could have tipped the scales against him when the board weighed otherwise equally excellent service records. It could only hurt his chances, and Spruance was pessimistic when the board convened. He needn't have been. The board selected Spruance for promotion to captain in late 1931.

In March 1933, Spruance was ordered to command USS *Vestal,* a twenty-six-year-old, 8000-ton repair ship. It was a dismaying assignment. Ambitious, first-rate officers sought command in the Battle Fleet rather than the lower-caste auxiliaries. Spruance was an officer on his way up. He had just been promoted to captain and had an excellent record in battleships and destroyers. The President of the Naval War College, Rear Admiral Harris Laning, had recommended that Spruance be promoted to flag rank "when due." Why then the orders to a lowly repair ship?

The assignment of naval officers was and is a complex business. Officers rotate frequently in a variety of assignments in order to gain broad professional experience. Whenever an officer moves, someone must replace him. Reassigning just one officer can trigger a series of moves for a half-dozen more. The result is a constant flow ("pipeline") of officers in and out of ships and stations.

The Bureau of Navigation gave first priority to the needs of the Navy. The next priority was the officer's personal desires. Often these two criteria were incompatible, for an officer's opinion of what was best for him frequently conflicted with the plans of the Bureau. The Bureau detailing officers—known as detailers—tried to be impartial and objective, but there were many pressures. Individual officers or their advocates would ask for special treatment. Senior officers would "requisition" favorite officers for their staff or ship. Detailer and officer frequently exchanged letters discussing future duty assignments if the latter was distant from Washington, or had discussed such assignments in person. Sometimes a detailer offered a choice of future duty. Sometimes orders were arbitrarily issued.

These procedures generated confusion. Orders frequently changed at the last moment, or long-awaited orders would be late in arriving. Planning for future duty (especially from the standpoint of the wife, who had household effects and children's schools to worry about) was fraught with uncertainty.

Detailers were both courted and held in contempt by other officers. Fleet Admiral Ernest J. King felt they were prone to vacillation and compromise. In his book, anyone associated with the Bureau of Navigation was a "fixer." He would always be suspicious of Fleet Admiral Chester Nimitz during World War II because of Nimitz's previous duty with the Bureau.

One can speculate that Spruance objected to his orders to *Vestal*. In any event, they were canceled, typically at the last minute. On 15 May 1933 he received urgent orders to report in two weeks as chief of staff to Rear Admiral A. E. Watson, Commander Destroyers, Scouting Force, three thousand miles away in California. Time was short. Spruance wanted to leave immediately, but there were two obstacles to a speedy departure. Edward was in limbo because the Academy entrance exam results were unannounced, and someone had to close the house and store the furniture.

The solution was to leave Edward behind. Edward would handle the house and stay with family friends until the examination results were known. Next morning Spruance, with wife and daughter, rushed from Newport in his 1932 Chrysler sedan. The sight of a very forlorn Edward, alone on the front porch, moved Margaret to tears. She was abandoning her son to an uncertain future. Halsey (then a War College student) reassured her. "Don't worry," Halsey said. "If Edward doesn't make it, I'll go to Washington and beat on doors. I'll take care of it."

Throughout the cross-country trip Spruance stopped at libraries to scan the *Army-Navy Register* for the list of successful candidates. In Salt Lake City he read the good news that Edward had made it.

Spruance reported to Rear Admiral Watson in late May in San Francisco. Watson commanded twenty-six destroyers in commission, one-third of the entire destroyer force. They were old, worn-out, and expensive to maintain. The Navy tried stopgap measures such as shuffling ships in and out of the mothball fleet or using one crew to maintain two ships. Such expedients were futile. New replacements were needed, but none had been authorized during the fourteen years following World War I.

The Great Depression was bad news for the civilian economy, but in a way good news for the Navy. Roosevelt's National Industrial Recovery Act had authorized a substantial shipbuilding program that would restore the Navy to treaty strength. The principal objective of the Act was to rejuvenate the economy. Civilians and Navy alike would benefit from the $238 million that Congress appropriated for thirty-two new ships.

In contrast, Congress forced the Navy to reduce its payroll as an economy measure. The measures seemed harsh: a 15 percent pay cut, the abolition of shipping-over (reenlistment) bonuses for enlisted men, and the elimination of longevity pay for everyone. Enlisted promotions were slowed. Officers could still be promoted but with no pay increase.

Yet Spruance and his brethren were smug and quietly content. Their regular paychecks and increased purchasing power provided financial security denied millions of civilians. Over 93 percent of all eligible sailors reenlisted for a naval career, owing to unemployment on the "outside." The naval profession became a closed shop. Only one out of every twenty-eight applicants was accepted for first enlistment, and the lower half of the Academy Class of 1933 was honorably discharged upon graduation because there was no room for them in the Navy.

The Secretary of the Navy despaired of manning his new ships. "It takes much time to train personnel," he wrote, "and, accordingly, when ships are laid down, Congress should authorize sufficient personnel to be trained and ready to man the ships when they are completed." Congress eventually increased the officer corps to meet the demands of a growing Navy, but President Roosevelt was reluctant to ask Congress for increased enlisted manpower, even in the last days before Pearl Harbor.

Watson was a difficult individual, but not to the degree of Rush and Andrews. Spruance, experienced by now with temperamental senior officers, soon established a comfortable working relationship with Watson. Spruance ran the force and Watson took it easy.

Shortly after Spruance came aboard, the Bureau of Engineering arranged to test several underwater sound devices aboard destroyers of the Scouting Force. For years the Naval Research Laboratory had sought methods to detect submerged submarines, and a group of scientists under Dr. Harvey West believed they had the answer. They would transmit an underwater sound wave which, when reflected off a submarine hull, would be detected by a sensitive receiver, thus locating the submarine's position.

Lieutenant (junior grade) David H. Hull had the task of installing and testing the experimental sound devices (later called SONAR—Sound Navigation and Ranging). Three destroyers were fitted with three types of equipment, and Hull approached Spruance to arrange the operating schedule. Spruance sympathized with young Hull, perhaps remembering the World War I years when he had sought permission to install and test new fire control equipment. He and his destroyers cooperated.

Spruance was not interested in the technical details, but the test results captured his attention. He was impressed. Five years later, when Edward had graduated and was serving as an ensign aboard the cruiser *Indianapolis,* he told his father that he wanted to become a submariner. "He advised against it," said Edward, "expressing serious doubts about the effectiveness of subs in a future war. Some new fangled device the British had, called ASDIC, would make the submarine a coffin."

As the Depression worsened in 1934, operating and maintenance funds nearly disappeared. Spruance tried to keep his deteriorating destroyers reasonably active and efficient, but the task was almost hopeless. In the mornings he hiked to Fleet Landing from his Coronado apartment over a mile away, often accompanied by Hull. Spruance confided his discouragement to his companion and once said a naval officer had no future. Hull remonstrated that Spruance should be pleased that he was a captain in a period when retiring as a commander with thirty years' service was considered a successful career.

Watson praised Spruance's performance and predicted that his career was far from over. "Fully qualified for command and promotion to admiral," wrote Watson.

Spruance was ambivalent about his next tour of shore duty—due in early 1935 after two years at sea—and requested at various times Washington, the Naval Academy, and the Naval War College. Finally he specifically requested the Naval Mine Depot at Yorktown, Virginia. The Bureau of Navigation seemed willing, and the Spruances made happy plans. The depot had comfortable quarters upon a grassy bluff overlooking the James River. They were shaded by tall trees and surrounded by peaceful, wooded Virginia countryside, where young Margaret dreamed of riding horses. The work was easy, and Spruance could roam and explore to his heart's content along the same river that he and Margaret had walked as newlyweds. Margaret loved that part of the country, and they eagerly looked forward to moving ashore.

Their dreams were shattered in March 1935. "We're not going to Yorktown after all," said a disheartened Spruance. "We are going back to the War College."

Said Margaret, "Upon hearing that news I collapsed."

Spruance did not want War College staff duty because it meant hard work, and neither his wife nor daughter liked Newport. All his shore duty over the years had been demanding, and he never had been able to relax in a big, comfortable house. He was tired, he was almost fifty years old, and the prospect of duty at Yorktown was irresistible. But it was not to be. The president of the college, Rear Admiral Edward C. Kalbfus, had asked for him, and that was that.

Spruance had become a pensive man dissatisfied with his duty assignments, tired of uprooting his family, pessimistic about his future, seeking solitude and peace. His quest for a contented life at a remote naval station persisted. He told young Margaret in 1939 that if he failed selection for admiral he wanted duty at the Naval Ammunition Depot in Hingham, Massachusetts, so he could retire in New England.

Spruance never really believed he would be selected for flag rank. He was haunted by the 1926 letter of reprimand. By choice he had not "played politics," and he was not particularly sociable. Both presumably were necessary in order to make admiral. Command of an isolated ammunition depot was not in the path to flag selection. Ambitious captains aggressively promoted their careers by pursuing tough, prestigious billets or by ingratiating themselves with powerful, influential people. Spruance was not one of them.

Spruance's third tour at the Naval War College lasted almost three years. At first he headed the junior course of five lieutenant commanders and seventeen lieutenants.[1] Their greatest concern at the time was promotion, because most had been passed over owing to the stagnation caused by the Depression. Some were apathetic and felt that the War College was a waste of time. Spruance soon diverted their attention to

1. The Naval War College in the 1920s and 1930s is the subject of a monograph by Michael Vlahos, *The Blue Sword: The Naval War College and the American Mission 1919–1941* (Newport, 1980).

the study of naval warfare. "Spruance was a tough taskmaster," recalled one student, "and the harder we worked the more he demanded of us. . . . He got to be very friendly with his class and became very proud of us."

The next year Spruance became head of the Senior Class Tactics Department. Commander Carl Moore, his old *Bainbridge* shipmate, was on the staff, and Spruance allowed him to run the war games. Spruance remained in the background.

In the summer of 1937 Spruance fleeted up to Head of the Operations Department, but he was overshadowed by his subordinate Head of Strategy, Captain Richmond K. (Kelly) Turner, a friend of many years. Turner was an aggressive, decisive, competitive, combative naval officer who mentally overpowered the students. His fiery debates with another stormy intellectual, Captain Robert A. (Fuzzy) Theobald, became legendary.

Turner undoubtedly was the greatest teacher of naval strategy since Mahan. "He worked our pants off," said one student. "It was the hardest year I ever spent. Turner corrected every estimate of the situation and final decision with red ink, and they were saturated with his caustic comment." Everyone agreed that Turner was a cinch for admiral. He eventually earned four stars and became a renowned amphibious commander under Spruance in the Pacific war.

Turner also initiated an impressive program of War College staff lectures, to which Spruance contributed by delivering several dry, scholarly talks on strategy and tactics. Turner's lectures were, by far, the most enlightened, and he emphasized that carrier and amphibious warfare would predominate in the future. But few listened. The battleship was still supreme at Newport.

Guest civilian lecturers occasionally spoke. Some were excellent, while others backfired. For example, the college was interested in anthropology on the theory that the "racial characteristics" of the enemy were an important factor in the Estimate of the Situation. The college's misguided efforts served primarily to reinforce the racial prejudices of the student body. For example, one visiting anthropologist argued against any form of integration with "colored races." "If you allow the colored people to come in," he said, "you're going to wind up with a nation like Venezuela in which there is nothing left because the genes intermingled."

Rear Admiral Kalbfus, the college president, had embarked upon a personal crusade that had the college in an uproar. Kalbfus maintained that the earlier versions of the Estimate of the Situation were superficial. Something better was needed, he said, so he began writing a treatise that would be the last word in solving naval warfare problems. Although he had good ideas he was a poor writer, and his magnum opus was cumbersome and prolix, as well as controversial. Yet he was so acutely sensitive to criticism that few dared to tell him of its defects.

Spruance normally was the first out the door at the end of the day, and he never brought work home. Kalbfus changed things. He insisted that Spruance (among others) review his treatise, entitled *Sound Military Decision* (*SMD*). Facing a deadline, Spruance was forced to read it at home in the evening. He thought *SMD* was useless and complained to his family about overtime work.

Not only did he dislike Kalbfus's writing style, he also disagreed with Kalbfus on the value of the so-called "Principles of War." There were nine of them: Objective, Offensive, Superiority, Cooperation, Simplicity, Economy, Surprise, Movement, and Security. The War College for years had maintained that they were essential to success in war. Spruance generally agreed. Kalbfus thought otherwise and felt that many officers wrongly believed that the Principles alone summarized all that one had to know about making war. War was too complex, he argued, to be reduced to nine simple rules, so he abolished them from the curriculum.

Spruance's boss, Captain J. W. Wilcox, had told Kalbfus that *SMD* was magnificent, and he forbade Spruance to tell Kalbfus otherwise. In Spruance's view, Wilcox lacked the moral courage to tell the truth and was deceiving the admiral. The two argued hotly. Finally Spruance disobeyed Wilcox and went directly to Kalbfus. Wilcox was furious and threatened to destroy Spruance's career in retribution.

The two angry men went before Kalbfus. He faced a dilemma. Wilcox was his strongest supporter of *SMD* and in theory had been within his rights to forbid Spruance to criticize the book. Perhaps Wilcox had equated dissent with disloyalty. Although Kalbfus always had admired Spruance for both his brains and his integrity, Spruance had disobeyed his superior, Wilcox. Now Wilcox demanded that Spruance be punished.

Kalbfus vindicated Spruance and overruled Wilcox. It was a humiliating rebuff to Wilcox. The rancor between the two captains never subsided. Once friends, they became bitter enemies.

Otherwise, life was pleasant. The students admired and respected Spruance and regarded him as a wise, scholarly officer who was as smart as Turner but much easier to live with. Spruance was content with the college the way it was and allowed his hard-charging subordinates to do the work.

The college continued to be shortsighted in many ways as it prepared its students for World War II. Although it considered Japan as an inevitable enemy, it ignored Germany and Italy. Kelly Turner, with his relentless, driving energy, was almost alone in advocating the study of new techniques in naval warfare. Spruance discussed the future and foresaw many of the advances in weapons and tactics, but he did not try to revise the college curriculum to make it current with the thinking and developments in the fleet. He would not have denied that he was too lazy to expend the effort, and no one else would do it for him. Turner could not change the curriculum by himself, but he tried.

Yet, for all its faults, the War College was extremely important. It bred an aura of professionalism and a unity of thought among its staff and students, who viewed the world through the same eyes and spoke a common language. They knew each other. They all understood the strategy that eventually defeated Japan. A War College education in the fundamentals of naval warfare helped the students to adapt to the new realities of World War II. The college taught the students to think as future naval commanders and made them realize that, if war with Japan were to come, ultimate victory would depend on them.

But war was several years away, and there was no sense of urgency at Newport.

Carl Moore summarized Spruance's third War College tour. "Spruance took his duties at the War College in his quiet, serene way," said Moore. "He never seemed under pressure of any sort and never seemed to exert himself to accomplish any particular task or to make changes in the curriculum. He enjoyed his outdoor activities [including challenging Moore to see who could take the last swim in the fall], he accomplished much in repairing and refurbishing furniture, and he liked the informal kinds of social activities. His tour of duty was a pleasant relaxation."

In the spring of 1938, Spruance was ordered to command the battleship *Mississippi*. It was the precise duty and the precise ship he had wanted. Spruance never felt he deserved any special consideration in the kinds of duty he was given—except command of a battleship. That he felt he had earned and deserved.

A captain needed a successful major command for any hope of promotion to rear admiral. Fifty-four ships were available: 16 battleships, 5 aircraft carriers, and 33 cruisers. Each year successive Academy classes rotated into these ships on a schedule that allowed them to complete their command tours just before they were considered by the flag selection board.

Therefore, Spruance and 53 other outstanding captains were competing with one another for the handful of yearly flag promotions. Their chances were based largely upon how well they commanded their great ships in the year or so allotted them. Some captains would be driven by ruthless ambition and would selfishly exploit their ships and their men. Their commands would be a nightmare for their people. Other captains would be excessively cautious, fearful of a mistake that would smirch their records. Their timidity would be equally demoralizing. Most captains simply would do their best and trust their fate to the selection board.

Twelve of the 54 captains were destined to become rear admirals.

The Navy had been revitalized since Spruance's last sea duty. New ships were enlarging the fleet, and Congress was reluctantly authorizing greater (yet still inadequate) numbers of officers and enlisted men. There were now 105,000 sailors in the Navy, compared to the 85,000 when Spruance had been *Mississippi*'s exec nine years before. The reenlistment rate was a gratifying 72 percent, and the hard core of naval careerists was continually strengthened for the looming wartime expansion. The Navy still could be selective in its recruiting. Fewer than one out of ten applicants were chosen. The sailor's life at sea had improved, because the newer ships were more habitable. Bunks were replacing hammocks, and large central cafeterias were replacing the small, widely scattered, and inefficient messes. High-capacity evaporators could produce enough fresh water to allow the men to bathe in showers rather than buckets.

The Secretary of the Navy made his annual plea for more line officers. He had 6500 but needed 2000 more. Some stopgap measures were tried. Congress enacted a law in June 1938 whereby officers who failed selection were not forced into retirement as in earlier years. Thus officers who were "best fitted" were promoted, and those who were "fitted" were retained on active duty in their present grade. Aviation cadets were beginning to man the cockpits of the burgeoning naval air forces, because the Naval Academy could not provide enough future aviators.

Spruance and Margaret left Newport in early April and drove at a leisurely pace across country, arriving in San Pedro in late April. *Mississippi* had returned from three months at sea from Fleet Problem XIX, and Spruance reported aboard shortly after she anchored in San Pedro Harbor.

Most large ships ran themselves. Commanding officers changed frequently, and ships and their professional crews easily accommodated the peculiarities of the incumbent during his brief tenure. The daily routine of a man-o'-war was so uniform and firmly ingrained that it normally mattered little who was in command.

There was no reason to prolong the command turnover periods, and they were usually short. The routine consisted of inspecting the ship and crew, the transfer of mysterious "secret" papers locked within the captain's safe, and a pleasant chat about mutual friends, the state of the Navy, and the idiosyncrasies of the ship and the division commander. Both officers would be anxious to get on with the Change of Command ceremony. There could be but one commanding officer and two was a crowd.

The time-honored Change of Command ceremony is a naval rite signifying the transfer of authority and responsibility from one commanding officer to another. The ship is cleansed, then festooned with signal flags and with bunting of blue and gold, the Navy's traditional colors. ("Blue of the seven seas, gold of God's great sun," sing Navy men. "Let these our colors be, 'till all of time be done.")

The *Mississippi* crew assembled in their finest uniforms and stood in symmetrical formations upon the fantail. All eyes focused on the elevated podium, on which their old leader and their new one would appear. Spruance soon would be the most important man in the lives of 72 officers and 1100 sailors. He, as with all naval commanding officers, was deified through law and custom that made his authority and responsibility absolute. Now he would embark upon the supreme moment of his career thus far.

For the past half hour, sleek captains' gigs and black-hulled admirals' barges had discharged their passengers, then hove to off the ship's stern, where they rocked in the swells. The naval hierarchy were piped aboard, the number of side boys corresponding to rank. (In the days of sail, visitors were hoisted aboard using a block and tackle, and the boatswain piped the hoisting orders to the straining side boys manning the falls. An officer's bulk increased with seniority. Two side boys could lift a nimble lieutenant, but eight were needed for a heavyweight admiral.) Nowadays the visiting officer climbs aboard, but the boatswain's mate still pipes, and the side boys still ceremoniously bring the notable aboard. The *Mississippi* symbolized that little had changed in the wonderful ways of a navy, despite the passage of centuries.

The visitors were seated. The crew went to parade rest. A bugle sounded attention. Spruance and his predecessor, Captain Ferdinand L. Reichmuth, mounted the platform in full dress regalia, a uniform closely resembling that worn in the days of Nelson.

The chaplain intoned his invocation, and Reichmuth read his orders. He was nervous and stumbled several times as he read. Spruance, in contrast, read his orders in a calm, quiet voice that one had to strain to hear. Then he turned to Reichmuth, saluted, said, "I relieve you, sir," and assumed command.

The *Mississippi* was his.

The brief ceremony ended with the National Anthem, then the chaplain's benediction with the band softly playing "Eternal Father" in the background.

"Amen." It was over. Spruance disappeared into his cabin. Fifteen minutes later he reappeared in civilian clothes, boarded his gig, and went home. Thus ended his first day of command.

Spruance and Margaret roomed in a Long Beach hotel when they first arrived. There they were reunited with Edward, then a rebellious ensign serving in the heavy cruiser *Indianapolis*. They had lunch and dinner together but passed most of the day in the hotel room. Edward dominated the conversation with scathing attacks against the naval establishment, based upon his year's experience at sea as a commissioned officer. For hours he stormed against dunderheaded senior officers; against the numbing mountains of paperwork; against unreasonable regulations and rules; against slavish attention to spit and polish. Nothing was spared. His bitter monologue was directed toward Margaret—who clucked sympathetically with her son—but the message was intended for his father, who represented the naval leadership that Edward condemned.

Margaret feared that her husband would be provoked by Edward's tirade. To her relief, he remained silent, and she later complimented him for his restraint.

"Everything Edward said was perfectly true," said Spruance, "and I felt the same way he did when I was an ensign. The Navy doesn't change, and every young ensign has to go through the same thing." Several nights later Spruance recounted the episode with friends at a party, all senior officers and their wives. They all laughed that an ensign would presume to criticize the Navy.

Spruance later called upon the flag officers present, one of whom flew his flag on the *Indianapolis.* Curious to see what Edward was doing to reform the Navy, he entered unannounced into his son's stateroom and found him prostrate in his bunk, nursing a hangover. Spruance informed Edward of his opinion of junior officers who slept during working hours.

Edward would not conform. As stubborn as his father, he lacked the elder's fatalistic acceptance of the ways of the Navy. For example, he was in charge of turret Number 3 and ran it contrary to standard procedures, which he believed were wrong. His unorthodox crew became known as "the Asiatics." He pursued a fast-paced bachelor's life ashore, using his parents' home as a base of operations and his father's 1937 Chrysler Royal sedan for transportation. One evening while driving to Los Angeles, Edward smashed up the car. Spruance was unperturbed. He simply extracted the cost of repairs from Edward's paycheck.

The *Mississippi* swung at anchor in San Pedro Harbor during the first weeks of Spruance's command. Spruance was soon regarded by his officers and men as a dignified gentleman, remote yet accessible, exacting yet tolerant, all powerful and all forgiving, as awesome and as majestic as the battleship he commanded.

Spruance first got *Mississippi* under way when she left harbor for an overhaul at Puget Sound Naval Shipyard at Bremerton, Washington. The crew was anxious to watch his performance at sea; the earlier captain had virtually lived on the bridge. Spruance was entirely the opposite. The ship got underway at midnight. Spruance sat wordlessly in his bridge chair while the navigator and senior watch officer weighed anchor and swung the battleship seaward. Upon clearing the Long

Beach breakwater, Spruance went to bed and shortly was followed by the exec, navigator, and senior watch officer. The OOD ducked into the chart house. His ensign assistant suddenly found himself alone, in charge of the 32,000-ton ship plowing through the dark, congested waters off Los Angeles.

A lieutenant standing his first OOD watch under Spruance was nonplussed by his captain's behavior on the way to Bremerton. *Mississippi* came upon a merchantman which, by the *Rules of the Road,* was obligated to stand clear while *Mississippi* held course and speed. Merchantmen were notorious for their reluctance to take evasive action. A collision seemed imminent, but the worried OOD could not get Spruance out of bed. Fortunately the merchantman changed course and the OOD entered Spruance's sea cabin to report it would miss the battleship.

"They will do it every time," Spruance responded. "Ease off a little if you think you should. Good night." Spruance rolled over on his side, hitched up the covers around his neck, dug his face into the pillow, and prepared for a comfortable sleep.

"I was stunned," said the officer. "Here was the brand new skipper of a capital ship, under way for the first time with a young watch officer he did not know, and he did not even get out of his bunk."

Yet he had other officers he would not trust. A new OOD was looking forward to his one big event of the watch—reversing course in the middle of the ocean in daylight with no other ships in sight. Just before the appointed time Spruance strolled onto the bridge. "I'll take it, son," he said. He ordered the new course, then returned to his cabin. The young officer was never allowed to order a course or speed change in his two years aboard.

Spruance enjoyed the company of his more interesting officers. Some would walk with him on the hike between home and Fleet Landing and were rewarded with a ride to the ship in the captain's gig. Others paced with him on the quarterdeck. He still advised promising officers not to volunteer for Navy air, although he admitted aviation was taking a larger role in naval operations.

He forgave mistakes and indiscretions—to a point. One of his ensigns got deeply in debt, and Spruance ordered the mess treasurer to take over his checkbook and manage his financial affairs. Unorthodox, but it worked.

After overhaul *Mississippi* rejoined Battleship Division Three.

Spruance no longer was independent and had to conform to the sometimes unwelcome dicta of the flag officers. At least once the Battle Force flagship shouldered her way in front of *Mississippi* while departing Long Beach harbor. Although the flag had the traditional right of way, Spruance had to choke down his rage at the admiral's bad sea manners.

Another admiral forced an impromptu personnel inspection. *Mississippi* was filthy from a drydocking, and Spruance decided to cancel the usual Saturday morning personnel inspection in order to hold field day. Her lifelines soon were covered with wet, scrubbed canvas, and men in dungarees holystoned decks, wiped down bulkheads, and shined brightwork. A message arrived by flashing light from the flagship. "There will be no deviation," it decreed, "from the normal battleship Saturday morning routine."

Spruance was furious. "Pipe captain's personnel inspection," he ordered, then went to his cabin. All hell broke loose: bunk bottoms were jerked from lifelines, hoses were stowed, dirty water was sloshed down scuppers, men shaved from buckets, and inspection uniforms were grabbed from lockers. In an incredibly short time the decks were dry, gear stowed, and the crew mustered in divisions for inspection.

Spruance popped out of his cabin in his dress whites, carrying rather than wearing his sword. He doubletimed up one rank and down the other without breaking stride, his face impassive. The men having been "inspected," he turned to his exec and announced, "Pass the word that the Captain is pleased with the appearance of the ship's company. Have the men leave their quarters and continue field day."

The men loved it.

These kinds of experiences caused Spruance to resent senior officers who interfered in the business of their subordinates. It happened far too often; he would not do it if he ever became an admiral.

Spruance capped his reputation with his crew in January 1939, when *Mississippi* transited the Panama Canal en route to the Caribbean for Fleet Exercise XX. The ship had unpredictable maneuvering characteristics. She responded sluggishly to the helm, slewed rather than turned, and she was down by the head. There were many sharp curves and narrow passages in the canal, and the pilot had the conn in accordance with regulations. Approaching Culebra Cut the pilot ordered right rudder to turn the corner. In her own mysterious, inexplicable way, *Mississippi*'s bow swung left, and the ponderous battleship bore down upon shoal water and a dredge anchored to port. The dredge's deckhands scrambled ashore, for they believed (as did the *Mississippi* crew) that *Mississippi* was in extremis. Collision and grounding seemed inevitable.

"I'll take her, pilot." Spruance's calm voice broke the tension. "Let go the starboard anchor and hold it," he commanded, followed by orders to back the starboard engines. As the anchor splashed and dug in, Spruance turned away from the forecastle and looked squarely at his signal officer. Spruance's hands were at his side, palms up, and he shrugged his shoulders and raised his eyebrows as if to say, "What more can I do? I've done all I can."

The anchor stopped the ship's swing, and Spruance soon had her headed far down the channel.

The entire United States Fleet had assembled in the Caribbean in early 1939 for Fleet Exercise XX. The tempo of operations quickened, and *Mississippi* became immersed in the stress and strains and anxieties caused by the vague threat of war with Japan.

Even before coming to the Caribbean, *Mississippi* and her sister ships had reacted to alarms that Japanese submarines were near the San Pedro Harbor anchorage. Liberty had been canceled, destroyers and aircraft had been deployed to cover the approaches to the anchorage, and a mild hysteria had set in. But nothing was found. Normality returned until the next scare. The false alarms had two adverse effects. Ships became tense and overworked, and the "cries of 'Wolf' " caused the fleet progressively to disregard warnings of suspicious Japanese movements—until Pearl Harbor.

The fleet made rendezvous at Guantánamo Bay, received bulky operation orders, then divided into Black and White forces. The fleet exercise included escort of convoys, raids, and the use of seaplane scouting forces. The operation dragged on for several days, and President Roosevelt came aboard *Pennsylvania* to watch the show. There was little to see, so the battleships conducted a fleet engagement to make things more interesting for the President. It was a poorly handled, dismal sight.

In two and a half years the Navy would be at war, yet it persisted in unrealistic exercises that manifested the fleet's unreadiness for air, amphibious, and submarine warfare. Its unpreparedness was not for want of energy. Everyone had worked long and hard, but no sooner was Fleet Exercise XX over than the staffs and crews began planning for their next exercise. No one had time to analyze what they had just done or to think much about the future. Exercise reports were submitted and filed, but no one read them to see what they were saying. Fleet commanders and commanding officers changed so rapidly that there was little continuity from one year to the next. Whatever lessons had been learned had to be relearned the next year. A contemporary observer remarked that the Navy was always trying to do too much.

In the midst of these frenzied efforts Spruance's crew had excelled in the yearly competitions, winning first places in gunnery and communications and a second place in engineering. Spruance had not earnestly sought these awards, but rather the crew had naturally done their best for their captain. Things happened to turn out well. Regardless of how they were achieved, *Mississippi*'s success in the yearly competitions would help Spruance at flag selection time.

Occasionally *Mississippi* slipped away to remote little islands in the Caribbean so the crew and their captain could unwind. While the ship was anchored off Culebra Island near Puerto Rico, Spruance summoned one of his favorite young officers to walk with him on Flamingo Beach.

"When we got to the beach," the officer later wrote, "I saw a small party of enlisted men standing around. A man in swimming trunks was hip deep in the fairly heavy surf, and two of the strangest looking small craft I had ever seen were lying just beyond the surf line. It was only then that Spruance said that we had come to observe a demonstration of two experimental landing craft.

"When the man in swimming trunks saw Spruance, he began to signal to the boats which began a series of full throttle runs straight through the surf, driving themselves on to the beach and retracting under their own power. Spruance stood silently, watching every detail. After a while the man in swimming trunks came splashing out of the surf and began talking to Spruance about the capabilities of the two boats. Spruance interrupted him and said, 'By the way, you two have not met. Lieutenant Oliver, this is Kelly Turner.'

"At the time Turner was commanding officer of the cruiser *Astoria,* and I pondered what connection a cruiser captain might have with experimental landing craft. Returning to Great Harbor, Spruance explained that Kelly Turner, a close personal friend and probably the smartest officer in the U.S. Navy, was determined to develop useable landing craft. He had squeezed some money out of the Navy Department, and we had just seen the first fruits of his labors. The object of the demonstration was to select the best boat so that it could be put into production when the time came."

Spruance had chosen young Robert J. Oliver to accompany him on the beach because Oliver several years earlier had watched dozens of ships' liberty launches attempt to land Marines in the surf. It had been a debacle, and the launches had either been sunk or seriously damaged. Knowing Oliver's interest in landing craft, he had taken him along. Oliver later became Spruance's flag lieutenant at the Battle of Midway.

Mississippi and the fleet had been scheduled to remain on the East Coast for most of 1939. However, another Japanese war scare in mid-1939 caused Roosevelt to return the fleet to the "unprotected" West Coast. Back through the canal she went.

As time approached for the flag selection board to convene, the conversation at home not unnaturally turned to Spruance's chance for selection. Spruance was fatalistic, although his fitness reports on the *Mississippi* had been outstanding.

One day his communications officer handed him a message. He and sixteen of his classmates had been selected for rear admiral. Fifty-five other classmates had been passed over. Spruance was fifty-three years old. He had been in the Navy for thirty-six years and had been at sea for half of them.

A "fresh caught" rear admiral needed duty ashore for "seasoning" before assuming command at sea. In line with this policy, Spruance became the first commander of the Tenth Naval District in early 1940.

His new shore command was mostly water. It comprised the entire Caribbean Sea and the West Indies, but the only American possessions in the district were Puerto Rico, the Virgin Islands, and the Guantánamo (Cuba) Naval Base. The remaining islands—the Bahamas, Greater Antilles, and Lesser Antilles—either were European colonies or were self-governing.

The Navy always had recognized the strategic importance of the Caribbean, but it never had developed naval bases in the area, other than the training installation at Guantánamo. Everything changed in the late thirties when Hitler began to menace Europe. The United States government started a $650 million base development program in the Caribbean in order to protect the area from possible German encroachment. Ten thousand men began a massive construction program that eventually included British-owned islands, leased in exchange for fifty old destroyers needed by Britain in her war against Germany.

The Tenth Naval District did not even exist until Spruance established his headquarters ashore in San Juan, Puerto Rico, in late February 1940. His staff—a handful of retired officers recalled to active duty—greeted him at the pier. They were living in hotels, had no idea where to begin, and simply had waited for Spruance to arrive and tell them what to do. San Juan was a somnolent, backward, undeveloped city that in no way resembled the lavish tourist haven of today. Although a naval base was under construction in the city, Spruance had no office to call his own. He rented a comfortable home on the beach and went to work.

His most important assistant was Commander (later Rear Admiral) Harold W. Johnson, Civil Engineering Corps (CEC), who supervised the entire construction program spread throughout Spruance's sprawling empire. Spruance provided Johnson with all possible support, and the two worked well together. Johnson was an outstanding civil engineer. Spruance later arranged for him to serve in the Pacific to supervise the base development of newly captured Japanese islands.

Although they had construction projects on remote West Indies islands separated by hundreds of miles of open water, their greatest problem was right in San Juan. It concerned the Navy's decision to build a naval air station upon a San Juan swamp misnamed Isla Grande, which had been chosen out of political expediency rather than engineering feasibility. Johnson remembered it as "a quivering lake of mud 20 to 30 feet deep." Thousands of piles were driven and tons of solid fill were dumped upon it, but Isla Grande remained a pile of mush, a civil-engineering nightmare. Buildings sagged, roads buckled, and water mains split. Spruance deplored everything about it but was powerless to change anything. The CEC officer in charge of construction already had complained long and loud. The Navy Department silenced him by writing, "You were sent to San Juan to build an airfield and not to select a site."

Spruance was against a naval base at San Juan because the restricted harbor was vulnerable to surprise attack. The Navy Department generally concurred. It pressed on with the San Juan plans but proposed building a major fleet base at Portage Bay on the south coast of Trinidad. Spruance objected strenuously. It was foreign territory, he said, it was not subject to American control, and the local government was unfriendly and uncooperative. Furthermore, it was not strategically well located within the West Indies.

Spruance recommended instead that the eastern end of Puerto Rico—later known as Roosevelt Roads—be developed as a major fleet base. The Navy Department agreed and construction began. It never was completed during World War II because of the emphasis on developing bases on the British-owned islands. After the war, however, work resumed. Roosevelt Roads became and now is the finest fleet anchorage in the western Atlantic.

Spruance's main task as commandant was dealing with people. One was a former naval officer named Virgil Baker, who years before had obtained a controversial long-term lease on some of the most valuable property in San Juan. For years the native Puerto Ricans had contested its legality and had tried unsuccessfully to break the lease in court. The Navy had better luck. Despite Baker's bitter protests, it seized some of his land for naval construction. Spruance was amused that Baker had been able to bamboozle the Puerto Ricans for so many years. Baker appealed to Spruance for help in retaining his land, but Spruance avoided him whenever possible.

Spruance's own staff constantly exasperated him. Although well-intentioned, they were bumbling and depended upon him for detailed guidance. The commanding officer of the emerging naval air station was also a constant irritation. Other than Spruance and the CEC officers, the Navy had not sent its better people to the nether regions of the West Indies. They were needed elsewhere. Spruance got what was left over. "He was very disgruntled most of the time," said Margaret.

Spruance was still a captain when he first arrived in San Juan, for he had to wait until enough senior admirals retired to open a vacancy for his own promotion. One evening Margaret was about to leave for the theater with neighbors. Spruance walked her to the car.

"What time do you think you'll be getting home tonight?" he asked.

Margaret said she didn't know. Spruance persisted.

"Why is it so important?" asked Margaret.

"Well," replied her husband, "it's not many women who can go to bed with a captain and wake up with an admiral."

Spruance's clever way of announcing his promotion found its way into the local newspapers, to the amusement of his friends and colleagues. He was not amused. His staff planned an elaborate celebration and invitations were prepared. Owing to a printing error they announced that the party was in honor of *Real* (rather than *Rear*) Admiral Spruance. Again everyone laughed, this time including the new admiral.

The senior Army officer in Puerto Rico was a brigadier general who recently had lost his wife and had become a brooding eccentric. Although he was senior when Spruance was a captain, he would be outranked by one star when Spruance became a rear admiral. In order to retain his seniority, the Army officer flew to Washington and got himself promoted to major general before Spruance received his promotion.

The general, two stars on his shoulder, attended Spruance's party and remarked that he never had seen such a lively affair.

France fell in the summer of 1940, and the French warships based at Martinique in the Windward Islands became an international issue. The United States and Great Britain both feared that Germany, through the Vichy government, might gain control of the ships. Britain would sink them before allowing that to happen. A Caribbean naval war was a real possibility.

Spruance went to Martinique and called upon Admiral Robert, the senior French naval officer present. Robert assured Spruance that he hated both the Germans and the Vichy. They would not get his ships. But his family were virtual hostages in France, so he could not openly collaborate with the Americans and British. His only course was neutrality, and he promised to inform the Americans of his own ships' activities. An American destroyer began a permanent patrol outside the French harbor. "He was a fine officer and a gentleman, in a tough spot," Spruance later said.

Rear Admiral Ernest J. King, commanding the Atlantic Fleet patrol forces, was a frequent visitor to the Caribbean. He invited Spruance aboard his flagship *Texas* to watch an amphibious landing exercise at Culebra Island in early 1941. Spruance accepted the invitation and met the senior Marine officer, Brigadier General Holland M. Smith. He and King had been quarreling constantly over amphibious tactics and doctrine, and Spruance was impressed by Smith's professional knowledge, his stubbornness, and his zeal. The Marine general obviously knew his business. Spruance received an eye-opening demonstration in the latest equipment and techniques of amphibious warfare. Smith was especially enthusiastic about his new "alligator," a tracked armored vehicle that could float on water and crawl over land. Two and a half years later the alligators would help win the battle for Tarawa.

Spruance decided that if he ever needed a Marine to command an amphibious assault, it would be Holland Smith.

As 1941 wore on, tensions mounted and America's preparations for war increased. That summer Spruance received orders to proceed to Pearl Harbor and take command of Cruiser Division Five.

II

The War

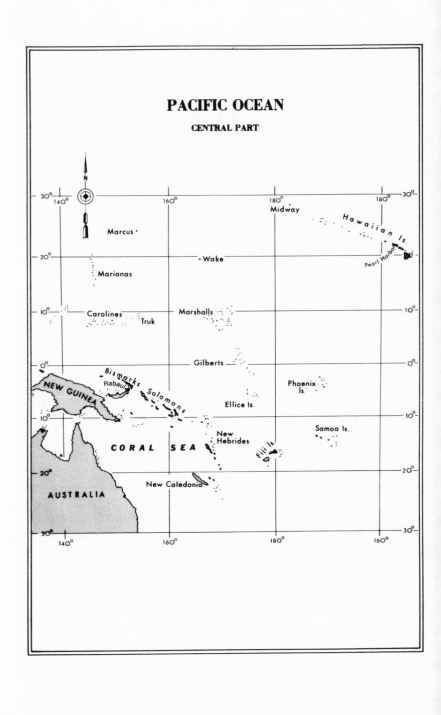

PACIFIC OCEAN

CENTRAL PART

Chapter 6

CRUISER DIVISION COMMANDER

S PRUANCE was disappointed with his orders to command the four heavy cruisers of Cruiser Division Five. He had wanted a battleship division. In fact, though, the orders were auspicious. He could have been stranded in Washington, because the Chief of the Bureau of Naval Ordnance had asked for him following his duty in Puerto Rico. However, Rear Admiral Chester W. Nimitz, then Chief of the Bureau of Navigation, decided—with the approval of Secretary of the Navy Frank Knox—that Spruance would fly his flag in the Pacific Fleet. The division would operate with a carrier task force commanded by Halsey. Spruance would be at the scene when the inevitable war against Japan began.

Spruance began his long journey to Pearl Harbor after he was relieved in Puerto Rico in August 1941 by Johnny Hoover. He first stopped in Washington for several days to review the latest intelligence on the Pacific; then with his wife and daughter he drove to San Francisco in order to sail on the passenger ship *Lurline*. En route across country he periodically checked for messages from Washington. When he got to Yellowstone Park, he apparently forgot his daily ritual. Young Margaret reminded him. "No," he responded, "I'm not going to do it." To her astonishment, her father had lost interest in communicating with the Navy Department.

As they neared San Francisco, Spruance repeatedly warned the women that they probably would not be allowed to accompany him to Honolulu. War was imminent, he said, and the President surely would prohibit dependents from leaving the continental United States. "That's what I would do, if I were President," he insisted.

They had a two-day wait in San Francisco. While walking to pass time Spruance met a friend who was visibly surprised to see him. "What are you doing here, Spruance?" the friend asked. "Ernie King is looking for you. He wants you to be his chief of staff. I thought you'd be in Washington." That was news to Spruance. Admiral Ernest J. King had just been appointed Commander in Chief, Atlantic Fleet, and in several months he would become CNO. Determined to avoid both King and Washington, his immediate reaction was an impatient urge to be away on *Lurline*. The women were unconcerned. They were happy simply to be with Spruance and to know that his predictions of a travel ban had been wrong.

Edward, by then a lieutenant, was serving aboard the submarine *Tambor*, based in Pearl Harbor. He and his new bride, Josephine, greeted the Spruances when they arrived, and he proudly introduced Josephine to his family. Shortly thereafter the five piled into a car and went sightseeing in the surrounding countryside. They stopped at a turnoff high on a mountain. Below them was a panorama of the Pacific Fleet berthed within Pearl Harbor. The ships looked so very vulnerable to young Margaret. "Dad," she asked, "what is to stop the Japanese from bombing our ships in the harbor?"

"They are not supposed to do it that way," he responded. His voice was heavy with sarcasm, reflecting his scorn with the theory that the Japanese probably would not attack Hawaii. It was too far from Japan, most people believed, and the first strike probably would be in Southeast Asia.

Despite his pessimism, Spruance felt there was a modicum of security within the harbor. He and Halsey later would visit during inport periods and would discuss the safety of the Fleet. Spruance reported that experts from the Bureau of Naval Ordnance had assured him that aerial torpedoes needed at least 70 feet of water to avoid hitting bottom after release. Pearl Harbor's depth was no more than 45 feet, so Spruance assumed that the ships inside the harbor at least would be safe from Japanese torpedo planes. He was not alone in this false hope.

Honolulu was trying to adjust to military and naval expansion. During the twenties and thirties Pearl Harbor had been no more than a submarine base and a shipyard. Everything changed in late 1939 when the Pacific Fleet came to stay. The naval base was enlarged to accommodate its needs, and frenetic preparations for war replaced a once-leisurely tropical routine. Swarms of sailors from arriving ships strained Honolulu's facilities to the limit.

Spruance hoisted his flag on the *Northampton* in mid-September 1941 and took command of four heavy cruisers: *Pensacola, Salt Lake City, Chester,* and his flagship.[1] They were so-called Treaty Cruisers that suffered from design defects caused by weight and armament limitations imposed by the 1922 Washington Naval Conference. Some rolled wickedly at low speeds, others vibrated at high speeds, and all had poor watertight integrity because internal bulkheads and strength members had been reduced to save weight. They were armed with powerful 8-inch guns, but their torpedo tubes had been removed and they were without effective antiaircraft armament. Another defect was poor ventilation. Portholes along their sides could be opened to admit fresh air, but at the risk of shipping green water if the ships were underway. When battened down for general quarters, the cruisers became unbearably hot.

Spruance's division and the Pacific Fleet had been in a quasiwar status for months. The fleet had "stripped ship" in April 1941 by removing all flammable, frangible, splintery, or otherwise dangerous or superfluous material. Everyone was tense and energetic—but the fleet was not ready to fight. It lacked aircraft, ammunition, antiaircraft guns, and fuel. Trained, experienced officers and men left to join new ships under construction. Admiral Husband F. Kimmel, Commander in Chief Pacific Fleet (CINCPAC), bitterly complained to Nimitz at the Bureau of Navigation about the loss of manpower. Nimitz replied that Roosevelt, for political reasons, had refused to ask Congress for the enlisted men needed by the Navy. "Don't bother me any more," said Nimitz, "and make do with what you have."

1. USS *Northampton* (CA 26), displacement 9,050 tons, main battery nine 8-inch guns, commissioned 17 May 1930 as a light cruiser (CL 26), but redesignated a heavy cruiser the next year. During 1942 she saw action in the early Pacific raids, at Midway, and in the Guadalcanal campaign. Japanese torpedoes sank her on 30 November 1942 during the Battle of Tassafaronga. DANAFS, vol. 5 (Washington, 1970), pp. 111–12.

Despite the danger of war, Kimmel chose not to keep the fleet in a constant state of vigilance, which would expend precious materiel and exhaust his men. Instead Kimmel concentrated on training at the expense of alertness. Spruance's main concern, therfore, was to exercise and prepare his cruisers for war. To assist him, Spruance inherited a three-officer staff that had been selected by his predecessor, Rear Admiral Sherwoode A. Taffinder. The flag secretary was Lieutenant Commander Victor D. Long, who served as paperwork controller, chief of staff, and principal planner. The flag lieutenant was Lieutenant William M. McCormick, who wanted to be a naval aviator but couldn't get his request approved. He would act as Spruance's personal aide and would supervise visual communications: flag-hoist, semaphore, and flashing light. Lieutenant William S. Parsons, the radio officer, completed the staff.

The staff was professional, competent, conscientious, and efficient. To a man, it contained career officers and Naval Academy graduates. Long and McCormick were future flag officers. All had been personally close to Taffinder, a warm and friendly character. But they were apprehensive about Spruance—about rumors that he was a "cold fish."

And Spruance was indeed a contrast to Taffinder: cool, remote, impassive, almost indifferent to his new staff. Spruance directed his officers to carry on as before. He would make no changes, and he expected them to handle all routine matters. A stand-up desk was installed in Spruance's cabin, and there he spent about ten minutes each morning reviewing correspondence with Long. Then he was alone the rest of the day. Unlike Taffinder, he also ate alone. The staff, assuming that Spruance was preoccupied, left him in peace and proceeded with their duties. Their new admiral silently approved and accepted what they did.

The staff wanted to entertain Spruance, hoping to melt his glacial reserve and to make a good impression. Long sounded him out. "Admiral," he said, "the staff would like to have a welcome-aboard party, so we can all get acquainted. What kind of party would suit you best? What would you like?"

"I like to walk," said Spruance. Then he silently stared at Long.

Long, dumbfounded, stared back. The thought of the staff and their wives hiking with the admiral was ludicrous, but Spruance offered no alternative. The silence became oppressive, and Long retired in confusion. The staff huddled and decided that Spruance must like the outdoors. Perhaps he would enjoy a picnic. Long approached him again, and Spruance agreed, but without enthusiasm. Unknown to Long, Spruance hated picnics.

On the appointed day, the officers and their wives gathered at an Army recreation beach to swim and cook steaks. The staff knew that Spruance wanted a fresh-water shower following his ocean swim, and they had tested it successfully earlier in the day. Inexplicably, it didn't work when he needed it that afternoon. Spruance was obviously uncomfortable after his swim, and the staff anxiously looked up the road for McCormick, who was bringing the steaks. When McCormick arrived, he had been delayed because his car had been in an accident. The men hoped that the worst was over and proceeded to light a cooking fire. Their appetites became whetted by the aroma of broiling meat. Their nerves calmed. A glorious sunset was followed by a full moon, rising over the windless bay. Lulled by the tranquil setting, they began to eat.

Suddenly, stinging, swarming mosquitoes attacked, and slaps and curses shattered the still air. Amid groans of despair, the defeated picnickers fled for their cars and home. The fiasco was crushing. The dejected staff had tried hard to please their admiral and had failed miserably. Spruance, impassive as usual, had said nothing the entire day. The picnic was never again mentioned.

The ill-fated picnic was a brief interlude in the midst of Spruance's efforts to ready his cruisers for war. He took them to sea three times from September through November, for nine-day periods. Sometimes he accompanied Halsey, who, flying his flag on the carrier *Enterprise,* commanded Task Force 2, which included Spruance's division. But generally he worked alone with his warships, which trained strenuously in obedience to the plans developed by the staff. From dawn to dusk, without respite, the division fired their guns, flew their observation aircraft, and crammed every waking hour with exercises and drills that improved their fighting efficiency. The schedule was so explicit that little had to be said or done. The staff ran everything; Spruance rarely spoke. He watched quietly, and he read. He was like a sphinx, inscrutable and uncommunicative, avoiding tasks he could get someone else to do for him. There were few exercises at night, and Spruance's sleep was regular and undisturbed.

After each underway training period, cruisers formed astern of the flagship and waited off Pearl Harbor until Vice Admiral Wilson Brown's Task Force 3 had sortied. Then the division entered and

moored, and the staff immediately began planning for the next underway period. Spruance went home.

At home he was worried and depressed. His daughter noticed that
he had lost his spark and never smiled. He expected war at any moment
and was discouraged about the readiness of the Navy and the United
States. He and Margaret discussed what they would do when war
began, whether she would stay in Hawaii or return to California. One
of his greatest concerns was whether Margaret could manage his financial investments. Spruance had amassed a complex portfolio of stocks
and bonds that needed constant attention and which his wife little
understood.

In early November, Japanese diplomatist Saburo Kurusu stopped in
Honolulu en route to Washington, where he would assist Ambassador
Nomura. Captain Ellis M. Zacharias, commanding *Salt Lake City,*
escorted Kurusu during the stop. Zacharias was fluent in Japanese and
was considered an expert on Japan. Kurusu was unaware of Japanese
war plans and in his ignorance was determined to maintain peace with
America. He impressed Zacharias with the peaceful intentions of his
country. After Kurusu left to continue his journey, Zacharias gave
Spruance his analysis of Kurusu's conversation. Citing his knowledge of
the Japanese language—which enabled him, he said, to understand the
Japanese mind—he declared that after talking with Kurusu he was sure
that there would be no war with Japan. Spruance listened without
comment.

Later, Margaret asked Spruance if he agreed with Zacharias's prophecy. He did not. Although Zacharias understood the Japanese language, Spruance said, he did not necessarily understand Japanese intentions. It was the clearest possible statement to his wife and daughter
that Spruance believed war was inevitable and imminent. He was right,
of course. One month of peace remained.

On 26 November 1941 Spruance issued an operations order for
another underway training period, very much as before. The division
would get underway with Halsey's task force on 28 November, resume
their training exercises near Pearl Harbor, and return to Pearl Harbor
on Friday, 5 December. Before leaving, Spruance asked Margaret to be
at Fleet Landing with Josephine when he returned. He wanted the two
women to dine with him aboard *Northampton* before he went home that
evening.

On the morning of the twenty-eighth, the *Enterprise,* three battleships, Cruiser Division 5, and the destroyer screen—Halsey's Task Force 2—filed out of Pearl Harbor as scheduled. Clearing the channel, Halsey split his force into two groups. One group, designated Task Force 8, comprised *Enterprise,* three of Spruance's cruisers, and nine destroyers. Halsey transferred command of the remaining ships—still called Task Force 2—to Rear Admiral Milo F. Draemel, the battleship commander. Halsey ordered Draemel to proceed to the normal operating areas to carry out the training plan. Halsey's force shaped course to the east. Spruance by then was aware that Halsey had disregarded the planned schedule, but he did not know Halsey's intentions. As commander of the accompanying cruisers and destroyers, Spruance screened his ships around *Enterprise* and awaited developments.

Once clear of Task Force 2 and sight of land, Halsey abruptly steered his force westward with instructions to arm for battle, sink any Japanese shipping sighted, and shoot any Japanese plane encountered. Halsey, apparently, was at war. Spruance eventually found that Halsey, operating in great secrecy, intended to deliver twelve Marine fighter planes to Wake Island in order to reinforce that island's defense against a probable enemy attack. The plan was Kimmel's, in reaction to the now-famous 27 November war warning. Only Halsey and two of his staff knew the plan when the force got underway, ostensibly for local training operations. Spruance knew nothing about either the warning or the Wake reinforcement mission.

Establishing the precedent for future operations, Halsey made the decisions and gave the orders. Spruance was an onlooker, largely concerned with making his ships responsive to Halsey's directives. As they steamed toward Wake, Spruance could only wait fatalistically for the dreaded war to begin. He had trained his cruisers, he had a competent, smooth-working staff—he had done everything possible to prepare for war. There was nothing more to do.

The planes were launched without incident near Wake, and Halsey reversed course toward Pearl Harbor. He planned to enter harbor on December 6, but he had to refuel his destroyers underway. Refueling underway required the warships to come alongside the oilers heading into the sea at moderate speed. The oilers passed over hoses which transferred the fuel. Larger combatants, such as carriers and battleships, also could refuel destroyers by the same method. Fueling, although necessary, frequently slowed a force of ships in transit, especially in heavy weather or when the oilers were forced to head away from the warships' destination. In this case, heavy weather slowed their progress, so Halsey revised his arrival time to Sunday afternoon, the seventh.

Margaret and Josephine, assuming that *Northampton* had been operating near Hawaii since leaving on the twenty-eighth, went to Fleet Landing on Friday the fifth for *Northampton*'s arrival, as Spruance had asked. They waited in vain; no ships came. Finally, Admiral Kimmel saw the women waiting and told them that *Enterprise* and *Northampton* would not be in that day, perhaps not even by the weekend.

They went home, and dates and parties were canceled because the ships were still at sea. Mother and daughter went to bed early, feeling rather sorry for themselves.

Chapter 7

WAR BEGINS

O N THE MORNING of Sunday, 7 December, *Northampton,* in company with Task Force 8, was two hundred miles westward of Honolulu. As Spruance was eating breakfast in his cabin shortly after 0800, his phone rang. It was McCormick, who was standing the staff watch on the bridge. He had just received a message, he said, from CINCPAC: "Air raid on Pearl Harbor. This is not a drill."

"Thank you," replied Spruance. "You know what to do."

Spruance earlier had issued a plan to the division, effective when war was declared. It invoked measures for increased alertness and intensified battle readiness. McCormick ordered the cruisers to execute the war plan. Nothing more had to be said.

Spruance came to the bridge and remained there for the next twenty-four hours. The initial reaction of the staff and ship to the reported attack was incredulity. No one remembers Spruance's reaction. If he said anything significant, the staff was too busy and preoccupied to notice it.

The airwaves became a pandemonium of conflicting messages. Japanese planes and ships were mistakenly sighted everywhere, commands were given and countermanded, and Halsey was reduced to frustrated rage trying to find the enemy. The Pacific Fleet—surprised, hurt, and shocked—thrashed blindly and wildly into empty air and ocean.

While Halsey groped for the enemy, Spruance tried to evaluate the babble on the radio circuits. Halsey had the same information that was available to Spruance, so Spruance kept his opinions to himself to avoid distracting Halsey. Halsey was in command, and Spruance trusted Halsey's ability to make the proper decisions and to do whatever was necessary. Spruance followed Halsey, operating his ships in obedience to Halsey's tactical commands.

As Sunday wore on, ships appeared over the horizon and joined Halsey's force. One admiral, whose ships had survived and had fled Pearl Harbor, reported that the battleships there had been "incapacitated." Other damage reports were similarly incomplete or misleading. Spruance could not find out the extent of the destruction at Pearl Harbor.

In the afternoon Halsey received a message locating the enemy to the southwest (although the Japanese were retiring to the northwest). Hoping to find the reported enemy force, Halsey sent Spruance and the surface ships on a fruitless search. The search burned precious oil, and it became imperative that Spruance's division enter Pearl Harbor to refuel. Fortunately, the Japanese had not attacked the fuel tank farms. The surviving ships were still mobile.

Northampton entered Pearl Harbor the next morning, Monday, 8 December. As the ship rounded Hospital Point, Spruance saw war's devastation for the first time in his life. The battleships—impregnable, familiar, enduring foundations of all he had believed in—now were shattered wrecks. The sight of his beloved battleships, so mortally stricken, stunned his senses. The years of reading and studying about war had not prepared him for what he saw that terrible morning.

Spruance clamped his jaw and was silent.

Northampton moored at noon. Spruance and McCormick went to CINCPAC headquarters to tell Kimmel that Halsey would enter harbor that afternoon. The wreckage of the staff reflected the wreckage of the fleet. Haggard and unshaven, they still were wearing their white Sunday uniforms, now crumpled and mud-splattered. Spruance had always admired Kimmel and was heartbroken to see him dazed and disheveled. Vice Admiral William S. Pye, an ardent battleship proponent, sat numbed and bewildered as though he couldn't believe that the attack had ever happened. The headquarters surged with hysteria, exacerbated by floods of panic-stricken rumors about Japanese ships surrounding the island, about paratroopers landing on Oahu, or about transports off the beaches. Spruance's pragmatic assessment was that the enemy was headed back to Japan, "well pleased" with the results of their attack. When Spruance reached home, his self-control dissolved. His wife and daughter were shocked—Spruance was a broken man. The three sat at a table, and he began to tell them what he had seen and felt. His voice choked with emotion, tears wetted his face, and he could scarcely speak. Yet he forced himself to talk about his shock and his grief, as though talking would purge his agony and suffering. Never before and never again would his wife and daughter see him in such despair. The destruction at Pearl Harbor was the most shattering experience of his life.

Most Americans damned the Japanese during those first days following the attack. An angered, aggrieved nation surged with abomination and vengeance. Naval officers vowed retribution against the despised "yellow race." But Spruance uttered not a word of condemnation. His wife and daughter saw him with every emotion laid bare. Hatred and vengeance were absent.

The next day, Spruance had recovered his poise and equilibrium. He never again spoke about his reactions upon seeing the sunken battleships for the first time.

December was a month of frustration for Spruance. Vice Admiral Pye had temporary command of the Pacific Fleet because Kimmel had been relieved, and Nimitz, his replacement, would not arrive until 31 December. Pye was reluctant to engage the enemy and allowed the Japanese to capture Wake Island unmolested by the Pacific Fleet. Spruance and his cruisers, in company with Halsey and *Enterprise,* steamed in futile patrols north of Oahu. Spruance impatiently waited for Nimitz, hoping that he would inject some fighting spirit into the demoralized CINCPAC staff.

Occasionally *Northampton* entered port to fuel, and Spruance spent every possible moment with his family. He no longer was strained and worried as he had been, before 7 December. The waiting was over. His family was reassured to see that he could smile again. He wanted to get on with the war and chafed at Pye's indecisiveness.

After Nimitz took command, Spruance was elated. "Then we commenced to go places and fight," Spruance later said. Nimitz's aggressive confidence invigorated the Fleet; where gloom and defeat once pervaded, hope and optimism were restored.

Both Nimitz and King were eager to lash back immediately at the

Japanese, but the Japanese retained the initiative in early January, forcing Nimitz to react rather than to attack. Indications were that the enemy might invade Samoa, a move which would endanger the indispensable Hawaii-Australia lines of communication. Marine reinforcements were en route to Samoa from San Diego escorted by Task Force 17 (Rear Admiral Jack Fletcher in *Yorktown*). Nimitz ordered Halsey to reinforce the convoy. When the Marines had been delivered safely, Halsey and Fletcher were to dash north to raid Japanese bases in the Gilberts and Marshalls, an offensive action which would do much to satisfy King's demand for an attack on the enemy.

Spruance said goodbye to his wife and daughter on 10 January 1942. They had taken stock of the future. The women wanted to stay in Honolulu as long as possible, even though the Navy was evacuating dependents to the mainland. Spruance, too, wanted them to remain as long as possible but suspected they would soon have to leave. Characteristically, he would not use his influence to keep them in Honolulu. When they parted on the pier, he had no assurance they would be in Honolulu when he returned.

Halsey in *Enterprise,* Spruance in *Northampton,* cruisers *Salt Lake City* and *Chester,* and six destroyers got underway for Samoa on 11 January 1942. Nimitz's tersely written orders for the operations after Samoa were to strike either the Marshalls or the Gilberts, with targets to be selected by Halsey. The written objective was to weaken the enemy and gain intelligence about his island fortifications. The actual objective was to satisfy King and to improve American morale. Nimitz's orders were necessarily vague because there was no intelligence about the Japanese forces, fortifications, or installations on either of the island groups. The Japanese had occupied the Marshalls for twenty years, and they had forbidden foreigners to visit. What they had done there to prepare for war was guesswork. The Gilberts recently had been seized by the Japanese from the British, and they probably had been fortifying and developing those islands as well. Halsey was not enthusiastic about the mission, despite his pugnacious character.

On 25 January the Marines arrived safely in Samoa, and Halsey's Task Force 8, in company with Task Force 17, steamed north by northwest toward the Marshall Islands, 1800 miles away. Halsey, responsible for selecting the targets, issued his final attack plan based upon a submarine's reconnaissance report that the Marshalls were lightly defended. The Americans would hit on the first of February. Fletcher would strike Makin in the northern Gilberts, and Mili and Jaluit in the southern Marshalls. *Enterprise* aircraft would strike Kwajalein, Roi, Wotje, and Taroa in the northern Marshalls. Simultaneously, Spruance with *Northampton, Salt Lake City,* and destroyer *Dunlap* would bombard Wotje Atoll; cruiser *Chester* and two destroyers would bombard Maloelap. The war was almost two months old. The raid would be America's first offensive action in the Pacific.

For thirty-nine years Spruance had prepared himself for this moment. His mind had been trained and exercised by hundreds of military problems at the Naval War College. Now, for the first time in his life, he was faced with a war game that was not a game. In stark contrast to the relaxed, remote rooms of Luce Hall on Coaster's Harbor Island, he was aboard a man-o'-war headed for combat. All over the world, professional American military and naval officers were experiencing the same transition from peace to war. Some would excel in fighting; others would fail. There was no way to predict such matters.

The most immediate problem for Spruance was the absence of information about what to expect on Wotje. He could not use cruiser scouting aircraft in advance to see what the Japanese were doing. The planes would betray the Americans' presence. With a vulnerable force audaciously venturing within range of Japanese land-based aircraft, the Americans could not afford to be detected. Surprise was paramount. They had to guess what they would find when they attacked. They could only hope it would not be more than they had bargained for.

Working under this severe handicap, Spruance addressed the problem. Navigation charts, based upon old and unreliable surveys, showed a typical Pacific atoll: an elliptical coral reef enclosing a lagoon. Wotje Atoll's twenty-five-mile axis ran east-west, with a series of islands surmounting the eastern half of the coral reef. The easternmost island, and by far the largest, was Wotje Island, shaped like a reversed "C" along a one-and-a-half-mile north-south axis, the northern portion a half-mile wide, the southern half tapering to a narrow peninsula. There were several anchorages inside the lagoon, reached through two channels piercing the southern reef.

Spruance studied the obsolete charts, the sailing directions, and the scanty data contained in the CINCPAC intelligence reports. There were many possible targets and defenses on the atoll. Spruance had to plan for those most likely, yet remain flexible for other possibilities.

The principal use of Japanese-held islands was to provide airfields, and Wotje Island was the only island on the atoll long enough for a landing field. Spruance reasoned that all the shore installations (and thus his targets) would be on the island. Enemy ships would probably be in the lagoon anchorage immediately to the west of Wotje Island, although they could also be at other anchorages inside the lagoon, or even entering or leaving the lagoon.

Spruance next established his target priorities. Enemy ships were most important because they could move and escape. *Enterprise* fighters would strafe any enemy aircraft on the ground. Shore installations were second priority after ships.

Spruance next considered the probable Japanese defenses. He reasoned that the shore batteries would be located on the eastern side of Wotje Island, covering the island's seaward approaches. Batteries might also be located on the smaller islands that flanked Wotje Island to the north and south. Guessing that the largest Japanese gun would be 6-inch caliber with a range of 10 miles, he decided to stay beyond that range from Wotje Island and to use his cruisers' 8-inch guns that could fire at 15 miles. Once they had silenced the Japanese 6-inchers, he could close to 6 miles and use his secondary 5-inch batteries, as well.

The navigational considerations were disturbing. The currents were strong and unpredictable. Erikub and Maloelap Atolls were nearby, south of Wotje Atoll. Erikub had submerged coral reefs with uncertain locations. All the islands, low and flat, would be poor navigational references. Spruance's force would have to close Wotje Atoll at high speed, at night, through dangerous waters—dangerous both because of hidden reefs waiting to tear out ships' bottoms and because of a hostile enemy defending those waters. The navigators would have to use dead reckoning procedures, estimating their position while using navigational charts in which they had little faith.

The staff had worked closely with Spruance in developing the estimate of the situation. Now Victor Long proposed the approach and bombardment plan: approach from the southeast—launch cruiser aircraft to spot gunfire, identify targets, and take reconnaissance photos—sink any ships in the lagoon—destroy enemy shore batteries—close in to destroy shore installations. The southeastern approach seemed best because it covered ships escaping from the lagoon and permitted enfilade fire against the north-south axis of Wotje Island.

Spruance accepted Long's suggested plan. He then had to decide how he would control the movements of the two cruisers and one destroyer during the bombardment. Doctrine called for forming the ships in column, with the admiral leading his ships into battle as a cohesive group, navigating in obedience to his commands. Spruance decided to follow standing doctrine. He would maneuver his ships in unison, uncovering their batteries in order to enable them to fire broadsides at the enemy ships.

On the other hand, the Navy had little experience in shooting at shore targets. Later in the war the Navy would realize that, in order to be accurate, ships had to steam slowly and employ measured, deliberate fire. But no one knew that in January 1942. So Spruance decided to fire at the shore targets in the same way he would fire at the ships: at high speed with the cruisers under his immediate control.

On 29 January, forty-eight hours before the attack, Spruance sent his plan to his force. Halsey had said he would operate to the northeast of Wotje Atoll and would open the show with a fighter sweep on Wotje Atoll from 0658 to 0715 in order to suppress enemy air. The remainder of the attack would be up to Spruance and his cruisers.

The cruisers would launch observation planes before sunup and by 0715 would be 10 miles southeast of Wotje Island in order to observe the enemy ships in the lagoon anchorage. Spruance would then maneuver his two cruisers by simultaneous turn movements on courses selected to close the range while maintaining broadside fire against the enemy ships, meanwhile determining the location and strength of the shore batteries. Eventually he would shift fire to shore targets, closing the range, if possible, to permit the cruisers to use their secondary batteries.

On the night of 31 January, Spruance's force began their approach. Victor Long navigated, and he was worried, especially about the hidden reef at Erikub. All through the night, he and the *Northampton* navigator used every bit of their skill and experience to steer the three ships safely through the dark and hostile waters.

In the early evening, Spruance's steward rigged a cot on the wing of the flag bridge. Soon Spruance appeared, turned in, and slept soundly through the night, oblivious to the tension of a ship about to go to war.

Chapter 8

THE MARSHALLS RAID

WHILE Spruance slept, his task group closed Wotje Atoll at 21 knots. Halsey's carrier group was somewhere to the north. An hour before sunrise, radar contacts appeared and were assumed to be *Enterprise* aircraft. Spruance awoke, went below to eat breakfast, then returned to the bridge in sharply pressed wash-khakis and shined shoes. At morning half-light the cruisers turned into the wind to launch the scouting aircraft; twenty minutes later they turned back toward Wotje.

Strident bugle calls blared over the *Northampton* general announcing system, followed by the gravelly voice of the boatswain's mate calling the crew away to general quarters. *Northampton* reverberated with pounding feet and slamming doors and hatches. Then she became quiet. Her turrets rotated, and her 8-inch guns elevated up and down, as if she were flexing her muscles before the fight. All hands topside wore lifejackets and steel helmets. Spruance, asserting an admiral's prerogative, never wore battle dress in battle.

Lookouts reported land ahead, then ships in the Wotje Island anchorage. Precisely at sunrise, Halsey's fighters roared in and began strafing Wotje Island. Simultaneously a scrappy Japanese gunboat loomed ahead and closed to do battle. "Take it," said Spruance to *Dunlap*. The destroyer peeled off and, after a half hour's firing (far too much time), sank the diminutive defender of Wotje Atoll.

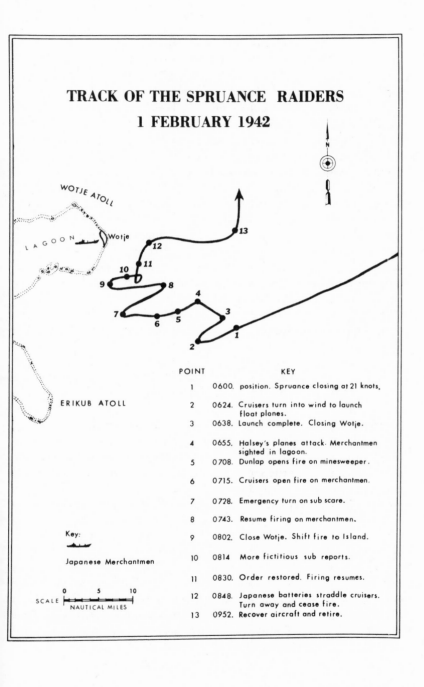

TRACK OF THE SPRUANCE RAIDERS
1 FEBRUARY 1942

WOTJE ATOLL

LAGOON Wotje

ERIKUB ATOLL

POINT	KEY
1	0600. position. Spruance closing at 21 knots.
2	0624. Cruisers turn into wind to launch float planes.
3	0638. Launch complete. Closing Wotje.
4	0655. Halsey's planes attack. Merchantmen sighted in lagoon.
5	0708. Dunlap opens fire on minesweeper.
6	0715. Cruisers open fire on merchantmen.
7	0728. Emergency turn on sub scare.
8	0743. Resume firing on merchantmen.
9	0802. Close Wotje. Shift fire to Island.
10	0814. More fictitious sub reports.
11	0830. Order restored. Firing resumes.
12	0848. Japanese batteries straddle cruisers. Turn away and cease fire.
13	0952. Recover aircraft and retire.

Key:

Japanese Merchantmen

SCALE 0   5   10
NAUTICAL MILES

Spruance and the cruisers, meanwhile, continued to close the atoll. As they came within range of the anchorage, they turned left to unmask their batteries. The *Enterprise* aircraft departed. Spruance ordered open fire on the ships in the lagoon, by then identified as small merchantmen making heavy smoke, lighting off their boilers and raising steam. All went well for eleven minutes. The cruisers' salvo splashes fell gratifyingly close to the frantic merchantmen, and the float planes reassuringly reported that the flanking islands were without shore batteries. Spruance could be well pleased with his plan and his ships' performance.

Suddenly, *Northampton* reported a periscope on the port beam. Spruance didn't want to believe it. He had considered the possibility of submarines at Wotje, decided there would be none, and had dismissed the submarine threat from his mind. He reluctantly ordered cease-fire and reversed course in an emergency turn. When the cruisers had steadied up, he ordered them to resume fire. But their accuracy was temporarily impaired; any radical change of course or speed disrupted the gunnery fire control solution.

The raid became a deadly game of hide-and-seek. The cruisers sped back and forth outside the lagoon, firing erratically, trying for a clear shot at the merchantmen inside the lagoon. The merchantmen, scurrying for survival, ducked behind the islands interposed between them and the warships. The spotter planes were hindered by clouds and often were unable to distinguish targets. Spruance's orderly plan degenerated into a melee.

After forty-five minutes of firing, the cruisers had sunk few, if any, of the evasive merchantmen. In order not to waste any more ammunition, Spruance ordered them to close Wotje Island and to shift fire from the merchantmen to the shore installations. By then the Japanese shore batteries had unlimbered, and enemy shells splashed close aboard both cruisers. A shell exploded in the water abeam the flag bridge. Long instinctively ducked. Spruance, standing alongside him, remained erect and unflinching. Seeing Spruance's composure, Long felt foolish. Spruance made no comment on Long's behavior.

The submarine scare would not abate. Zacharias in *Salt Lake City* had been sure, before the raid, that Japanese submarines would defend Wotje. Fictitious submarine sightings confirmed his fears: a scout plane reported two submarines leaving the lagoon; a surface ship inside resembled a submarine tender; empty, bobbing gunpowder cases that had been thrown overboard were identified as periscopes by jumpy lookouts. Almost everyone except Spruance soon was convinced that submarines had surrounded the American ships. The cruisers twisted and turned to avoid torpedoes that their captains believed were streaking toward them. Spruance signaled his cruisers to disregard the "periscope" sightings, to no avail. Tactical discipline had broken, the guns could no longer fire, and Spruance watched helplessly as his panicked cruisers fled from imaginary submarines.

Eventually he restored control and again turned the cruisers toward Wotje Island. The range closed, and the secondary batteries joined in the bombardment. Several large fires erupted that "burned," as Zacharias said, "with a full, rich orange flame." But the cruisers' inexperience in firing at shore targets became evident. Shells, randomly flung ashore, hit targets by chance rather than by design.

The Japanese shore batteries increased their accuracy and volume of fire, straddling both cruisers. The cruiser gunners, their vision obscured by smoke and excitement, were unable to find and silence the dangerous Japanese guns. Spruance was imperturbable amidst tumult and remained on the open bridge rather than inside the armored conning tower, his ostensible battle station. The enemy shells and shrapnel got thicker.

"Admiral," McCormick insisted, "don't you think you'd better get back in the conning tower?"

"No," replied Spruance, "but maybe you'd better, because you have so much longer to live than I have."

His ships in danger and his guns ineffective, Spruance turned away from Wotje Island and ceased fire an hour and forty-seven minutes after the attack had begun. He ordered the float planes to strafe and bomb, and then they were recovered. The cruisers sped toward Halsey and rejoined him in early afternoon.

Halsey had been busy, having launched and recovered countless strikes against the adjacent islands. For nine hours he had maneuvered *Enterprise* within sight of Wotje and had been unmolested. But he had pushed his luck to the limit; Japanese planes would surely find and soon attack him. When Spruance joined, Halsey wisely decided it was time to quit. He retired to the northeast at high speed. Thus began the legendary club, "Haul Ass With Halsey."

Japanese planes belatedly appeared in midafternoon. The cruisers fired energetically but ineptly. Fortunately the Japanese accuracy was no better.

During the three-day return to Pearl Harbor, Spruance assessed the destruction his ships had wrought and decided it wasn't much. Possibly two small ships were sunk and several damaged. The shore bombardment had started three large fires. The extent of damage to other shore installations was unknown or indeterminate. His ships extravagantly had fired 690 eight-inch and 1300 five-inch rounds to achieve those scanty results.

Halsey's force returned to Pearl Harbor in great triumph and were welcomed as heroes. Ships shrilled their sirens, blared their whistles, and clanged their bells. Thousands cheered. Halsey wept and was not ashamed. The objective of improving American morale had been achieved.

Margaret had gone. The barge coxswain brought the news that she and young Margaret had been evacuated to the mainland several days earlier. Spruance reacted with mixed feelings. He had hoped she would still be in Honolulu; he didn't think she would be gone so soon. Spruance was disappointed that he couldn't be with her, yet he knew that it was best that she had left the war zone. She had been his confidante. Now he was alone.

Spruance remained aboard in the isolation of his flag cabin. Late that evening his new flag lieutenant, Robert J. Oliver, reported aboard for duty. Spruance had allowed McCormick to enter flight training and had selected Oliver as a replacement because of their earlier close relationship on *Mississippi*. Invigorated with the heady atmosphere of victory that day in Pearl Harbor, Oliver was shocked when he stepped into Spruance's cabin.

Spruance was exhausted. His head jerked from side to side from what appeared to be a nervous twitch in his neck. His usually lustrous eyes were dull. "Good God!" thought Oliver. "What has happened to this man?"

Spruance greeted Oliver warmly, and they briefly exchanged small talk. Oliver, sensing Spruance's fatigue, felt he should leave. Spruance told him to stay—he wanted to continue talking.

The Wotje raid, Spruance said, had been a bitter disappointment. His cruisers had not performed well in battle. Their antiaircraft fire was ineffective. The false submarine scare had thwarted his bombardment plan and had destroyed tactical discipline. "The ships scattered in all directions, and no amount of signalling got them back," he said. "I had lost control." The episode was particularly galling because of his certainty that there never had been a submarine threat to begin with.

Spruance recalled the first weeks of the war and his frustration with the lack of direction and purpose within the CINCPAC staff. Their vacillation made Bill Halsey so upset, he said, that Halsey "had almost put the telescope to the blind eye."[1]

As Spruance talked, he gradually became more optimistic. On the whole, he felt, the Marshalls raid had been worthwhile, particularly the air attacks on Kwajalein. He praised and admired both Halsey and Nimitz for their leadership and fighting spirit. Without question we had been badly hurt, Spruance admitted, and the struggle to recover would be long and painful. "But don't be discouraged, Oliver," he said. "Things will be better." Having thus reassured his young companion (who perhaps felt the admiral needed more reassuring than he did), Spruance ended his soliloquy and Oliver left. Spruance's vigor and peace of mind were apparently restored by next morning.

Spruance had to adjust to life without Margaret. It would be difficult, because he was dependent upon her in many ways. His letters to her immediately following his return to Pearl Harbor in early February reflect his melancholia. "I need my wife to keep me cheered up," he wrote. "I don't believe that I am going to enjoy the beauties of this part of the world, nor the war either, nearly as much without you. Life has certainly lost its interest for me since you left, and the worst of it is that I have no definite date to look forward to when I shall see you again."

Although uncertain whether he ever again would see his wife, he pragmatically suggested that she find a home in California. "I would rather have you on the West Coast," he wrote, "as something might turn up sometime to bring me there for a day or two. I don't see any prospect of it, but it just might." But his primary concern seemed to be Margaret's management of their finances. "You are very careless about such things, so please turn the job over to young Margaret to do, just as

---

1. A naval euphemism meaning to take aggressive action contrary to orders. Nelson had put a telescope to his blind eye at the Battle of Copenhagen so that he could not read his superior's flag signals to withdraw from the enemy.

Wotje Raid, 1 February 1942. Cruiser observation plane flies over burning
Wotje Island. The Spruance raiders are out of the picture to the left. The
lagoon and Japanese merchantmen are to the right.

you have in the past to me." He wrote detailed instructions on computing their income tax. "This will be a practical test of Vassar vs. Lake
Erie,[2] so get young Margaret to work on this job."

He wanted to tell Margaret about his first experience in combat, but
a self-imposed censorship forbade any disclosures. The most he would
say was, "We heard a radio report the Pacific Fleet had made a raid on
the Marshall and Gilbert Islands . . . you may have heard the same
news."

Meanwhile, Nimitz awarded Spruance the Navy Commendation
Medal, despite Spruance's private belief that the raid was a personal
failure. "For distinguished service," read the citation, "in the line of
his profession as Commander Cruiser Division Five and for his bold
and effective handling of the bombardment group during the action
on February 1, 1942. He pressed home his attack against strong
enemy positions in the face of enemy shore battery fire, silencing the

---

2. Referring to their respective colleges; Margaret went to Lake Erie, young Margaret to Vassar.

enemy guns and inflicting heavy damage on enemy shipping and shore installations."[3]

The war went on, and the Japanese were close to victory in Malaya, Bataan, and the Netherlands East Indies. King demanded additional carrier raids, so Nimitz ordered Halsey to attack Wake Island in late February. Nimitz had little faith that it would accomplish much of value.

3. Spruance originally received an individual letter of commendation from Nimitz. On 11 January 1944 the Secretary of the Navy created the Navy Commendation Ribbon to be worn by those receiving such letters. Not until 22 March 1950 was there authorized for wear the Navy Commendation Ribbon with Metal Pendant, later known as the Navy Commendation Medal. Those who had earned the Navy Commendation Ribbon were awarded the medal. Navy Department, *Navy and Marine Corps Awards Manual*, NAVPERS 15,790 (Washington, 1953), p. 9.

Chapter 9

MORE RAIDS

ON 11 February 1942 Nimitz issued written orders for Halsey's task force to raid Wake Island on 24 February in order to divert the Japanese from their sweeping advances in Southeast Asia. The objective was a delusion, because one aircraft carrier striking recently captured Wake Island could not possibly divert the Japanese armies from completing their conquests two thousand miles away. Nimitz specified some secondary purposes: weakening Japanese strength in the Central Pacific and gathering aerial intelligence photographs. But the mission was without valid strategic or tactical objectives and would be no more than another training exercise for the *Enterprise* air group and Spruance's cruisers. It would bring Halsey increased fame. Spruance would continue to be anonymous in Halsey's shadow.

One encouraging aspect was that more intelligence on enemy dispositions would be available for planning. The island, which until recently had been in American hands, was well charted. Nimitz promised to send a plane to deliver recent aerial photographs after Halsey had gotten underway. Thus neither Halsey nor Spruance issued their own attack plans, preferring to wait until they received the new intelligence material at sea.

Task Force 16 left Pearl Harbor on 14 February, with *Enterprise, Northampton, Salt Lake City,* and six destroyers. The transit to Wake would be long—two thousand miles—and Spruance faced days of boring steaming and the absence of any pressing duties. He collected every book and paperback he could find and devoted his waking hours to reading. The war had changed many things in the early months, including naval dress. Spruance's uniforms and grooming always had been meticulous, and he required adherence to *United States Naval Uniform Regulations,* which he seemed to know from cover to cover. As the war progressed, wash khakis replaced dress whites as the warm-weather uniform. But officers still wore ties, even pilots in combat flight gear. One day Nimitz radioed the fleet that ties no longer were required. Spruance read the message and removed his tie. So did the staff. Then Spruance rolled up his sleeves and removed his cap. Handing cap and tie to his Marine orderly, he remarked, "Now we can get on with this business in comfort."

The photographs of Wake finally arrived by air the afternoon before the planned strike and were distributed among the ships of the force. Spruance assigned each member of his staff a specific task in developing the bombardment plan, urged them to hurry, then waited for them to return.

Oliver would select the targets. Thrusting the aerial photographs into Oliver's hands, Spruance told him to lay to the flag cabin, break out Spruance's navigation kit, and there he would find a magnifying glass.

"Use the glass and find our targets," Spruance commanded.

Oliver scurried below, found the glass, and looked uncomprehendingly at the photos taken from a B-17 at twenty thousand feet. Knowing nothing about photo interpretation, he was perplexed. How did one identify targets? A typical Pacific atoll, islands upon a four- by nine-mile coral reef, a lagoon in the center—nothing else was immediately apparent on the photographs. Time was short. In desperation he located several "targets"—presumably shore batteries and buildings—and rushed back to flag plot. Spruance grabbed the photos and, without a glance at what Oliver had selected, thrust them at Long. "There are your targets," he said.

Long, meanwhile, had developed a proposed approach and bombardment plan. He reasoned that the Japanese defenders would have difficulty seeing the Americans at dawn against the darkened western horizon, and Japanese patrol boats most likely would be searching to the northeast, toward Honolulu. He therefore proposed an attack from the west at sunrise. Spruance concurred. Satisfied that the staff work was completed, he began to write his attack plan. He paused briefly from time to time and stared at the bulkhead. When finished, he tore the sheet from the pad and handed it to Long. "Is this all right?" he asked.

The staff clustered around, all trying to read it at once. It was a perfect dispatch operation order without an erasure or correction. Not one of the staff could have produced it without a reference book.

"Admiral," the radio officer remarked, "the Navy is wasting money supplying you pencils with erasers." Spruance almost smiled.

Spruance's force—two cruisers and destroyers *Maury* and *Balch*—separated from Halsey that evening to begin their night approach. Halsey's plan scheduled the *Enterprise* aircraft to strike at 0710, ten minutes before sunrise. Spruance would hide his force over the western horizon, then dash in once the aircraft began their attack.

Next morning Halsey could not launch on schedule because of bad weather, but he wouldn't break radio silence to tell Spruance, miles away on the opposite side of Wake. Unaware that Halsey's planes would be delayed, Spruance began to launch his scouts on schedule and to close Wake at 15 knots.

The Japanese were not surprised. *Northampton*'s radar revealed aircraft closing the force from Wake. Soon they were sighted visually—Japanese seaplanes, shadowing beyond gun range. Spruance pressed onward, still launching his own planes, still assuming Halsey's aircraft were over Wake. He was forced to maintain a windward course, slightly away from Wake, until *Northampton* had completed launching her four aircraft. (Spruance had a low opinion of his flagship's efficiency and rarely spoke to her captain. *Northampton*'s aircraft handling provoked some of Spruance's greatest criticisms.) As the last *Northampton* plane cleared the catapult, Spruance turned his ships—then in column—on a direct course toward Wake.

The gun director officers, meanwhile, could not see their targets in their optical range finders. The atoll lay directly in line with the rising sun, and the glare on the water was blinding. Long, chagrined that his western approach had failed, expected Spruance to castigate his poor judgment. Spruance said nothing.

Having circled the force for twenty minutes, the Japanese float planes suddenly dived to attack, and the ships reacted with their usual ineffective antiaircraft fire. McCormick earlier had told Oliver that he would inherit a problem with Spruance: he needlessly exposed himself in battle. McCormick said he had tried in vain to persuade Spruance to take cover when bombs and shells were flying, and he was relieved to pass the problem on to Oliver. Now Oliver looked up and saw a Japanese plane roll over and dive straight for *Northampton*'s bridge. The flag lieutenant instinctively looked for cover. Spruance didn't move. Completely exposed, he calmly watched the plane become closer and larger. When the plane released its bomb, Oliver was certain it would hit the bridge. Still Spruance did not move. Suddenly Oliver realized that Spruance had no intention of taking cover. *Northampton* jammed her rudder hard over at the last moment, and the bomb narrowly missed.

The force shook off the air attacks and came within range of shore targets on Wake Atoll. The ships opened fire, triggering a spirited response from the shore batteries, whose muzzle flashes could be seen winking in the light of dawn. Presumably the ships' intended course would keep them beyond the range of the Japanese guns, but the enemy salvoes crept uncomfortably close. Spruance seemed oblivious to the lethal splashes converging on his ships. Oliver thought Spruance didn't see them; looking astern, Oliver discovered that *Salt Lake City* was straddled. Alarmed, he yelled at Spruance and pointed. Spruance lowered his binoculars slightly. "Yes, I see them," said Spruance, his voice tinged with annoyance as though Oliver had pestered him with trivial details.

Within a half hour the ships fired 2300 rounds of 8- and 5-inch ammunition, which raised great clouds of dust but exacted slight damage. The high speeds, long ranges, and glaring sun had prevented accurate gunfire. In Spruance's mind he was wasting ammunition, so he ceased firing and withdrew. The float planes dropped their bombs and were recovered. *Enterprise* planes belatedly attacked with meager results.

As the action subsided, Spruance was in high spirits. Oliver decided to force the issue of Spruance's refusal to protect himself under fire. Taking Spruance aside, he sternly told him that his behavior was folly. Spruance patiently listened to Oliver's arguments. Then, with a mischievous gleam in his eye, he said, "Oliver, you shouldn't be so nervous."

"But sir, I'm not nervous."

"If you weren't nervous," Spruance said, "why did you smoke so many cigarettes?"

Oliver abandoned his futile admonishments, but he never could dispel his concern for Spruance's safety.

Spruance's intent—to be brave—is understandable, because a naval commander traditionally has been expected to exhibit courage under fire. Spruance often remarked that warriors like Nimitz and Marine general Roy Geiger were "born brave men," and he extolled Nimitz's "utter fearlessness." In contrast, Spruance would admit to fear, which he suppressed. "Some of us," he once said, "have steeled our nerves, to a certain degree, to be brave." He had disciplined himself, after years of sea duty, to remain calm during periods of stress and danger. Bombs and bullets headed his way were no more than a magnification of the hazards he had overcome before the war. His self-discipline overcame the most powerful instinct of all, self-preservation. He never flinched, never ducked, never faltered.

Yet his sorely worried subordinates argued that, whatever the benefits of his example of personal courage, those benefits were not worth the risk of losing him. His death would be in vain. They argued he owed it to the Navy to stay alive. Perhaps he had scant faith in the negligible protection provided by the thin-skinned flag bridges against armor-piercing bombs and projectiles. Better fatalistically to stay in the open. And he was a fatalist, believing he would die when his time had come, and he could not control when that time would be.

He could have gone inside the more heavily armored conning towers, but then he couldn't see what was happening outside. As a student at the Naval War College, he once had listened to Admiral Behncke, a German who had fought at the Battle of Jutland. Behncke had stressed that the admiral in battle must be outside where he could see things. Perhaps such advice from veterans of naval battles had impressed Spruance. John Paul Jones and Admiral Lord Nelson always had exposed themselves in battle. Spruance had plenty of precedent. A naval commander did not go into battle hiding from personal danger.

With the Wake raid nearly over, two unfortunate Japanese patrol vessels crossed Spruance's path. One had been damaged by *Enterprise* planes, and *Maury* administered the coup de grace. The other blundered into the force several hours after the bombardment. It was no more than a sampan mounting one small gun. Spruance ordered *Balch* to sink it. The destroyer quickly closed, then at point-blank range slowed, turned, and trained her guns upon the doomed vessel.

Moments passed, but *Balch* delayed firing. Oliver pictured the scene on the destroyer's bridge: the commodore admonishing the captain not to embarrass the destroyer force in front of Spruance, and the captain on the telephone to the gunnery officer reminding him to make it good. The *Northampton* flag bridge was packed with spectators, and the scene before them resembled a condemned prisoner before his executioner. Spruance stood among the crowd of witnesses, steadying his binoculars by leaning his elbows on the windshield. Still not a shot, and the tension grew. Finally Long said, "I pity those poor devils."

Spruance straightened up, his binoculars falling to his chest, and he turned his back on the scene as if he couldn't bear to watch. He walked slowly to the opposite side of the bridge. "Yes," he remarked, "I feel very sorry for those poor men."

Then he stopped abruptly, spun on his heel, and exclaimed, "But after all, we did not start this war." He rushed back, jostled his way into the crowd, and raised his binoculars to watch *Balch* blow the picket boat to pieces, bit by bit.

With miles to go before rejoining Halsey, Spruance received the bad news that *Northampton*'s new radar antenna had been jarred off its pedestal by the shock of her gunfire. Spruance was worried. Many hours of daylight remained, and a Japanese search plane was shadowing his force. *Enterprise* was too far away for air cover. Surely the Japanese would send planes from the Marshalls to attack him during withdrawal, and he now was unable to detect them at long range because he had no radar.

His concern was justified. As the day wore on, the lookouts' attention became transfixed on the omnipresent search plane. Just before sunset, two bombers sneaked overhead and were undetected until their bombs began to fall. Spruance ordered an emergency turn, and the bombs narrowly missed.

His troubles worsened as his ships plunged into dense fog. Lacking radar and under radio silence, the task of finding Halsey would be tricky. When Spruance arrived at the rendezvous next morning, the fog persisted. The two forces groped for each other, unable to see and unwilling to talk. Someone on *Northampton* suggested sending Morse code by ship's whistle. Spruance agreed. A signalman tapped out a message on the electric whistle, and a muffled chorus of whistled "Rogers" answered in return. Spruance and Halsey had made a perfect rendezvous.

* * *

Everyone hoped they would return to Pearl Harbor, but Nimitz ordered Halsey by message to "retire" toward Japan and raid Marcus Island. Marcus was 999 miles from Tokyo. Other than that, Halsey knew little about it. The force refueled, raided Marcus without incident, and finally headed toward Pearl Harbor. They would be underway almost four weeks before returning to port.

Life for Spruance under Halsey had become monotonous. Brief hours of exciting action were small compensation for weeks of tedium. He exhausted the ship's library, retired early, and got a full night's sleep.

"I wish I had something more to do," Spruance later wrote Margaret, "as most of the time I ride around as a passenger and might as well be ashore. This last time out, for instance, I was off on my own for only two days and a half. However, Bill Halsey is a grand man to be with. He is a splendid seaman and will smack them hard every time he gets a chance."

During the long, inactive days at sea, Spruance used the idle time to train the staff by assigning theoretical operational problems for them to solve, similar to those at the Naval War College. Oliver used *Sound Military Decision* for guidance, and Spruance one day asked if he found it useful. Oliver, without much thought, said he found it so. Noticing that Spruance's eyes had begun to sparkle with bedevilment, Oliver suddenly felt he was about to be trapped, and he became wary.

"That's fine, Oliver," Spruance persisted, "but do you understand everything in it?"

Oliver hedged—there was *one* part that was a little vague.

"Show me the part you don't understand," Spruance commanded. Spruance took the notorious green book and read a few lines, then fixed Oliver with a withering stare.

"Don't you understand that?" Spruance demanded.

Miserably: "No, sir, I don't."

Spruance glared at Oliver, who was increasingly embarrassed that his stupidity had so displeased his admiral.

Then Spruance's eyes softened into their familiar merry twinkle. "Well," he said, "Kalbfus wrote it, and it's nothing but words, words, words." Pleased with his morning's amusement, Spruance walked off. Oliver was bewildered, not knowing until twenty years later about Spruance's past stormy association with *Sound Military Decision* at the Naval War College.

The task force returned to Pearl Harbor in mid-March, feeling none of the elation that followed the earlier Marshalls raid. Nimitz, reflecting the attitudes of Halsey and Spruance, admitted that the latest raid had yielded low returns at great risks to the American ships. The press, however, exaggerated the significance of the raids, implying they were great American victories.

"The thing I don't like about our press," Spruance wrote Margaret, "is the constant overemphasis they give to comparatively unimportant events, with the result that the public gets a wrong picture of how things are really going. Then the public indulges in wishful thinking. I like the way Winston Churchill does not hesitate to tell the British when things are going badly." Continuing his self-imposed censorship, yet eager to tell Margaret what he had been doing, he suggested that she read the *Life* magazine that described Halsey's raids—even if they were "overemphasized."

While in port between raids, Spruance visited friends and took long hikes with Oliver. (The other staff officers avoided walking with Spruance, preferring the officers' club bar after a hard day's work.) During these walks Spruance talked about everything except the war. Save once. On that occasion Oliver had spoken disparagingly of the Japanese race. Spruance remarked that if the Japanese were as inferior as Oliver suggested, then it was ironical that the superior Americans were so worried whether they could beat them in war.

The stricken battleships dominated Pearl Harbor. They swarmed with continuous human activity. Cranes and winches and men struggled to salvage what the Japanese had destroyed. Ships' crews, leaving Pearl Harbor to make war at sea, passed close aboard Battleship Row. Nimitz and his admirals and their staffs, immersed in their planning to conquer Japan, could glance out their office windows and see the battleships and their salvors. The battleships were omnipresent and evoked mixed feelings within the hearts of thousands of avenging Americans.

For years before the war, beginning when Billy Mitchell had first sunk a dreadnought in the early twenties, debates had raged about the respective merits of battleship power and air power. Their arguments had been inconclusive—until December seventh. At first opportunity, Spruance inspected the shattered battleships. He crawled and climbed about their reeking, oil-slicked hulls, jagged and twisted and wrenched by the explosive force of Japanese bombs and torpedoes. He soon became absorbed in learning about air warfare.

In early March, Margaret wrote Spruance that young Margaret had tuberculosis, apparently contracted while she had been with her parents in Puerto Rico.

"I was distressed to learn that young Margaret was in the hospital," he wrote Margaret. "I am not worried about her condition, as I feel that she is in good physical condition generally and I don't believe the disease has gotten very far. So don't get yourself run down by letting your imagination and sentiments run away with your reason."

Then, knowing he would soon leave for the Tokyo raid, he wrote, "Perhaps there will be considerable news before I write again."

The Joint Chiefs of Staff (JCS) had initiated the Doolittle bombing of Toyko. Apparently the JCS felt that this dangerous yet spectacular adventure had a legitimate military objective in improving American morale.[1] Spruance was vocally critical of the entire operation, because it diverted two carriers and numerous cruisers and destroyers from the main Japanese area of operation, the southwest Pacific, and unnecessarily endangered these ships with no objective other than raising spirits at home.

Eventually the Pacific Fleet would have to confront the Japanese armed forces. The raids thus far had not slowed Japanese conquests in the least; they had been a minor irritation, a flea on a dog's back. The proper objectives were to sink Japanese ships, down Japanese planes, kill Japanese soldiers, halt Japanese offensives—and start pushing them back. Win some important tactical and strategic victories, Spruance believed, and morale would take care of itself.

"The Doolittle raid was very hush-hush," Spruance later wrote, "but Halsey told me about it before we left Pearl Harbor to rendezvous with the *Hornet*. The plan was to run in to 500 miles of Japan before launching. Unfortunately for us, the Japanese had fishing boats with radio as pickets about 700 miles off shore, so we were picked up and reported not long after daylight. Halsey ordered Doolittle's planes

1. Actually the Joint Chiefs of Staff were not the originators of the Tokyo Raid. It was the personal idea of Admiral King and was first proposed by a member of his staff, Captain Francis S. Low. See the excellent account of the JCS by Grace P. Hayes entitled *The History of the Joint Chiefs of Staff in World War II—The War against Japan* (Annapolis, 1982), p. 127.

launched from the *Hornet*. . . . I had a ringside view of the launch and felt much relieved when the last plane was safely in the air.

"The Doolittle raid was a spectacular operation, good for American morale; but, unless it caused the Japanese to retain at home forces which they intended to send to the South Pacific, it did not impress me as particularly valuable from a military point of view."

On the return voyage to Pearl Harbor, the weather grew colder. One by one the staff shifted into the warmer blue uniform; Spruance persisted in wearing lightweight khakis. He was obviously cold, so cold that his teeth were almost chattering, despite his transparent efforts to mask his distress. The staff told Oliver to prevail upon Spruance to be sensible and shift to warm clothing.

Oliver reluctantly approached Spruance. "Admiral, it is too cold for you to be up here dressed like that."

Spruance recoiled at his aide's affront, wheeled about and stomped about the wing of the bridge. His face covered with guilt, he returned to Oliver.

"If you want to worry about me," stammered Spruance, "do it when it gets hot. I can stand the cold." Spruance angrily fled down the ladder and returned shortly in blues. Oliver was much relieved and again perplexed by Spruance's inexplicable behavior.

Oliver, who thought he knew Spruance well, could not have known that, forty years before, Spruance had plunged into the bitter winter weather without warm clothing, snapping at his scolding grandmother, "I won't be mollycoddled!"

Chapter 10

MIDWAY PRELIMINARIES

Halsey's Tokyo task force returned to Pearl Harbor on 25 April 1942 for rest and replenishment. They would not remain long. Nimitz was mustering his few available forces to oppose imminent Japanese invasions of Port Moresby in southeastern New Guinea and Tulagi in the Solomons. The carriers *Yorktown* and *Lexington* were in the South Pacific and available to confront the Japanese invasion forces. Nimitz dispatched Halsey with *Enterprise* and *Hornet* as reinforcements.

Halsey's Task Force 16 (which as usual included Spruance and his cruisers) left Pearl Harbor on 30 April, too late to help. As Spruance had feared, the Tokyo raid had diverted American forces needed elsewhere. *Yorktown* and *Lexington* alone fought in early May what became known as the Battle of Coral Sea. Each side lost a carrier. Neither side was a clear winner. But the Americans thwarted the invasion. Still belatedly steaming southward, Halsey received message orders on 16 May to return with haste to Pearl Harbor.

No one in the task force knew why Nimitz had ordered the task force to return. But during the long return transit, Nimitz began sending reams of intelligence messages to Halsey and Spruance. Spruance and the staff studied them intently; the messages indicated that the Japanese, using powerful naval forces, intended to seize Midway and the Aleutians. Spruance was puzzled why the Japanese would want Midway. He felt the American island, twelve hundred miles northwest of Honolulu, had little strategic importance. Japanese operations against the Aleutians seemed equally illogical.

"If we only knew what they were thinking," he mused aloud. He doubted that their real objective was capturing Midway. He was correct. The Japanese objective was to destroy the outnumbered American fleet in decisive action. The seizure of Midway Island was a ploy to draw the Pacific Fleet into battle and ultimate annihilation.[1]

On 26 May the task force entered Pearl Harbor. Spruance was anxious to call on Halsey, a custom after each return from sea, but *Northampton* delayed interminably in mooring to the buoys on East Loch. Spruance, dressed in formal white uniform, impatiently paced the quarterdeck. When his black-hulled barge finally pulled alongside, Spruance and Oliver quickly boarded, then headed for *Enterprise*. As they approached the carrier, they sensed something was wrong. The ship's quarterdeck was quiet, and the watch did not announce Spruance's arrival over the PA system. The usual bustle of quarterdeck ceremonies for an arriving flag officer was missing. Moreover, Halsey was not tending the side to greet Spruance, as he had always done so punctually in the past. Yet his absentee pennant wasn't flying. Where was Halsey?

They looked at each other in bewilderment.

"What is wrong, Admiral?" asked Oliver.

"I don't know," Spruance replied. "We had better go and see."

As Spruance stepped aboard the lower platform of the accommodation ladder, Halsey's flag lieutenant, William H. Ashford, bounded down the steps. He told Spruance that Halsey was not aboard, that he had seen Admiral Nimitz, and that Halsey now was in the hospital. Nimitz wanted to see Spruance immediately, because Spruance probably would take command of the task force. He would use Halsey's staff but could bring his own flag lieutenant.

"Let's go to the Sub Base," said Spruance to Oliver.

Spruance was silent during the short boat ride ashore. When they arrived at CINCPAC headquarters, Spruance told Oliver to visit the Fleet Intelligence Office while he saw Nimitz. The conference with the

---

1. For the strategic background of the Coral Sea and Midway campaigns, see in addition to the books cited in the introduction the following: Rear Admiral Edwin T. Layton, U. S. Navy (Ret.), *"And I was there," Pearl Harbor and Midway—Breaking the Secrets* (New York, 1985), and John B. Lundstrom, *The First South Pacific Campaign* (Annapolis, 1976).

white-haired admiral was brief. Halsey was sick with a skin rash, Nimitz said, and Nimitz had confined him to the hospital. Halsey, knowing he was too sick to fight, had recommended that Spruance command the task force, and Nimitz had agreed. The task force would get underway in forty-eight hours, having refueled and replenished, Nimitz continued, and it would fight the Japanese fleet threatening Midway. Rear Admiral Frank Jack Fletcher in battered *Yorktown* would arrive shortly from the Coral Sea. If that carrier could be patched up in time, Fletcher would join Spruance's force and would assume tactical command of the American striking force.

Nimitz had one other message: Spruance would become his chief of staff when the battle was over. Having disliked his two previous tours of staff duty, Spruance was displeased. He did not want a staff job ashore now that the war at sea was heating up. About to fight the most crucial sea battle of the Pacific war, and knowing he soon would come ashore, perhaps for the duration of the war, Spruance left Nimitz's office with mixed emotions.

On the return trip to *Northampton,* Oliver told Spruance that there was nothing more to add to the information he had already received from Commander Edwin J. Layton, the Fleet Intelligence Officer: that the code revealing Japanese intentions had been broken. Layton had assured Oliver that the information was valid and that Spruance would immediately be informed of any new developments. The only uncertainty was the date of the Japanese attack.

Then Spruance confided to Oliver that Nimitz had given him two sets of orders. His written orders were to meet and defeat the Japanese. But Nimitz had told Spruance not to lose his force. If things went badly, Spruance was to withdraw and allow the Japanese to take Midway. "They can't hold it," Spruance said, "and we can get it back later."

Spruance told Oliver that Oliver would accompany him to *Enterprise;* the remainder of the staff would remain aboard *Northampton.* "You and I had better get packed as soon as possible," Spruance warned. "If I were you, I wouldn't take anything I didn't need, because we might get hit and lose everything."

Before Spruance left *Northampton* with his bags packed, one of the staff officers asked Spruance if he had any concern about commanding a carrier task force. No, Spruance said, he was not concerned; he would have all the technical brains of Bill Halsey's staff at his disposal.

That question was on many minds that day. The command of a carrier task force presumably required a flag officer who was a naval air warfare expert. Spruance, without experience in carrier aviation, was relieving Halsey, who, although a late starter, had served continuously in carrier aviation for eight years. Halsey had commanded a naval air station, a carrier, a carrier division, and finally all Pacific Fleet carriers. Small wonder that Spruance was surprised, perhaps astounded, that Nimitz had chosen him to replace Halsey.

Halsey's recommendation that Spruance relieve him was not impulsive. He recognized, after years of intimate friendship, Spruance's ability to command. That ability had been tested in war, confirming Halsey's faith. He was forever praising Spruance to his staff. On the return to Pearl Harbor from the South Pacific in late May, Halsey knew that his acute dermatitis would demand hospitalization. He told his staff that he would recommend to Nimitz that Spruance replace him.

The day before Halsey entered Pearl Harbor, he expressed his faith in Spruance in an official letter. "Rear Admiral Spruance has consistently displayed outstanding ability combined with excellent judgment and quiet courage," Halsey wrote. "I have found his counsel and advice invaluable. From my direct close observation I have learned to place complete confidence in him in operations in war time.

"I consider him fully and superbly qualified to take command of a force comprising mixed types and to conduct protracted independent operations in the combat theater in war time."

Halsey's explicit endorsement of Spruance was for the record. Yet most who wore wings on their breasts knew nothing about Spruance— except that he was not an aviator. The aviators were uneasy going into the battle of their lives led by a stranger, a shadowy figure who had been riding about in the cruisers. In their hearts, every aviator in the force wanted Halsey to lead them at Midway.

That afternoon Spruance and Oliver called on Halsey in his hospital room. Halsey lay naked in bed; his body, smeared with a soothing ointment, was covered by a single sheet. He was cheerful but uncomfortable, constantly rubbing his arms, chest, and shoulders. The two admirals did not talk of the war or the looming battle: they knew each other so well, and they so often had spoken about what they would do should Spruance have to assume command. Rather they spoke as old friends, one sick and the other wishing him a speedy recovery. Spruance was entirely relaxed.

Halsey then asked Oliver to leave so he could speak privately to Spruance. They were briefly alone; then Spruance left.

Spruance received his written orders on the evening of 27 May, the night before he got underway. They comprised ten succinct pages. All operation orders in the early stages of the war were terse, reflecting the command philosophy of King, Nimitz, and the better admirals. That philosophy was to tell the subordinate commander what you wanted done, give him the necessary resources, provide as much information as you could about the enemy, and then let him alone so he could accomplish his mission. King would upbraid any commander for the sin of oversupervising subordinates with complex, overly detailed directives. The intent was to encourage the on-scene commander to use his initiative and not to inhibit his freedom of action. Spruance's personal belief was that the commander responsible for accomplishing the mission should develop the necessary plans; the proper role of the next highest command echelon was to establish the objective and to *suggest* how the objective might be achieved.

Nimitz's orders assigned Spruance two carriers—*Enterprise* and *Hornet*—six cruisers, and twelve destroyers, designated Task Force 16. Fletcher would command Task Force 17: crippled *Yorktown,* two cruisers, and six destroyers. Fletcher, senior to Spruance, would exercise tactical command of both task forces, and he would be responsible for coordinating the combined task force operations.

The order then described the enemy intentions. The huge Japanese fleet outnumbered the Americans. It would attempt to seize Midway in the near future with a force of 2 to 4 battleships, 4 to 5 carriers, 8 to 9 cruisers, 16 to 24 destroyers, 8 to 12 submarines, as well as transports carrying a landing force. One or two carriers would attack Midway and destroy her defending aircraft, surface ships would bombard the island's fortifications, and Japanese amphibious troops then would seize the island. A powerful covering force of the remaining carriers, the fast battleships, and the submarines would interpose itself between the island and the approaching American fleet, thereby isolating Midway and preventing American interference during the amphibious landing. The Japanese carriers probably would approach Midway from the northwest. If they discovered the American carriers early in the operation, the American carriers would likely become the prime target.

Nimitz had given Spruance a detailed intelligence annex which amplified the basic intelligence contained in the operation order. For example, the annex identified each Japanese ship that would be involved in the operation. This wealth of information, obtained by breaking the Japanese radio code, provided Spruance with an extraordinary advantage: knowing the Japanese *intentions* was enormous compensation for his inferior numbers of ships and aircraft.

Nimitz's orders directed Fletcher and Spruance to lie in wait northeast of Midway, stationing them on the left flank of the Japanese carriers attacking Midway from the northwest. Should the Japanese close from the northeast, the American forces then would be astride the Japanese path of advance. Either way, the Americans would be in position to intercept the Japanese.

Fletcher and Spruance were to inflict maximum damage on the enemy by employing strong attrition tactics, *but*, they were not unnecessarily to risk heavy American losses. Nimitz issued a separate letter of instruction to amplify the latter point. "You will be governed by the principle of calculated risk," wrote Nimitz, "which you shall interpret to mean the avoidance of exposure of your force without good prospect of inflicting, as a result of such exposure, greater damage to the enemy."

The mission of all the American forces, including the American troops and land-based aircraft on Midway, was to *hold Midway*. This mission was explicitly stated in the written operation order signed by Nimitz. But there were many unwritten implications. Spruance knew he was not to hold Midway at all costs. Nimitz had told him orally that conserving the precious American carriers was more important than saving Midway. To be sure, if Midway fell and Spruance's carriers survived, Spruance could well be damned for not saving the island, regardless of Nimitz's oral and written escape clauses. Yet if Spruance held Midway but lost his carriers, then he would have disobeyed Nimitz's principle of the calculated risk. Worst of all, Spruance could lose both Midway *and* his carriers. If the Americans lost the Battle of Midway, the repercussions would be horrendous. With the American fleet sunk, Honolulu would be defenseless, and a second and more devastating Pearl Harbor inevitably would follow. The effects on the American war effort and public morale would be incalculable. Even then the American press was visualizing an Axis invasion of California.

The United States could not afford defeat at Midway.

Spruance doubtless appreciated the hazards of the impending sea battle, but by his nature he would not allow his imagination to magnify the threat and paralyze his thinking. Certainly he was gratified that he had an independent command and was finally coming to grips with the enemy after months of ineffective American raids against unimportant Japanese atolls. Now he could fight a legitimate fleet action, the decisive battle for which he had trained his mind for years. Although the capital ships would be carriers and not battleships, and although he probably would not even see the enemy ships, this was his kind of war, his life's profession.

Moving into Halsey's recently vacated cabin on *Enterprise,* Spruance planned his strategy, based upon a council of war with Nimitz and Fletcher on 27 May. Spruance wanted to hit the Japanese carriers before they hit him. He would attack as early as possible with all his available air strength. His planes would concentrate on the enemy carriers in order to sink them. He did not want to spread his attack over all the Japanese ships, because they might only be damaged and live to fight another day. If he sank the Japanese carriers, and if he had any planes left, then he would concentrate on sinking battleships and cruisers.[2]

His plan was a gamble with grave risks, but it promised great rewards. Spruance would commit his entire force of aircraft in one massive attack, holding nothing in reserve. If Spruance's aircraft could pounce upon the stronger Japanese forces and catch them unaware and unprepared, the Americans could demolish the enemy carriers in one stroke, and the Japanese would be unable to retaliate. On the other hand, if the Japanese found him first, their superior power would overwhelm Spruance's force.

Surprise was vital to Spruance's plan. The Japanese must know that the Americans were waiting for them at Midway. Spruance therefore imposed radio silence on his task force. Under no circumstances were ships or planes to use radios, even to help a lost search plane find its carrier.

2. USS *Enterprise* (CV 6), displacement 19,800 tons, main battery eight 5-inch guns, 85 aircraft, commissioned 12 May 1938. Arguably the most famous aircraft carrier in history, "The Big E" saw combat in almost every major action in the Pacific War, including every carrier battle except that of the Coral Sea. She earned 20 battle stars for World War II service. Decommissioned on 17 February 1947, she was sold for scrap eleven years later, despite fervent efforts to save her as a memorial. DANAFS, volume 2 (Washington, 1968), pp. 356–58.

Miles Browning as a student at the
Naval War College, 1936

Finally, despite his meticulous plans, Spruance knew he would need luck as well as surprise in order to win. Critics later called him cautious, saying that he lacked boldness and was not aggressive. They were wrong. His plan was bold and daring. He was going for the Japanese jugular.

Spruance's newly acquired staff were nervous and apprehensive. Halsey had talked of Spruance so often and in such glowing terms that they envisioned him as a superman. They were fiercely loyal to the ebullient Halsey. Spruance was a chilling contrast.

The chief of staff was Captain Miles R. Browning, an experienced aviator who would be Spruance's principal aviation advisor. Browning recently had received a meritorious early promotion to captain and a Distinguished Service Medal for having recommended and planned the tactics for the Marshalls raid in February. *Life* magazine called him a hero. He had achieved a well publicized reputation as a brilliant naval air warfare expert.

Browning was enjoying an unexpected esteem within naval circles, because failures and controversy had buffeted his career. A lean, hawk-like man, he was emotionally unstable and evil-tempered, becoming angry, excited, and irrational with little provocation. He drank too much, too often, and had a capacity for insulting behavior, especially when drunk.

Over the years Browning had made many enemies, especially among the aviators. Halsey had saved him. He could control Browning and used his brilliant ideas while disregarding his wilder schemes. Browning had once been passed over for commander; thanks to Halsey, he was meritoriously promoted to captain over many of his classmates. Yet he was a mediocre chief of staff. His erratic, irascible behavior demoralized the staff officers. Halsey was not an administrator, and Browning was worse yet. The message files were a shambles when Spruance came aboard, manifesting the staff's sloppy administration. Yet Browning was the man upon whom Spruance was expected to depend for advice.

Spruance embarked in *Enterprise* on 26 May, accompanied by Oliver. The jittery staff officers immediately cornered the young flag lieutenant and deluged him with worried questions. What did Spruance like? Dislike? What were his methods? Oliver's answers were meant to be reassuring, but the staff couldn't believe that Spruance would be the undemanding admiral that Oliver described.

On the morning of 28 May the task force prepared to leave Pearl Harbor. Oliver preceded Spruance to the flag bridge and met Browning. The chief of staff was wearing a tie and noted that Oliver was tieless.

"What is the admiral's policy on ties?" Browning asked.

"Sir, he does not wear a tie," Oliver replied. "He does not wear a cap, and he goes around with his sleeves rolled up. If you follow the motions of the admiral, everything will be fine."

Browning, much relieved, tore off his tie and jammed it into his pocket, then unbuttoned his collar.

The staff messed with Spruance on *Enterprise,* and the first meal was painfully awkward. The staff officers ate silently and stared at their plates. As coffee was being served, Spruance began to talk, about nothing in particular, and nothing about the forthcoming battle. Then his eyes began to sparkle, and he raised his voice so it could be heard at the farthest end of the table. "Gentlemen," he said, "I want you to know that I do not have the slightest concern about any of you. If you were not good, Bill Halsey would not have you."

Oliver later recalled, "In a few words, Spruance had broken the ice, melted it, and poured it down the scuppers. That was the last silent meal in the admiral's mess."

Gradually the staff relaxed. Although Spruance usually remained in his cabin or on the open flag bridge atop the island,[3] he occasionally visited the flag mess between meals. A staff officer stumbled upon him there, sitting in an easy chair and reading the radio news. Seeing Spruance, he froze and began to retreat. Spruance looked up. "Come in and relax," he said. "This is our home. We have nowhere else to go."

The staff chuckled at their new admiral's breakfast routine. The steward placed a four-cup Silex coffee maker at his one hand, a toaster at the other, and a large bowl of canned peaches in the center. Spruance thereupon brewed his coffee, toasted his toast, and ate his breakfast. He once explained he had developed this routine because in his early Navy days refrigeration was unreliable, and fresh provisions were not available for long periods at sea. His invariable menu could provide an adequate breakfast, refrigeration or no, and so his habit had developed.

Spruance deliberately began preparing himself for the major decisions he would soon be making. He removed himself from the details of running the task force. When he had commanded his cruiser division, he had (perhaps because he was bored) participated in everything that went on. Although he never had interfered with his staff, he had watched them closely. Yet on *Enterprise* he remained in the background, allowing Browning and the staff to direct the activities of the force. It was an unusual and unexpected sight to Oliver.

With his force underway, Spruance drafted a dispatch to his ships. Soon the shutters of the *Enterprise* signal lamps began to clatter, the flashing lights attracting the attention of the ships in company. Signalmen on the other ships blinked their lights in response, then began chanting the words flashing in Morse code from the flagship's signal bridge. Apprentice signalmen—"strikers"—began recording the message.

"An attack for the purpose of capturing Midway is expected," the message read. "The attacking force may be composed of all combatant types including four or five carriers, transports and train vessels. If presence of Task Force 16 and 17 remains unknown to the enemy we should be able to make surprise flank attacks on enemy carriers from a position northeast of Midway. Further operations will be based on

3. The carrier's superstructure above the flight deck.

result of these attacks, damage inflicted by Midway forces, and information of enemy movements. . . ."

Naval tradition holds that great leaders must speak heroic words designed to inspire subordinates in battle: "I have not yet begun to fight," or "Damn the torpedoes! Full speed ahead!" Spruance apparently felt he should do the same, but he ended his message with a declaration that was awkwardly phrased, almost an afterthought: "The successful conclusion of the operation now commencing will be of great value to our country."

Halsey had established a command post, known as the flag shelter, on top of the *Enterprise* island. It was simply furnished with a chart table, a voice radio handset, sound-powered phone outlets, two settees, and metal book racks that stowed tactical publications. Spruance would fight the battle from that location.

Spruance carried a rolled-up twenty-inch-square maneuvering board,[4] fastened by a paper clip. He was never without it, and when he entered the flag shelter he would casually toss it upon the book rack. There it remained until he retrieved it upon leaving. No one asked him to explain his mysterious maneuvering board.

He would use it to make the most important decision of the Battle of Midway.

4. A paper form containing a compass rose and a distance scale, used by mariners to solve relative motion problems at sea.

Chapter 11

THE BATTLE OF MIDWAY

SPRUANCE refueled his force from an oiler on 31 May and took station 325 miles northwest of Midway. Fletcher, in hastily repaired *Yorktown,* joined in midafternoon on 2 June and assumed tactical command. He began implementing the plan that Nimitz, Fletcher, Spruance, and their staffs had developed during their council of war at Pearl Harbor on 27 May.

Fletcher directed Spruance to operate his Task Force 16 ten miles southward of Fletcher's Task Force 17, allowing the two forces to remain within visual signaling range. They did not merge into a single disposition because current doctrine held that carriers could best operate in combat by maneuvering independently. Fletcher also directed Spruance to have *Enterprise* and *Hornet* cocked and ready to launch attacks on short notice. *Yorktown* would provide the defensive fighter patrol (called CAP, for combat air patrol) and the necessary search planes. On the morning of 3 June *Yorktown* and the cruisers launched their searches and the Americans continued their vigil. People were jumpy. The force went to general quarters when a bogey (unidentified aircraft) approached. The CAP intercepted the bogey and reported it was friendly—that is, American. The nervous crews stood down from their battle stations.

Spruance had earlier met with the *Enterprise* pilots and told them what to expect. Now he patiently waited for someone to find the Japanese, hoping that Nimitz's estimate of the Japanese intentions had been correct. If Nimitz had guessed wrong, and if the Japanese intended to attack somewhere else—such as Pearl Harbor or even the West Coast—it would have been absurd for the Navy to be waiting in empty ocean near Midway.

Midmorning of the third brought reassuring news. Midway patrol planes had sighted the Japanese landing force 700 miles west-southwest of Midway, exactly where Nimitz had said they would be. The report confirmed in Spruance's mind that the Japanese were going after Midway. If Nimitz also was right about the Japanese carriers, then those carriers would be attacking from the northwest early next morning. That night Fletcher moved the force slowly southwest so that it would be positioned to strike the Japanese carriers' left flank at daybreak—if they appeared.

The dawn of the fourth of June promised fair skies with heavy white clouds, good visibility, smooth seas, and cool temperatures. The gentle wind from the southeast would force the American carriers to charge away from the enemy at high speed, in order to generate enough relative wind across their flight decks to operate aircraft.

The pilots had been ready to attack since before daybreak. Twice they had manned their planes, only to be called back to the ready rooms. Just before sunrise *Yorktown* launched ten planes to search to the north, in the event the Japanese intended to attack from the northeast. (In that case the Americans would be astride their path, and Fletcher did not want to be surprised by an unexpected approach.)

Spruance awakened early and went to the flag shelter, joining Browning, the operations officer, Commander William H. Buracker, Oliver, and the staff watch officer. A radio loudspeaker was tuned to the Midway Island search plane frequency, in order to monitor contact reports.

The men sat and waited.

At 0534 they heard a message from a Midway search plane: "Enemy carriers." The Japanese were nearby. But where?

At 0545 the same plane reported many enemy planes closing Midway from the northwest at 150 miles. That report confirmed that Japanese carriers were somewhere to the west of the Americans. But where were they *exactly?* And how many? And were they headed toward Midway or toward the American carriers? The inconclusive reports had an unintended and malignant effect upon the staff officers, wrenching their nerves and intensifying their anxiety. Anticipating that the next message surely would locate the enemy, they could scarcely contain their impatience and excitement.

The message burst through the loudspeaker at 0603: two carriers and battleships heading for Midway at high speed, 180 miles to the northwest of the island. The effect was explosive. Browning, Buracker, and the staff watch officer lunged in a body toward the navigation chart, all grabbing for the single measuring dividers. For a moment it looked as if someone might get stabbed by the instrument's sharp points.

Spruance, meanwhile, calmly rose from his seat, picked up his maneuvering board, and unrolled it. Oliver had wondered for days what it contained. To his astonishment, he saw it was blank, without a pencil mark upon it.

Spruance stood quietly behind his staff officers as they feverishly plotted the reported enemy position. When they finished, he asked that the contact report be read to him.

Someone read it.

Was it authenticated?

It was.

Then he asked for the ranges and bearings from Midway to both his force and to the enemy. These he plotted on his maneuvering board, allowing him to measure the distance from him to the enemy. Using his thumb and index finger as dividers, he estimated the distance was about 175 miles, within the maximum range of his torpedo planes.

He rolled up the maneuvering board and tossed it aside.

"Launch the attack," he said.

Spruance's order was a gamble. He knew the enemy fleet contained four or five carriers, but that only two had been reported. His quick decision to launch an immediate attack, based upon the 0603 contact report, indicated he did not intend to wait in order to find the rest. He obviously hoped the other enemy carriers would be near those already sighted.

The wind was blowing from Midway toward the Japanese carriers. Spruance assumed that they would continue to close Midway, heading into the wind in order to recover their first launch against the island. Having rearmed and refueled their aircraft, they then could launch a second strike, either at Midway or against his own force *if discovered.* Time was short. Japanese search planes could find him at any moment. Perhaps Japanese attack planes were headed his way even then.

Spruance's decision—to launch his attack immediately—was therefore well reasoned but risky. If he was lucky, he would catch all four or five Japanese carriers in one place. If he was unlucky—if the Japanese carriers were split—he would have launched his entire air group against only a part of the Japanese carrier force. Any enemy carriers that he did not hit on his all-or-nothing attack would pose a terrible threat to his outnumbered force. That was the calculated risk.

The American aircraft could not leave the flight deck instantaneously with Spruance's decision. The actual time of launch required complex calculations that took some minutes to complete. Many factors were involved: the relative motion of the two opposing forces; wind velocity and direction; the possibility that the reported enemy position was inaccurate; the payload and fuel capacity of the American planes; the time needed to man and start the planes; the time interval between the launch of the first and last planes of the attack group; their endurance and combat radius; and finally, the time required to send the attack order by flashing light on the *Hornet.* Spruance long before had intended to launch everything when he was within range of the enemy, that is, 175 miles. Computing the exact time of launch was now up to Browning. But it had to be without delay. Spruance wanted his planes up and flying at the earliest possible moment.

Browning began barking orders. *Enterprise* sounded general quarters; the force turned westward and increased speed to 20 knots. Fletcher signaled to close and attack the enemy, a superfluous order because Spruance was on his way. Fletcher remained behind to recover his search planes and CAP; Spruance was on his own. Shortly he turned his force slightly left to a course west by southwest and increased speed to 25 knots, in order both to lead and to close the enemy carriers presumably still headed toward Midway. Browning by then had recommended a 0700 launch time. Spruance accepted the recommendation. The order was transmitted to *Enterprise* and *Hornet.*

Spruance planned a coordinated attack, the *Enterprise* and *Hornet* air groups flying in company, then each attacking one Japanese carrier respectively. In accordance with current doctrine, the dive bombers would hurtle from above while torpedo planes simultaneously skimmed the surface, all the while being protected from the Japanese CAP by American fighter escorts. This kind of coordinated attack would divide the Japanese defenses and increase the chances for American success.

Enterprise intended to launch 64 aircraft. At 0700 she turned into the gentle southeast wind. Her aircraft gunned their engines, thundered down her flight deck, and became airborne. The launch seemed agonizingly slow. After thirty minutes it was only half completed. Then Spruance received a report he knew was inevitable: a Japanese scout plane was on the horizon. The Japanese had found him. Now, more than ever, he had to hit the Japanese without delay. Yet his attack aircraft continued to circle overhead, burning fuel, waiting for the remainder of the air group to launch and rendezvous. Meanwhile the range between the Americans and the Japanese widened, as the contrary wind forced Spruance's carriers to rush away from the enemy.

The torpedo planes remained to be launched, but Spruance could wait no longer. At 0745 he signaled Lieutenant Commander C. W. (Wade) McClusky, the *Enterprise* air group commander, to proceed and attack with the bombers then aloft. The torpedo planes would have to attack later and separately. Spruance had consciously and deliberately abandoned his plan for a coordinated attack in order to get *something* headed toward the Japanese without further delay.[1]

The last torpedo plane lifted off the *Enterprise* flight deck an hour and six minutes after launching operations had begun. After *Hornet* had completed her launch, Spruance ordered the force again to close the Japanese at 25 knots. The American planes disappeared from view, then faded from the radar screens. The CAP circled overhead, AA gunners searched the skies, and radar operators stared at their phosphorescent scopes, all looking for the Japanese aircraft which surely would attack at any moment. *Hornet* had opened in order to operate independently with her screen; Spruance signaled her captain, Marc A. Mitscher, to remain within range, if possible. *Yorktown* was not in sight, so Spruance had no idea where Fletcher was or what he was doing. The excruciating wait began.

The airwaves were silent. Later, when the American planes had

1. Spruance actually did not know his task force had been spotted by the enemy until nine minutes after the last planes left the *Enterprise*'s flight deck. He became impatient with the slowness of the *Enterprise*'s takeoffs, because he could see the *Hornet* had already launched all of her planes. See John B. Lundstrom, *The First Team* (Annapolis, 1984), pp. 334–35, 338.

found the enemy, they presumably would radio the information back to the task force. One, then two hours passed. The estimated time of intercept came and went with no contact report, and the staff's worry and concern mounted. Finally at about 1000, Lieutenant J. S. Gray, the skipper of Fighting Squadron 6 (whose fighters had escorted the *Enterprise* attack group), reported that he was running low on fuel and soon would have to return. After an interval, the staff heard him again; he had sighted the enemy force of two carriers, two battleships, and eight destroyers heading north, without a CAP.

The Japanese had been found. But where were they? And where were the American attack planes? What in the hell was happening? Browning could not restrain himself. He impulsively grabbed the voice radio and shouted, "Attack! Attack!"

After a pause, McClusky's voice: "Wilco, as soon as I find the bastards."

More agonizing minutes. Then McClusky again: "Tally ho!" followed by instructions to his dive-bombers assigning targets.

The staff was flooded with relief. At last McClusky had found the Japanese carriers and was attacking. But Spruance could not assess whether McClusky's forces were winning or losing. The radio crackled with snatches of cryptic exchanges between the attacking aviators. Apparently they were successfully hitting some of the enemy ships. But Spruance's carriers were 135 miles away from the Japanese; he would have to wait until his pilots returned before they could report fully what they had seen and what they had done. Not until then could Spruance determine the damage they had wrought—or the loss in American aircraft.

The surviving American pilots who had weathered the Japanese defenses began their long return journey across the ocean toward their own carriers. Some crewmen were wounded, some planes were damaged, and all were short of fuel. Many of the *Enterprise* dive-bombers became lost. They radioed for navigational directions, and Lieutenant Commander L. J. (Ham) Dow, the staff communicator, responded with the carriers' location. The bombers tried to reach the carrier, but many ran out of gas and were lost at sea. Browning and the staff had blundered.

An aircraft carrier, unlike an airfield, is not stationary. It will constantly move while an aviator is flying his mission, and when he returns, the carrier may be located as much as a hundred miles away from its earlier position. The pilots therefore had to know where their carrier would be when they returned, a navigational reference point called "Point Option."

The staff was responsible for predicting the task force movements, computing Point Option, then telling the pilots—before they left— where it would be. If it changed radically while the pilots were away on their mission, the staff normally would radio a revision to the pilots. It was particularly important that morning because the planes had been launched at maximum range and would have little reserve fuel. Browning was responsible for promulgating Point Option, a routine detail that Spruance assumed would be handled competently by the staff, given their months of operational experience.

Browning did not broadcast Point Option before the *Enterprise* and *Hornet* planes began their 0700 launch. The pilots had been trained in such a way that, if they had not received the information before launch, they were to assume that the carriers would continue to close the enemy at high speed. Therefore they individually computed Point Option on that premise. But the fickle southeast wind prevented the carriers from closing the enemy. Time and again they turned away from the enemy in order to launch and recover both the CAP and the early stragglers from the attack group.

About 1100 the returning *Enterprise* dive-bombers began circling what they believed to be Point Option. (The *Hornet* bombers had missed the Japanese and had landed on Midway. Later they returned safely to the *Hornet*.) The ocean beneath them was empty, because *Enterprise* was forty-four miles away to the east. Browning and the staff had inexplicably failed to radio the revised Point Option to the pilots. Not until McClusky radioed for help did anyone on the staff attempt to guide the pilots home. Many crashed at sea, their fuel exhausted. Some survivors had as little as five gallons of fuel remaining when they landed.

Waves of deafening noise inundated Spruance in the hour before noon: the roar of airplane engines; the amplified voice of the air boss directing flight deck operations; the radio loudspeaker blaring a continual chatter between airborne pilots and their shipboard controllers.

The returning pilots, excited by their morning's adventure, climbed the ladders to the *Enterprise* island to report to Spruance and the staff.

The fog of war began to lift with their narratives of the battle. They had discovered four Japanese carriers, two more than the Midway search plane had reported. Spruance's hunch had been right. But the enemy carriers were located far to the north of their predicted position, and they had been closing the American carriers. They had not been damaged despite the earlier attacks by Midway-based aircraft. When discovered, the Japanese carriers had been headed into the wind, their flight decks jammed with aircraft about to be launched, probably against the American carriers.

The American attack had been piecemeal and uncoordinated. The fighters had failed to protect the slow-moving torpedo planes from the enemy CAP, allowing the Japanese Zeroes to slaughter the torpedo planes. The *Hornet* dive-bombers never did find the Japanese carriers. But then the Americans' luck had changed. Fletcher had launched the *Yorktown* planes an hour behind the *Enterprise-Hornet* launch, and all three air groups had searched independently for the enemy. Providentially, the *Enterprise* and *Yorktown* dive-bombers had simultaneously discovered and attacked the enemy fleet, each unaware of the other's presence. When their brief, slashing attack was over, three Japanese carriers had been hit and left burning fiercely. One undamaged carrier remained.

Enterprise reported heavy aircraft losses. Ten of 14 torpedo planes gone. Eighteen of 32 bombers had failed to return. McClusky reported that his bombers had been almost unopposed because the Japanese Zeroes had been on the deck demolishing the torpedo planes. Spruance therefore assumed that most of his bombers were lost later because Browning had fouled up Point Option. His confidence in Browning must have been severely shaken by high noon.

Another distraction summoned Spruance's attention: *Yorktown* reported she was being attacked by Japanese aircraft. Spruance had not thought about Fletcher during the morning; now he could see *Yorktown*, almost out of sight on the northwest horizon. Black puffs from her AA bursts speckled the sky. Spruance could not close to help because *Enterprise* and *Hornet* still were recovering aircraft, forcing the ships to steam away from the endangered carrier. As Spruance watched from afar, a large black column of smoke rose ominously over *Yorktown*. She was obviously hit hard, but Spruance had no way of knowing how badly she was hurt. He sent two cruisers and two destroyers from his force to help.[2]

---

2. The Task Force War Diary (cited in the introduction) shows that Spruance and Fletcher communicated several times late that morning.

It was a time of crisis. A hundred details clamored for Spruance's attention.

The admiral detached his mind from the bedlam surrounding him in order to think and to decide what he would do for the remainder of the day. He knew that one undamaged Japanese carrier remained nearby, whose planes at that moment were attacking *Yorktown* with great success. It was the most dangerous threat to his force, and he decided that his next objective was to destroy that carrier. But its location was unknown. It had last been seen at 1000, over two hours before, and its trail had grown cold. Steaming at 25 knots, it could move many miles before the Americans would be ready to launch a second attack in the early afternoon. Therefore Spruance decided to delay until he could confirm the Japanese carrier's new position.

His decision was both a calculated risk and a decided change from his earlier way of thinking. In the morning he had launched everything on the basis of one sighting report, because he wanted to hit the Japanese first at all costs. Yet in the afternoon he delayed launching, even though he knew the approximate location of the fourth carrier and realized he would expose his own force to the risk of subsequent attacks while he delayed, the exact situation he wanted to avoid earlier in the day.

Why, then, his decision to wait? Spruance's analysis of the morning attack highlighted the hazards of finding an elusive enemy based upon an hours-old contact report. His planes had wandered about the ocean in scattered groups, and the *Hornet* dive-bombers had missed the Japanese entirely. The American attacks had been haphazard and piecemeal, allowing the Japanese to demolish the torpedo planes. Other American planes had been lost at sea, having wasted their fuel in futile searches. The morning attack could have been a fiasco. Its success was owed to Wade McClusky of *Enterprise,* Lieutenant Commander M. F. (Max) Leslie, the *Yorktown* air group commander—and luck.[3]

Another consideration was that *Enterprise* and *Hornet* needed more time to get organized. The planes which had returned from the morning attack needed rearming, refueling, and repairs, but the carriers

---

3. Lieutenant Commander Leslie was actually commander of Bombing Squadron Three. The *Yorktown* air group commander was Lieutenant Commander Oscar Pederson, who remained on board as fighter director. An excellent new study on the *Yorktown* is Robert Cressman's *That Gallant Ship: USS Yorktown (CV 5)* (Missoula, Montana, 1985).

were burdened with handling the CAP and landing *Yorktown* survivors. (The *Yorktown,* ablaze and crippled, could not operate aircraft.) These distractions interfered with the flight deck crews who were preparing aircraft for a second attack.

Given all this, Spruance undoubtedly reasoned that an immediate second launch easily could degenerate into a wild-goose chase. Browning, however, contested Spruance's decision and urged an immediate launch. But Spruance was adamant. He would delay until he knew the exact location of that fourth carrier, allowing his own carriers plenty of time to ready their remaining attack planes. He would accept the risk of his being attacked in the interim.

Curiously enough, Spruance did not launch any search planes, a potentially fatal omission in view of his concern with finding the Japanese carrier. He could have employed carrier planes, cruiser float planes, or both. He used neither. Apparently he was content to wait for someone else to find the enemy. Perhaps he and the staff were too preoccupied to plan and organize a search. Another possibility is that he had suffered heavy aircraft losses in the morning attack and did not want to spare his remaining aircraft as scouts, leaving even fewer on deck to launch a second attack. Furthermore, he may have reasoned that Midway Island and *Yorktown* were responsible for air searches, and the latter, although hurt, possibly could have launched a search patrol before she was hit. Fortunately for Spruance, Fletcher had had the presence of mind to maintain continuous searches. While Spruance waited, *Yorktown* scout planes were indeed searching for the remaining Japanese carrier in the early afternoon.

By midafternoon, *Enterprise* and *Hornet* were ready to launch another attack; still Spruance held off until someone else found the Japanese carrier. The situation worsened. At 1430 a second wave of Japanese planes from the elusive enemy carrier attacked *Yorktown.* Again Spruance could only watch helplessly at a distance. Luckily for Spruance's Task Force 16, but unluckily for her, *Yorktown* was interposed between the enemy and the other two American carriers, thereby becoming the focus of the Japanese attack. She was hit again and went dead in the water at 1443. Her radios fell silent, an ominous indication that she had lost all her electrical power.

Spruance's decision to delay looked bad.

Two minutes later, a *Yorktown* scout plane reported a Japanese force of one carrier plus other heavy ships and destroyers 110 miles to the west of the American force. A very relieved Spruance now knew where his enemy was. He told Browning to launch the second attack of the day.

But the staff failed miserably in carrying out their admiral's order. Spruance's decision to wait should have allowed Browning and the staff adequate time to prepare a coordinated attack. Yet they bungled every aspect of the planning and execution of the second launch. At 1515—a half hour after receiving the *Yorktown* plane's contact report—someone on Spruance's staff signaled *Hornet* that Spruance did not know the position of the enemy carrier whose planes were attacking *Yorktown*. Three minutes later the staff sent *Hornet* a corrected message relaying the contact information received on *Enterprise* a half hour earlier. Still *Hornet* did not receive an order to attack, although Spruance had given the order to Browning thirty minutes earlier.

Meanwhile (probably through a telephone call to her bridge), the staff had told *Enterprise* to attack. At 1530 the flagship turned into the wind and began launching twenty-four bombers, many of them *Yorktown* survivors. Mitscher on *Hornet* must have wondered what was going on. Why was *Enterprise* launching while he still was without orders?

Finally, belatedly, the staff signaled *Hornet* at 1539 to launch her attack group less fighters. (Apparently the remaining fighters were to remain behind to protect the carriers.) She began launching at 1605. Her 16 bombers went aloft and headed west, trailing the *Enterprise* planes airborne thirty-five minutes earlier. For the second time during the day, the two carrier air groups had failed to mount a coordinated attack and again were embarked upon their separate ways, this time toward the remaining Japanese carrier.

The staff had collapsed. Midway was their first test of sustained combat against powerful forces. Their earlier raids against weakly defended islands had not prepared them for the demands of a fleet action. They were a free-wheeling staff, accustomed to impulsive decisions and hasty plans. Before Midway they had muddled through without any major mistakes. The staff officers were capable and willing, but erratic Browning provided neither leadership nor cohesion. Thus the staff became progressively more confused and disoriented as the battle progressed, unable to cope with the need for disciplined planning and the coordination of complex task force operations.

Less than an hour after launch, the American planes found and attacked the fourth Japanese carrier. Assuming that its destruction was assured, Spruance could think again of the immediate future. Although battered *Yorktown* had been abandoned, Fletcher was alive and well in his temporary flagship, the cruiser *Astoria,* and he was still OTC (Officer in Tactical Command). Many decisions had to be made, such as plans for the night and the disposition of the *Yorktown,* which was still afloat. Spruance did not know what Fletcher wanted to do or what Fletcher wanted him to do. Accordingly, he sent Fletcher a message: "*Hornet* and *Enterprise* groups now attacking fourth carrier reported by your search planes. *Hornet* about 20 miles east of me. Have you any instructions for further operations?"

"Negative," the senior admiral replied. "Will conform to your movements."

Spruance interpreted Fletcher's reply to mean that Spruance now was in command of the entire force. Apparently Fletcher felt that he could not direct an air war from a cruiser; Spruance was in a better position on the *Enterprise.* Everyone had to know who was in command. Fletcher now had made it clear. Spruance was everlastingly grateful for Fletcher's message.

The *Enterprise* aviators returned and reported that they had hit and heavily damaged the fourth carrier, but that it had not sunk. The escorting force of Japanese battleships and cruisers had not been damaged. With this information, Spruance set his mind to another estimate of the situation. His primary mission, he reminded himself, was to prevent the capture of Midway. The Japanese could press on with their invasion plans despite their losses, or they could quit and retire. They were capable either of making an amphibious assault on Midway or of seeking a fleet action to avenge their loss of their four carriers. The unscathed Japanese battleships and cruisers were a hundred miles to the west. Possibly other forces were nearby as well. If Spruance went westward during the night in order to close the enemy, he would risk colliding with the lethal Japanese surface ships, who were as fast as his carriers and whose big guns could shoot accurately at night.

Spruance was unwilling to take that risk. He decided not to steam westward in order to avoid an ambush. Instead, he wanted to be in a position next morning whereby he could either oppose a landing on Midway or regain contact with any Japanese naval forces still near Midway, such as crippled carriers and their escorts. Spruance and the staff debated the alternatives, but his advisors were little help. "Put me someplace where I can deal with them in the morning," Spruance demanded, but the staff seemed unable to offer any acceptable recommendations.

Spruance decided for himself. He would keep moving to avoid submarines, head eastward until midnight, turn north for an hour, then again head westward, allowing him to be within supporting distance of Midway at daybreak while avoiding Japanese surface forces at night.

There being no other business, Spruance went to bed.

At midnight the force changed course to the north, as planned. Forty-five minutes later the staff watch officer received a report of a radar contact on the surface, fourteen miles to the northwest. It could have been part of the dreaded Japanese surface force that Spruance wanted to avoid. He ordered an emergency turn to the east, dispatched a destroyer to investigate, and telephoned Spruance in his sea cabin. The watch officer assumed Spruance would call his ships to general quarters, as Halsey surely would have done. He was stunned with Spruance's response. "Very well," said the sleepy admiral. "When you lose the contact, resume the base course and speed. Good night."

Another report interrupted Spruance's slumber shortly after 0400. Submarine *Tambor* (with his son Edward aboard) had sighted many unidentified ships ninety miles west of Midway. Perhaps the Japanese were pressing on with the invasion. Spruance increased speed and headed toward Midway.

Several hours later *Tambor* reported that two Japanese cruisers were retiring from Midway; then an American patrol plane sighted them streaming oil. (They had collided at night, it later was learned, while maneuvering to avoid *Tambor*.) These reports indicated that the Japanese had canceled their landing on Midway. Spruance went to breakfast.

After breakfast the staff excused themselves and hurried off, anticipating more fighting. Oliver rose to follow.

"Come sit with me for a while," said Spruance. Oliver protested that he wanted to get to the signal bridge where he belonged.

"They don't need us up there," Spruance assured him. "Besides, you and I had a busy day yesterday, and it won't hurt us to relax for a while." Oliver rejoined his admiral.

Spruance was cheerful, relaxed, and philosophical. He reviewed the events of the previous day's fighting, then remarked that it had been a typical major battle. You go in with a good plan, he said, and hope that it will work. Then the fog of battle sets in, and you are never quite sure what is going on. But you must have faith, and much depends on luck. His only regret was that he had to lose so many brave men.

Later, when Oliver arrived at the flag shelter, he was confronted by the staff officer who had been on the midwatch. He took Oliver aside. "What kind of man is Spruance?" the staff officer demanded. "He refused to get out of bed for a radar contact report that could have been the Japanese fleet."

Oliver replied that, if it would make him feel any better, he too had trouble getting the Old Man out of his bunk.

Having finished his leisurely breakfast, Spruance went to the flag shelter and was met by an agitated Browning. The chief of staff was certain that the enemy fleet was retreating; he urged Spruance to speed up and attack as soon as possible, before the Japanese escaped. Spruance demurred. He doubted that the Japanese were offensively minded after losing four carriers. Still, they had the capability to attack Midway. A fifth Japanese carrier also might be in the area, ready to attack after he had committed his dwindling force of aircraft against the Japanese battleships and cruisers. Furthermore, the morning's weather was bad for flying. In view of these considerations, Spruance disregarded Browning's recommendation and decided to await developments. The fog of war had settled again.

Inexplicably, Spruance again did not launch search planes to help him find the enemy. Perhaps he was influenced by the bad weather and a desire to conserve his carrier planes for attack and self-protection. Although he could have used his cruiser float planes, they never were flown. With his planes immobilized on deck, Spruance was at a serious disadvantage: he was literally blind and had to depend upon submarines and Midway patrol planes. The latter did send contact reports throughout the forenoon, which indicated the Japanese fleet was withdrawing, but their performance was as inept as it had been the day before. Spruance needed but could not get continual reports of the enemy's composition, location, and movements. To his frustration, the land-based planes would not maintain contact, but rather broke off and returned to Midway, and the enemy again disappeared from view.

Nevertheless, both the weather and the situation were clearing. By midmorning Spruance assumed that the Japanese would not attack Midway, and he decided to seek and attack the retreating fleet. Apparently it was in two groups, one to the west and the other to the northwest of Midway. The latter was farther away but contained the more "profitable" targets—according to reports, a burning Japanese carrier and two battleships. Spruance chose that group as his objective and began a stern chase at 25 knots. By early afternoon, the Americans had not received amplifying reports on the northwest group they were pursuing. The trail grew cold. Any attack would have to be on the basis of stale information; the enemy's location would have to be a guess.

Browning developed an attack plan based upon the enemy's last known position, course, and speed, then recommended a 1400 hours launch with dive-bombers armed with 1000-pound bombs. Spruance, assuming that the senior aviator was competent in such matters, accepted the recommendation. Browning issued the attack plan.

Within minutes, Wade McClusky stormed into flag shelter protesting Browning's plan, accompanied by a squadron commander and by Captain George D. Murray, the *Enterprise* skipper. McClusky disputed Browning's calculations, arguing that the range was too great, the bombs too heavy, and that the planes would not have enough fuel to return. McClusky wanted to delay the launch an hour and load only 500-pound bombs in order to carry more fuel. Even then the planes' fuel reserve would be dangerously low. Browning stubbornly refused to change his plan. The two men's tempers rose, and they began shouting.

Spruance could not ignore the tumult; he had to quell the argument. He joined the tight knot of angry men. "Admiral," said one, "we will go if *you* tell us to. But if we go, we won't be coming back."

Spruance, without a word to Browning or the staff, turned to McClusky. "I will do what you pilots want," he said.

Browning was first astounded, then enraged that Spruance had overruled him. He supposedly was the final expert on aviation tactics and Spruance's principal advisor. Now the admiral had publicly disgraced him by acceding to McClusky. Hurt and humiliated, Browning stormed off the shelter and fled below to the bridge. There he lost all control; he wept and raged and screamed. Finally he went to his cabin, where he sulked until a staff officer persuaded him to return to the flag shelter.

Perhaps Browning had miscalculated the payloads and ranges because of his anxiety to launch the strike at the earliest moment using the largest available bombs. During their argument, McClusky had accused Browning of being unfamiliar with the bomber's operating characteristics; Browning, rather than checking his figures with McClusky's, arbitrarily told the air group commander to "obey orders." Already disillusioned by

Browning's performance the day before, Spruance finally lost all confidence in his chief of staff that afternoon.

The American force continued to close the enemy, whose estimated position was becoming increasingly doubtful. A flight of Midway-based B-17 bombers passed overhead toward the enemy, then returned without sighting anything. Nevertheless at 1500 the attack was launched, with Spruance hoping for the best and expecting the worst. His planes found only two small ships, attacked them without success, and returned in the growing darkness.

Now Spruance had to make yet another crucial decision. The planes were low on fuel and would have to land without delay. Yet they had little or no experience in night landing; many might perish in the dark. Their best hope of survival was to illuminate the ships, both to provide navigational beacons and to illuminate the flight decks.

Spruance ordered the force to turn on their lights. Many considered his decision rash. Ships were habitually darkened at night in order to prevent detection by the enemy, principally submarines. Others considered him a courageous humanitarian, risking his ships for the lives of his aviators. The fact was that Spruance was entirely pragmatic. In his view a carrier without its aircraft was disarmed and impotent, a liability and not an asset. He considered the risks before the launch, not after. He later explained that if planes are to be flown so late in the day that a night recovery is likely, and if the tactical situation is such that the commander is unwilling to do what is required to get the planes back safely, then he has no business launching the attack in the first place. On the afternoon of June fifth he believed he was chasing the damaged fourth carrier. The only enemy who could see his lights would be, at most, a submarine or two. Granted, submarines were a threat, but he was even more worried about the ability of the pilots to land at night, even with the flight decks illuminated. They were fatigued after two days of combat, and they never before had done what they had to on the night of June fifth. To his intense relief, all but one landed safely.

Another disquieting report came to Spruance's attention. He wondered why some of *Hornet*'s dive-bombers had returned before the *Enterprise* group. He discovered that a large number of *Hornet*'s aircraft had carried 1000-pound bombs in disobedience of his orders. With less fuel, their range was also less. He was already irked that the *Hornet* bombers had completely missed the enemy the day before. Now his opinion of the *Hornet* and Mitscher was steadily worsening.

Spruance considered his plans for the second night. The late afternoon attack had been futile, and he had been lucky to recover the air group intact. He had lost the Japanese fleet. The two small ships his planes had attacked surely would warn the remainder of the enemy fleet—wherever they were—of Spruance's estimated location. The fleeing Japanese force had two options: to continue northwesterly in order to hide in developing bad weather, or to turn westward toward Japan possibly to elude the Americans if they continued to the northwest. There was no reason to head into the heavy weather to the northwest. Aircraft couldn't operate and the Japanese could successfully hide and escape. On the other hand, if they had changed course to the west as an evasion tactic, Spruance still would have a chance to find them. He therefore decided to change course to the west.

Within minutes after the course change, *Northampton* reported a submarine on the starboard bow. Browning had by then returned to duty. He immediately picked up the TBS (voice radio) and snapped an order to the force for an emergency left turn. (Spruance cited this event to the author as an example of Browning's quick, intelligent thinking. He never mentioned Browning's faults, only his virtues, in his conversation with the author.)

A half hour later Spruance again turned to the west. Hoping both to avoid a chance encounter with Japanese battleships in the darkness and to conserve his destroyers' diminishing fuel supply, Spruance chose a safe, economical speed of 15 knots.

No longer willing or able to rely upon Midway search planes to find the elusive Japanese, Spruance finally decided to launch his own search at daybreak. Then they went to bed.

The third day, the sixth of June, began with good news. At daybreak, *Enterprise* search planes reported two distinctly separated groups of Japanese battleships, cruisers, and destroyers about 130 miles to the southwest, heading slowly toward Japan. Spruance, having been plagued with unreliable sighting reports, wanted more information. He ordered the cruisers to launch their scout planes in order to help in the hunt. If they found the enemy, they were to maintain continuous surveillance. The previous two days' practice of making only one report and then breaking contact had bedeviled the admiral. Now he wanted someone watching those enemy ships every moment, so he would know at all times what they were, where they were, and where they were going.

During the early hours of the morning, Spruance had received a message from Nimitz saying that Ensign Gay of *Hornet*'s Torpedo Squadron 8 had been rescued, the only surviving crew member of the ill-fated torpedo planes that had been slaughtered on the fourth. On the basis of Gay's eyewitness description of the battle, Nimitz was certain that the Japanese were now without carriers. He suggested that the time was appropriate to seek out and destroy the remainder of the Japanese fleet. Spruance needed no urging. At 0800 *Hornet* launched twenty-six dive-bombers plus a fighter escort. Spruance ordered *Enterprise* to recover her search planes and prepare for a follow-up strike.

At 0930 the *Hornet* bombers reported they were attacking a Japanese force consisting of one battleship, one cruiser, and two destroyers. Later they reported that they were getting hits and that a cruiser was badly damaged, but that the enemy ships were not sinking. As the *Enterprise* bombers were being spotted aft for their next launch, Spruance asked Browning how many torpedo planes were still available. They had begun with forty-one slow and obsolescent Devastator TBD's. Browning replied that only four remained, three of them operational. Spruance called for McClusky and the senior surviving torpedo pilot, Lieutenant (junior grade) Robert Laub.

When they arrived, Spruance spoke to them. "Now listen carefully," he said. "I want to put that cruiser down, and the surest way to do it is to put some torpedoes into her. [Spruance by then had recognized that the American bombs were not armor-piercing. They wrecked the superstructures but did not sink heavily armored ships.] I want the bombers to silence their guns before you make your run. But if there is one single gun firing out there, under no circumstances are you to attack. Turn around and bring your torpedoes home. I am not going to lose another torpedo plane if I can help it. Do you understand?"

They nodded, and the torpedo planes were launched. The cruiser's guns were still firing when the *Enterprise* group attacked. The torpedoes were not used.

The *Enterprise* pilots reported many hits on both cruisers. Still they refused to sink. Spruance ordered *Hornet* to launch a third attack. Her bombers left and were soon poised above the wretched cruisers. The group commander's voice, ordering the attack, blasted over the radio in the *Enterprise* flag shelter. The staff rushed to the radio speaker to get as close as possible. Spruance, by adroit footwork and sheer drive, forced his way into the middle of the pack. Suddenly the speaker blared forth with wild yells and bursts of profanity as the punch-drunk pilots swooped down upon their helpless victims. All radio discipline vanished, and the dialogue was rich with invective. The bedlam continued for a few minutes, then ended. "Come on," radioed the air group commander, "let's go home."

Spruance backed out of the clustered staff, straightened up, crossed his arms over his chest, and began tapping his toe. He turned to Browning and said, "Send for Dow."

The flag communications officer arrived, panting, cap askew, sweat wetting his khakis. His face was pallid, because he feared that the stern and severe Spruance would hold him responsible for the collapse of radio discipline. The staff hovered in the background, embarrassed to watch yet curious to see what Spruance would do. Dow froze at attention.

"Dow, do you have a transcript of that air circuit?"

"Yes, sir!"

"Dow, are you sure?"

"Yes, sir!"

"Dow, I mean a verbatim transcript."

"Yes, Admiral!"

"Dow, I mean I want every word. Can you produce that?"

"I had two of my best men copying," said Dow. "I am sure I can produce it."

"Very well, have a smooth transcript typed up," replied Spruance. "I want to send it to Admiral Nimitz so he will know what our boys think of the Japs."

Dow's rigid body relaxed and he smiled sheepishly. As Dow turned to leave, Spruance had an afterthought and called out, "While you are at it, make a copy for me. I want it for my personal files."

When Spruance mailed the transcript to Nimitz, he wrote, "One or two of these would not pass the censor, but I think you will enjoy them as much as we did at the time . . . the pilots apparently were having a thoroughly enjoyable time." Normally, Spruance did not approve of swearing and followed a puritanical morality. The only time his family heard him curse was when he once sputtered "son of a bitch" while changing a tire. In 1964, a publisher asked Spruance to comment upon a novel about the Pacific Navy in World War II, filled with explicit sex scenes and raw language. That kind of book deeply offended Spruance. He defended naval morality by asserting that the sexual activities of Navy men and women in Honolulu during the war in no way resembled those in the book. Then he talked about swearing.

"The use of foul language in a wardroom mess on board ship was something that was never tolerated in my days," he wrote the publisher. "I do have a vivid recollection of listening in on the radio the third day of the Battle of Midway . . . and our people were thoroughly enjoying the day. Their language, as it came over the air, was vivid and picturesque and appropriate to the occasion."

Spruance was irritated and puzzled. Despite three intensive bombing attacks the Japanese cruisers would not sink. And still he was unsure of their identity. Some of the returning aviators reported at least one battleship, while others insisted both were cruisers. Furthermore, he was misled to believe that two distinct groups of ships lay over the horizon. His planes actually had been attacking a single group of two cruisers and two destroyers. Confusion arose because the early-morning search planes had given faulty contact reports. All had seen the same group of four, but their reports differed considerably both as to composition and location. Even after three attacks, combined with additional searches by cruiser float planes, Spruance still believed the enemy ships comprised two separate groups. Such is the fog of war.

In order to clarify the conflicting reports, Spruance dispatched two reconnaissance planes to photograph the thrice-attacked ships, so he could see for himself what his planes had been fighting all day. When the two planes returned, the pilots hustled up to Spruance for interrogation. His patience waning, he eagerly asked what they had seen.

"Sir, I don't know," one young pilot drawled, "but it was a hell of a big one." The casual, nonresponsive answer provoked Spruance's anger, and it grew when the second pilot confessed he didn't know what he had seen either; he had forgotten to take his ship recognition cards.

Spruance excoriated the two careless pilots for failing to identify the targets. His fury finally abated when the photographer reported he had taken some excellent photos, which he promised to deliver shortly. They revealed a devastated *Mogami* class cruiser about to sink. There had been no battleship.

The sun was setting over the helpless Japanese ships just over the horizon. What next? thought Spruance. His destroyers were low on fuel, his aviators were exhausted after three days of continuous combat, and he was coming within range of land-based Japanese aircraft on Wake Island. He had decided long before that he would not expose his force to the Wake air threat.

Spruance decided to end the battle. He had pushed his luck to the limit. The force turned back toward the northeast to rendezvous with his oilers. It is well that it did. The Japanese even then were trying to lure Spruance within range of Wake Island aircraft, while simultaneously organizing an ambush with their still-powerful surface forces.

Task Force 16 seemed to realize the battle was over. The pilots, pleased with their success and thankful to be alive, opened private bottles of liquor and celebrated. The staff had neither shaved nor changed clothing for three days. Halsey considered a shaved face as bad luck during battle, and Spruance conformed to that custom by growing a stubble with the rest of the staff. Now everyone shaved, bathed, and wore fresh clothes for dinner.

After dinner and during coffee, the staff read copies of the radioed press news (their first opportunity to do so since the third of June) to discover what was happening in the outside world. One news item concerned a particularly grisly murder in the United States, prompting two officers near Spruance into a philosophical discussion of a murderer's mentality. Murder was such an unnatural act, one commented, that only a man with a deranged mind would do such a thing. Overhearing the remark, Spruance lowered his paper and said dryly, "What do you think I have been doing all afternoon?"

The following days were anticlimactic. Nimitz ordered Spruance north to the Aleutians to take on the Japanese diversionary forces there. Spruance dreaded the hazards of operating aircraft in that area's exceedingly foul weather, and he was much relieved when Nimitz canceled the order and called the force home.

Returning to Pearl Harbor, Spruance resumed exercising on *Enterprise*'s expansive flight deck. As he marched to and fro, he was often accompanied by an escort of aviators, who described their adventures with swooping hand and arm gestures portraying aircraft in flight. One day McClusky met Spruance on deck with a radio news dispatch. "Admiral," he said, "you had better count to ten before you read this." It was the Army Air Corps official version of the Battle of Midway. It claimed that B-17 bombers had sunk the Japanese carriers and belittled the Navy's role in the battle. Predictably, Spruance was incensed, and he hotly damned the press release and those who wrote it. He knew that the B-17's had not touched the Japanese ships despite numerous attacks. Nevertheless, the bombastic Army publicity created a widely held and long-lived myth that ships at sea were vulnerable to high-altitude, level flight bombers. That impression would persist throughout the war. Nimitz's version of the battle was released too late to counter the impact of Air Corps assertions.

Spruance apparently saw no useful purpose in resurrecting the failures of the staff, even though his personal relationship with Browning degenerated into reciprocal animosity. "Halsey's splendid staff made my job easy," he wrote Nimitz after the battle. He never disputed the acclaim they were awarded. Browning later received the major credit for the victory at Midway, both by many historians and by the Navy. On Halsey's recommendation he was rewarded with the Distinguished Service Medal. The citation read in part: "By his judicious planning and brilliant execution, [he] was largely responsible for the rout of the enemy Japanese fleet in the Battle of Midway."

As far as it is known, Spruance neither publicly nor privately criticized Browning's performance. It would only have aroused bitter controversies, which he believed were destructive to the good of the Navy. When he had been a midshipman, the infamous Sampson-Schley controversy had blighted the reputation of the service, and the American naval victory in the Spanish-American War was discredited by selfish naval officers. Spruance would not allow the triumph at Midway to be marred by personal squabbles between him and Browning. He was content to let everyone share the credit. He said nothing to suggest that he and Halsey's staff had been other than an efficient, harmonious team.

Spruance's disapproval of Mitscher's performance on *Hornet* was discreetly expressed in his written endorsements to Mitscher's battle report. He indirectly blamed Mitscher for *Yorktown*'s loss, because the *Hornet* dive bombers had failed to locate the Japanese carrier force on the morning of 4 June.[4] If they had found the enemy force, Spruance observed, they could have hit the fourth carrier in the morning, thereby

----

4. The performance of the *Hornet* air group was unfortunately worse on 4 June than Spruance ever realized. See Lundstrom, *The First Team,* chapter 15, for recently discovered details on the *Hornet* at Midway.

preventing any further attacks on *Yorktown*. Furthermore, Mitscher falsely reported that all his bombers had carried 500-pound bombs on the late afternoon attack of 5 June, yet Spruance knew that some had carried 1000-pound bombs in disobedience of his orders. He directed an understated slap at Mitscher's objectivity: "As a matter of historical record," Spruance wrote on his endorsement, "the HORNET report contains a number of inaccuracies. The ENTERPRISE report is considered accurate and should be relied upon for reference."

Spruance's judgment of Mitscher was unfortunate, because he would harbor a built-in prejudice for the wizened aviator when Mitscher later commanded Spruance's Fifth Fleet carriers, the famous Task Force 58.

Spruance's force returned almost unnoticed and without fanfare to Pearl Harbor on a late Saturday afternoon. Months and years of analysis would be required in order to assess the true extent of the victory. Spruance knew only that he had sunk three Japanese carriers, damaged and perhaps sunk a fourth, damaged other surface ships, and prevented the seizure of Midway.[5]

Spruance had accomplished his mission and was awarded the Distinguished Service Medal. Its abbreviated citation was less than descriptive of his role at Midway. "For exceptionally meritorious service in a position of great responsibility as Task Force Commander, United States Pacific Fleet," it read. "During the Midway engagement which resulted in the defeat of and heavy losses to the enemy fleet his seamanship, endurance, and tenacity in handling his task force were of the highest quality."

Spruance received credit for "seamanship, endurance, and tenacity," and Browning received credit for the "judicious planning and brilliant execution" that defeated the Japanese. Such are the ironies of war.

In 1948, after years of study and analyses, the Naval War College summarized what Spruance and his forces had accomplished. "The

5. The Japanese lost the carriers *Hiryu, Soryu, Akagi,* and *Kaga;* cruiser *Mikuma;* 258 aircraft, and 2500 men. One Japanese oiler, one heavy cruiser, and two destroyers were damaged. On the American side, *Yorktown* was finally sunk by an enemy submarine, which also sank the destroyer *Hammann.* The Americans lost 148 aircraft operating from the carriers and from Midway Island. Approximately 307 Americans were killed.

Battle of Midway was . . . an overwhelming American strategical and tactical victory," said the report. "By destroying four of Japan's finest aircraft carriers together with many of her best pilots it deprived the Japanese Navy of a large and vital portion of her powerful carrier striking force; it had a stimulating effect on the morale of the American fighting forces; it must have had a sobering effect on the morale of those members of the Japanese fighting forces who witnessed the destruction of the four carriers; it stopped the Japanese expansion to the east; it put an end to Japanese offensive action which had been all conquering for the first six months of war; it restored the balance of naval power in the Pacific which thereafter steadily shifted to favor the American side; and it removed the threat to Hawaii and to the west coast of the United States."

Samuel Eliot Morison best described Spruance at Midway: "Fletcher did well, but Spruance's performance was superb. Calm, collected, decisive, yet receptive to advice; keeping in his mind the picture of widely disparate forces, yet boldly seizing every opening. Raymond A. Spruance emerged from the battle one of the greatest admirals in American naval history."

Chapter 12

CHIEF OF STAFF

O N 18 June 1942 Spruance reported aboard CINCPAC headquarters in Pearl Harbor as chief of staff to Nimitz. It was an assignment with vastly increased responsibilities. In his previous billet as Commander Cruiser Division Five, Spruance had largely been a spectator to Halsey's adventures. Now he was responsible for coordinating the activities of a seventy-five-officer staff that was ever enlarging, and he also served as principal advisor to Nimitz. [1]

Nimitz wore two hats: Commander in Chief, Pacific Fleet (CINCPAC), whereby he commanded all naval and Marine Corps units in the Pacific; and Commander in Chief, Pacific Ocean Areas (CINCPOA), a combined command which gave Nimitz authority over all American and Allied naval and military forces in the Pacific theater, except those in MacArthur's Southwest Pacific Area.

The task with the highest priority for Nimitz in the summer of 1942 was the seizure of Guadalcanal in the Solomon Islands. Admiral King had insisted upon a "defensive-offensive" strategy in the Pacific in order to wrest the initiative from the Japanese, continually victorious in the

---

1. The whole question of Spruance's role as chief of staff to Nimitz and his influence on the upcoming Guadalcanal campaign remains infuriatingly mysterious, because very little of the conversations between the two admirals was recorded.

Southwest Pacific and only recently checked in the Central Pacific by the Battle of Midway. Prodded by King, the JCS in the summer of 1942 directed Nimitz to seize Guadalcanal and adjacent Tulagi.

The Japanese, having been defeated at Midway, redirected their attention to the South Pacific and coincidentally sought the same physical objectives as did King: Guadalcanal and Tulagi. The powerful Japanese navy and the understrength American Navy thereby collided in mortal combat on those two miserable islands in August 1942. For the next six months Nimitz and the staff would focus their attention and anxieties on the battles and crises of that protracted campaign.

Nimitz and Spruance had not known one another personally when Spruance joined the staff in June, but they knew each other's reputations. Nimitz had selected Spruance before the Battle of Midway, and that battle had substantiated what Nimitz already knew: that Spruance was a fighter, a clear thinker, and an experienced planner and strategist who was wasting his talents under Halsey. He was the perfect man to serve as Nimitz's chief of staff.

Nimitz lived in a large, comfortable four-bedroom home in the Makalapa compound, an officers' community of newly built bungalows located on the crater of an extinct volcano with a panoramic view of Pearl Harbor. Spruance moved into the Nimitz house, because Nimitz apparently wanted both a close personal and professional relationship. The third occupant was Captain Elphege A. M. Gendreau, the fleet medical officer, presumably included because he was good company and because Nimitz was concerned about his own health and the health of his senior officers who lived nearby.

The routine at CINCPAC headquarters did not outwardly reflect the desperate fights and galling defeats at Guadalcanal those last five months of 1942. Nimitz and Spruance would emerge each morning from their home and walk together to the nearby headquarters building, a large white concrete structure adjoining the Makalapa compound. Other senior officers, clean-shaven and wearing starched, pressed khakis, also would leave their bungalows and stroll past the manicured lawns and well-tended gardens toward the building. Another day in the war would be underway.

Nimitz and Spruance would go to their separate offices and read the accumulated message traffic, mostly bad news about Guadalcanal from Vice Admiral Robert L. Ghormley, the South Pacific area commander.

Spruance, as usual, worked at a stand-up desk, installed shortly after he arrived.

At 0900 the staff would assemble with Nimitz for his invariable morning meeting, in order to review the progress of the war and the latest intelligence. Future plans normally were not discussed at this time. The meetings were relaxed and informal, and everyone was heard. Most of the day was unstructured. Impromptu meetings would be convened when decisions had to be made and future plans considered. The atmosphere at headquarters reflected the personalities of Nimitz and Spruance: serene, confident, poised, and efficient.

At 1100 each morning Nimitz would receive the commanding officers of every ship that had recently arrived at Pearl Harbor. "He wanted to have a chance to size them up," recalled one staff officer, "and for them to know that they had an identity with the fleet commander. It was an important element in morale."

Knowing Nimitz's concern for morale, Spruance made a recommendation that benefited the fleet for the remainder of the war. During the Battle of Midway, the naval aviators had told him that their future was hopeless. If they survived Midway, they simply would continue flying in later operations until their number was up. There was scant possibility of being relieved before they eventually were killed.

When Spruance came ashore as chief of staff, he soon persuaded Nimitz to establish a rotation program that sent fresh aviators to relieve those that had been in the front line for long periods. For the remainder of the war, a substantial reserve of replacement squadrons always was available for the fleet carriers. After the war, Nimitz emphasized to a military audience that his men—especially his aviators and submariners—had been his most important asset. He wanted them to be fresh, alert, and well rested. Rotation and recreation programs had been essential.

The two admirals got on well professionally. The commander in chief entrusted many details and decisions to Spruance. These included screening the hordes of visitors, both official and unofficial, that wanted to intrude upon Nimitz's valuable time. They first had to pass Spruance. Everyone stood when stating their business to the chief of staff. He never offered chairs. It was a powerful incentive to be brief.

Spruance's philosophy for winning battles emerged during this period. A staff planning officer proposed that a modest cruiser-destroyer force be assigned to carry out a minor operation. Ships were scarce, and

Nimitz and Spruance, 1945

the planner felt his proposed number of ships could do the job without undue risk. Spruance said he wanted the force doubled. The planner protested that it was unnecessary, that Spruance would be cracking a walnut with a sledgehammer.

"That's the way to win wars," Spruance replied. He wanted all the fighting strength he could get to increase his chances of winning a battle. His most vocal and persistent critic—naval aviator Vice Admiral John H. Towers—once said that Spruance wanted a "sledgehammer to drive a tack" for the Tarawa assault. The sledgehammer phrase apparently was popular around CINCPAC headquarters.

Spruance was later characterized by his critics as being overly cautious. They felt he missed opportunities to inflict greater damage upon the enemy. Spruance conceded that perhaps he was cautious in the sense that he carefully weighed each alternative to determine the relative degree of danger to his forces. Recognizing that in making war danger was unavoidable, he sought to minimize rather than to avoid danger. Every decision was deliberate. He never could afford even one bad decision—it could lose thousands of lives, or a battle. He would admit to that kind of caution.

Toward the end of the war, a fellow admiral remarked to Spruance that every successful commander must be a gambler. Spruance replied that if this was so, he was one of the professional variety—he wanted all the odds stacked in his favor.

Nimitz and Spruance ended their workday in mid- or late afternoon so they could exercise or relax. The older man enjoyed horseshoes and persuaded Spruance to try, which he did with little success. Frequently the extinct volcano crater next to the compound echoed with the sound of pistol shots, and everyone knew that Nimitz was enjoying himself on the pistol target range.

Oahu Island had miles of interesting mountain trails for Spruance to hike upon and explore, and he was often accompanied by Nimitz. Other times they went to the beach for strenuous swimming and more walking. Nimitz was a superb swimmer, and frequently he took guests and new staff officers to test their endurance. Invariably, the admiral still would be swimming long after his invited companions had quit. Shortly after Spruance arrived the two men entered the water and began to swim, paralleling the beach. The staff was shocked to see Nimitz was the first to run out of steam. Leaving the water, he walked back to his towel, while Spruance continued swimming.

Spruance frequently swam with other companions, such as reluctant staff officers. He soon noted that the younger men always swam between him and the beach. As he suspected, they were running along the bottom in order to keep up. "It was a sad day," recalled a former staff officer, "when he decreed that in the future all junior officers would swim outboard of the Admiral. I do not recall any drownings, but a number had close calls."

Occasionally Edward Spruance visited his father when *Tambor* was in port. His most lasting impression of his dinners in the admirals' mess was the admirals' absolute confidence that the United States was going to win the war.

Nimitz, Spruance, and Gendreau ate well in their private mess: filet mignon, pineapple, avocados, papaya, mango ice cream, fresh local lichee nuts, and Chinese gooseberries flown in from New Zealand. Fresh vegetables and salad greens grew in the stewards' organic garden, in soil fertilized by their domestic rabbits. Cocktails preceded dinner, Spruance enjoying an elaborate drink he had discovered in Puerto Rico containing rum, juices, and sherry. In Gendreau's absence he mixed other drinks as well, and he became proud of old fashioneds he prepared for the guests whom they frequently entertained.

Their many friends and visitors included both military officers and civilians. Nimitz and Spruance were invited time and again to the elegant homes of Hawaiian society, and the von Holts, Campbells, Dillinghams, and Castles became their good friends. The civilians' hospitality was reciprocated with dinners in the Nimitz-Spruance home followed either by first-run movies at the Navy theater or by USO shows at the Fleet Recreation Center. Several of the older society women grew especially fond of Spruance and became self-appointed guardians of his social welfare.

The admirals introduced one another to their personal avocations. Nimitz enjoyed classical music, and he played his extensive record collection during dinner and into the evening. Spruance acquired a taste for the music and could eventually recognize what he was hearing, although he had no musical ear.

Spruance, in turn, introduced Nimitz to the delights of fine coffee and converted his household companions into connoisseurs. He procured the coffee raw, such as Kona from Hawaii and Espíritu Santo from the South Pacific. Following his practice of many years, he roasted the beans, then brewed them in his four-cup Silex, timing with his old, familiar gold watch. He drank the usual one daily cup at breakfast, leaving the remaining three cups for those smart enough to join him for breakfast.

Spruance also introduced schnauzers into their home. The dogs made life complete, he wrote Margaret, and he proudly announced that a litter of puppies had been successfully delivered.

Spruance and Nimitz needed all the rest and diversion they could get that summer and fall of 1942. The war was going badly. The Americans lost four cruisers at Savo Island to attacking Japanese cruisers, who were attempting to sink the American troop transports anchored off the Guadalcanal beaches. The Savo Island debacle presaged the savage, see-saw battles of the prolonged and indecisive campaign. The Japanese persistently attacked with sea, air and troop reinforcements, which Ghormley viewed with increasing alarm.

The murderous melees seemed to favor the Japanese. "Tension increased and at times reached a pretty high level," recalled a former staff officer. "Few words were spoken. In every instance it appeared we were taking a terrible beating. Early reports were mostly from our damaged ships, and damage to the enemy frequently was unknown for days or weeks. I suppose later the staff got used to it."

Nimitz and Spruance were far removed from the scene of action and relied upon the local commanders to make all the tactical decisions. Spruance occasionally recommended that they radio long-range advice when their distant commanders seemed to be overlooking an opportunity or were about to make a bad move. Nimitz would not allow it. "Leave them alone," he said. "Looking over their shoulders will only inhibit them. As long as the local commanders have the responsibility, they must retain the initiative to do what they think best."

Yet Nimitz was fast losing confidence in Ghormley. In October 1942 he sent Spruance to the South Pacific to get a firsthand report on the deteriorating war at Guadalcanal and to find out the problems and needs of the American forces. Halsey, recovered from his dermatitis and ready for action, accompanied Spruance in order to take command of the South Pacific carrier forces. When their plane arrived in Nouméa, Halsey received message orders from Nimitz to relieve the faltering Ghormley as area commander.

"Jesus Christ and General Jackson!" Halsey exclaimed. "This is the hottest potato they ever handed me."

The sudden orders were a surprise to Spruance as well. Apparently Nimitz did not confide everything to his chief of staff.

Nimitz's sacking of Ghormley was not inconsistent with his philosophy of noninterference. He allowed his subordinates freedom of action (as did King), but if they could not perform, Nimitz fired them. Ghormley's messages had become unduly pessimistic, almost defeatist, and Nimitz believed that Ghormley no longer was capable of commanding in time of crisis. And if Nimitz ever was slow in replacing a nonperformer (as he sometimes was), King would do it for him. It was a "perform or perish" policy.

Taking leave of Halsey, Spruance visited his old friend Rear Admiral Kelly Turner and remained overnight aboard his flagship. Turner commanded the amphibious forces at Guadalcanal, and he doubted that he could stop the Japanese from throwing the Americans off the island. His forces had neither air nor naval superiority; the Japanese were constantly landing reinforcements, and their ships and planes were incessantly attacking the American troops and installations. Spruance's report to Nimitz would be grim.

Fortunately, Turner was wrong. Weeks of hard fighting remained, but Halsey's optimism and combative spirit invigorated his forces. The Japanese lost their hold on Guadalcanal. By late November 1942, Spruance had time to think of other things, both past and future.

Early in the war, Spruance had realized the imperative need for accurate, timely intelligence. He had been handicapped in the early Wotje-Wake raids by the lack of it, and immensely helped at Midway by its abundance. In discussions with Commander Edwin T. Layton, the Fleet Intelligence Officer, Spruance discovered that only four officers and one yeoman were assigned the task of collecting, evaluating, and disseminating intelligence information. Layton had urged Nimitz to expand this effort, but Nimitz was reluctant to enlarge his staff. Although Spruance favored small staffs as well, he supported Layton's recommendations.

Nimitz relented and established the famed JICPOA—Joint Intelligence Center, Pacific Ocean Areas—which eventually comprised a large body of experts that provided indispensable intelligence to Nimitz throughout the war.

After a morning meeting in the fall of 1942, during which Layton had given his usual intelligence summary, Spruance asked Layton to remain behind for a private talk. His request was not unusual, for the two men on several occasions had discussed intelligence trends and developments. But that morning Spruance wanted to talk about the Battle of Midway.

Officers on Nimitz's staff had criticized Spruance's action in that battle, especially his reluctance to close the crippled yet dangerous Japanese fleet on the nights of 4 and 6 June. They contended that he had been overly cautious and had missed opportunities to sink or damage additional ships. The Japanese fleet without carriers had been a paper tiger, they argued, and Spruance had allowed the enemy battleships and cruisers to escape. Spruance could shrug off the criticism from the officers on Nimitz's staff, but some weeks later Vice Admiral Pye, the new president of the Naval War College, repeated their arguments in a gratuitous War College analysis of the battle. King's endorsement of the college report had tended to agree that Spruance had been too cautious.

Pye's analysis was one of many criticisms that embittered Spruance against self-proclaimed experts, absent from the scene of action, who criticized battlefield commanders' decisions. "Important studies must not be injured in value by indulging in controversial criticisms," Spruance wrote after the war. "I have always hesitated to sit in judgment of the responsible man on the spot, unless it was obvious to me at the time he was making a grave error in judgment. Even in that case I wanted to hear his side of the matter before I made any final judgment."

Spruance's concern about Pye's analysis became evident as he spoke to Layton. (Regardless of his motives, Pye might have been right—at least King had thought so.) Spruance asked if Layton had any intelligence about the movements of the Japanese forces during the battle, from sources such as POW's and captured documents. Becoming aware of the admiral's uncharacteristic tenseness, Layton replied that the Japanese movements generally were unknown. Spruance finally explained the source of his anxiety, and Layton promised to be alert for fresh information.

Four days later, Layton's vigilant staff found a captured Japanese track chart and radio message log that reconstructed the Japanese movements. The documents established that if Spruance had continued westerly on the night of 4–5 June, he would have collided with the overpowering Japanese surface force. Layton went to Spruance's office, found him alone at his stand-up desk, and told him that his Midway decisions now were vindicated by the facts. Then they carefully reviewed every item in the captured documents, Spruance now and then pausing to take notes. When they finished, the chief of staff was visibly relieved.

"Now I have a basis to rebut Pye's criticism," he said. "Take this information up to Admiral Nimitz. The weight of a score of years has been lifted from my shoulders."

As Christmas approached, there was a lull in the war. Guadalcanal was secured, and no action was contemplated in the immediate future. Spruance took leave to visit his family, whom he had not seen for almost a year. He arrived unannounced in Monrovia, a small town in southern California, where Margaret had rented a home in order to be near the sanitarium where young Margaret was recovering from tuberculosis.

Spruance took long hikes in the hills around Monrovia; otherwise he wanted to be alone with his family. He was eager to talk about the Battle of Midway and reconstructed the action on the kitchen table with his wife and daughter as spectators. It was the only time when he was home on leave that he wanted to talk about the war.

Over the years he always had been depressed at Christmas. Christmas 1942 was particularly saddening because he had but a few days' leave, and he was disturbed by his daughter's sickness. He returned to Honolulu on a long, melancholy flight, alone among strangers.

The year 1943 lay before Nimitz and Spruance. With Guadalcanal secured, they could think about the rest of the war: specifically, what to do next against Japan. During the January 1943 Casablanca Conference, King and General Marshall, the Army Chief of Staff, had insisted that the Allies maintain pressure on Japan while pursuing the "Germany First" strategy. Having received reluctant agreement from the British to take limited offensive action against Japan, King wired Nimitz on 9 February 1943 for comments on the feasibility of seizing the Gilbert Islands in the near future. Nimitz replied that he had neither sufficient ships nor troops to assault the Gilberts in early 1943.

Nimitz must have hated to say no, because he and the naval high command wanted to start an offensive against Japan as soon as possible. King and Nimitz wanted to drive through the Central Pacific: the Marshall, Caroline, and Mariana island groups. This strategy had been naval dogma for years. But before anything could begin, Nimitz needed the approval of the Combined Chiefs of Staff (CCS). Its members were both the JCS (Admirals Leahy and King, Generals Marshall and Arnold) and the British Chiefs of Staff. King, as the American naval spokesman, had to convince the other members of the soundness of the Navy's Pacific strategy.

General MacArthur had other ideas. He was commander in chief of the Allied forces in the Southwest Pacific Area—outside Nimitz's Pacific Ocean Areas jurisdiction. MacArthur scorned the Central Pacific approach and advocated an offensive through New Guinea and the Philippines. He, of course, would be in command. Nimitz and the Pacific Fleet merely would provide naval support to MacArthur's campaign.

Nimitz had no intention of being subordinate to MacArthur. Ever. The Nimitz staff, including Spruance, deeply distrusted the general. Spruance felt that MacArthur was motivated by presidential ambitions, that he sought personal glory, and that he would not cooperate with the Navy in defeating Japan.

In March 1943, Nimitz's forces under Halsey were about to intrude into MacArthur's theater of operations, precipitating a jurisdictional dispute. The problem was bucked to the JCS, who scheduled a conference in Washington to determine future plans for joint action by MacArthur and Halsey in the South Pacific. Nimitz sent Spruance as his surrogate, with instructions to proselytize for the best interests of the Navy. In particular, Nimitz charged Spruance with obtaining JCS approval to recapture Attu and Kiska in the Aleutian Islands off Alaska, which the Japanese had seized as a diversion during the Battle of Midway. The Japanese occupation of those fog-shrouded, remote American islands was a continual irritant, and the frustrating campaign for their recapture had dragged for months, diverting naval forces needed elsewhere. Nimitz wanted to eradicate the Japanese once and for all with a decisive amphibious assault.

Spruance duly went to Washington for two weeks in mid-March 1943 and "educated" King's staff as to Nimitz's way of thinking. Undoubtedly Spruance also intended to counter moves by MacArthur's representatives, who would be intensively lobbying for a dominant role for MacArthur in Pacific war strategy.

The final conference convened on Sunday morning, 21 March. Leahy, King, Marshall, and Arnold presided. Major General Sutherland represented MacArthur, and Miles Browning represented Halsey. Many of the JCS staff sat in as well. King and Spruance were prepared to work in harmony, both to oppose MacArthur's arguments and to influence the other chiefs on the wisdom of a Central Pacific strategy.

Spruance was silent during most of the meeting, listening to the others discuss how MacArthur and Halsey might work in concert against the Japanese in the South Pacific. The dialogue revealed that neither had adequate resources to execute the offensive operations already approved for their theaters. King seized the initiative. He was opposed, he said, to tying up the Pacific Fleet in the south while land operations there were bogged down for want of resources. He wanted to examine where else the fleet might be profitably used, thus implying the Central Pacific. The other conferees, however, would not be diverted from the main issue and remained focused on land operations in the south. The subject was dropped—until Spruance's turn came to speak. He had plenty of suggestions about what to do with the Pacific Fleet, in response to King's leading questions.

Nimitz was much concerned about the Japanese fleet, said Spruance. It had been "pinned down" during the Guadalcanal campaign, but now that the Americans had permanent control of that island, the Japanese fleet had gone and could roam at will. The Americans did not contemplate any offensive actions in the near future that would pose a threat severe enough to influence the enemy to commit his fleet into action. Furthermore, the Japanese had changed their radio encryption procedures since Midway, so the Americans no longer knew their intentions: the Japanese fleet was a clear and present threat to all American bases in the Pacific, but particularly to Pearl Harbor.

In order to protect Pearl Harbor, Spruance continued, Nimitz wanted at least part of the fleet returned from the South Pacific, and he wanted to recapture the Japanese-occupied Aleutians as soon as possible in order to release the large numbers of American ships committed to that area. Furthermore, General Emmons, commanding the Central Pacific Army Air Forces, wanted medium bombers as protection against the Japanese carrier threat at Pearl Harbor.

But Nimitz did not propose to wait passively for the Japanese to attack Hawaii, said Spruance. Rather, he wanted to seize the Marshalls and the Gilberts to remove the threat to Hawaii. He would need plenty of carriers to smother Japanese air power, which was well established on mutually supporting airfields on adjacent islands in the Marshalls and Gilberts. Once those islands were seized, the Pacific Fleet needed enough forces to remain on the offensive and to consolidate its gains.

Spruance's argument for a Central Pacific offensive—to remove a threat of Japanese carrier raids on Pearl Harbor—was curious. He failed to mention any number of sound, valid, strategic reasons for using the Central Pacific approach, reasons which emphasized offensive actions to defeat Japan rather than defensive actions to protect Pearl Harbor. Perhaps King, Nimitz, and Spruance felt that the "Pearl Harbor" argument had the best chance of being accepted at that time.

King endorsed Spruance's thesis. With operations bogged down in the south, King said, the Japanese surely would strike elsewhere. What then, he asked rhetorically, is the best thing for the fleet to do in order to maintain the initiative and "beat the Japs to it"? A stalemated campaign in Southwest Pacific jungles certainly was not the answer. "We must consider the Pacific as a whole."

He and Spruance had subtly shifted attention from MacArthur's activities in the Southwest Pacific to the Navy's role in the Central

Pacific. Their arguments that day were comparatively restrained, a muted forerunner to the later divisive conflicts between the Army and Navy over strategy in the Pacific.

Without recorded comment, the other chiefs predictably redirected their attention to the problems in the South Pacific, which was the purpose of the meeting. They had not met to debate the merits of a Central Pacific strategy, but King and Spruance had made their point. The JCS now sat in closed session, then announced that MacArthur and Halsey could proceed with limited operations in the south. Nimitz could proceed against the Aleutians. The question of overall strategy in the Pacific remained unanswered.

While in Washington, Spruance frequently visited his old friend and shipmate, Captain Carl Moore, who was serving on the staff of the JCS. Moore had failed selection for admiral, primarily because he had run his cruiser aground in December 1941. Many passed-over captains are consigned to naval limbo, but Moore's considerable talents as a strategist and planner were needed in Washington. So without hope of flag rank, Moore conscientiously toiled long and grueling hours, hoping he could return to sea. The reunion was a happy respite for both men.

Spruance also felt obliged to pay his respects to Mrs. Nimitz and her daughters, who were living in Washington. Spruance—typically—did not forewarn them of his visit. When he called, the Nimitz apartment was a mess and the daughters were not dressed for visitors. Spruance, acutely embarrassed in the sea of feminine disorder, retreated at the first possible moment.

Returning to the West Coast, Spruance stopped in San Diego to confer with Major General Holland M. Smith, whom he last had seen in Puerto Rico during the 1940 landing exercises at Culebra. They had much to discuss, because the Marine general was now training the amphibious ground forces that would seize Attu and Kiska. Smith impressed Spruance with his attitude and his knowledge of amphibious warfare, so much so that Spruance later would choose him to lead Spruance's amphibious troops across the Pacific.

Spruance's final stop was in Monrovia to see his wife and daughter. He remained for several days and was encouraged by young Margaret's progress toward recovery. When he returned to Honolulu, Nimitz—thoughtful as always—met him at the plane.

The American offensive to recapture the Aleutians began to roll in April and May, but the JCS remained mute on future strategy in the Pacific. Finally in mid-June 1943 they announced their decision: American forces would close Japan *both* through the Central Pacific under Nimitz *and* through the Southwest Pacific under MacArthur. The CCS had reasoned that a two-pronged offensive would generate continual pressure against the Japanese and would keep them off balance. The Central Pacific offensive would begin in the Marshall Islands, and the JCS directed Nimitz to plan for their seizure on 15 November 1943.

Elated with the JCS approval, Nimitz and his staff began to consider ways and means to seize the Marshall Islands. They had no precedent, no experience for the task ahead. Although the Guadalcanal and Aleutian campaigns provided some guidance, they had been haphazard, shoestring affairs which no one wanted to repeat. And neither campaign had involved seizing small, heavily defended coral atolls, such as those in the Marshalls. Therefore the planning would have to be original and creative, incorporating guesswork and unproven theory. The CINCPOA headquarters churned as naval officers, having ignored amphibious doctrine for years, finally were forced to begin realistic amphibious planning under Spruance's general supervision.

They began with an estimate of the situation. The opposing fleets were about equal strength. The Japanese fleet, having abandoned Guadalcanal, was free to operate on interior lines of communication from their major bases at Rabaul in the Bismarcks and Truk in the Carolines. Japanese air power was strong and aggressive and could operate from mutually supporting air bases within the Marshalls, reinforced via the Caroline Islands and the island air pipeline that originated in Japan. The amphibious objective, once selected, would have to be isolated from all Japanese air, naval, or submarine forces that could threaten the American assault troops. The Americans had been unable to establish control of the sea and air at Guadalcanal and had nearly lost the battle. They could not allow a recurrence in the Marshalls.

By far the greatest problem was the lack of intelligence about the Japanese defensive installations in the Marshalls, because American land bases were too remote for land-based air reconnaissance.

The CINCPOA War Plans Division proposed a five-pronged attack against Kwajalein, Maloelap, Wotje, Mili, and Jaluit. Spruance objected to their scheme. The green American forces, he said, would lack the training and the experience necessary to seize the five islands. Spruance assumed they were heavily defended. Handicapped by the lack of intelligence information, he could not safely assume otherwise. Furthermore, the American fleet supporting the landings would be split five ways and would be vulnerable to a concentrated Japanese naval counterattack. Finally, there was no suitable anchorage reasonably near the Marshalls to serve as the advance fleet base needed for logistical support of the attacking forces.

Captain Forrest P. Sherman (chief of staff to Vice Admiral Towers, then Commander Naval Air Force Pacific Fleet) was a respected planner with a different proposal. He recommended seizing Wake Island first in order to use it as a base for the air reconnaissance of the Marshalls that Spruance had insisted upon. But Spruance opposed this plan also. The Japanese islands that the Americans would buy with their own blood had to be useful as future bases. Thus a potential amphibious objective ideally provided both a fleet anchorage and an airfield, and it also was expected to improve American lines of communication. Wake would provide an airfield only. It had no deep-water lagoon suitable as an anchorage, and it was remote from American lines of communication that ran south of the Marshalls.

Accurate air reconnaissance (which provided the amphibious planners with intelligence on beach gradients, water depths, reef locations, and defensive installations) became the controlling factor. Spruance knew it would be suicidal to try to seize a heavily defended island without this essential information. As he vetoed plan after plan, the admiral began to realize that a direct assault on the Marshalls was unfeasible. Yet he and Nimitz could not admit to the JCS that they were stymied, not after the Navy had put its reputation on the line by advocating a Central Pacific offensive.

Spruance found a solution, a plan that incorporated a "preliminary" operation: seize the Gilbert Islands first, then proceed to the Marshalls. It contained persuasive reasoning.

• American aircraft would reconnoiter the Gilberts from airfields in the Ellice and Phoenix islands, less than a thousand miles to the east-southeast of the Gilberts.

• Land-based aircraft on these same islands could provide air support to the amphibious assault troops, and air reinforcements could be provided from air bases in the Hawaiian Islands and the South Pacific.

• The Gilberts would provide experience for later assaults in the

Marshalls. Spruance dreaded using inexperienced troops in a major operation against the heavily defended Marshall Islands. Instead he wanted an objective that was tough enough to try the Americans but not so tough that they would suffer heavy losses—or perhaps even lose the battle. Thus the Gilberts would be a "training ground" in preparation for the greater battles to come.

• Most important, the physical objective had to be strategically valuable. The Gilberts fit the bill by providing bases for an assault against the Marshalls, the ultimate objective. Gilbert airfields would provide both air reconnaissance and air support; Gilbert lagoons would provide the fleet anchorages; Hawaii–South Pacific lines of communication, passing nearby, would be strengthened and improved.

Spruance initially received little backing for his proposal, and he was a voice crying in the wilderness of the CINCPOA headquarters. In time, however, Nimitz agreed with him, and the plan was forwarded to the JCS in early July for approval. The JCS approved and on 20 July directed Nimitz to seize Tarawa Atoll and Nauru Island in the Gilberts on 15 November 1943. The operation was given the code name GALVANIC.

In the spring of 1943, long before the JCS had defined the final GALVANIC objectives, Nimitz was reasonably certain of two things. The JCS would authorize some kind of Central Pacific strategy, and many new ships soon would augment his fleet. He began to consider who would command the forces that would lead the projected offensive.

One May morning he and Spruance were walking from their home to the headquarters building. Out of the clear, Nimitz said, "There are going to be some changes in high command of the fleet. I would like to let you go, but unfortunately for you, I need you more here."

"Well," replied Spruance, "the war is the important thing. I personally would like another crack at the Japs, but if you need me here, this is where I should be." And he thought no more about it.

During the next morning's walk Nimitz again spoke: "I have been thinking this over during the night. Spruance, you are lucky. I decided I am going to let you go after all."

But the fleet commander did not specify Spruance's new billet. The composition of the Central Pacific forces and their initial objectives—Gilberts or Marshalls—were undetermined. Furthermore, King had to approve all flag officer assignments, and he would be particularly selective about who would lead his cherished Central Pacific offensive. In view of the uncertainties, all Nimitz could promise was that he would recommend to King that Spruance be promoted to vice admiral and be given a major command at sea.

Nimitz intended to confer with King in San Francisco in late May and would try to get the CNO's approval at that time. Nimitz left for the meeting. The first indication that he was having success with King was a dispatch from Washington on 30 May 1943 that promoted Spruance to vice admiral. That afternoon the CINCPAC signal staff gave Spruance a new three-star flag, and when he loaded his car with companions for a beach party, he noted that his driver had installed a three-star ID plate on the bumper. The staff enlisted men, in their own mysterious, clairvoyant way, had anticipated that King would approve Spruance's promotion.

Spruance was confident of a major sea command even before the King-Nimitz conference, and he began thinking about forming his personal staff. He wanted a chief of staff who was a hard worker, a good administrator, and an expert planner. Spruance functioned best when he talked to others and thought aloud, but the complicated, tedious translation of his decisions and ideas into intricate written plans was a chore he disliked and could not do well. Carl Moore was a sound, logical thinker who wrote clearly, just the man to do the work that Spruance wanted to avoid. After seeing Moore in March, he knew that his friend was unhappy in Washington and wanted a change, so Spruance wrote Moore and asked him to be his chief of staff. Moore responded immediately that he accepted the offer. Spruance also asked him to choose the staff officers, except for the flag lieutenant, whom Spruance would personally select.

When Nimitz returned from San Francisco in early June, he told Spruance that King had approved his command of the forces that would attack the Marshalls. Spruance now had a vital interest in the operation, and he was "highly motivated" to see that his Gilbert Islands concept was approved.

Spruance would be commanding the first major amphibious assault of the Pacific war, but he was without experience in amphibious warfare. He needed qualified subordinate commanders: an admiral to command the ships that would carry, land, and support the troops; and a Marine general to command the troops after they were ashore.

Spruance wanted Kelly Turner to be that admiral and Holland Smith to be that general.

His choice of Turner was logical. Turner was brilliant, he was a

Charles J. Moore, 1943

proven fighter, he was experienced in amphibious warfare, and Spruance knew and trusted him after decades of friendship and close association.

Smith was a fighter who was the Marines' foremost authority on amphibious warfare, owing to his years of experience in developing amphibious tactics and equipment.

Turner was working for Halsey in the South Pacific, and Smith was training amphibious forces in the United States. Possibly they would not be available because they were too valuable and were needed elsewhere. But Spruance decided he should at least try to get them by asking Nimitz. It worked, and they were assigned to Spruance.

Spruance also needed a commander for the carrier forces. In this case he had no strong preference because he did not know the qualifications nor the availability of aviator flag officers. Nimitz made the choice, Rear Admiral C. A. (Baldy) Pownall, a senior and experienced naval aviator.

Spruance expected to be detached as chief of staff in early August. He had served for thirteen months and had become a Nimitz disciple. "It has been an inspiration working for Nimitz," he wrote Margaret, "and I hope watching him has taught me more patience and tolerance. He is one of the finest and most human characters I have ever met, yet has all the energy, courage, determination and optimism that are needed in a great military leader." He repeated his admiration in a later letter. "I have learned a lot from watching Nimitz for over a year," he wrote. "He is a marvelous combination of tolerance of the opinions of others, wise judgment after he has listened and determination to carry things through."

The two men had enjoyed a special relationship of mutual trust, professional respect, and intimate friendship. "The Admiral thinks it's all right to send Raymond out now," a staff officer is said to have remarked. "He's got him to the point where they think and talk just alike."

Chapter 13

PLANNING FOR THE GILBERTS

THE Gilbert Islands include sixteen widely scattered atolls that straddle the equator, two thousand miles southwest of Pearl Harbor. The Japanese had seized the islands from the British shortly after the war began. Lieutenant Colonel E. F. Carlson's Marine Raiders had raided Butaritari Island on Makin Atoll in August 1942, an ill-considered venture that motivated the Japanese to fortify the islands against further American attacks.

One of Spruance's physical objectives was Betio Island on Tarawa Atoll, chosen because it contained an airfield that the Americans wanted. The triangular atoll lies 80 miles north of the equator. Its eastern and southern legs are chains of long, narrow islands, 18 and 12 miles long respectively, covered with palm trees. The western barrier reef contains two deep-water entrances to the lagoon.

Betio is a 290-acre island, 2 miles long and 500 yards wide, nestled in the southwest corner of the atoll. It was heavily fortified by the Japanese with beach obstacles, artillery and machine-gun emplacements, and ingenious bombproof shelters constructed with concrete, steel, coconut logs, and coral. The well-planned fortifications would be stoutly defended by 4500 able Japanese troops.

The other physical objective was Nauru Island, 380 miles southwest of Tarawa. The Japanese had constructed an airfield on the island that

NORTHERN GILBERT ISLANDS

MAKIN

Butaritari I.

MARAKEI

ABAIANG

TARAWA

Lagoon

NAURU 380 MILES

Betio I.

MAIANA

SCALE | 0   10   20   30 |
NAUTICAL   MILES

was protected by formidable defenses deeply imbedded in the island's rugged cliffs and hills.

The islands in themselves would be hard to capture. Adding to the hazards, the Japanese were capable of attacking American amphibious forces in the Gilberts with aircraft flying from bases in the Marshall Islands, 300 miles to the north; with the Japanese fleet operating from the main naval base at Truk 1300 miles to the west-northwest; and with submarines.

Nimitz had lacked the naval and military power to seize the Gilberts in early 1943, but by fall he was ready. American industry was in high gear and had supplied the ships, planes, and guns that Nimitz needed. The JCS promised Spruance over 200 ships, 35,000 troops, 117,000 tons of cargo, and 6,000 vehicles. (The large number of vehicles is difficult to understand considering the restricted size of the physical objectives.)

The magnitude of Spruance's command was enormous: 6 attack carriers; 5 light carriers; 7 escort carriers; 12 battleships; 15 cruisers; 65 destroyers; 33 large amphibious transports; 29 tank landing ships (LST); 6 miscellaneous ships; 90 Army bombers; 66 Navy land-based bombers and scouts; and almost 200 Marine aircraft. Another 22 ships such as oilers, tugs, and tenders would provide logistical support. Ten submarines would participate, primarily as scouts. Spruance, although a naval officer, also would command all the ground forces: the 2nd Marine Division and the 27th Infantry Division. His subordinate commanders included sixteen rear admirals, three Marine generals, and two Army generals.

Thus the JCS had given Spruance his mission and the resources to accomplish that mission.[1] He was responsible both for organizing his assigned forces and for developing the plans for seizing Tarawa and Nauru. The CINCPOA staff had developed preliminary plans in the late spring and early summer of 1943, but Spruance's staff and his principal subordinate commanders would have to produce the final detailed plans and operation orders.

By the end of July 1943, three and a half months remained to plan and prepare for the seizure of the Gilbert objectives. Spruance's as-

1. The ships under Spruance's command were designated the Fifth Fleet. The forces under his command—Army, Navy, and Marine Corps—were designated the Central Pacific Force. In 1944 the latter title was dropped, and his command was called simply the "Fifth Fleet." For clarity, the term "Fifth Fleet" will be used throughout.

signed ships and troops were scattered over half the world, his staff had not arrived, and Kelly Turner and Holland Smith were still in the United States. Considering the perils and uncertainties that lay ahead, time already was short. For the moment, Spruance was very much alone.

Carl Moore arrived in Pearl Harbor by plane on 30 July and moved into the Nimitz-Spruance house. Dr. Gendreau had been killed while on an inspection trip, so Moore occupied his vacant room. Rear Admiral Charles H. (Soc) McMorris, Nimitz's new chief of staff, was the fourth occupant.

If Spruance was anxious to start the Gilberts planning, it was not apparent to Moore. Spruance simply was happy to have Moore with him and seemed primarily concerned with his friend's health and welfare. He knew that Moore tended to work himself into mental and physical exhaustion; with a long war ahead, he did not want Moore to burn himself out. So Spruance set about to improve Moore's stamina with exercise and relaxation before addressing the business of war—an ordeal to come soon enough. During the first few days in August the two friends took ten-mile hikes in the mountains, and Moore's unused walking muscles ached. Moore preferred to relax by pitching horseshoes with his star-studded neighbors and by enjoying the cuisine and amenities of the Nimitz household.

Meanwhile the remainder of the staff began to arrive. Spruance had told Moore—who selected the staff—to keep it small. "My ideas on staffs," Spruance later explained, "are that they should be composed of the smallest number of first class men who can do the jobs. I have little sympathy for the enormous staffs that we have today. They may be all right in theory, but a lot of energy is expended in overcoming internal friction, and it is very difficult to get an answer out of such a staff until you get to the top. The subdivision is so great that it takes a long time for the paper to pass through the hands of everyone who may have a possible interest in the problem."

Many of Spruance's new staff had served in Washington since the war's beginning and were without combat experience. Most were strangers to one another. They arrived in Pearl Harbor with only hazy conceptions, at best, of what GALVANIC was all about.

The operations officer was Captain Emmet P. (Savvy) Forrestel, a tall, lean destroyerman who had graduated nineteenth in his 1920

Academy class of 460 members. Although he never attended the Naval War College, he nevertheless was experienced in operational planning. Forrestel was a taciturn, competent professional with an intelligent, orderly mind. A future flag officer, he was responsible for organizing, deploying, and assigning tasks to Spruance's sprawling, complex forces. He also developed the broad concept of operations that described how those forces would work in harmony to accomplish the primary mission.

The logistics officer was Captain Burton B. Biggs, similar in intelligence, physique, and experience to Forrestel. Like Forrestel, Biggs had not attended the Naval War College. His staff position was new and unprecedented. Before the war, logistics was a dull subject that the Navy largely had ignored—no fleet staff had included a "logistics officer." But the war in the Pacific painfully demonstrated that logistics controlled nearly every naval operation. In order for fleets to roam the broad Pacific, thousands of miles from fixed bases, the Navy had to devise methods to provide logistical support: fuel, food, ammunition, repair parts, consumable supplies, and the means to repair damaged ships and to replace lost aircraft and pilots.

Spruance had absorbed these lessons while serving as CINCPAC chief of staff and realized the need for a staff logistics officer. The Americans would be fighting a dangerous enemy two thousand miles away from Pearl Harbor, with no intermediate bases in between. American supply lines—the interior lines of communication—would be stretched thinly across a hostile ocean. "In starting to plan our Central Pacific operations during World War II," he later said, "three questions immediately engaged my attention. First, was adequate logistic support available and could it be gotten to the combatant forces where and when they needed it? Second, was our line of communications secure? Third, how could we get and keep control of the air in the theater of operations? When these questions were satisfactorily answered, we had a firm foundation on which to build the highly complex amphibious operations. . . ."

Biggs had to provide answers to the first question. Although his only related experience had been command of a provision ship before the war, he was an enthusiastic logistics proponent. He had an agreeable personality that promoted cooperation among the logistical support commands, as well as a keen, creative mind well adapted to solving seemingly insoluble problems. Biggs eventually became a vice admiral and a renowned logistical authority.

The most overworked man on the staff was the communications officer, Commander Justus R. (Red) Armstrong. Communications planning was a nightmare for want of a communications doctrine for amphibious warfare. Hundreds of disparate units, scattered over thousands of square miles of ocean, would have to communicate with one another with reliability, security, and reasonable speed. The communication equipment available had a random mixture of frequencies, ranges, and operating characteristics that compounded the planning complications.

Armstrong and his assistant, Lieutenant Commander William B. McCormick, had to devise a coherent plan out of chaos. Although both were war experienced communicators, their enormous tasks would require superhuman efforts. The pressure made them short-tempered and irascible, and—with their laboring young communication watch officers—they were not a congenial element of the staff. Armstrong, high-strung and volatile, eventually committed suicide after the war.

The flag secretary was Lieutenant Charles F. Barber, responsible for controlling the blizzard of papers—correspondence, orders, and plans— that was generated or received by the staff. Chuck Barber was a Reserve, a lawyer by training and education, and a former editor of the *Harvard Law Review* who had been selected as a Rhodes Scholar. The war in Europe prevented American students from attending British universities, so Barber was commissioned from the NROTC and served on the secretariat of King's staff in Washington in the early war years. Moore, impressed with Barber's intellectual abilities and administrative competence, brought the young lawyer with him to Pearl Harbor.

Barber never became a naval planner or strategist, but he was vital to the smooth and efficient operation of the staff. His law training enabled him to absorb and retain great quantities of facts, and he became a walking encyclopedia for others who needed accurate information. A refreshing and open-minded young intellectual, he was a fascinated observer of professional officers at war, frequently serving as an unbiased sounding board for their ideas. After the war he studied at Oxford and today is chairman of the board of a large corporation.

Barber also was important to Spruance as a companion. He was one of few with enough stamina to keep pace with Spruance's exercising.

Moreover, he was a good conversationalist, pleasing Spruance, who loved to talk while walking. Nimitz worried when Spruance swam alone in the ocean and was much relieved to learn that Barber was a good swimmer. Unknown to Spruance, Nimitz assigned Barber to be his unofficial lifeguard. The staff naturally was happy with Barber's role, for it allowed them to work uninterrupted by summonses from the admiral.

Another important staff member was Commander Russell S. Smith, a destroyerman and ordnance specialist. After recent service on a Pacific Fleet cruiser, he joined the staff as "gunnery officer." That title was a misnomer, because he served as fleet navigator and assistant operations officer. He prepared all the charts for the planned operations and was responsible—with a crew of four Reserve ensigns—for plotting the locations of every ship in Spruance's command as well as the location of all known enemy forces.

These seven officers—Moore, Forrestel, Biggs, Armstrong, Mc-Cormick, Barber, and Smith—formed the nucleus of the staff. They were primarily responsible for supporting Spruance. The remainder of the staff either were specialists or were junior Reserve officers who served as communications watch officers and plotting room officers. The specialists included an aviator (who rarely was consulted), a meteorologist, a Japanese language expert, an intelligence officer, a Marine Corps liaison officer, and an Army liaison officer (who was astounded by the staff's small size). Spruance consulted with these experts when he needed specialized information; otherwise they never became heavily involved in the overall planning.

The only officer Spruance personally selected was his aide and flag lieutenant, an ex-enlisted man named E. H. (Squee) McKissick. He was a curious choice, because earlier flag lieutenants had been bright young Annapolis graduates who were treated as sons. McKissick was a stolid older man, unschooled in the social graces normally expected of a personal aide. Spruance had no interest in that aspect. He wanted an expert in visual communications, the traditional role of the "flag" lieutenant, so Spruance chose McKissick because he was a former signalman. Spruance apparently anticipated frequent periods of radio silence at sea and wanted assurance he could communicate with his ships by semaphore, flag hoist, and flashing light.

Moore had selected the kind of small, competent staff that the Fifth Fleet commander wanted. Its few members would work longer and harder than their opposite numbers on larger staffs. For example, Halsey's fleet staff was twice as large. Moore and company were keenly aware of this disparity and took grim pride in the fact that any one of them did as much as two or three of Halsey's officers. That knowledge was some compensation for their grueling workload.

Carl Moore was responsible for organizing the arriving staff but was not having much success. They were groping about, trying to find out about GALVANIC, trying to get aquainted with each other and with the other staffs involved in GALVANIC planning. "About half of them are here," Moore wrote his wife on 5 August. "We don't fit in any place, and it's hard to get down to work. No proper desks, pen, ink, and so forth. No questions that I ask are answered, and no questions that are asked me are answered. It's a little frustrating, but otherwise delightful. . . . I don't understand all that goes on here."

The situation had not improved by the seventh. "Yesterday," Moore wrote, "I was busy running around and finally got to the office at 1630 expecting to go to work. I found a message saying I am to play horseshoes with four, three, and two stars at 1700. No work, all play. . . . The food is grand. . . . "

Spruance wanted to see the South Pacific battlefields and talk with those commanders in that region who would work for him during GALVANIC. Thus, ten days after Moore's arrival, he and Spruance boarded an elephantine seaplane and headed south. They visited many islands, and Spruance—ever the tourist—explored them all, walking with his enormous energy while sore-footed Moore hobbled far behind. The beautiful, languorous Fiji Islands were untouched by war, and Spruance and Moore enjoyed the gracious hospitality of their civil governors. At Suva, Fiji, both were impressed with the vast stockpiles of poison gas containers. They got closer to the war when they landed at New Caledonia to visit Halsey, who was commanding American forces in the Solomons. Moore plumbed Halsey's chief of staff, Robert B. (Mick) Carney, for advice on preparing for a major amphibious operation. Carney was cooperative but unable to offer much of value, because Halsey was an area commander and Spruance would be a fleet commander, two dissimilar jobs.

Next they journeyed to New Zealand to visit the 2nd Marine Division, which would be fighting at Tarawa. The Marines, debilitated from their ordeal on Guadalcanal, were recuperating in remote Wellington, a city as cold as Guadalcanal had been hot. Major General Julian C. Smith—a calm, impressive man—was in command. Although he had only a vague idea of what to expect on Tarawa, he knew what he needed to get ready. Many of his men were new, and none were experienced in amphibious operations. Smith needed amphibious ships immediately for training and rehearsals. Spruance also would have to arrange for the Marine general to rendezvous with Rear Admiral Harry W. Hill, commanding the ships that would support the amphibious troops.

Thence to Guadalcanal, where they saw the aftermath of protracted jungle warfare, followed by a nostalgic visit for Moore to the Samoa Islands, where his father had been governor forty years before. They resumed their journey by calling again on Halsey and by stopping at Espíritu Santo in the New Hebrides for conversations with Admiral Hill. They returned to Pearl Harbor on the afternoon of 22 August after a thirteen-day odyssey covering 12,000 miles.

The landing was a near disaster, because the retractable port pontoon would not lower. The port wing was in danger of dipping, snagging the water, and wrecking the ponderous seaplane. The pilot improvised an ingenious scheme. Just as the plane touched down, the four-man crew scurried out through a topside hatch onto the starboard wing. Their counterweight stabilized the plane, and it landed safely.

Upon their return Moore had hoped to get moving on the GALVANIC plans, but Spruance and the other admirals would not turn him loose. The more frantic Moore became, the more often Spruance would insist that Moore join him for a walk or a swim or an evening of listening to classical music.

The pace quickened when Kelly Turner arrived in late August. "R. K. Turner will arrrive tomorrow," Moore wrote, "and I expect him to stir things up some." Later: "Turner is here, and he is not any more open minded than ever, but I am glad he is here, as he moves and I like movement."

Moore finally was unshackled in early September, when he was quietly and ungracefully evicted from the Nimitz house to make room for an arriving flag officer. But now the chief of staff could work, free from the distractions and temptations of his congenial messmates.

Holland Smith arrived shortly after Turner. In short order he began sputtering about too many dress uniforms and too many parties with Honolulu society. He had come to fight, not play. But eventually he grudgingly bowed to the subtle pressure of his peers and occasionally was seen wearing starched whites in lieu of combat greens. [1]

Turner and Smith both were blunt, tactless, strong-willed, and stubborn. They immediately clashed over the vexatious problem of who would command the amphibious troops, and when. The problem was unique to amphibious warfare. At times all the troops would be afloat, other times they all would be fighting ashore, and at still other times some would be afloat and some ashore. The troops never could be independent of the ships that supported them. Thus a cooperative relationship had to be established between the admiral and the general whose responsibilities were so closely intertwined. This vital issue had to be resolved, because during the first hours the landing operation would be precarious, critical decisions would have to be made, and everyone would have to know who was in command to make these decisions.

Spruance ignored the squabble, so Turner and Smith separately cornered Moore to vent their complaints. Turner raged that Smith was uncooperative; Smith, in turn, castigated Turner. Their vituperations ricocheted around Moore's office, and the Navy captain despaired of resolving their arguments. In desperation, he asked Spruance for help.

Spruance refused, for he was uncomfortable when confronted with angry people. "Oh Carl, don't worry about it," Spruance said. "They know what I want to do, and they're not going to make any trouble. They'll do exactly what I want them to do. I know them both so well, and they know me, and they'll be all right."

Moore replied in exasperation that Spruance was missing the point—everyone had to understand who was in command.

"Oh, fix it up to suit yourself," said Spruance, and he dismissed the matter, unwilling to face his rampaging commanders.

Moore finally hit upon a simple solution whereby the Marine general would command the troops once he had established his headquarters ashore. Turner and Smith accepted Moore's solution in principle, but their command relationship continued to fester and flare throughout the war.

1. The best study of H. M. Smith remains the unfortunately unpublished Ph. D. dissertation by Norman V. Cooper, "The Military Career of General Holland M. Smith, USMC" (University of Alabama, 1974).

Moore's concern for command relationships was well founded. Holland Smith resented naval authority. He was acutely sensitive to any imagined slights or discrimination against his beloved Corps, and he would often overreact when he sensed an affront. His command relationship with Kelly Turner eventually had to be resolved by King and Nimitz. The Army, in turn, resented Holland Smith, who had authority over the infantry divisions assigned to the operations. To complicate matters at sea, aviator admirals, commanding fast carrier task groups, frequently gave orders to the senior surface admirals who commanded the screen.

Thus an amphibious assault generated complex command problems. The Savo Island debacle at Guadalcanal in August 1943 was a costly example of the potential hazards.[2] No one had known who was in command when the Japanese had struck, and in the confusion the Allies had lost four cruisers. "Everyone has to understand who is in command," Moore insisted, and this resolve was reflected in every Commander, Fifth Fleet, operation order. Thanks to Moore's meticulous supervision, every subordinate commander knew to whom he reported, who reported to him, and what Spruance expected everyone to do.

But Turner and Smith, seemingly irreconcilable, continued arguing on other aspects of the amphibious planning. At times the Marine sounded unlike a general. "All I want to do is kill some Japs," he grumbled. "Just give me a rifle. I don't want to be a commanding general. Just give me a rifle, and I'll go out there and shoot some Japs. I'm not worrying about anything else around here."

Their incessant quarrels wore on Spruance, and he began to wonder if GALVANIC would get planned before there was an irreversible rupture between the two men he had selected to capture places for him. Yet he never did adjudicate their differences.

Barber was familiar with JCS planning procedures, and he was struck by the fact that GALVANIC was entirely different. In Washington the initial planning was accomplished by writing memoranda, proposals, studies, and estimates. In Pearl Harbor the initial planning was largely oral. Staff officers gathered for impromptu discussions in corridors or before maps and charts within the offices. Time was short; decisions and agreements had to be made quickly; planning had to be

---

2. The date for the Battle of Savo Island is 9 August 1942.

both concurrent and coordinated. Therefore the many commands and organizations involved in GALVANIC congregated under one roof at the headquarters building. Talking logically preceded writing.

"Planning for the conduct of active war operations ought to be done by the people who are going out to conduct those operations," Spruance later wrote. "Because the time factor is often so short, this means concurrent planning by the different echelons. The people in the forward areas must be given a considerable voice in the objectives and in the timing.

"At least in so far as the Navy was concerned," he continued, "there was often considerable discussion as to the objectives that were to be captured. The best solution was usually obtained only after a considerable exchange of views between all of us. This freedom to exchange ideas back and forth I consider most important to success in war planning."

Beginning in midsummer 1943 the CINCPOA staff had developed the basic plan for the seizure of Tarawa and Nauru. Turner and Smith were unable to examine the plan until early September. The Marine general promptly protested that Nauru's defenses were too strong. He sought Turner's support to eliminate Nauru and to substitute Makin. Turner agreed, and the two approached Spruance for his approval.

Spruance was sympathetic. He had always disliked Nauru for strategic reasons. It was 380 miles from Tarawa and close to Truk, the powerful Japanese air and naval base. Spruance could not cover both Nauru and Tarawa simultaneously should the Japanese fleet attack. Ideally he wanted to concentrate his own fleet in one place to support Turner and Smith, which he could do if Makin and Tarawa were the targets. Therefore Spruance asked Nimitz to substitute Makin for Nauru. Nimitz, however, was reluctant to forward Spruance's request to the JCS.

Smith persisted with his objections, adding a new argument that he had neither enough troops to seize both Tarawa and Nauru nor enough transports to bring in additional forces. Spruance, impressed with Smith's new and compelling argument, told him to express his objections in writing. Spruance would pass the letter to King, due to arrive shortly for the regular bimonthly King-Nimitz conference, and thereby force the issue.

On 25 September 1943 King arrived in Honolulu, accompanied by his plans officer, Rear Admiral C. M. (Savvy) Cooke. As the admirals and generals assembled in the CINCPAC conference room, Turner passed Smith's letter, with Turner's endorsement, to Spruance. Spruance read the letter and gave it to Nimitz, who read it and handed it to King.

King read the letter and turned to Spruance. "What do you propose to take in place of Nauru?"

"Makin," replied Spruance.

A brief discussion followed on the merits of Makin over Nauru. Cooke said the JCS initially had chosen Nauru "to broaden our front" (a questionable rationale). King soon agreed to the substitution and said he immediately would forward the recommendation by message to the JCS for approval.

The conference agenda for the second day included planning for the seizure of the Marshalls. The JCS had ordered an assault date of January 1944, less than two months after the seizure of the Gilberts. The question of *which* Marshall islands to capture had been heatedly and continually debated at all levels of command. Nimitz favored Kwajalein, Wotje and Maloelap. He was determined to present a united front before King in order to stifle any further debate and delay.

The second day's conference began auspiciously. King reported the JCS had radioed its approval of Makin for Nauru, and soon everyone generally had agreed on the scheme for capturing the Gilberts and the Marshalls.

Spruance, however, still had reservations. He wanted land-based air support for the assault on Kwajalein, and he and Moore felt the Americans should first seize nearby Ujae Atoll to provide an additional airfield. Spruance had not discussed this proposal with either Nimitz or King and had decided to spring it on them the second day of the conference. Spruance, however, did not attend the conference and sent Moore as his surrogate with orders to bring up Ujae when Kwajalein was under discussion.

Nimitz was purring with contentment at the smooth-running conference when Moore interjected that Spruance wanted to take Ujae. Nimitz became furious. He turned on Moore and berated him for implying in King's presence that Nimitz's subordinates were not in accord with their commander. "Now you come up and bring up a perfectly strange proposition here," he snapped. Moore responded that he was carrying out Spruance's orders.

King laughed wickedly at Nimitz's discomfiture, because he had been suspicious of the unusual air of unanimity. King continued to needle until Nimitz peevishly declared that the discussion was closed.

Moore was both amused and slightly embarrassed by the episode. But he was not sorry. Many flag officers in the Pacific with whom he would deal once had been his contemporaries or juniors, so he was unawed by their rank and position. He became fatalistic about his own chances of promotion to flag rank and was unconcerned if he perturbed some admirals from time to time.

Moore reported to Spruance about the rhubarb he had precipitated. Spruance was unruffled. "That's all right. I'll fix it up," he assured Moore, and he immediately went to Nimitz. Nothing more was ever said.

By October Spruance was allowing Moore the time he needed to direct the planning. The staff toiled until midnight, and Moore labored mightily to recoup lost time. His biggest chore was keeping Spruance in the office and out of the foothills. With few weeks left until the assault, he urgently needed Spruance for decisions and guidance as the planning problems compounded concerning materiel, ships, equipment, troops, and personalities. Smith and Turner were still wrangling over matters such as whether amphibious landing tractors (LVT's) would supplement the landing craft. D-Day loomed, and Spruance prepared for it by abandoning Moore and taking long walks.

Moore described his frustrations in letters home. "Raymond is so funny," Moore wrote. "When he feels the urge for exercise, nothing can stop him. He won't stop for anything but goes tearing off, usually with me grabbing at his coattails trying to get him to sign something or give me some decision that will let me proceed until he gets back. He invariably begs me to come along, knowing darned well that I won't, and that if I did the work would stop. When he gets back, it's hard to make him pay attention long enough to read and sign before he flops into bed. What a life I lead."

Spruance's awareness of his relationship with his staff was reflected in his letters to Margaret. "I have trouble getting away for exercise as frequently as I used to," Spruance wrote. "There is a lot to do in a short time, and Carl is so conscientious that I don't like to walk out and leave him plugging away at his desk. Carl is a horse for work, but he is always pessimistic about getting things in order and worked out in time. It certainly is fortunate that I have someone like Carl to put the ideas in orderly form on paper and to marshal the mass of details involved and get things in orderly shape.

"Carl likes to commit his thoughts to paper, which is something I never do if I can help it. Details and writing get me bogged down immediately. I hate to write, get my best results by talking to people and thinking out loud, but I get bogged down as soon as I have to assemble my ideas on paper. I can do so if necessary, but I have go off alone, be completely undisturbed, and labor excessively.

"My staff has been working up to midnight every night," Spruance continued, "and I have been working during the day but refuse to go on the night shift. Their labors are almost over now, I hope."

The staff viewed Spruance's extreme walking and sleeping habits with feelings ranging from annoyance to amused tolerance. Probably they did not realize that the admiral was reacting to mental stress. When the tensions and pressures of high command became overwhelming, he closed his mind and escaped into the foothills. He returned with his psychological equilibrium restored.

Now even his sleep had become affected, although his staff would never know of it. "My only night work is purely involuntary," he wrote Margaret. "It comes from waking up at 3:30 to 4 A.M. and, with no loving wife near to distract my thoughts, starting to cogitate on numerous unsolved and partially solved problems that are pressing for solution."

As D-Day neared, his sleep became even more disturbed. "I turned in at 9 P.M., woke up at 2 A.M., started to cogitate on unsolved future problems and finally decided to close the windows, turn on the light and write to you."

Spruance continued to seek relaxation in the evenings and, as before, frequently dined with the wealthy and glamorous of Honolulu society. He recognized that his social life was a marked contrast to the enforced inactivity of his wife and daughter, who were depressed with dull, drab Monrovia. Searching for a way to rationalize their unhappy isolation, he wrote, "I am sorry you and Margaret haven't a more interesting and exciting life. When you get bored or down-hearted, just think of all the wounded and crippled people who may be months and years getting back in some kind of shape."

Music also continued to provide relaxation. "I can recommend Dvorak's New World Symphony, Beethoven's Pastoral Symphony, and

Schubert's Unfinished Symphony—all beautiful music. Also Marian Anderson singing 'Sometimes I feel like a marvellous [sic] child' . . . these records have stood the test. Some of the modern things are just a lot of discordant sounds that we listen to once and then quickly return to their owners."

Visiting firemen provided diversions. "Mrs. Roosevelt came to our house for dinner," Spruance wrote, "and I had the pleasure of sitting next to her. She is very simple, charming, and has a delightful sense of humor. Whatever one may think of the possibility of achieving her ideals, she certainly has them and she has a deep faith in the underlying goodness in the ordinary human being. She is certainly a very fine person."

By early fall Spruance had decided upon a broad concept of operations for GALVANIC. His primary concern—in addition to American inexperience in amphibious assaults—was the Japanese fleet and landbased enemy aircraft. They would be particularly threatening when his transports were anchored off the landing beaches, discharging troops and cargoes. Spruance counted on three factors to counter that threat: surprise, speed, and his new carriers.

In any operation he commanded, Spruance always sought surprise. He would have it in the Gilberts. The Japanese occupied or controlled hundreds of Pacific atolls, many of them potential American objectives. If the GALVANIC plans were kept secret, the enemy would not know which islands the Americans wanted. The Japanese fleet probably would be hundreds or thousands of miles away on D-Day.

However, once the landings had begun, the alerted enemy would be capable of counterattacking with its fleet and land-based aircraft. Therefore Spruance wanted to seize Tarawa and Makin with "lightning speed," so that his fleet would not be pinned down in close support of the transports and the ground forces any longer than necessary. He did not doubt his ability to defeat the Japanese fleet; he simply wanted freedom to maneuver, which would be denied if he had to stay near the helpless transports immobilized off the beaches. The transports had to be unloaded and moved out of danger as soon as possible.

The Fifth Fleet commander had mixed feelings about exposing his ships to land-based air attacks from the nearby Marshalls. He was inculcated with the dogma that a fleet—including carriers—was vulnerable to attack by land-based dive-bombers and torpedo planes. He would aggressively attack enemy air bases with his carriers, but he recognized that a fleet was foolish to stay within their range indefinitely. The proper doctrine was to run in, attack, and then run out. But that doctrine couldn't be used during the Gilbert assault. Spruance was determined to keep the fleet—and the carriers—tied down within range of the Marshalls to provide close support to the troops. He would accept the risk of land-based air attacks.

The senior naval aviators vigorously disputed Spruance's decision. Led by Towers,[3] they wanted the carriers free to roam the oceans, using their mobile power to destroy Japanese air power at its source before it could counterattack the amphibious forces at Tarawa and Makin. In contrast, Turner wanted the carriers to provide a protective umbrella near the landing beaches. Japanese aircraft and ships had burned him far too often at Guadalcanal, while the American carriers were "roaming" at sea, too far away to help.

Spruance compromised. He directed the carriers to raid Japanese air bases shortly before the assault, but once the landings began they were to return and provide a barrier around the Gilberts in order to intercept all Japanese counterattacks. If the Japanese fleet appeared to do battle, Spruance anticipated the kind of classic fleet engagement that had been Naval War College doctrine: a line of battleships flanked by cruisers and destroyers, with carriers behind the battle line to provide air support.

The aviators were appalled. Rather than aggressively seeking out the enemy, the carriers would have to wait for the enemy to come to them, at a time and place chosen by the Japanese. They protested and complained, but Spruance would not change his decision. These kinds of argument set the pattern for continuing hostility between Spruance and Towers, and aviators and surface officers in general.

If Spruance's staff had any potential weakness, it was that all but one of its members were without aviation experience. The sole aviator did not have well-defined duties and rarely became involved in the planning, even though the carriers played a decisive role in every Fifth Fleet operation. As the war progressed, Spruance and the staff would

3. Vice Admiral John H. (Jack) Towers was a naval aviation pioneer, who won his wings in 1911 to become Naval Aviator Number 3 at age twenty-six. He was the senior naval aviator in the Pacific during the war and was the spiritual and administrative leader of the Pacific Fleet aviators.

become increasingly susceptible to criticism from the naval aviation community.

The staff yeomen began typing the final plan on stencils in mid-October. Things had begun to coalesce under Moore's direction. The chief of staff demanded exacting standards, sometimes to the staff's discomfiture, and he wanted all the details expressed in clear language that everyone could understand. For example, Biggs had developed a perfect scheme for the underway refueling of the invasion force, and he gave it to Moore for review and approval. Moore growled at Biggs that the wording was "rotten" and that no one would be able understand the plan. He wanted clarity, so he rewrote the refueling plan himself, much to Biggs's chagrin.

Although the staff chafed under Moore's fussing and prodding, they soon recognized that he was a master planner and organizer. "He was a tower of strength," Forrestel recalled years later. "Anything you wanted to know about planning, Carl Moore had at his fingertips. He was the backbone of the staff."

Moore's insistence that plans be lucidly written was rewarded in the Gilberts and all subsequent campaigns. The Fifth Fleet plans were always thorough, timely, and easily understood; everyone knew in advance what they would be expected to do. On the other hand, the same subordinates dreaded operating under Halsey. Although he was a great combat leader, Halsey rarely followed an established plan. His orders often were impulsive, denying his commanders adequate time to prepare for the next day's operation. Although Halsey's moves kept the Japanese off-balance, his commanders would be equally disconcerted by his unexpected brainstorms. Operating under Spruance was a pleasure. He would issue good plans and stick to them.

Spruance presented his final plan to Nimitz and the CINCPAC staff in the war game room in the headquarters building. It was discussed and debated over charts, and the staffs tried to visualize every possibility. As a result Nimitz knew what Spruance intended to do, and Spruance could benefit from the comments and suggestions from Nimitz and his staff. When the meeting adjourned, everyone understood the battle plans. These meetings became a standard procedure before each major operation.

Spruance's plan organized his carriers into four task groups under

Pownall, collectively designated Task Force 50. A Northern Attack Force, Task Force 52, commanded by Turner using units from the 27th Infantry Division under Major General Ralph C. Smith, would seize Makin. A Southern Attack Force, Task Force 53, commanded by Hill, would seize Tarawa, using the 2nd Marine Division under Major General Julian C. Smith. Rear Admiral Johnny Hoover would command the land-based forces, Task Force 57, and, using Seabees and garrison troops, would build and develop the bases and airfields on Betio and Makin after they were seized.

As the 20 November 1943 D-Day approached, few were satisfied with their readiness for war. Planning had been rushed by exhausted staffs working long, grueling hours. Men, equipment, and tactics were new and untried. But everyone knew that the longer the Americans waited, the more entrenched the Japanese would be.

Crises large and small persisted until the last moment. Turner was stricken with malaria in late October. His loss would have jeopardized the entire operation, but he had a quick recovery. Moore toppled into a deep drainage ditch in the dark following an evening's work session and nearly dislocated his shoulder. (Later, the staff Marine advisor broke his leg just before the Marshalls campaign.)

Barber accumulated a growing pile of papers that would comprise the Fifth Fleet operation order. Over 300 copies had to be mimeographed and distributed, and each copy contained over 300 pages and weighed more than three pounds. When the last page had been typed one October night, Barber assembled a platoon of Marines and a dozen or so staff officers who were the authors of the various sections (annexes) of the plan. With Barber supervising, the Marines formed an assembly line, collected the annexes from each responsible staff officer, then assembled, packaged, addressed, and accounted for every bundle of plans. By 0400 the work was done and the plans were on their way to the GALVANIC forces by officer messenger.

Barber was amazed that the senior staff officers would willingly participate in such a tedious clerical task. Their cooperative attitude reflected their high morale as well as their anxiety to ensure that their individual annexes were included in every package. The procedure proved so effective and efficient that it became a trademark of the staff and a source of friendly joshing both during and after the war. "Barber is a great youngster," wrote Moore, "and we just couldn't put out the work we do without him."

Their work completed in late October, Spruance and the staff relaxed while preparing to go to sea for their first battle. "My social life is drawing to a close," he wrote Margaret, "for I shall be moving on board ship in about a week. I am sorry my letters are so routine and dull, but perhaps I may be able to improve them in the future after a rest and a change of scenery for a while. This is the last letter you will receive from me in some weeks—possibly until about Christmas time—as I shall be too occupied with other matters to do any writing."

Chapter 14

THE GILBERTS

IN November 1943, Spruance prepared to go to sea to make war. He would welcome the change from shore duty. "It's fine to be ashore," he once said, "but it's great to be at sea, away from the noise and the distractions, and it makes us appreciate our wives more."

He needed a proper flagship. It had to be fast enough to keep pace with the carriers and to operate without escorts, powerful enough to defend itself, and with enough endurance to steam long distances without refueling. It had to be designed as a flagship and had to contain ample communications equipment. One of the magnificent new battleships fresh from the building yards would have seemed appropriate.

But that kind of ship would not do. Spruance intended to roam his ocean battlefield, going where he was needed or where the action was. He would not weaken his forces by withdrawing a large and powerful flagship whenever he hauled out over the horizon. The flagship also had to be expendable. He wanted a close view of the landings and fighting ashore and thereby would deliberately hazard his flagship to enemy fire. Should it be hit and put out of action, he did not want its loss to seriously weaken his fleet.

The twelve-year-old heavy cruiser *Indianapolis* fitted his specifications.[1] She was a "Treaty Cruiser" with the same kinds of design deficiencies that had plagued *Northampton,* Spruance's earlier flagship. *Indianapolis* once boasted a beautiful teak quarterdeck and a reputation for impeccable honors and ceremonies, performed by a Marine Guard whose every man was six feet or taller, wearing specially tailored uniforms. After Pearl Harbor, the cruiser had been stripped for war. The teak deck had been removed, the Marines wore fatigues, and the admiral's barge and the accommodation ladders had been left ashore as excess baggage. Visiting flag and general officers now arrived by landing craft, clambered up a steep, vertical sea ladder, and were piped aboard by a boatswain's mate in dungarees.

Although *Indianapolis* had been designed as a flagship, she had been intended for a division commander's staff of four or five officers. Spruance came aboard with thirty-two officers, who—when squeezed into the cramped, crowded staterooms—suggested that the congestion be relieved by leaving some of their number ashore as a rear echelon. Spruance refused to consider that recommendation; no one would remain behind. The staff's size would be limited to the number that could be accommodated aboard *Indianapolis.* He later used that argument when anyone attempted to force additional officers upon him. It was pragmatic insurance that the staff would remain small and efficient.

The flag cabin was quickly modified for Spruance's peculiar needs. Carpenters installed the familiar stand-up desk and a large chart board. Fleet navigator Smith posted a chart of the Pacific Ocean that showed the location of all Fifth Fleet ships and all known Japanese contacts. The young Reserve plotting officers, standing a twenty-four-hour watch, would keep the data current. Thus Spruance would instantly know the location of every ship in his fleet, any hour of the day. The

1. USS *Indianapolis* (CA 35), displacement 9,800 tons, main battery nine 8-inch guns, commissioned 15 November 1932. Away from Pearl Harbor at the outbreak of war, she participated in two of the early 1942 raids before being detailed to the North Pacific Area for operations in Aleutian waters. As Spruance's principal flagship for the Fifth Fleet, the *Indianapolis* saw action in almost every major amphibious invasion in the Central Pacific. Her last mission was to deliver parts of the atomic bomb from the West Coast to Tinian, where she arrived on 26 July 1945. On her way to rejoin the fleet at Leyte, she was sunk early on the morning of 30 July 1945 by the Japanese submarine *I-58.* No distress message was received, and survivors were first sighted by chance on 2 August. Loss of life was extremely heavy, and the sinking to this day remains controversial. DANAFS, volume 3 (Washington, 1968), pp. 432–36.

watch officers became Spruance's constant cabin companions; he was alone only behind his bedroom door.

On 5 November 1943, *Indianapolis* broke Spruance's flag—three white stars on a blue field—at the truck, signifying that the admiral soon would lead his fleet to sea and to battle. But in his cabin below, a worried Spruance wondered if he would have enough warships. Halsey was attempting to seize Bougainville in the Solomon Islands, and the Japanese navy was resisting with strength and vigor. Halsey had needed reinforcements, so Nimitz had transferred five carriers, five cruisers, and three destroyer divisions from Spruance to Halsey. Nimitz wanted them returned in time for the Gilberts assault, but Spruance was not reassured. What if those ships were sunk or damaged? What if Halsey's situation became so desperate that he needed them indefinitely? Bougainville was 1200 miles away from Tarawa. Too many things could go wrong.

Nimitz agreed that he could not guarantee that Halsey could return the borrowed ships on time, so he told Spruance on 5 November to prepare an alternate plan based upon the assumption they would not be available. Next day Nimitz slipped D-Day by twenty-four hours, to 21 November, to allow extra time for the borrowed ships to rejoin Spruance.

Despite the confusion of moving his staff aboard ship, Spruance quickly issued his alternate plan. If his borrowed forces did not return, he would use what remained to seize Tarawa first, followed by the seizure of Makin. He also wrote two letters to Nimitz.

He had two plans, Spruance wrote, and he didn't know which he would use until he had a firm return date for his borrowed ships. Soon the Fifth Fleet would be underway. It was scattered about the ocean and had to follow complex schedules to arrive on time at the appointed rendezvous. Any last-minute schedule changes had to be made, he wrote, with the greatest care in order not to disrupt the movement plan. (Perhaps Spruance was warning Nimitz and the CINCPOA staff not to tinker further with the plan. The last-minute diversions to help Halsey had been ominous.)

Spruance then summarized his contingency plans, based upon whether all, some, or none of his borrowed ships returned. He also had a contingency plan in the event bad weather inhibited the scheduled landing. Sometime *after* he left Pearl Harbor, yet well *before* D-Day, someone would have to decide which plan would be used. It couldn't be

Spruance and his principal staff officers, early 1944,
on forecastle of USS *Indianapolis**

*Spruance did not want to pose with the group but finally assented when Carl
Moore threatened to use force. Left to right: R. S. Smith, assistant operations officer;
C. F. Barber, flag secretary; R. W. Morse, aviation officer; C. F. Coleman, electronic
warfare officer; B. B. Biggs, logistics officer; G. M. Slonim, Japanese language officer;
C. J. Moore, chief of staff; M. C. Burns, aerological officer; Spruance; J. R. Armstrong, communications officer; E. P. Forrestel, operations officer; G. S. Eckhardt,
Army liaison officer; C. H. Murphy, intelligence officer; W. B. McCormick, assistant
communications officer; J. E. Jones, Marine Corps liaison officer; E. H. McKissick,
flag lieutenant

Spruance. He was determined to surprise the enemy by maintaining radio silence. Someone would have to make the decision.

Spruance asked Nimitz to bear that responsibility and to broadcast from Pearl Harbor which of Spruance's plans would be used. "The directives issued," wrote Spruance, "should conform with the general plan of movement, and should fit in so far as possible without delaying either combatant forces or fleet oilers." He even told Nimitz what to say in the message, if the alternate plan were executed: "Commander Central Pacific Force Operation Plan No. Cen 5-43 effective." The first impression was that Spruance was telling his boss how to do the boss's job. But the two men were so close that they must have agreed orally beforehand, the letters serving as written confirmation.[1]

Next day, 8 November, the cruiser *Birmingham,* on loan to Halsey, was torpedoed and badly damaged. She was scratched from GAL-VANIC. Her loss was a bad omen, but by the day before sailing, 9 November, the picture improved. Halsey ordered the borrowed cruisers to return to Spruance. The status of the five carriers and their destroyer screens, however, remained unresolved.

To complicate his immediate problems (which compounded as sailing day approached), Spruance was distracted with follow-on plans for the Marshalls. The JCS had directed that the Marshalls be seized before 1 February 1944, and just before sailing, Nimitz told Spruance that D-Day would be 17 January 1944.

Spruance protested that it would be impossible to seize the Marshalls before 1 February. Nimitz was unmoved and told Spruance that 17 January was firm. Spruance, realizing that he could not begin planning for *any* D-Day until he returned from the Gilberts, decided to defer his objections until after GALVANIC.

Spruance was also confronted with a problem of less importance but great annoyance. The press was aware of GALVANIC and wanted to interview Spruance. They knew nothing about him and regarded him as a new and probably newsworthy discovery. Spruance, however, refused to see any war correspondents, telling Moore that he wanted no personal publicity for fear of being exploited for the benefit of the press.

---

1. The letters wisely illustrate that any important oral agreement, even between the closest of friends, should be confirmed in writing to avoid unintentional misunderstandings.

Spruance expressed his antipathy toward the press and toward those who sought publicity in a letter to Margaret. "Everyone in the country," he wrote, "seems to feel at liberty to express his opinions on the strategy of the war and to publish his ideas to the largest audience that will listen to him. If enough smart commentators and not so smart public officials air their ideas, they will probably cover the entire range of possible action. Then the Japs, having everything to choose from, will be no better off than they would have been if no one had said anything—something which Americans have never learned to do. I have always wondered how our Guadalcanal-Tulagi expedition was able to catch the Japs so flatfooted, for our people were gathered all around and they had a most obvious objective. I guess the Japs must have thought that no white enemy would ever dare attack them."

Moore finally convinced Spruance that he had a duty to at least talk to one or two of the war correspondents. Spruance relented and allowed several to visit with him before the operation. He treated them courteously, refused to talk about himself, and spoke only of the war and the need for a team effort by all the services. The frustrated journalists, who understandably wanted to write a human interest "profile," could not crack the admiral's passive exterior. They turned to others for an insight into Spruance's personality; predictably, they were misinformed.

Correspondent Frank D. Morris wrote a wildly inaccurate article entitled "Our Unsung Admiral" that was published in the 1 January 1944 issue of *Collier's*. Morris opened by saying that reporters feared Spruance, but that he had found him "to be as formidable as an old shoe. When Admiral Spruance isn't walking, he's driving himself and his subordinates and his ships and the enemy. He's a demon for work. . . . If he possesses one fault, it is that he believes too much in work and doesn't get enough play."

Spruance admired and respected Robert Sherrod of *Time* for his accurate and objective reporting of battles, but Sherrod's 26 June 1944 *Time* cover story about Spruance was anything but accurate. Unaware of Spruance's carefully concealed warmth and humanity, Sherrod called him a "cold, calculating, mechanical man," a "modified version of his starched icy-eyed Commander-in-Chief, Admiral Ernest King." Quoting a misleading statement from Vice Admiral W. L. Calhoun, Sherrod also wrote that Spruance was "a cold-blooded fighting fool."

The correspondents pressed for permission to accompany Spruance on *Indianapolis*. He refused and his refusal stuck, with minor exceptions.

On 10 November 1943 Spruance left Pearl Harbor in *Indianapolis* in company with many of the other ships of the Fifth Fleet. Slower ships had been underway for many days, from many ports. Spruance's scattered forces had begun their inexorable journey toward their coral island destinations. The fifty-seven-year-old vice admiral was embarked upon a dangerous, complex mission using untried men, equipment, and tactics. He still did not know which plan he would use nor what forces ultimately would be available. Despite these uncertainties, he had anticipated the most probable contingencies and had a plan for each. Spruance had done all he could do to be prepared. Now he relaxed and established the at-sea routine that would prevail throughout the war.

Spruance's resolve to remain aloof from details and distractions frequently was tested by Moore. Moore was a driver, accustomed to working hours late and long, who incessantly questioned, badgered, and goaded the staff in order to achieve his rigorous standards of efficiency and performance. When a problem arose, the chief of staff would be impatient and tackle it regardless of the hour. Eager to press on with his work, Moore frequently tried to involve Spruance in his concern of the moment. Spruance resisted Moore's irrepressible intrusions and often would ignore or brusquely dismiss his friend in order to preserve his rest and privacy.

"He is the most wonderful boss I have ever known," Moore later wrote his wife, "but he has exasperated me no end a good many times. I can understand what Margaret means when she says he is a bear when he doesn't get his exercise or his sleep or his coffee and so forth. He never gets ruffled or excited, never gets exasperated with me when I get disagreeable. When he doesn't want to do business, he just pretends not to hear and goes to bed or walks off and doesn't answer.

"He eats quantities of raw sliced onions for his health, and walks me for miles up and down the forecastle with no shirt on to get me brown. Never mind stacks of work to do. This goes on until I insist the war has got to be won, and my tan is really of no importance." ("On board ship," wrote Spruance to Margaret, "I have to spend an hour and a half to two hours walking up and down the forecastle every afternoon with no shirt on to get sun and exercise and keep my digestion in good order.")

"He turns in about eight and doesn't like to be disturbed except for something most important," wrote Moore. "He won't sleep in his emergency cabin because it is stuffy. He has read dozens of books and doesn't like to be interrupted. I refer almost nothing to him except matters of vital importance, and he lets me strictly alone except on those matters. He is most appreciative of my efforts and says, 'I don't know how I could have gotten along without you, Carl.' As long as I will stay and do the work and he can walk and read and sleep, he'll be contented.

"I expect no reward," Moore concluded. "In the presence of rank I am ignored, which is as it should be, I suppose. He'll chat for hours with a visiting friend when he knows I need only a minute of his time to get ahead with my work. The staff is fine. They work hard, take my ill humor, and all do their stuff."

The transit from Pearl Harbor to the Gilberts took ten days. *Indianapolis* steamed in company with Turner's Northern Attack Force, and Spruance directed Turner to act as Officer in Tactical Command (OTC). In this capacity, the amphibious commander controlled the courses, speeds, drills, exercises, and tactical dispositions of the immediate force, and *Indianapolis* conformed to his orders.

Spruance rarely acted as OTC. His staff controlled the general movements of the fleet as a whole, but they were not prepared to control the minute-by-minute operations of a single task group of a dozen or so ships. That kind of responsibility was the proper concern of the subordinate task force and task group commanders—flag officers junior to Spruance.

Historian Samuel Eliot Morison accompanied the invasion force and wrote a vivid account of that passage from Pearl Harbor to the Gilberts, typical of the many ocean journeys to war that would be made by Spruance and his forces. "There was little rest for anyone [other than Spruance] on the nine-day passage to Makin," Morison wrote. "Turner knew from abundant experience the value of constant training, and some of the ships under him were fresh from shakedown. A prearranged zigzag plan was imposed on the basic course, but the task force seldom followed it an hour without Turner's ordering some sort of workout. Radio silence was maintained, but signal flags snapped and blinkers

The two men whom Spruance selected to capture places for him:
Holland M. Smith (left) and Richmond Kelly Turner (right)

flashed his orders; groups of cruisers or battleships deployed to repel
imaginary air or submarine attacks or steamed over the horizon to
practice division tactics; transports, looking like indignant old ladies
being pushed around, made emergency turns and steamed in line of
bearing; carriers swung into the wind to launch or recover planes as
their pilots played at submarine hunting, searching 175 miles northward of the formation; destroyers continually dashed about, screening
other vessels or shooting at towed sleeves. Not one submarine or air
contact was made en route, but this training was all to the good. Each
ship was a floating college of naval warfare; officers studied intelligence
control, anti-aircraft gunnery and all manner of subjects. A succession
of perfect winter tradewind days slipped by with everyone busy and in
high spirits, eager for a fight and confident of victory."

The staff initially had felt green and awkward at sea, but Spruance
seemed confident that they would do well. His self-assurance helped to

dispel their jitters. Gradually the staff became accustomed to *Indianapolis* and to working with each other. The relationship between any staff and the flagship crew is always a potential source of friction. Staff members frequently are regarded as intruders and can make life miserable for a ship's company. Fortunately, the Fifth Fleet staff and the *Indianapolis* crew were compatible throughout the war.

As they neared the equator, the ship became almost uninhabitable. Ventilation was poor, and when *Indianapolis* buttoned up for general quarters she became unbearably hot. The ventilation fans created static that interfered with the radar, so the fans were secured and the crew sweltered. The temperature in Moore's stateroom near the smokestack rose to over a hundred degrees.

By 13 November the borrowed ships had returned to Spruance, so that he could proceed with his original plan to seize both Tarawa and Makin. Hoover's aircraft, based in the Ellice Islands, began their prearranged strikes and reconnaissance missions against the Gilberts and Marshalls, and Hoover reported good weather and light opposition. The carriers peeled off and began the pre-D-Day strikes that would smother enemy land-based aircraft within range of Tarawa and Makin.

On the morning of 18 November, Hill's Southern Attack Force, coming up from the south out of Efate in the New Hebrides, made rendezvous with Spruance and Turner's Northern Attack Force. Tarawa was 400 miles to the northwest. *Indianapolis* left Turner and joined Hill, who was going after Tarawa. That was where Spruance wanted to be. A destroyer passed a letter from Hill.

"My dear Raymond," it said. "We had a fine training period in Efate and I think the boys are all prepared to do their job in good fashion provided we get a break in the weather and tidal conditions on the beach. I have had a little trouble convincing some of my fire support boys that when I say I want close fire support I mean *close.*"

Hill shared Spruance's concern about the need for surprise and for quick consolidation of the occupation of Tarawa before the Japanese could react: "The 2nd Division has done a fine job in their loading and are streamlined down to a point where I fully hope we may get the transports completely out of the area in approximately twenty-four hours. They have been a wonderful crowd to work with and I think will put on a good show."

Hill closed on a hopeful note: "With best wishes to you and Carl and the hope that this force may prove a credit to your command on D-Day, I am Sincerely, Harry."

Kelly Turner anticipated the impending assault with a religious fervor. "I lift my spirit with this unified team of Army, Navy and Marines whether attached to ships, aircraft or ground units," he said by message, "and I say to you that I know God will bless you and give you strength to win a glorious victory."

While darkness fell on the eve of battle, Spruance as usual watched a movie in the wardroom. He had few companions. The movie over, the admiral went to bed.

In the black of night, Hill's force and the *Indianapolis* began their final deployment to surround unsuspecting Tarawa Atoll. Nerves jangled when a destroyer reported the navigation lights of an approaching surface vessel. Hill and his commanders tensely debated on the TBS whether the contact was friend or foe. Fearing discovery, Hill ordered his force to attack, and a cruiser and destroyer began firing guns and torpedoes. The contact immediately disappeared, leaving two green flares hovering in the sky, the signal of an American submarine.

Moore and the staff were sickened when they realized what had happened. Hill had fired on the submarine *Nautilus,* patrolling off Tarawa. Hill had not been told she would be there, owing to an oversight during the rush to complete the final plans. Fortunately, *Nautilus* was not sunk by the shelling. The Pacific Fleet subsequently developed elaborate precautions to preclude firing upon friendly submarines.

Surprisingly enough, the firing and the racket on the TBS had not alerted the Japanese on Tarawa. The atoll lay hidden in the darkness, visible only on the shimmering radar screens. The ships dispersed and began their stealthy approaches towards their final attack positions. *Indianapolis* took station on the eastern leg of the atoll in order to bombard gun emplacements and ammunition dumps located on the chain of smaller islands north of Betio, while the main force encircled Betio Island on the southwest corner of the atoll. Toward midnight a Japanese searchlight pierced the darkness, flashed intermittently for a half hour, then flicked off. The ships were in position. The defenders were asleep.

Red flares rose over the atoll just before sunrise—the Japanese finally had discovered the invasion force. In the last moment of silence, before all hell broke loose, 4500 Japanese defenders rushed to their guns and their bunkers and looked disbelievingly at the transports disgorging

USS *Indianapolis* (Official U.S. Navy photo, National Archives)

the vanguard of 18,600 Marines into landing craft. Battleships, cruisers, and destroyers trained their turrets and mounts towards Betio, which in response menacingly sprouted gun and cannon muzzles from its sand and coral. The island and its ring of attacking ships were at point-blank range.

Then the guns began to fire.

At first Spruance could only hear and not see what was happening on Betio. (*Indianapolis* had been around the corner on her independent bombardment mission.) But clouds of smoke confirmed that the ships were hitting their targets. Shortly after 0600, carrier aircraft bombed the island, then withdrew, and the ships resumed their barrage.

When *Indianapolis* drew near Betio, Spruance could see the first wave of Marines approaching the beach in their squat, unwieldy LVT's. The flagship joined in the bombardment, and Betio writhed under the impact of hundreds of high-explosive projectiles. A pall of smoke and dust hovered over the island, obliterating any view of individual targets, so the ships shifted to area fire that swept the island from end to end.

"Fires were burning everywhere," Moore remembered. "The coconut trees were blasted and burned, and it seemed that no living soul could be on the island . . . the troops approached the beach, and it looked like the whole affair would be a walkover."

Spruance watched the LVT's clamber up on the beach, but he could not see what the Marines were doing because of the smoke. Then to his horror, he saw the blunt-bowed landing craft, following the LVT's, ground on the barrier reef that extended hundreds of yards offshore. The water over the reef was too shallow. A high tide, high enough for those boats to clear the reef, had been forecast. But the forecast was wrong, and the landing degenerated into a bloody disaster.

Some boats withdrew. Others lowered their ramps, and the Marines jumped into the water to wade ashore. They were mercilessly exposed as they struggled across the hundreds of yards of open water between them and the protection of the beach. Shell and bullet splashes peppered the water. Marines fell, and LVT's and landing craft burst into flame. Despite the massive bombardment, the Japanese defenders of Betio were alive and fighting.

The Americans were in desperate trouble. A babble of agitated voices jammed the airwaves as radio discipline collapsed. Spruance did not know it at the time, but Harry Hill and Julian Smith on the flagship *Maryland* could not communicate with the Marines ashore. The *Maryland*'s 16-inch salvos had so jarred and damaged Hill's delicate radio equipment that it was inoperative. The Marines ashore were no better off; their radio equipment was watersoaked.

Reinforcements could not get ashore by landing craft owing to the unpredicted low tide over the barrier reef. Boats circled offshore in confusion with nowhere to go. American ships and planes poured more steel and explosive into Betio, and more smoke and fire and dust erupted. Spruance had no way of knowing what was happening in the inferno ashore. Were his forces winning or losing? He silently watched through his binoculars and waited.

In the early afternoon Julian Smith radioed Holland Smith at Makin. He reported heavy casualties at Betio, and requested permission to land the reserve regiment. "The issue is in doubt," Julian Smith concluded.

The staff viewed the request with apprehension. If Julian Smith wanted to commit the reserve so early in the battle, things ashore were going very badly indeed. Forrestel was shocked at the "issue in doubt" statement. The last time the Marines had used that phrase was just before Wake Island fell to the Japanese in December 1941.

The chaos and clamor accentuated the air of crisis. The staff, detached observers rather than harried participants, felt they had a broader, clearer picture than those involved in the actual fighting. They could see situations develop that required action and decisions, and they pressed Spruance to send messages to alert Hill and Smith. Spruance refused. "I pick men who I believe are competent to do the job," he said, "and I'm going to let them do it." The matter was closed.

Spruance calmly watched and waited. Night fell, and the fighting lulled. Most of the ships stood out to sea, except for several destroyers who provided call fire throughout the night. Next morning the ships returned and the fighting resumed.

After three days of savage combat, the Marines completed seizing Betio. The Army required three days on Makin, but for different reasons. The slow progress on Tarawa was understandable, but Spruance was exasperated with the Army on Makin Atoll. The 27th Division had landed 6500 assault troops on Butaritari Island, which was defended by about 800 lightly armed Japanese troops and laborers. Spruance expected the Army to seize Butaritari in a day so that he could withdraw his fleet in order to avoid possible enemy counterattacks from the nearby Marshalls.

An island under assault was like a magnet. Ships in support nearby were effectively immobilized until the island was secured, tempting targets for Japanese ships, aircraft, and submarines. During the unnecessarily prolonged three-day Makin assault, the carrier *Liscome Bay* had been supporting the Army. A Japanese submarine had sunk her with great loss of life. Spruance was convinced that if the Army had won swiftly, *Liscome Bay* could have been withdrawn earlier and would not have been lost.

Kelly Turner reported by letter to Spruance what had gone wrong. "Makin was a pushover," wrote Turner, "without enough defenders to put up a real fight. It should have been taken in a day and a half at the most, instead of nearly three days. For your eyes alone, I will say that the 27th Division is the fourth National Guard Division with which I have been intimately associated in connection with action against the enemy. All of them were approximately alike, although I believe that the 27th Division is somewhat below the other three in effectiveness. These divisions simply do not have the leadership and the staff work that the regular divisions have. Until they have to learn the hard way,

Betio Island on Tarawa Atoll secured, D+6 Day
Transports in the lagoon unload supplies

The 600-yard-long pier, spanning the deadly barrier reef that lay exposed
and glistening at low tide

they are not very good. . . . I would like to have you talk with some of the soldiers about some of the things that went on ashore in Makin during the occupation. I am not blaming anyone in particular; I feel that it is the natural result of the system, and of the inexperience and lack of moral fiber of the officers and non-commissioned officers. Frankly, they were jittery before starting and they stayed jittery."

Turner's criticism was restrained and moderate compared to that of Holland Smith, who had gone ashore to speed progress. He was furious at the Army's sorry performance. "One of the worst nights I ever spent in the Pacific was at the Command Post ashore on Makin," wrote Smith, "when I slept under a mosquito net, on a cot set outside the tent. This was the first time the 165th Regiment had been in action and I hoped the presence of Ralph Smith, their Commanding General, and myself would be a good influence on the sentries posted around camp. I was mistaken. Shots whizzed over my head from a 25-yard range, drilled holes in the command post tent and clipped coconuts off the trees. I crawled out from under my net and implored the sentries to stop shooting at shadows. There wasn't a Japanese within a mile of the Command Post."

The Army's inept performance on Makin and Holland Smith's wrath would have tragic repercussions during the remainder of the war in the Central Pacific. Joint Army–Navy–Marine Corps operations required close cooperation, but interservice relations were poisoned on Makin and would steadily deteriorate.

By 27 November both atolls were secure. Garrison troops and base development teams had begun to land, and the assault troops were ready to withdraw. Nimitz flew in with an entourage of flag and general officers to view the conquests. Spruance prepared to meet them on Betio.

Indianapolis steamed into the lagoon and a landing craft came alongside. Spruance and members of his staff got in, and the coxswain gunned his engines, spinning the boat's head toward the beach. It would be Spruance's first close look at his conquest.

Betio was so low that at a distance its hundreds of shattered palm trees seemed to rise from the water. Soon the island appeared, carpeted with a welter of indistinct shapes that were the wreckage of war. The boat thunked against the end of the long pier that extended into the lagoon. It had been the focus of some of the heaviest fighting.

Spruance got out and began walking up the six-hundred-yard-long pier, spanning the deadly barrier reef that lay exposed and glistening at low tide. The rubble ashore became distinct. Scores of shattered LVT's littered the beaches. The island was strewn with debris that once had been guns, tanks, trucks, buildings—and men. Over 20,000 warriors had fought on a patch of sand and coral. The concentrated firepower had ripped and torn and shredded and blasted and burned the battlefield into a vast, ghastly junkyard of destruction.

Spruance quickly discovered why the massive prelanding bombardment had failed materially to soften the island's defenses. Every square foot of the island seemed to contain bunkers, barricades, foxholes, pillboxes, trenches, and tunnels. Reinforced concrete and piles of coconut logs had protected the defenders from naval gunfire. Only direct hits with large-caliber naval projectiles had penetrated the almost indestructible defenses.

Spruance stood in a Japanese gun emplacement and looked across the landing beaches and the barrier reef, a quarter-mile wide. A few days earlier, Marines had floundered across that reef in waist-high water, and Spruance now could visualize the Japanese field of fire that had killed the helpless Americans. The survivors must have had the same feelings as Willie and Joe surveying the Anzio beaches in Bill Mauldin's cartoon: "My God! Here they wuz an' there we wuz."

The Marines had buried their own dead, but the air stank from rotting, unburied Japanese bodies, swelling and bursting in the equatorial sun. Although some enemy dead had been gathered in bomb craters and covered by bulldozers, the larger command posts and bunkers were filled with charred, mangled, putrified flesh. No one wanted to bury the horrid messes inside.

Carl Moore saw a pair of Japanese shoes and casually kicked them aside. The owner's feet, he found, were still inside. Another staff officer peered into a demolished pillbox. The sight and the stench engulfed him in a wave of nausea, and he nearly vomited. Later, as he reflected on the sights he had seen, he became deeply troubled by the carnage that pervaded the island. His roommate, on the other hand, hated the Japanese, because he had been a lucky survivor of the Japanese invasion of the Philippines. He viewed the enemy dead with satisfaction.

The living Marines were unshaven, dirty, hot, hungry, thirsty, bloody, shocked, and weary. Yet they were working hard: on the airfield, their gun positions, or their bed for the night. Others were

The concentrated firepower had ripped and torn and shredded and blasted and burned the battlefield into a vast, ghastly junkyard of destruction. Betio, 27 November 1943

hunting Japanese survivors. The fascinated staff officers explored with a morbid curiosity, and they were surprised that the Marines were indifferent to their surroundings. Death and destruction for them were all too familiar. "What they have been through during that week," wrote Moore to his wife, "I'll never appreciate."

Some of the staff felt guilty as they mingled with the exhausted troops. While the Marines had been fighting, suffering, and dying ashore, life on the *Indianapolis* just a few miles away had been relatively pleasant. The flag mess meals had been excellent, the staff had bathed in warm showers, had slept between clean sheets, and had worn crisp

*Mutilated Japanese bodies, strewn everywhere, were casually ignored
by the conquering Americans, who regarded the hideous corpses as
inanimate battlefield debris. Marine burial details, equipped with what
appeared to be large hay rakes . . .*

khakis fresh from the ship's laundry. One staff officer wrote home, "I
must say that I felt inwardly embarrassed when I saw the boys in
Tarawa still eating K and C rations out of cans."

Spruance joined the Nimitz group. Their faces were grim,
Spruance's an impassive mask. Julian Smith affirmed that a thousand
Marines had been killed.

Spruance's inspection of Tarawa was his first direct contact with the
horror of war. War had been an abstract theory most of his life, and
even after World War II began he had been without contact with a
smoking battlefield covered with blood and torn bodies. He had visited
wounded men in hospitals, but the wards were clean and antiseptic, far
removed from the sights and sounds and smells of mortal battle.

Spruance's earlier experiences with the sight of human blood had
been unnerving. Always fascinated with the physiology of the human

. . . dragged the putrid bodies into bomb craters, later to be covered by bulldozers.
Roi-Namur, February 1944

body, as a young man he had speculated whether he could have been a physician. To satisfy his curiosity, he had watched an appendectomy—and fainted. On another occasion, when Edward as a small boy once passed red urine, Spruance was certain his son had an internal hemorrhage. He called for a doctor and became highly agitated, to a degree that Margaret had never seen before or since. The doctor's diagnosis was that Edward had eaten a large quantity of red berries.

Spruance kept his thoughts to himself as he walked about the Betio battlefield. Only his wife got a hint of his feelings. He wrote Margaret that when he inspected the main Japanese blockhouse "it was so full of dead Japs that one look was all I could take."

Tarawa proved that the Japanese were fanatical fighters who never would surrender, despite hopeless odds. Spruance wrote Margaret that in order to defeat them, every Japanese soldier would have to be dug out and killed on every island that they defended against American invaders. There would be a continual slaughter ahead. The curtain had just been raised at Tarawa.

Killing Japanese was not difficult for most Americans, who regarded them as little more than vermin. American propaganda inflamed the worst instincts in Americans, and exterminating the despised enemy was elevated to a noble and patriotic duty. Spruance did not hate his enemy, however. Hatred was an emotion that interfered with rational thought. Instead he respected the Japanese, recognizing their ability to fight, and used his intellect—unencumbered with emotion—to make war. He would be guided by reason rather than instinct.

In late 1944 Spruance passed a compound in Pearl Harbor containing Japanese prisoners of war, awaiting transfer to POW camps in the United States. He compulsively walked over to the wire fence and began gesturing and speaking in pidgin English. "You Japanese good fighters," he said again and again to the startled captives. Both Americans and Japanese were astounded at the sight of a four-star admiral speaking so earnestly to the enemy.

But Moore wasn't surprised. He had accompanied Spruance to hospitals to visit both American and Japanese wounded. The admiral's compassion for men torn and disfigured by war was genuine and indiscriminate. He was as concerned for the Japanese as he was for the Americans.

Spruance returned to the *Indianapolis,* anxious to be away for Pearl Harbor. The time had come to begin planning for the Marshalls assault. But he was forced to remain in the Gilberts for two additional weeks because of delays in unloading supplies and equipment for the garrison and base development forces.

The staff became immersed in reorganizing task forces, coordinating ship movements, and in refueling and repairs. Japanese planes and submarines occasionally harassed the Americans and damaged several ships, but the enemy had conceded the Gilberts. Finally everything was safely ashore, and Hoover took over. The fleet left. *Indianapolis* arrived in Pearl Harbor on 11 December 1943.

The postmortem began. Spruance took the blame upon himself for the shelling of the *Nautilus,* and that incident was closed. But controversy had begun as to whether Tarawa had been a legitimate objective worth a thousand lives. Spruance never would deny that the price had been heavy, but he defended both the tactics and the strategy in seizing the Gilberts. The results, he maintained, were worth the cost. Shortly after the Gilberts operation, he visited with Edward in Honolulu. His son recently had returned from leave in the States, and he told his father that many Americans were shocked at the heavy losses at Tarawa. Spruance replied that if his superiors didn't like the way he was doing his job, they could replace him. He never publicly doubted the decision or the wisdom of the Tarawa assault.

Chuck Barber was an astute and sensitive observer of the thinking of senior officers. He carefully watched and listened to Nimitz and visiting flag and general officers as they viewed the wreckage on Betio on 27 November. They ultimately would pass judgment on Spruance's performance in the Gilberts.

"Everyone topside seems to think Spruance has done a good job," Barber wrote home several days later. "That's swell because we have a long road ahead, and the nation and I will be riding in his ship."

In retrospect, Spruance's advocacy of seizing Tarawa was sound. The Americans were not prepared to seize the Marshalls in late 1943 for want of both experience and photographic intelligence. Tarawa provided both: experience for later assaults on the Marshalls and beyond, and bases for airborne reconnaissance and supporting air strikes.

The heavy American casualties were caused by two factors: an inadequate prelanding bombardment that allowed too many defenders to survive and fight; and the low tide that prevented landing craft from reaching the beaches for many hours. Spruance cannot be faulted for either. All the amphibious planners apparently believed that an intense

D-Day bombardment of several hours' duration was going to be enough. Everyone was wrong. They learned that a prelanding bombardment required days, not hours.

The planners had known that in the past there had been "dodging" tides at Tarawa—irregular neap tides which ebb and flow several times a day at unpredictable intervals, and which maintain a constant level for many hours. The Americans could not predict the dodging tides for want of accurate tide tables for the Gilberts; they gambled for a high tide on the morning of 20 November and guessed wrong. War is a risky business. Much depends on luck. The low tide was bad luck.

Some historians question why the Navy always seemed to pick Central Pacific islands that were heavily defended, while MacArthur moved along the northern shore of New Guinea by seizing lightly held objectives. The answer is that almost every American objective was chosen for use as an airfield. In order to be suitable, a prospective site needed three criteria: adequate length; the long axis in the direction of the prevailing wind; and adequate construction materials.

Most of the northern New Guinea coast was suitable, and MacArthur could go where the Japanese weren't. In contrast, few Central Pacific atolls could support an airfield. Those that could already were occupied and heavily defended by the Japanese. Nimitz and Spruance had no choice other than to meet the enemy head on.

As the *Indianapolis* glided into Pearl Harbor on 11 December 1943, a signal light flashed from the control tower, transmitting a message to Spruance.

CINCPAC IS VERY PROUD OF THE WAY YOUR TASK FORCE COMPLETED ITS RECENT MISSION. FOR YOU AND YOUR FLAGSHIP A SPECIAL WELCOME. WELL DONE. NIMITZ.

Chapter 15

PLANNING FOR THE MARSHALLS

THE Gilberts had been only a prelude to the ultimate objective: seizure of the Marshalls.

The Marshall Islands comprise 32 island groups and 867 reefs scattered over more than 400,000 square miles of ocean. The island groups are largely coral atolls enclosing lagoons, many of them excellent anchorages. The Japanese had occupied the islands for two decades and had developed a large number of fortified airfields. The hub of the enemy's defenses was Kwajalein Atoll, containing both anchorages and airfields. Kwajalein was shielded by encircling island air bases: Kusaie, Jaluit, and Mili to the south, and Wotje and Maloelap to the east. Eniwetok, 360 miles northwest of Kwajalein, was the main conduit for aircraft reinforcements entering the Marshalls from the Mariana-Caroline pipeline.

Comparing distances, Kwajalein was 565 miles northwest of recently captured Tarawa. The major American naval base at Pearl Harbor was 2100 miles northeast of Kwajalein. The major Japanese naval base at Truk was 980 miles west of Kwajalein.

Spruance quickly became involved in a month-long series of squabbles and debates, revolving about three questions: (1) *which* islands shall be seized? (2) *when* shall they be seized? (3) *how* shall they be seized in order to avoid the magnitude of the casualties at Tarawa? Spruance

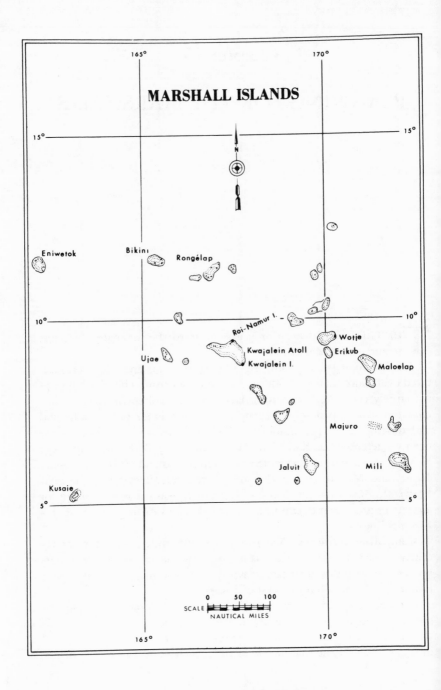

MARSHALL ISLANDS

N

Eniwetok

Bikini

Rongélap

Roi-Namur I.

Ujae

Kwajalein Atoll

Kwajalein I.

Wotje

Erikub

Maloelap

Majuro

Jaluit

Mili

Kusaie

15° 15°

10° 10°

5° 5°

165° 170°

165° 170°

SCALE 0   50   100

NAUTICAL MILES

intended to force a decision on the first question at the earliest moment. The only directive he had in writing was a CINCPAC plan of October setting a 1 January 1944 D-Day for three unspecified objectives, which he understood to be Kwajalein, Maloelap, and Wotje Atolls.

Upon his return from Tarawa, he immediately went ashore and conferred with Turner and Holland Smith, who had preceded him to Pearl Harbor and were familiar with Nimitz's intentions. The commander in chief still wanted a simultaneous attack on the three atolls. Spruance, Turner, and Smith quickly agreed that they would oppose that plan. Their sobering experience in the Gilberts had made them cautious and conservative about future amphibious assaults, and they believed they did not have enough forces for a simultaneous three-pronged attack. They spoke with Nimitz, who agreed and canceled his plan. There was no immediate decision on which objectives would be substituted.

Following the morning's conferences, Spruance dashed off for the beach to swim and exercise, disappearing from view for the remainder of the day. He did not see Moore, who, when besieged by questions from the staff, had one answer: "I don't know."

Within the next few days, Spruance learned that Nimitz had a new plan. He proposed to seize Kwajalein Atoll, then send his fast carriers to the South Pacific, as directed by the JCS, to support amphibious assaults in that theater. Spruance was astonished. He did not fear the Japanese Kwajalein defenses and did not question his ability to seize the atoll. What he did doubt was whether he could hold the atoll once the carriers left. In his mind, the surrounding Japanese air bases then could sever the American lines of communications into Kwajalein. Kwajalein would be isolated. As much as Spruance respected his chief, he strenuously objected to Nimitz's plan.

Turner and Smith supported Spruance. All three favored the seizure of Maloelap and Wotje, which would provide suitable bases for an eventual assault against Kwajalein. Determined to scuttle Nimitz's plan, Turner concocted a scheme to persuade Rear Admiral Forrest Sherman (who had become Nimitz's plans officer) to intercede in their behalf and to convince Nimitz to abandon the "Kwajalein first" proposal. Spruance agreed.

Moore invited Sherman to Spruance's office (located on the third floor to discourage casual visitors), and Spruance, Turner, and Moore began their coercion. Sherman stubbornly resisted. He was a brilliant, strong-willed man, and a future CNO. The plan had been his in the first place, he had recommended it to Nimitz, and he was loath to change his mind. Indeed, Sherman forcefully defended the Nimitz decision and implied that Spruance and Turner had an exaggerated fear of Japanese land-based air power. The discussion ended and Sherman left. Although Sherman was tactful under duress from Spruance and Turner, he later bitterly complained to Moore about the episode, telling Moore that he had resented being pressured.

Nimitz met with Spruance, Turner, and Smith on 14 December in order finally to resolve the controversy. He listened as the three again recommended Maloelap and Wotje and again argued against Kwajalein. Then Nimitz again confirmed that Kwajalein would be the objective. Turner became angry and frustrated. Nimitz's plan was dangerous and reckless, he argued, and he continued to protest, supported by Spruance.

Nimitz lost his patience. Despite his congenial nature, he could be ruthless. He gave his rebellious commanders an ultimatum: either obey his orders or he would replace them with someone who would, from among the many competent flag and general officers itching for their jobs. That ended the arguments. Spruance, Turner, and Smith quickly accepted Nimitz's decision.

Nimitz did compromise, however, to the extent that he allowed them to prepare alternate plans for Wotje and Maloelap, in the event that Kwajalein had to be scrubbed.

Spruance, still skeptical, returned to his staff. He resignedly told them to prepare plans for seizing the islands of Kwajalein and Roi-Namur, located on Kwajalein Atoll, as well as the alternate plans. Moore soon made a suggestion that brightened the picture. He recommended that Majuro Atoll, 230 miles southeast of Kwajalein, be seized as a simultaneous objective. Recalling his Naval War College studies of Pacific atolls, Moore explained that Majuro's splendid lagoon would provide a fleet anchorage where ships could assemble for repairs, resupply, and rest. Spruance agreed. It certainly would give him a better chance to seize and hold Kwajalein. When he presented the proposal to Nimitz, Spruance also said the 16 January D-Day was impossible. Nimitz concurred on each count. By 23 December the JCS had approved both the addition of Majuro and a revised D-Day of 31 January.

The selection of 31 January 1944 as D-Day for the Marshalls invasion, codenamed FLINTLOCK, was a compromise between King and Spruance, with Nimitz acting as an intermediary. King wanted to maintain an offensive momentum against the Japanese through relentless attacks both in the Central Pacific and in the Southwest Pacific, in order to deny them time to reorganize and to consolidate defenses. He was adamant that the Marshalls be seized on 16 January 1944, even if the American forces were not entirely ready. King was a student of the Civil War, and he likely was aware that Lincoln's generals lost many opportunities to shorten the war by failing to maintain pressure and offensive momentum against the Confederate armies.

Spruance appreciated King's motives, but he also knew that the earliest date he could assemble his forces off the shores of Kwajalein was 1 February, owing to the long distances they would have to travel. Nimitz negotiated by message with King, and the CNO finally agreed to 31 January. Spruance conformed to this date by landing artillery on undefended islands adjacent to Kwajalein and Roi-Namur, but the main assault did not begin until 1 February—the date Spruance had wanted from the beginning.

The staff, experienced by now, began developing plans to implement these late December decisions. Spruance, as usual, was impatient to take to the hills, with Moore, as usual, objecting. On one occasion Moore demanded that Spruance devote several hours to office work. Spruance insisted on walking and promised to return in a few hours.

"All right," said Moore, "you go ahead, and when you get through you come back here. I'll be waiting for you, and then you can read these papers."

"All right, Carl," replied Spruance. "Just keep quiet. I'll be right back."

Moore waited in vain. Hours passed. Spruance did not return. Finally in the early evening the admiral rushed into the office, apologizing that he had forgotten his commitment. Following his walk, Spruance explained, he had gone home for supper; later, something had reminded him about his promise to Moore.

Christmas approached, normally a time that depressed Spruance and made him unpleasant to be with. Christmas 1943 was different. It began with a sumptuous Christmas Eve dinner party with his wealthy civilian friends.

"This has been a gay Christmas here," he wrote Margaret. "I have received more presents than I have in the past twenty years." He was embarrassed that he was unable to give suitable gifts in return. "At times like this and at social events when names fail me," he wrote, "I need you very badly."

On Christmas Day, Spruance conscientiously labored with Moore in the office from eight to five. When he wanted to leave to attend another dinner party that evening, Moore became furious. "I had to spoil the day somewhat by bawling Raymond out," Moore wrote his wife. "I hope it hurt him as much as it did me. I worked until five and probably would have kept on if I hadn't gotten mad at the boss."

Spruance was unabashed and reported to Margaret, "I went and had a delightful time."

Margaret was unhappy in the isolation of Monrovia, and her letters reflected her loneliness for her husband, whom she had not seen for nine months. Spruance could offer little encouragement. Nimitz frequently urged him to take home leave, but he always declined. "When and if I do take leave," he wrote Margaret, "I hope it will be for more than three or four days. I would not enjoy coming if I had a lot of important work backing up, and people wanting decisions every day that I was gone and cursing me because I was not present to make them.

"You know that I am never so happy as when with you," Spruance continued, "but a lot of men's lives depend upon how well I am able to do my job now, so the war must take first place. The Japs started this war and they are going to have to say when they want us to stop it—on our terms."

Spruance predicted that they would be permanently reunited "when this war is over two years hence or earlier if I get bounced from out here." He concluded that leave was a remote possibilty before then, "so don't get your hopes up."

But in the midst of the burdens and distractions of war, he found time for an occasional repartee with Margaret. She teased him that Nimitz probably had given him a new khaki belt for Christmas because he was too stingy to buy one for himself. Spruance responded hotly, "Your ideas about my belt are surmise not based on fact." Then he unconsciously revealed his frugality by admitting he knew how to refurbish his old belt to make it last indefinitely, so he would not have to buy a new one.

They gossiped about mutual friends and about his seeing Edward in Pearl Harbor—and even about tomatoes. "Your tomato plants are an improvement over the ones I had in Coronado in 1920," Spruance wrote, "but there is some little trick about tomatoes that neither of us understands. I suggest you read up on the subject."

Most of his letters ended with apologies for their dullness and the explanation that he had little free time to write and "my thoughts have been mostly on official business."

That business was planning how to seize Kwajalein without the magnitude of casualties of Tarawa. Spruance's doctrine for seizing islands while avoiding casualties by now had evolved. *He would use violent, overwhelming force, swiftly applied.* After the war he explained to an audience of Marines why the Tarawa experience had convinced him that a preponderance of strength was essential in an amphibious operation.

"On going into action for the first time," he said, "we found that our best thought-out plans required later modification in the light of actual combat experience, and that exceptional valor in the troops was called for in order to make good unforeseen deficiencies in our planning. *As a matter of fact, even with the best of planning and of preliminary training, I always have had the feeling that the margin between success and failure in an amphibious operation conducted against strongly defended positions was a narrow one.* I would never want to conduct such an operation with troops poorly trained, poorly led, or of poor quality. To do so would be to court defeat, and I do not think we can afford to risk defeat in an amphibious operation." [Emphasis added.]

Turner and Smith endorsed Spruance's concept. The two had become cooperative once the fighting began at the Gilberts, and Spruance was relieved that they no longer fought each other.

The amphibious warfare experts had candidly analyzed their mistakes in the Gilberts and had devised new methods and procedures to avoid the same mistakes in the Marshalls. For example, the LVT's had proven their value, and many more would be used against Kwajalein. Turner and his assault force commanders would operate from specially designed command ships, equipped with new, reliable communications equipment that would not fail as it had at Tarawa. Most important, the preassault bombardment would last for three days, rather than three hours as at Tarawa.

But there were major impediments to the concept of "overwhelming force, swiftly applied." The Army was accustomed to advancing slowly and methodically after intensive artillery preparation, all the while protecting the flanks and keeping intact the line of advance. On the other hand, the Marines advocated swarming ahead, hell-for-leather, overrunning the enemy positions and later mopping up isolated pockets of resistance. The Marine Corps held that winning quickly produced fewer casualties than the Army's more deliberate tactics. Spruance naturally favored the Marine Corps doctrine, which reduced the time needed to keep his ships on station to support the forces ashore.

Another major problem was the Army Air Force. Spruance never forgave their false claims at the Battle of Midway, and his prejudice was reinforced by his assessment of their later performance in support of his Central Pacific campaigns. The Air Force bombed in level flight from high altitudes, and Spruance believed their accuracy (compared to Navy dive-bombers) consistently was as poor as their claims for success were exaggerated.

The Air Force bombers and fighters that supported Spruance's offensives were commanded by Rear Admiral Hoover, who exercised that command through Major General W. H. Hale. Hoover and Hale were incompatible and frequently disagreed on doctrine and tactics. Hoover urged the Air Force to fly lower for improved accuracy; Hale refused because his pilots were skittish about antiaircraft fire and wanted to fly above the range of enemy guns. Hale, in turn, wanted his aircraft in massed formations, which Hoover felt yielded mediocre results. Following the Gilberts campaign, Hale complained to Lieutenant General Robert C. Richardson, commanding all Army forces in the CINCPOA theater, who in turn severely criticized Hoover's use of Air Force aircraft in a letter to Nimitz.

Spruance knew the Air Force resented Navy control and wanted to be rid of the dour, ill-humored Hoover. But Spruance needed those Air Force aircraft, despite their shortcomings, and they had to be responsive to his orders. He did not trust the Army's cooperation. Hoover would do what Spruance wanted done—Hale might not. Therefore Spruance never would allow the Air Force to operate independently whenever they were attached to his forces. An admiral (Hoover) remained in command of the assigned Army Air Force units and was accountable to Spruance.

But the Air Force problems were surpassed by Spruance's mounting problems with his own naval aviators. Pownall, commanding Spruance's fast carriers at the Gilberts, had struck Kwajalein in early

December. Towers felt that Pownall had been excessively cautious, so much so that he asked Nimitz to fire Pownall. Nimitz did, selecting Rear Admiral Marc Mitscher as Spruance's new carrier task force commander without Spruance's knowledge or concurrence.

The fait accompli angered Spruance. He had been pleased with Pownall's performance and saw no justification for Nimitz's decision. Although Spruance had not observed Pownall in action, another admiral had been present in Pownall's task group. The admiral, a battleship division commander, wrote Spruance that Pownall's task group "was superbly handled. It was a joy to observe its air operations, and its fighter direction was perfect." Spruance was further distressed with Mitscher as a replacement because he had reason to mistrust Mitscher's competence after his uneven performance at the Battle of Midway.

Now Towers had accused Pownall of losing the confidence of his aviators. Nonsense, thought Spruance, Towers acted on the basis of self-serving and ambitious motives. (Perhaps Spruance felt that Pownall's only mistake was that he was one of the few senior aviators who had been friendly and cooperative with Spruance.) Spruance now regarded Towers as an enemy. Towers was, in fact, one of the few men he ever hated.

In early January, Nimitz flew to San Francisco for one of his periodic meetings with King. In his absence, Spruance and Towers wrangled over the doctrine for fast carrier employment during FLINTLOCK. Spruance was obsessed with the danger from Japanese air power operating from the Marshall air bases that Nimitz had decided to bypass; he was certain that the Japanese air would blast his forces. In order to reduce those "inevitable losses," he demanded that the carriers suppress that threat before the amphibious forces arrived at Kwajalein, and as long thereafter as necessary.

The details of the disagreements between Spruance and Towers are unclear and must be inferred. What is certain is that the aviator admiral could not accept having a battleship admiral commanding his carriers. Neither could he accept having the carriers pinned down to direct support of the amphibious assaults. Towers had criticized Spruance's use of the carriers in the Gilberts, and Spruance intended to use them the same way in the Marshalls, restricted to well-defined roles in well-defined geographic areas. Towers, as with most aggressive air admirals, cherished the carriers' mobility. The carriers, in the aviators' minds, were the spearhead of the fleet, and they should range over the ocean destroying Japanese ships and bases. When Spruance "downgraded" the carriers to a supporting role, the carrier admirals predictably became resentful.

The prime objective—in the eyes of the aviators—was the "fleet engagement," and they cited Clausewitz and Mahan (out of context) in stating that the primary objective in war is the destruction of the enemy's army (or fleet). Destroy the enemy fleet, urged the aviators, and the war would be won. This doctrine had previously troubled Spruance. When planning for the Gilberts, Spruance was distracted by a memorandum written by Vice Admiral John S. McCain, an ardent aviator. The McCain memorandum, entitled "Proposal for Future Operations," advocated that the Pacific Fleet gather around the carriers and sally into enemy waters, remaining as long as necessary in order to force the Japanese fleet to come out and fight. Nimitz asked for Spruance's comment on the proposal.

Spruance replied that McCain's proposal amounted to a raid in force with major limitations: Japanese air forces were too strong and would inflict unacceptable losses, and the Pacific Fleet could not logistically support a large carrier task force operating for extended periods at great distances from Pearl Harbor. Furthermore, the Japanese would not oblige the Americans with a decisive fleet engagement unless the Japanese thought they could win.

Spruance's reply enunciated the basic philosophical disagreements between him and the aviators. Spruance believed that the Japanese would be defeated primarily through amphibious warfare. The aviators, on the other hand, wanted both to avoid the cost and drudgery of amphibious warfare and to defeat the enemy primarily through carrier air power alone. Spruance felt that the aviators were unrealistic, that they ignored vital considerations such as logistics, and that raids for the sake of raids were not valid military objectives and would not defeat Japan. Rather, for Spruance, the proper objective of carrier raids was to support amphibious operations.

These arguments resembled the Army debates within the European theater. The air power advocates held that strategic bombing would precipitate Germany's defeat. The ground forces, however, believed that infantry and armor would have to kill Germans and capture enemy territory before Germany would surrender, and Army ground generals wanted Air Force to provide close air support rather than diverting their efforts to long-range bombers.

In his arguments with the senior aviators, Spruance was motivated by another basic Spruance principle for waging amphibious warfare: *isolation of the objective area,* a corollary to his doctrine of "violent, overwhelming force, swiftly applied." This principle influenced his every decision and plan for the amphibious campaigns that he commanded from the Gilberts to Okinawa. "Isolation" implied not only sea and air superiority in the immediate area of the physical objective, but also secure lines of communication so that the amphibious forces could safely move to the objective. But even beyond that consideration, Spruance wanted secure lines of communication after his forces had seized the objective in order to ensure safe passage for the many ships that would bring supplies and men to develop the newly won base.

Spruance's anxiety about the hazards of Nimitz's plan was understandable. He had given much thought to the problem of isolating Kwajalein and had developed a carrier employment scheme that would give the amphibious forces a chance for survival. He inwardly seethed at Towers' obstructionism. "If you were not an admirer of Towers and did not play on his team," Spruance later wrote, "your path was not made smooth if he could help it. . . . Towers was a very ambitious man."

The original CINCPAC plan (undoubtedly influenced by Towers) scheduled the carriers to hit the Marshalls for two days, then to withdraw without returning until the amphibious assault began. Spruance objected, because he wanted continuous air cover to keep Kwajalein isolated. Determined to prevail, he told the aviators precisely what he wanted the carriers to do. At D-2 Day, 29 January, the carriers would strike the Japanese air bases at Wotje, Maloelap, Eniwetok, and Kwajalein. Hoover's land-based aircraft, operating out of the Gilberts, would suppress the enemy air forces at Mili and Jaluit. Immediately following the strikes, said Spruance, fast battleships from the carrier screen would peel off and bombard the airfields in order to prevent their reinforcement. One carrier task group would stand by Eniwetok to plug the aircraft corridor from the Carolines and Marianas.

Sensing Towers' hostility to this plan, Spruance made a mental note to check the carrier task groups' final operation orders in order to verify that the aviators intended to do precisely what he had ordered them to do.

Throughout these protracted and unpleasant arguments, Spruance was often tempted to lose his temper. Although he patiently listened to

Towers and the other aviators, and weighed what they said, Spruance's restraint belied his decisiveness. Once Spruance made his decision he rarely changed his mind. The aviators discovered that further arguments and entreaties then became futile and superfluous.

The decisions made, the staffs labored to develop the implementing plans. Spruance would lead a force considerably larger than he had commanded at the Gilberts. The Southern Attack Force, commanded by Turner, would seize Kwajalein Island, using 22,000 assault troops from the 7th Infantry Division. The division, veterans of the dismal Aleutians campaign, was well led and well trained. Their opposition would be about 1800 Japanese soldiers and Marines and about 2800 laborers and base support personnel.

The Northern Attack Force was commanded by Rear Admiral Richard L. Conolly, a veteran of amphibious landings in the Mediterranean. Roi-Namur Island would be his objective, to be seized by 21,000 Marines of the 4th Marine Division. The division was unblooded and needed more training before D-Day, but it ran out of time. Some 345 trained Japanese fighters would defend Roi-Namur, backed by 2100 Air Force personnel and a thousand miscellaneous "ineffectives."

Harry Hill would seize lightly defended Majuro, using an infantry battalion of 1600 men. In addition, he would command the floating reserve, a regiment each of Marines and infantry, totaling 9300 assault troops.

Mitscher's Task Force 58 was awesome: 6 heavy carriers, 6 light carriers, 8 fast battleships, 6 cruisers, 36 destroyers, and 700 carrier aircraft. Some 475 land-based Marine and Air Force aircraft, based largely in the Gilberts and commanded by Johnny Hoover, would supplement Mitscher's air power.

In broad figures, Spruance would command 375 ships, almost 85,000 troops, and over a thousand aircraft.

"Our work now is almost wound up," Spruance wrote Margaret on 9 January 1944. "I tried to get Carl to declare a holiday for himself and the staff, but he refused on the ground that there was too much pressure of work. In a few days I hope to be able to send a lot of my people over to the Damon house [a recreation facility] to get full of restful health. They are a fine hardworking crowd of men and all pull together like a good team."

A week later Spruance finally persuaded Moore to take a breather. "I took Carl out to the beach yesterday afternoon," Spruance wrote, "and he spent the night there to rest and relax. It is now noon and he is still away, so I hope he gets a bit of a change."

Spruance wanted Moore to be a rear admiral. Following the Gilberts campaign, Spruance wrote an official letter to Nimitz recommending that Moore be promoted. Nimitz agreed and forwarded the letter to the Chief of Naval Personnel, who pigeonholed the recommendation. Moore was embittered and correctly suspected that King would not approve his promotion to flag rank. Moore was too old, and captains who grounded their cruisers had no hope of promotion, regardless of recommendations by Nimitz and Spruance.

It was time to leave again for war. "My letters will be irregular from now on," Spruance wrote Margaret, "but keep on writing regularly yourself. Mail will reach me at intervals and it means a great deal to me to hear from you.

"This war is an interesting business," he said, "especially when things go off well. . . ."

Chapter 16

THE MARSHALLS

SHORTLY before Spruance got underway for the Marshalls campaign in late January 1944, he studied recent reconnaissance photographs of Eniwetok Atoll. The photographs revealed that the atoll was almost defenseless when compared to the Japanese fortifications on Tarawa. He also saw that the Japanese recently had reinforced Eniwetok with several thousand troops, who certainly would hasten to improve the atoll's fixed defenses.

Spruance told Nimitz that he wished the Fifth Fleet could immediately press on to Eniwetok after seizing Kwajalein, in order to attack the Japanese before they were dug in. But the JCS wanted the carriers to go south to assist Halsey in his contemplated assault against Kavieng, just north of Rabaul, in early April. They would not return until the tentative D-Day for Eniwetok, 1 May 1944. The Japanese would have two and a half months of grace to strengthen their Eniwetok defenses, at the expense of increased American casualties. Spruance left Pearl Harbor on 19 January 1944, assuming that the JCS would adhere to their plan to strip his carriers to support the Kavieng assault.

On 24 January *Indianapolis* anchored in Tarawa lagoon, and Spruance viewed the base construction progress with approval. "Our heavy earth-moving construction equipment certainly can do marvelous things in building airfields, roads, etc.," he wrote Margaret. "The Japs have to rely largely on hand labor, at which they are probably much better than we are. They can build a lot of things, such as dugouts, which require mostly hand labor, very well; but when it comes to roads and airfields they are entirely outclassed."

Then Spruance meditated on the destruction of war, expressing himself with the metaphor and euphemism that frequently characterized his writing. "If it were possible to start with a brand new island always," he wrote, "with no modern improvements, the going would be a lot easier than it is to take one that has been completely wrecked and then have to clean up the wreckage before you can start to rebuild. Sometimes, however, the corner lot in question has so much value that the disadvantages of wrecking the old building before you can start the new one have to be accepted. Sometimes you have to buy the old lot to get rid of undesirable neighbors."

The Betio airfield was operational, and Spruance watched Army bombers and fighters leave for strikes against Japanese airfields in the Marshalls, the first step in his plan to smother the Japanese land-based air before the landings on Kwajalein Atoll.

On the evening of 26 January, *Indianapolis* weighed anchor in order to rendezvous with the fast carrier group commanded by Rear Admiral Alfred E. Montgomery. Next morning the flagship joined the task group. Together they headed for Kwajalein.

Montgomery's task group was responsible for destroying Japanese air installations on Roi by carrier air attack, followed by a battleship bombardment to keep the airfield inoperable. To Moore's surprise, Spruance began reading Montgomery's operation order. Normally Spruance paid little attention to such details. But this time he was suspicious of the aviators. After the protracted arguments in Pearl Harbor, he sensed that they might try to deviate from what he wanted them to do.

His suspicions were confirmed. Montgomery had not provided for the battleship bombardment. Spruance was furious. His staff was shocked at the intensity of his anger. Grabbing paper and pencil, he wrote a bristling message to Montgomery. "It was my expressed desire that Roi be made inoperative by surface ship bombardment at the earliest possible time," wrote Spruance. Then he described in detail precisely what Montgomery's battleships were to do. Montgomery quickly complied.

On 29 January 1944, Task Force 58 swooped down upon the Marshall Islands. Its hundreds of carrier planes swarmed over the Japanese air bases and obliterated every vestige of Japanese air power. At day's end, not a single Japanese airplane survived. That evening the fast battleships glided in toward the airfields and lobbed one-and-a-half-ton projectiles that prevented the Japanese from repairing their runways and landing reinforcement aircraft. In less than a day, Spruance's forces had isolated Kwajalein Atoll and were masters of the surrounding sea and air. The air and surface bombardments continued through the thirtieth. The assault troops moved in for the kill, undisturbed by Japanese planes or ships.

On D-Day, 31 January, Spruance's ships and planes systematically demolished the remaining Japanese fortifications on Kwajalein and Roi-Namur islands. *Indianapolis* joined the Roi-Namur bombardment group and shared in the destruction of the island. Conolly's transports steamed into position for the major landings on 1 February.

That evening Hill reported he had seized Majuro Atoll without opposition. The lagoon anchorage had been surveyed and buoyed, and was ready to receive American ships. Anxious to use the anchorage at the earliest possible moment, Spruance immediately released messages directing repair and supply ships to head for Majuro.

Next morning Spruance watched the bombardment of Roi-Namur roar into a crescendo, the weight of steel and explosive far exceeding that at Tarawa. The island, shuddering with explosions, belched spectacular fires and towering columns of smoke. Offshore, however, Conolly's LVT's and landing craft were milling about in chaos, owing to the fatigue and inexperience of the drivers and coxswains. Realizing the futility of attempting to restore order, Conolly ordered everything afloat to head ashore, and the disorganized mass of small craft began to move. They hit the beach without opposition, and the Marines moved inland to grapple with the surviving Japanese defenders.

Spruance was particularly pleased that Conolly's resourcefulness had untangled the early-morning confusion. "Seeing this," he remarked to Barber, "proves that you can put complete faith in the men you have selected to do a job." Barber was impressed that Spruance had said nothing to Conolly when Conolly's landing force was in hopeless disarray. "If there ever was a person who was the paragon of coolness," he wrote his parents, "it is Admiral Spruance. When our big day comes— if ever—the Admiral will do a superb job, not because he has a great capacity for hard work and detail (as is said of Napoleon), but because he cannot be flustered or excited, and trusts his subordinates to handle *all* detail."

After the war, Spruance expanded upon this philosophy of command. "Things move so fast in naval actions, and the consequences that hang on the results of these actions are often so momentous, that fast teamwork is essential," he said. "Teamwork is something that comes best from association, training, and indoctrination. There are too many variables possible in war for everything to be foreseen and planned for ahead of time. Our plans can be made out in great detail up to the time we hit the enemy. After that, they have to be flexible, ready to counter what the enemy may try to do to us and ready to take advantage of the breaks that may come to us. To do that the man on the spot must know where he fits into the operation, and he must be able to act on his own initiative, either without any orders at all, because radio silence may be in effect, or on very brief orders because there is no time for long instructions."

As the day progressed, the reports from ashore indicated that the Marines were winning and rapidly advancing. The island became a killing ground. Spruance and the staff watched from grandstand seats aboard *Indianapolis,* slowly cruising no more than a few thousand yards from the battle arena where men fought savagely in dirt and filth. At lunch time aboard *Indianapolis,* the staff retired to the flag mess and ate from china and linen, the food hot and the water cold, while the sound of gunfire and hand grenades drifted in through the open doors and portholes.

Within twenty-four hours the Marines had seized Roi-Namur, and Kelly Turner reported that the 7th Army Division was slowly winning Kwajalein Island, forty-five miles to the south. The estimated American casualties on Roi-Namur were light, about a hundred killed compared to the thousand dead at Tarawa. The only major damage to the fleet was a serious collision at night between the battleships *Washington* and *Indiana.* Spruance sent them to Majuro for a safe haven and temporary repairs. Moore's wisdom in advocating Majuro as a fleet anchorage was quickly becoming evident.

The Roi-Namur assault attracted visitors, including James V. Forrestal, the Under Secretary of the Navy. Spruance called on Forrestal and then went ashore. Roi-Namur had once been a bustling base and airdrome, a rear area rather than a front-line fortress. The three-day bombardment had razed the island, creating the popular phrase, the "Spruance haircut." The bombardment's ferocity and duration had eradicated fortifications and killed or stunned most of the defenders. Mutilated Japanese bodies, strewn everywhere, were casually ignored by the conquering Americans, who regarded the hideous corpses as inanimate battle debris. Marine burial details, equipped with what appeared to be large hay rakes, dragged the putrid bodies into bomb craters, later to be covered by bulldozers.

"Dead Japs were very plentiful," Spruance wrote Margaret, "but not so ripe as at Betio, or else I am getting used to the flavor, although I still cannot say that I enjoy it."

By 2 February, the rapid progress on Kwajalein Atoll convinced the American high commanders that Hill's floating reserve of 9300 assault troops would not be needed. Suddenly everyone—King, Nimitz, Spruance, Turner, and Smith—conceived the idea of pressing on to Eniwetok at the earliest moment and seizing it with the uncommitted reserve. A flurry of messages passed between Washington, Pearl Harbor, and Kwajalein. The upshot was that by the third of February the JCS had approved an assault against Eniwetok in late February, as well as a covering strike against Truk. Spruance would be allowed to keep his carriers to support the Eniwetok landings, a cause for great satisfaction after his earlier pessimism about the entire Marshalls operation.

On the morning of 3 February, *Indianapolis* weighed anchor off Roi-Namur, steamed south to Kwajalein Island, and reanchored. Spruance had another grandstand seat for the fighting ashore, this time performed by the troops of the 7th Infantry Division. In accordance with Army doctrine, the soldiers were moving forward slowly and deliberately behind heavy artillery preparation. The contrast between the Marine and the Army styles of fighting again was apparent. Although the 7th Division fought well, it required four days to seize Kwajalein Island, while the Marines had seized Roi-Namur in one day.

Each service believed that its way of fighting would best reduce casualties. The results at Kwajalein Atoll were inconclusive. Both forces suffered approximately equal casualties—less than 200 dead each—although the Army had twice the number of wounded, 1,037 to the Marines' 545. Both divisions landed about the same number of assault troops (more than 20,000 each), although the Army faced about

5,000 defenders compared to the 3500 that opposed the Marines on Roi-Namur.

The light American casualties (for which everyone was truly thankful after Tarawa) can be attributed to a number of factors: American know-how from lessons learned at the Gilberts; air and sea supremacy; a high ratio of assault troops to defenders; and bad Japanese tactics—both the Japanese defenders and the fortifications were inferior to those at Tarawa.

On 5 February Nimitz and a company of VIP sightseers arrived at Kwajalein to view the spoils. Their mutual delight in the swift, cheap victory was euphoric, and all the services praised each other for selfless cooperation and splendid teamwork. For a few brief moments, rivalries and disputes were forgotten on the field of victory at Kwajalein. Total harmony prevailed for the first and last time in the Central Pacific amphibious campaigns.

"So far, everything has gone off according to schedule," Spruance wrote Margaret, "and I hope our good fortune continues. It is a pleasure to plan and pull off one of these operations when everything goes the way you want it to and everybody pulls together. We have a fine team working now. . . ."

The staffs worked feverishly to generate plans for the Eniwetok assault, while Spruance conferred with Nimitz, Turner, Smith, and others. They agreed that D-Day for Eniwetok would be 17 February, code name CATCHPOLE. In order to prevent any interference by the Japanese air force or fleet, Task Force 58 simultaneously would raid the major Japanese naval base at Truk 660 miles southwest of Eniwetok. Everyone was eager and anxious to press on and seize Eniwetok before the newly arrived Japanese reinforcements could get dug in.

The war councils adjourned, and on 8 February *Indianapolis* entered Majuro lagoon. The sight of the assembled power of the Fifth Fleet was breathtaking. The lagoon, twenty-four miles long and five miles wide, was filled with ships from end to end. The might of the Fleet—the carriers, battleships, and cruisers—shared the vast anchorage with destroyers, amphibians, repair and supply ships, and sturdy tugs moving lighters to and fro. The combatant ships gulped oil and swung aboard pallets of ammunition and stores as they girded for the assault against Truk and Eniwetok. A week earlier the lagoon had been empty; now it was a huge, pulsating naval base, protected from both submarines and heavy waves by the encircling coral reef.

The brute strength of the Fifth Fleet finally could be appreciated. Heretofore Spruance's ships had been scattered over the ocean. Now they were together, and they were awesome. Spruance, seeing his massive fleet stretching to the horizon, was moved to share his thoughts with Barber. "What we are now trying to do," he confided, "is to convince the Japanese that they cannot win the war. Our fleet has devastated the enemy and will do it again and again. And soon the Japanese will come to believe they are hopelessly inferior."

Spruance visited ashore and relished the beauty of Majuro's islands. The Japanese had left them undefended, and the Americans had seized them without destruction. Spruance walked through a lovely park beneath towering (and unshattered) palm trees. The Seabees intended to build an airstrip on Majuro Island, but the civil affairs officer was opposed. The native population lived at the proposed airfield site, the highest and most habitable area on the atoll, and they would have to be dispossessed. Unwilling to disturb the tranquil island or to intrude upon the natives' privacy, Spruance agreed and canceled the airfield plans.

Spruance later visited the natives, who by his orders were untouched by war and were living in isolation from the naval installations on the adjacent islands. A Navy boat took him within several hundred yards of the beach, whereupon the natives took him ashore in an outrigger canoe. The "king" of the atoll, a barefooted dignified elder wearing a clean starched white suit, greeted Spruance. The natives were agreeable hosts, and he explored the village and the island as a happy and inquisitive tourist.

On 10 February Spruance received a message that he had been promoted from vice admiral to admiral. Inwardly pleased, but outwardly embarrassed with the effusive congratulations from his shipmates, he wrote Margaret, "Getting this rank was something that was beyond my utmost expectations." Spruance had become the sixth ranking officer in the naval service, and at age fifty-seven the youngest naval officer ever to become a full admiral.[1] "Four stars!" wrote Chuck Barber

1. But Spruance was considerably older than the Army four-star generals who were promoted a year later at the average age of fifty-four. Eisenhower was fifty-three when he became a full general in February 1943.

to his sister. "That makes him a very big man in the world today. . . . Our star is still rising, may the sky be clear." Spruance had been a vice admiral for less than nine months.

Kelly Turner was simultaneously promoted to vice admiral, but Carl Moore remained a captain. A four-star admiral rated a rear admiral as chief of staff, so Moore could expect either to have a later promotion or to be relieved by a rear admiral. The latter alternative was the most probable.

The day before Spruance received the promotion news, he and the staff shifted from the *Indianapolis* to the new battleship *New Jersey*.[2] The huge man-o'-war seemed a fitting flagship in view of Spruance's promotion. He was the only full admiral flying his flag at sea. Her spacious, luxurious accommodations were a welcomed change from the hot, cramped old cruiser flagship.

That same day Spruance issued his operation order for CATCHPOLE and the Truk raid. Hill would seize Eniwetok Atoll with one regiment each of Marines and infantry, supported by one fast carrier task group. The other three carrier task groups, collectively Mitscher's Task Force 58, would raid Truk.

The Truk raid was essential to success at Eniwetok. Truk was regarded by most American naval officers as one of Japan's most powerful

2. USS *New Jersey* (BB 62), displacement 45,000 tons, main battery nine 16-inch guns, commissioned 23 May 1943. Serving temporarily as Fifth Fleet flagship was only the first of many illustrious combat assignments for this superb *Iowa*-class fast battleship. She earned nine battle stars for World War II and served mainly as close escort for fast carrier task forces. She was decommissioned on 30 June 1948, but recommissioned on 21 November 1950 for the Korean Conflict, where she added four more battle stars to her tally. The second decommissioning came on 21 August 1957, and she was placed in the "mothball fleet." On 6 April 1968, the *New Jersey* was again brought into service for fire-support missions off Vietnam as the world's only operating battleship. She was again decommissioned on 17 December 1969. By the early 1980s it appeared that the fast battleship could again play an important naval role, being well protected by armor and a large platform for sophisticated new weapons. The *New Jersey* was recommissioned on 28 December 1982. In the fall of 1983 she was despatched to the Mediterranean, where in December she conducted shore bombardments against hostile positions in Lebanon. As of this date she remains on active duty, joined by her sister *Iowa*-class battleships, *Iowa* and *Missouri,* and the soon-to-be-recommissioned *Wisconsin*. DANAFS, volume 5 (Washington, 1970), pp. 432-36; personal communications from the Naval Historical Center. A very recent book on the *New Jersey* is Paul Stillwell's *Battleship New Jersey* (Annapolis, 1987).

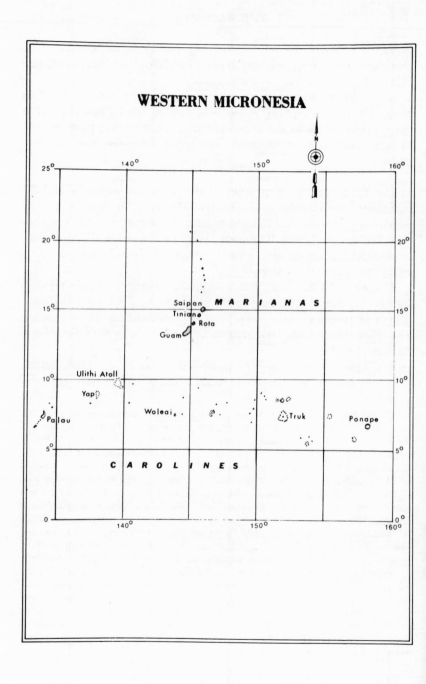

bases. In early February 1944, South Pacific search planes had sighted many Japanese combatant ships in Truk anchorages, and the Truk airfields certainly would contain several hundred aircraft. Those ships and planes, so close to Eniwetok, were a menace to Hill's amphibious assault forces.

As if to accentuate the threat from Truk, the Japanese demonstrated the vulnerability of American amphibious forces to air attack. In the darkness of early morning on 12 February, a half-dozen Japanese sea-planes from Saipan via Ponape bombed the Marine supply dump at Roi and the nearby landing ships unloading at the beach. Their accuracy was perfect. Twenty-five Marines were killed, 130 were wounded, and several ships were lost. Over 80 percent of the Marines' supplies were destroyed in a stupendous conflagration, and the garrison had to live on emergency rations for two weeks until fresh supplies were landed. The successful Japanese air raid was an impetus to protect the Eniwetok amphibious assault forces from similar attacks.[3]

Spruance had shifted his flag to the battleship because he hoped to catch a large number of Japanese ships in the Truk lagoon anchorages. Once Mitscher's carrier planes began their attack, the Japanese war-ships would flee for open water, and Spruance wanted to be there to greet them. The *New Jersey,* with her 32-knot speed and 16-inch guns, would be in the thick of action, and Spruance wanted to be where the action was.

Spruance in his new flagship got underway from Majuro and rendez-voused with Task Force 58 on 14 February. The ships refueled from fleet oilers and shaped course for Truk. Spruance assumed tactical command, a departure from his normal practice of allowing the next senior admiral (in this case Mitscher) to act as OTC. The staff thus became unexpectedly busy in controlling the movements of the three carrier task groups, comprising 9 carriers, 7 battleships, 10 cruisers, and 28 destroyers.

The task force steamed on, apparently undetected, with Spruance maintaining firm control of the course, speed, and cruising disposition. On the fifteenth Spruance broadcast his intentions for the next day's strike: the force would close Truk from the northeast to 60 miles, then at 0630 would change course to east-northeast (the direction of the esti-

---

3. Spruance and Moore began using a curious phrase about this time, "if we can get away with it," when talking about future operations. Perhaps they recognized how much their plans depended on luck. This phrase continued throughout the war.

mated wind) and increase speed to 20 knots. Not until then would he allow Mitscher to act as OTC and to begin launching the air attack. Spruance had usurped Mitscher's prerogatives by issuing such detailed instructions, normally the province of the carrier task force commander.

Spruance's action was contrary to his recent reaffirmation of the wisdom of trusting his subordinates. Why, then, his iron grip on the carriers for the approach on Truk? His reasons must be inferred. The Truk raid was extremely dangerous. If Task Force 58 made one bad move, the alerted Truk air and sea forces could hit Spruance before he hit them. He knew that he might be forced rapidly to modify his plans. If quick decisions were needed, he did not want to take the time to discuss alternatives with Mitscher by message. One suspects, also, that Spruance was not entirely confident that the carrier admiral could execute the raid without making a potentially fatal error in judgment.

Spruance had Baldy Pownall aboard as his trusted aviation advisor, and he could rely upon Pownall to help devise the aviation tactics. Spruance later wrote Margaret that Pownall "has been of great assistance. He is a splendid officer, an excellent shipmate and a very fine character. He is going to relieve Towers, which pleases many persons." (Towers became Deputy CINCPAC, ostensibly to handle logistics, and Pownall relieved Towers as Commander Naval Air Forces, Pacific. Pownall's new job was almost entirely administrative, and it was more a sop than a promotion. It is unclear who the persons were that Spruance felt would be pleased.)

Another possible reason for Spruance's tight control of the carriers was that he believed that MacArthur had rashly jeopardized the entire Truk strike. Just before issuing his strike plan on the fifteenth, Spruance received a copy of the radio press news, announcing that MacArthur's forces had just landed on Green Island in the Solomons, a hundred and twenty miles away from the main Japanese airbase at Rabaul. He flared with anger and began damning MacArthur with a cold fury. Knowing that MacArthur's forces lacked naval support, Spruance was certain that the Japanese would violently react to an American landing so close to Rabaul. If the Japanese air and naval forces attacked MacArthur at Green Island, Spruance reasoned, Task Force 58 would have to go to the rescue, cancelling the Truk strike and jeopardizing the Eniwetok assault.

Spruance's concern, however, was shared by neither the JCS, MacArthur, Nimitz, nor Halsey (who had conceived and who commanded the Green Island assault). All had approved the plan. Green Island was a pushover, so much so that no one thought Spruance needed to be forewarned about it. Thus when Spruance learned about the landings on the fifteenth, he was surprised and suspicious. More than ever, he distrusted MacArthur as a selfish opportunist.

On the morning of the sixteenth, the carriers turned into the wind and began launching. Their aircraft arrived over Truk about 0800, and their first reports indicated that they had surprised the enemy and that targets were plentiful. At midmorning the planes reported that several Japanese ships had escaped from the lagoon and were fleeing seaward. That was the news Spruance had been waiting for. He decided to head them off at the pass.

Spruance formed a task group of the battleships *New Jersey* and *Iowa,* cruisers *Minneapolis* and *New Orleans,* and four destroyers, then announced they would circle Truk in order to locate and destroy any escaping enemy ships. Mitscher was to continue the carrier strikes; Spruance would rejoin him in the morning. Spruance assumed tactical command and formed the four heavies into a column with the destroyers screening ahead. His task group proceeded on a leisurely westerly course, passing north of Truk. In the early afternoon a Japanese plane appeared and dropped a bomb close aboard *Iowa,* and Moore began to worry about enemy air attacks. He urged Spruance to change the formation from a column into a circle, in order to provide better AA protection. The admiral indignantly rejected Moore's recommendation. "We're not out here fighting aircraft," he snapped. "We're out here fighting surface vessels. I want to remain in column." Realizing the futility of arguing with Spruance once he had made up his mind, Moore said no more.

By midafternoon the task group was a dozen miles north of the northern entrance to the Truk lagoon, allowing the Americans a splendid view of the dark green cone-shaped islands that were the tops of a submerged mountain range. The islands rose to 1500 feet, a contrast to the Gilbert and Marshall islands, which were not more than 20 feet above sea level.

Moore began to suspect that Spruance's motive for his independent expedition was sightseeing rather than ship hunting. Truk always had been a source of fascination to American naval officers because of its strategic importance, and many considered it an impregnable fortress. The chief of staff surmised that Spruance was merely satisfying his curiosity about the mystical Japanese base that he had studied intently for years but never had seen. What other reason, thought Moore, would Spruance have for being here? Certainly a powerful force of two battleships and two cruisers was unnecessary. Mitscher's planes could have handled any Japanese ships in the area.

Spruances's motives that day *did* seem obscure, a departure from his pragmatic, no-nonsense way of making war. In retrospect, his intention, whether deliberate or not, may have been to assert the symbolic ascendency of American naval power over Japan. A few days earlier Spruance had said that one of his immediate objectives was to convince the Japanese that they were militarily inferior and that their cause was hopeless. What more striking display of American naval superiority than his battleships and cruisers steaming with impunity before the once-mighty but now-impotent Truk naval fortress? "I doubt if their morale was raised any by the operation," wrote Spruance to his wife.

And what greater satisfaction for Spruance, the senior admiral afloat, than flying his flag aboard America's most powerful battleship while personally commanding the force that represented American naval supremacy over the weakened Japanese navy? The impact of his display of power can be appreciated if one considers the equivalent if the roles were reversed. If after the Japanese attack on Pearl Harbor two years before, Admiral Yamamoto in his battleship *Yamato* had cruised off the entrance to Pearl Harbor flaunting his strength and defying the Americans to fight—that would have been the equivalent to Spruance's action off Truk on 16 February 1944.

Was Spruance thereby avenging the attack on Pearl Harbor? The explanation is tantalizing.

Shortly after 1500, the Americans sighted smoke over the horizon, and two crippled, burning Japanese ships hove into view, under attack from American carrier planes. Interposed between was a Japanese patrol craft. The slaughter began. The van destroyers fired upon the patrol craft as they passed by, hitting the vessel and causing it to stop and burn. The destroyers pressed on and began shooting at the two larger ships, a cruiser and a destroyer. Although the Japanese were dead in the water, their guns continued to fire, and they were as dangerous as cornered, wounded tigers.

Spruance's staff began to flounder. They were accustomed to making more unhurried strategical decisions that were implemented by subordinate commanders, and they were without experience in a fast-moving close-in slugging match with enemy ships. Moore and the staff had not exercised the quick reflexes that were needed at that moment, and they were surprised that Spruance did not pass tactical command to either Rear Admiral Olaf M. Hustvedt in *Iowa* or Rear Admiral Robert C. Giffen in *Minneapolis,* whose staffs were accustomed to handling ships in a fluid tactical situation. But Spruance retained tactical command. Moore did the best he could, suggesting to Spruance that Giffen and the cruisers engage the two Japanese ships. Spruance decided that the cruisers would take the enemy cruiser, and the battleships the destroyer. As the task group closed the two Japanese warships, the *New Jersey* passed close aboard the crippled patrol craft and ripped a point-blank broadside of ten 5-inch guns into the unfortunate vessel, which disintegrated in a spectacular explosion.

The range had continued to close when Moore noticed two flashes in quick succession from the enemy destroyer's deck; he did not attach any significance to what he had seen until a salvo of torpedoes straddled *New Jersey.* Moore was mortified—he suddenly realized that the flashes had been impulse charges launching the torpedoes against the *New Jersey.* Had he been alert, he would immediately have maneuvered the ships to evade the torpedoes, but instead Moore had allowed the task group to blunder into the torpedoes' path. It had been a near thing, and the torpedoes had missed the battleships through luck alone.

Spruance was undisturbed and unconcerned. With eyes twinkling, he commented that had the torpedoes hit, "that would have been embarrassing." Moore was furious at both Spruance and himself. "We have no business being in tactical command," said Moore, and he demanded that Spruance allow Giffen to take control. Spruance was unmoved and retained control of the force.

Spruance's determination to retain tactical command, despite his disarrayed staff, never has been explained. Without question he was unnecessarily hazarding his ships, apparently on a whim. Perhaps it was the culmination of a dream to lead a battleship division into a fleet action. He loved battleships, and for more than three decades Spruance had prepared himself to lead them into war. But once war began, he realized that a fleet action with thundering battle lines was a remote possibility; the Truk raid might be his last chance to fight a surface action with the Japanese fleet. Possibly, then, he hoped to command and maneuver a battle line at least once, with the two newest and mightiest battleships in the Pacific Fleet, in order to satisfy a lifelong ambition. If so, the ambition was not truly fulfilled. "The Truk party went off as well as could be expected under the circumstances," Spruance later wrote Margaret, "but unfortunately the Japs had not left any of the valuable naval units in Truk which we had hoped to find there and sink—only small fry and merchant ships."

Spruance's warships closed in for the kill, and the Japanese cruiser and destroyer perished beneath a storm of fire and steel, their guns courageously firing to the last. Their sinking was acutely distressing to both Spruance and Moore. The two naval officers had witnessed every possible form of destruction on land, sea, and air, and Moore had rationalized dead Japanese soldiers as justifiable vindication for the Pearl Harbor attack. But both agreed that "sinking ships in war at sea is the hardest thing to take." Their feelings may appear callous, for it is hard for the layman to understand how the death of an inanimate ship could apparently invoke more pity than the deaths of American and Japanese warriors. Perhaps the reason is that Spruance and Moore had devoted their lives to ships and the sea. To them, a ship was a viable entity, possessing both beauty and dignity, which seagoing men sought to protect and preserve. The destruction of a ship therefore offended their most deeply ingrained sensibilities, however misdirected their feelings may appear in retrospect.

An American plane reported that a Japanese destroyer was escaping over the horizon. Spruance ordered *New Jersey* and *Iowa* to fire, using the aircraft's spotting, and the two battleships surged forward at more than 30 knots. *New Jersey*'s huge 16-inch rifles fired dead ahead, and the great ship bucked with each recoil, as if she had collided with an invisible wall. The massive projectiles arched in a 16-mile trajectory, but the unseen destroyer dodged the salvos and opened the range, so Spruance ordered cease-fire.

Sensing that no more Japanese ships would appear, Spruance repositioned the four heavies into a circular formation. The fighting was nearly over. In the late afternoon, *Iowa* mistakenly shot down an American aircraft that had glided toward the formation, and the plane's crew perished. Toward evening the force discovered another small Japanese patrol craft. Spruance ordered that it be sunk and prisoners taken. A destroyer promptly dispatched the patrol craft, but it had trouble seizing prisoners. The survivors dived under water and fought like fury when the destroyer's boat crew tried to bring them aboard, another stark reminder that Japanese soldiers and sailors would fight to the death rather than surrender, even when treading water under the guns of two battleships. Six Japanese ultimately were delivered to Gilven M. Slonim, the Japanese language officer, for interrogation.

In the early evening, Spruance finally passed tactical command to Giffen with instructions to continue circling Truk counterclockwise. Next morning Spruance rendezvoused with Mitscher and the carriers. The carriers continued strikes throughout the morning of the seventeenth, except for the carrier *Intrepid,* which had been hit during the night by Japanese torpedo planes and was limping back to Majuro.

The Japanese had exploited an American weakness: American carrier planes could not fly at night. But Japanese planes effectively could and did. Fearing another night torpedo plane attack, Mitscher wanted to open the range from Truk before nightfall. Spruance concurred, and at noon he and Mitscher decided it was time to go home. Mitscher's carrier planes had destroyed an estimated 200 planes and had sunk or damaged almost 40 ships, surprised at anchor in the Truk lagoon. Only 17 American planes had been lost in two days.

The force withdrew, rendezvoused with oilers, and refueled. Spruance planned next to strike Ponape, a Japanese seaplane staging base 360 miles east of Truk. That scheme changed when Nimitz suggested by message that the task force raid the Japanese airfields in the Marianas before returning to the Marshalls. Spruance and Mitscher by flashing light discussed the raid's feasibility. The Marianas were 600 miles northwest of Truk. a thousand miles west of Eniwetok, and 1250 miles from Tokyo. They never before had been raided, and they would be defended by hundreds of Japanese aircraft.

The two admirals decided in favor of the raid. Spruance must have been favorably impressed with Mitscher's handling of the carriers during the Truk air strikes, because he decided to allow Mitscher to go it alone against the Marianas. Moore certainly was impressed. "I have profound respect for these aviators," he wrote, "from the vice admirals down to the ensigns who fly the planes. They know their stuff and they do their stuff, fearlessly and quickly and without equivocation. . . . There is no doubt about it, the Jap aviators are overwhelmed by them."

Refueling completed, Mitscher and the carriers headed west. Spruance in *New Jersey,* with a one-destroyer escort, steamed eastward for Kwajalein.

On the long return trip, Spruance had no pressing duties and was

isolated from both the assault on Eniwetok and the impending raid on
the Marianas. He had been under tension for many weeks and had
reacted toward Moore (but not the staff) by being grouchy and "sometimes quite disagreeable. He was a queer egg in many ways, there's no
doubt about it," Moore recalled. "And you had to adjust yourself to his
peculiarities. Our very close relationship and mutual affection and
understanding put me in a position where I could cope with these
peculiarities of his. And he could put up with my peculiarities and
disagreeable features too."

Spruance wanted and needed sleep, and he sought his bed in the
early evening, assuming that nothing could happen to *New Jersey* to
disturb his sleep.

Late one night as Spruance slept, Moore was called by a staff watch
officer who was bothered by a bogey, detected on the radar screen, that
seemed to be trailing the flagship. It could have been a Japanese
torpedo plane, the kind that had damaged the *Intrepid* a few nights
before. The contact would not go away, as if it were stalking the
battleship. Against his better judgment (knowing that Spruance's sleep
was sacrosanct), Moore decided to inform Spruance about the worri-
some bogey.

Moore entered Spruance's pitch-black bedroom, wakened him, and
reported they were being shadowed.

"Well," snapped Spruance from the darkness, "is there anything I
can do about it?"

"No," replied Moore.

"Then why wake me up?" Spruance growled. "You know I don't like
to be wakened in the middle of the night." He rolled over and went
back to sleep.

In the early afternoon of 19 February, *New Jersey* entered Kwajalein
lagoon and anchored. From all reports, Hill's assault on Eniwetok was
proceeding on schedule, but Spruance apparently had no desire to
watch the battle. For the next several days he visited with Turner,
Hoover, and visitors from Pearl Harbor, and read a backlog of personal
mail.

Meanwhile he waited for a report from Mitscher on his Marianas
raid, scheduled for 22 February. The night before the strike, he received a message from Mitscher: "We have been sighted by the enemy.

We will fight our way in." Surprise was lost, and Mitscher surely would be attacked by aroused swarms of Japanese land-based airplanes. Moore asked Spruance if he wanted to cancel the raid owing to the increased hazard to Mitscher's carriers.

Spruance was indignant. "No," he said.

The subject was dropped, and Moore had suffered yet another brusque rebuff from Spruance. Yet Moore was not discouraged, because he felt Spruance wanted and appreciated his suggestions, despite Spruance's often curt dismissals. "I never let that bother me very much," said Moore. "If I had something to say to him, I said it." But once Spruance had made up his mind, he was decisive. "He knew what he was going to do," said Moore, "and there was no fooling."

Mitscher later reported that his attack was successful despite heavy enemy air opposition. He estimated he had destroyed over 100 Japanese aircraft, had sunk or damaged a dozen noncombatant ships, and had strafed and bombed installations ashore. None of Mitscher's ships had been hurt, and he had lost only six aircraft.

The raid over, Spruance and Moore waited for Mitscher and Task Force 58 to return to Kwajalein. "What a time I have with Raymond," Moore wrote home. "I wrote a complimentary dispatch to Mitscher and gave it to Raymond to release, about an hour after dinner tonight. He read it, put it in his pocket, and went to bed. Not a word spoken." Moore never could accept that Spruance would not make decisions in the evening that could be postponed until morning.

"Tomorrow the heroes [Task Force 58] will arrive," wrote Moore, "and they will be in a state of mind, as there is no food for them. . . . I never seem to get caught up. These post-campaign times are worse than the pre-campaign times in many ways. The forces have to be reorganized and some ships sent home and others to other places. They all need fuel and food and repairs and ammunition and bombs, and it's a general mess. Just as we think it all out and get things moving, CINCPAC comes along and wants it done some other way. That is what drives me wild."

Subordinate commanders streamed to the flagship, "all wanting to do something different than what they had been told to do, or me telling them to do something else than what I had told them to do 24 hours ago. I bear the brunt of the whole thing," Moore concluded, "as Raymond refuses to be bothered with administrative details, and chats along in a social way while I am trying to get business done. Biggs and

Forrestel, though, are towers of strength to me, and all are working well and hard."

Harry Hill reported by letter from Eniwetok. "I think you might be interested in hearing some of the details of our little show here," he wrote. "We really ran into quite a hornet's nest and had to shuffle and reshuffle our plans several times before the job was finished. However, in a couple of months more it really would have been a tough place to take, and there is no question about the soundness of your decision to move in when you did. You have done a wonderful job at Truk and Saipan-Tinian. We never even saw a Jap plane during the 17 days of the Eniwetok assault."

By the end of February, the Marshalls were secured. The campaign had been a triumph for the United States.

It was a strategic victory. The United States now possessed air and naval bases in the Marshalls that could be used to stage amphibious assaults against either the Caroline Islands or the Mariana Islands, the next logical offensives in the Central Pacific. With the war slightly more than two years old, the United States had seized the offensive initiative, and Japan now would be forever on the defensive. American industrial might was providing an ever-increasing abundance of ships, planes, and weapons that the Japanese could never match.

It was a tactical victory. The Pacific Fleet had largely perfected the equipment and the techniques for both amphibious and carrier warfare. The expensive lessons of Tarawa had been recognized and successfully applied in the Marshalls. The amphibious naval commanders—Turner, Hill, and Conolly—had proven themselves. And Mitscher had proved that he was a shrewd, aggressive, and competent leader of Task Force 58, who could exploit the full potential of the carriers' power and mobility.

It was a moral victory. The heavy casualties at Tarawa had damaged public confidence in naval strategy and tactics. In seizing Betio Island alone, just one small island, 1000 marines had been killed. By contrast the total American deaths in seizing the entire Marshall Island archipelago were less than 600. Over 12,000 Japanese had died defending the islands. American morale soared at such a swift victory with so few losses. The Marshalls restored public confidence in the ability of the Pacific Fleet to defeat the Japanese. On the other hand, the Japanese morale was severely eroded. The overwhelming American naval power, and its aggressive use by King, Nimitz, Spruance, Turner, and Mitscher, presaged an ultimate Japanese defeat. If American carriers could so successfully raid Truk and the Marianas in early 1944, then those bastions of Japan's outer defensive perimeter were doomed, and so was Japan.

It was a personal victory for Nimitz. He had decided to seize Kwajalein Atoll despite the protests and against the judgment of Spruance, Turner, and Smith. Nimitz had been right and they had been wrong. As Nimitz had suspected, Kwajalein was ill-prepared for self-defense, and its quick, cheap seizure allowed the subsequent early seizure of Eniwetok and the carrier raids on Truk and the Marianas. Kwajalein had been the key to the stunning American victory.

And finally, it was a personal victory for Spruance. King and Nimitz made the strategic decisions, but Spruance had to make their decisions look good. Despite his grave personal reservations about Nimitz's Kwajalein decision, Spruance was determined to make it work and focused his attention on the broad concept of operations, particularly the isolation of the objective area through gaining air and naval superiority before D-Day. After the campaign began, it expanded into an operating area of over two million square miles. Spruance and his staff had to coordinate and control hundreds of ships and planes and more than 100 thousand men, fighting separate actions hundreds of miles apart within that vast ocean battlefield. Spruance succeeded because he elevated his mind above the details in order to maintain a broad perspective of his forces and the enemy as a whole.

Spruance had a good plan, and he trusted his subordinate commanders and his staff to carry out that plan. And they did. When major decisions or general directives had been needed, Spruance provided them. Otherwise Spruance had silently watched his plans unfold.

When Spruance returned to Kwajalein in late February, following the Truk strike, he was still a vice admiral, because he needed a physical examination for promotion. He wouldn't spare the time before then. "The day before yesterday," he wrote Margaret on 23 February, "I found time to have my physical examination for promotion, and, when it was successfully over, I put on my four stars. I told the doctor that this was the last time I would ever have to bother the Medical Corps for an examination for promotion."

The quartermaster of the watch hoisted a blue flag with four white stars to the *New Jersey* foretruck.

February 1944 had been a very good month for Raymond Spruance.

Chapter 17

MARIANAS PRELIMINARIES

THE unexpectedly swift conquest of the Marshalls in February 1944 left Allied planners without definitive plans for the next move against Japan. MacArthur, as usual, deprecated the Central Pacific strategy and advocated an advance along the north coast of New Guinea into the Philippines, followed by the eventual invasion of Japan, with MacArthur in command. His rival Nimitz, by contrast, wanted to seize Truk in the Caroline Islands. For decades it had symbolized Japanese naval power in the mid-Pacific, and naval officers at the Naval War College had captured Truk during innumerable Orange-Blue war games. It was common knowledge among the high command that one of Nimitz's great personal ambitions was to fly his flag over the Japanese naval base.

As before, the CCS and the JCS had to adjudicate the ultimate Pacific strategy and the specific objectives for the remainder of the war. The members of those august bodies had been debating that very issue for many months.

King had always regarded the Mariana Islands as the key to conquering the Western Pacific. The Marianas intersected Japanese lines of communication between the home islands and the Japanese bases in the Caroline Islands and Bismarck Archipelago, and they protected the eastern flank of the Japanese economic lifelines to the Philippines and

Southeast Asia. In American hands, King argued, the Marianas could provide bases for further westward advances (probably through Formosa), eventual landings on the China coast, and the ultimate blockade and economic strangulation of Japan.

Marshall, however, was not receptive to King's views, and the resolution of long-range Pacific strategy was stalemated. Then in late 1943, General H. H. Arnold, the Army Air Force Chief of Staff, became a King ally. The Air Force had developed the long-range B-29 bomber and was anxious to use it against Japanese cities and war industries. Arnold believed that the Marianas would provide ideal airfields and was more than willing to allow King's Navy and Marine Corps to capture the islands for that purpose. Therefore, King and Arnold sought the same physical objective, although for entirely different reasons.

The King-Arnold alliance provided the impetus needed to break the impasse on strategic planning in the Pacific. At the Cairo Conference in December 1943, the CCS authorized the seizure of the Marianas in October 1944. The CCS also reaffirmed that Nimitz would advance in the Central Pacific simultaneously with a MacArthur advance in the Southwest Pacific.

Spruance did not express a preference for the next step to follow the Marshalls conquest. It was a contrast to his earlier explicit recommendations for the objectives in the Gilberts and Marshalls. He seemed content to wait for word from the JCS about the future course of the Pacific war. That word came in February 1944 from Nimitz: the JCS had authorized the seizure of Truk in the summer of 1944, followed by the Marianas in the fall. When he received this news, Spruance did not discuss it with Moore and did not indicate whether or not he agreed with the JCS decision.

Moore, however, contested the entire concept of seizing either Truk or the Marianas. On the return to Kwajalein following the mid-February Truk raid, Moore drafted a lengthy memorandum to Spruance that expressed his reasoning. The chief of staff urged that Truk be bypassed; an amphibious assault would be too costly and Truk now was without strategic value to either Japan or the United States. Nor was it a threat to the Americans; the Japanese apparently no longer intended to use it as a naval base and Task Force 58 had proven its vulnerability as an air base. Yet Truk still was heavily defended with troops and guns, many Americans would have to die seizing it, and it would have little strategic value to the Americans after they had captured it. Furthermore, Moore concluded, Truk would remain a liability to the Japanese as long as they held it, for its bypassed garrison would require supplies that were needed elsewhere.

Moore, recalling the strategy he had helped develop while on duty in Washington early in the war, visualized a landing on China as the ultimate act that would defeat Japan. In his mind, neither Truk nor the Marianas contributed to the objective. Instead they would divert resources from the main effort to reach China. And how did Moore feel the United States could best reach China? Through New Guinea and the Philippines, he said. Moore, unaware of the background to the JCS decision, had unknowingly advocated the very strategy that MacArthur was seeking—and which was anathema to King.

Moore gave his memorandum to Spruance just before or shortly after the *New Jersey* returned to Kwajalein on 20 February. Spruance read it, returned it to Moore without comment, and walked off. Moore also gave a copy to Pownall, who would leave shortly for Pearl Harbor to relieve Towers. Pownall asked Spruance if he could show the memorandum to Nimitz. Spruance readily assented, but he remained mute on his personal opinion about what Moore had written.

Several weeks later Pownall wrote Spruance that Nimitz would take copies of Moore's memo to his next meeting with King. "I think Carl should feel quite happy that his memo has received such serious consideration by the higher echelons at this time," wrote Pownall. "Please tell him 'well done' from me."

Spruance continued his refusal to discuss the merits of Moore's memorandum, despite Moore's attempts to elicit some word of approval or disapproval. Spruance disliked emotional conflicts and arguments and probably did not want to oppose his friend on a point about which Moore felt so deeply. In that Moore's objections to the Marianas were academic, having been overtaken by events, Spruance's attitude was not to "fight the problem," probably hoping that Moore eventually would drop the subject. Yet Spruance respected Moore's strategic thinking, and he allowed Moore to get a hearing with Nimitz when Pownall passed on the memorandum.

Not until months later did Moore discover—to his astonishment— that the JCS had chosen the Marianas primarily to provide B-29 bases, and that he unwittingly had supported MacArthur's strategy while opposing that of King. Moore then naturally regretted his opposition and wondered why Spruance never had told him about the B-29 issue.

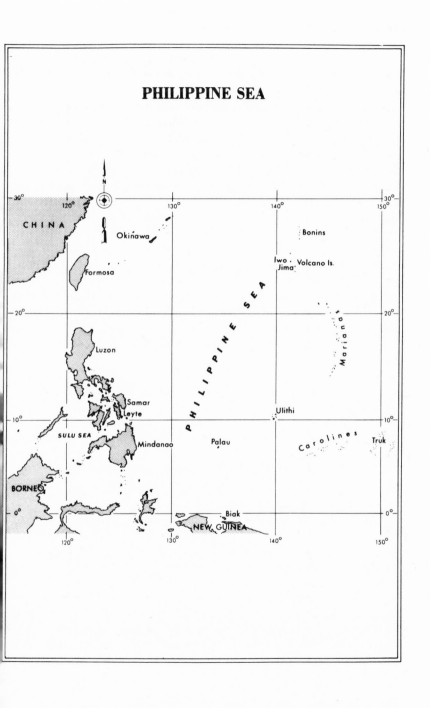

PHILIPPINE SEA

CHINA

Okinawa

Bonins

Iwo
Jima

Volcano Is.

Formosa

PHILIPPINE SEA

Luzon

Mariana

Samar
Leyte

Ulithi

SULU SEA

Mindanao

Palau

Carolines

Truk

BORNEO

Biak

NEW GUINEA

Moore, however, did maintain that his reasoning for bypassing Truk was sound, and his judgment was vindicated when the JCS eventually dropped Truk as an objective.

Meanwhile, MacArthur disputed the CCS and JCS decisions to seize the Marianas, and he reiterated that the entire American offensive effort should be concentrated in his Southwest Pacific theater. His intransigence forced the JCS to call yet another conference in Washington to resolve the Pacific strategy. Nimitz attended the conference, convened in early March. When it ended, the JCS had made two crucial decisions: (1) Nimitz would bypass Truk; (2) Nimitz would seize the Marianas in mid-June rather than in October. The JCS also decreed that MacArthur would have to accept a simultaneous limited offensive leading toward the Philippines, regardless of his own feelings.

With his objectives finally nailed down, Nimitz returned to Pearl Harbor in mid-March, summoned Spruance from Kwajalein, and told him about the JCS decisions. Spruance's most immediate concern would be a Task Force 58 raid against the major Japanese air and naval bases in the Palau Islands, which would cover MacArthur's offensives on the north coast of New Guinea, five hundred miles south of the Palaus.

Spruance returned to the *New Jersey* in Majuro on 20 March and told Moore to plan the carrier raid on the Palaus. The eternal struggle again resumed, with Moore insisting that Spruance work in the evening and Spruance refusing. "Gee, he makes me mad," wrote Moore, adding, "Raymond hasn't told me a single word about what he found out in Pearl Harbor, except our immediate business."

Spruance, as usual, removed himself from the planning details and continually proselytized Moore and the staff to the Spruance program for physical fitness. "Raymond has just appeared and wanted me to walk up and down the deck," wrote Moore. "He's rigged out in a new pair of gaudy Hawaiian bathing panties. Quite disgusted when I declined to go. I am tired and don't want to walk and talk just now. Can't see much rest for the next several months." On another occasion Moore wrote that he constantly was "being interrupted by Raymond, and when I am busiest he wants to argue or take me walking or drag me to the movies."

Spruance's solicitude for Moore's health and welfare was well founded. Moore was tormented by overwork, by foreboding over the decision to seize the Marianas—and by apprehension about his future. Since the beginning of the war, the naval aviators had complained that surface admirals had commanded most of the important fleets and task forces. The aviators wanted more high-level commands because of the growing importance of carrier air power. King compromised by decreeing that fleet and task force commanders and their chiefs of staff could not both be aviators or both be surface officers. As Spruance was a surface officer, his chief of staff had to be an aviator—which Moore was not.

It seemed only a matter of time until Moore would be replaced, regardless of his value to Spruance. His only hope was that Spruance had enough influence in Washington to keep him on his staff, irrespective of King's announced policy. Moore's chances would be immeasurably improved by a promotion to rear admiral, a rank more appropriate for the chief of staff to a four-star admiral. In the event that Moore failed promotion, Spruance suggested that he could remain as an assistant chief of staff after the inevitable aviator rear admiral came aboard. Moore, however, had no desire to be demoted to an inferior staff position.

The uncertainty frayed Moore's nerves, and he was approaching both mental and physical exhaustion. Spruance could not cope with Moore's personal problems, and their relationship became badly strained. "Sometimes I have the greatest sympathy for Margaret," Moore wrote, "for Raymond is hard to live with. I know he is devoted to me, as he is to his family, and perhaps that is one reason that makes him difficult. He just doesn't have to put himself out to be pleasant or even polite. I can't complain because I am not any too congenial company myself. I get so fed up with his personal cracks sometimes that I am not always courteous myself."

The laboring staff, however, retained their harmony and good humor. "One becomes a veteran of this game awfully quick," Barber wrote his parents. "We have seen it now—and from this point on it becomes a grim and exciting business. We're more casual now—relaxed—you might say less serious. We take it in stride, much as the Admiral did, to our amazement, on our first show."

That less serious side of the business of war surfaced time and again among the staff. During a swimming expedition in Majuro, Burton Biggs, who preferred sunning to bathing, accidentally fell overboard fully clothed. Moore became helpless with laughter at Biggs's startled

"He's rigged out in a new pair of gaudy Hawaiian bathing panties."
Spruance pounds the forecastle with Burton Biggs, left,
and Vice Admiral John S. McCain, right.

expression as he toppled downward—and when Biggs thrashed and sputtered alongside the boat. As if in retaliation, the staff enticed Moore topside one day while *New Jersey* was bombarding the bypassed Japanese on Mili Atoll in the Marshalls. Moore unwarily wandered toward the engaged side of the bridge, wondering why the staff was clustering on the opposite side. Suddenly *New Jersey* unleashed a full 16-inch broadside, and the guns' concussion walloped Moore with stunning force. Somehow he landed on his feet; dazed and shaken, he saw his staff laughing hilariously at their clever ploy.

Spruance and Moore had lighter moments also, owing to their enduring comradeship. Moore began to notice that Spruance had become

mysteriously subdued and quiet, had ceased his walking and exercising, and was resting more than usual. His curiosity aroused, Moore
watched the admiral closely and soon discovered the ship's medical
officer examining Spruance with a stethoscope and listening to his
heart. Moore, knowing that Spruance was a hypochondriac, decided to
tease his friend. "I guess it was plain meanness, nothing else," he later
admitted.

"What's the matter with you, Raymond?" Moore asked when they
next met. "You're not acting yourself at all. You sick? What are you
worried about?"

"Oh, nothing," replied Spruance. "It's all right."

"It's not all right," Moore persisted. "You're not acting normally at
all. You're worried about something."

"I didn't think I was showing it."

"You're showing it all right. What's the matter—are you sick?"

"Well," Spruance admitted, "I had a little murmur or something in
my heart, and I thought maybe I'd better have it looked at."

Moore chuckled about the incident years later. "I never let on that I
was cheating," he said. "I just wanted to get a little fun out of it."

Moore loved to tease his friend. The large overstuffed chairs and
sofas in *New Jersey*'s flag cabin were uncomfortable for Moore, and he
often curled his legs beneath him while sitting. Spruance viewed
Moore's habit with disgust and irritation and "would turn up his nose
as if he smelled something bad."

"I wish you wouldn't put your feet on the furniture," complained
Spruance.

"Well, why not?" Moore responded. "The deck is perfectly clean.
It's just as clean as the chairs are."

Moore maliciously continued to pester Spruance by furtively slipping his feet on and off the furniture. If Spruance intended to sit where
Moore recently had rested his feet, he would fastidiously brush off the
cushion, grumbling, "I don't want my trousers to get all dirty sitting
where you've had your feet."

Within a day of Spruance's return from Pearl Harbor on 20 March,
his unflagging staff completed the operation order for the raid on
Palau. Task Force 58 would consist of 11 carriers, 6 battleships, 13
cruisers and 48 destroyers organized into three carrier task groups
under Mitscher. The carriers' planes were to find and destroy the Japa-

nese fleet at anchor. The planes would also mine the anchorage entrances, an innovation in naval air warfare, as well as hitting installations ashore. On subsequent days the force would strike nearby Yap and Woleai. The distance from Majuro to Palau was more than 2000 miles. The 78 ships of the task force would need thousands of tons of fuel, so the plan provided for elaborate refueling arrangements from strategically located fleet oilers.

On 23 March *New Jersey* steamed majestically from Majuro lagoon and stood out to sea. Spruance's fleet gathered about the flagship and shaped course to the southwest. Hoping to avoid detection by Japanese search planes based in the Carolines, Spruance intended to steam on a sweeping southern arc along the equator in order to pass 500 miles south of Truk and less than 150 miles from once-mighty Rabaul, still held by the Japanese but no longer used as an air base. Halfway to Palau, however, Japanese search planes discovered his force. The enemy now knew that Task Force 58 was 1000 miles away from Palau and closing, and Spruance reconsidered his original plans.

The American aviators were without photographic intelligence to assist their planning. They knew only that the Palaus contained many small islands with steep cliffs and lush vegetation, together with innumerable potential anchorages. No one knew the locations of the ships and airfields, which were primary targets. Therefore Nimitz had arranged for Halsey to photograph the main Palau anchorage on 26 March with Southwest Pacific aircraft and to deliver the pictures by air to Spruance when he passed Green Island on the twenty-seventh. The Palau attack date was April first.

Moore had long before abandoned hope for surprising the Japanese fleet. Halsey's planes intended to photograph at night using high-intensity flares, a clarion announcement to the enemy that an attack was imminent. That plan was a "fiasco," Moore snorted. Spruance could not disagree. He reasoned that the Japanese fleet, alerted both by Halsey's air reconnaissance and by the Japanese discovery of Task Force 58, would immediately evacuate the Palaus. Therefore he decided that his best chance to catch at least some of the forewarned Japanese shipping would be to attack as soon as possible without waiting for Halsey's photographs, which in any event would be out-of-date by the time Spruance received them. Accordingly, Spruance advanced his attack by forty-eight hours—to 30 March—and asked Nimitz to inform everyone concerned.

Task Force 58 continued its westward approach along the equator and topped off with fuel on 28 March. Just before noon another Japanese search plane sighted the force. It escaped unharmed—the CAP was having no luck in splashing the Japanese snoopers. The Japanese by now had pinpointed the American position. Doubtlessly they were arming their airplanes on Palau for an attack while their big ships fled. Surprise was irrevocably lost.

Fueling completed, the oilers and their escorts dropped behind. *New Jersey* steamed alone as guide in the center of the formation, the carrier task groups on the horizon, each group occupying a 120-degree sector and maneuvering independently to launch and recover CAP. Occasionally one of the task groups disappeared over the horizon as the carriers chased the wind, causing Moore to fret about the loss of contact for visual signaling. Voice radio was forbidden. But the formation, suggested earlier by Pownall, worked well and allowed Spruance to control his huge task force without restricting the carriers' sea room.

Spruance advised Mitscher that he intended to approach Palau from the south-southwest and to head into the wind at daybreak on the thirtieth when a hundred miles from the target. At that point Mitscher would take over. Mitscher concurred.

As expected, Japanese aircraft began sporadic attacks against the approaching Americans threatening their Palau bases. But the almighty fleet rolled purposefully forward, shaking off the meddlesome enemy planes with ease.

Also, as expected, the Japanese fleet had escaped. American submarines surrounding Palau reported that ships of all sizes were fleeing, and *Tunny* claimed two probable torpedo hits on a battleship. All hope of catching the Japanese fleet had vanished.

On the day of the strike Spruance passed tactical command to Mitscher and became a spectator to the air show. The ships wheeled into the wind, occasionally spurting puffs of black smoke from their stacks as boilertenders lighted off extra burners to generate more steam. The morning sky swarmed with aircraft climbing and turning to rendezvous with their flight leaders. After a time, the squadrons shaped course toward Palau with parade-ground precision, the throbbing roar of their engines fading and finally disappearing.

Spruance kept vigil on the bridge of his battleship, easily keeping pace with the carriers. The first aircraft over Palau reported no suitable targets for the battle line—*New Jersey*'s guns would not fire that day.

Spruance, hoping that not everything had escaped, ordered Mitscher to search northwest of Palau, but nothing was found.

Spruance knew not what was happening over Palau, for his carriers were scattered over the ocean and his planes continually were coming and going. Mitscher continued his attacks throughout the day but was unable to provide Spruance with a damage appraisal, owing to the difficulty of analyzing reports from hundreds of returning aviators. Next day, the thirty-first, Mitscher resumed his strikes against Palau and sent one task group to hit Yap. The second evening Spruance was still without a damage estimate from Mitscher. Spruance assumed tactical command of the two Palau task groups and sped at high speed through the night, in order to position his carriers for an attack on Woleai on the third day.

By noon of the first of April, the carriers had completed their whirlwind onslaught. After rendezvous with Spruance, they began the long return voyage to Majuro.

Secretary of the Navy Frank Knox was eager to publicize the raid and demanded immediate information on the results. Spruance had sent Nimitz a preliminary report, saying only that many Japanese aircraft had been destroyed and that all the ships in the anchorage had been sunk or damaged. Spruance also reported that no American ships were damaged and that he had lost 25 planes.

Nimitz, under pressure from Washington, asked for more details. But Spruance would not respond for two reasons. First, he wanted to authenticate the aviators' damage reports. Spruance abhorred extravagant claims of success, which were so common among many Pacific military commands. Realizing that aviators' action reports often were inaccurate, Spruance sent a visual dispatch to Mitscher directing him to review the results conservatively.

Spruance's other reason for not replying to Nimitz was that he did not want to break radio silence while Task Force 58 was at sea, deep inside Japanese waters.

Knox apparently continued to press for information,[1] and Nimitz's messages to Spruance became increasingly insistent. Finally Nimitz

---

1. King resisted this kind of pressure by not telling Knox anything, because, as King once explained, "Knox tells all the newspaper men everything about what we are trying to do."

ordered Spruance to break radio silence, and Moore became apprehensive. But Spruance was imperturbable. "I'm not going to tell them anything," he said. "My job is to report to my superiors precisely what I have accomplished. When I have an accurate assessment, then I will report. If they want somebody to come out here and fight a publicity war, then they can relieve me."

New Jersey and Task Force 58 entered Majuro and anchored on 6 April. A messenger delivered Mitscher's damage appraisal report: 29 minor auxiliary ships sunk, 17 others damaged, 214 aircraft destroyed or damaged, and an indeterminate number of shore installations destroyed or damaged. Other than *Tunny*'s torpedo damage to a Japanese battleship, the Japanese fleet had escaped unscathed.

Spruance transmitted the report to Nimitz.

"PACIFIC NAVAL VICTORY!" heralded the Chicago *Sun* on 8 April 1944. "The giant guns of the battleships [which had never fired] joined those of smaller warships," claimed the *Sun,* in achieving "one of the greatest naval victories in history."

And yet, despite the distorted emphasis of newspapers like the *Sun,* the American public received one of the war's most truthful and timely reports of a major Pacific battle. The published damage figures were surprisingly accurate, a rare phenomenon in those days of exaggerated victory proclamations. Other newspapers and magazines, although impressed by the Navy's deep penetration into Japanese waters, muted their reports, realistically observing that the Japanese fleet had escaped to fight another day.

Nimitz visited Spruance in Majuro several days after Task Force 58 had returned. If Nimitz chastised Spruance for his refusal to break radio silence, Spruance's staff never was aware of it.

Task Force 58 had a week's breather in Majuro before its next operation in northern New Guinea to support MacArthur. Spruance, however, would not accompany the carriers, because he and the staff had to begin planning for the Marianas invasion. He transferred his flag to *Indianapolis* and returned to Pearl Harbor.

The ax had fallen on Moore. The mail in Majuro included two letters from the Chief of Naval Personnel. One said Moore had failed selection for rear admiral, the Navy way of saying that King, who controlled all promotions, would not promote Moore. The other said that in accordance with current policy, Moore would be relieved by an aviator rear admiral. Spruance was asked to select a new chief of staff from a list of three names.

Moore, disappointed and bitter, hoped that Spruance would more actively oppose the relief, but Spruance knew he could exert little influence. He earlier had officially stated that Moore should be both promoted and retained as his chief of staff. Now, distressed by Moore's unhappiness, Spruance searched for some way to help his friend. But recognizing the futility of arguing with the CNO, Spruance was reluctant to press King further.

"I am sorry for Raymond," wrote Moore, "as he won't get another chief of staff who will do all his work for him and give him hell when he needs it. We have been a team, and I doubt if he can find another partner who can play with him the way I have."

Spruance had to respond to King's ultimatum. He selected Rear Admiral Arthur C. Davis but qualified his reply by repeating his recommendation for Moore's retention and promotion, in one last effort to forestall the inevitable. Moore would not give up hope and became increasingly disturbed as weeks passed without a reply to Spruance's latest appeal. Spruance, typically embarrassed when confronting an emotion-charged predicament, tried unsuccessfully to comfort Moore. One day Moore had worked himself into a state of extreme agitation; Spruance grabbed his shoulders, shook him gently, and looked at him intently. "Come on, Carl," he said. "Quit fighting the problem. Let's get down and get to work." Moore temporarily regained his composure, but his mood remained morose.

In early May another letter from Washington confirmed Moore's fate, and he became resigned to having to leave Spruance following the Marianas operation in June. The mandatory changes of chiefs of staff already had swept the Pacific Fleet. Aviators Halsey and Mitscher, for example, reluctantly had to accept surface officers as replacement chiefs of staff. The Spruance-Moore team would be the last to go.

Spruance later wrote to Davis, who was assigned at the time to King's staff in Washington. "I apologize for asking for you," wrote Spruance, "as I know you would much rather have a command afloat. However, I wanted some one that I knew,[2] and I felt sure that you and I could work well together. Also, you will have all the latest Washington

2. Davis earlier had served on the CINCPAC staff when Spruance had been chief of staff.

background, which will be of great value. Winning this war in the shortest possible time is the thing that matters, and our personal desires have to take a secondary place.

"I shall be sorry to have to lose Carl Moore," Spruance continued, "as we have been close friends for over thirty years, and he has done splendid work for me as chief of staff. However, we both understand the situation which has caused the new policy, and you may rest assured that we shall be very happy to see you again when you arrive out here.

"Be sure to take any leave that you want, because you are coming to a job with plenty of heat and hard work. Good luck until I see you."

By mid-May the Marianas planning was completed. D-Day was a month away, so Spruance and several of the staff had time to fly to California for home leave. Although Spruance had not seen his family for more than a year, he arrived in Monrovia without telling the women he was coming. His wife and daughter were not at home when he arrived, and Spruance rummaged through the refrigerator and prepared a cold supper while he waited.

As with his earlier leaves at home, Spruance wanted isolation from the world. Despite the curiosity of his Monrovia neighbors, he generally was able to preserve his privacy with his family. Young Margaret was amazed at her father's tranquility in view of his heavy responsibilities in the Pacific. His wife thought he seemed tired at first, but he quickly relaxed with long solitary hikes into the hills and the love and warmth of his wife and daughter. In Margaret's eyes, her husband had not been changed by the war. And for a while the three discussed the war—until Spruance snapped, "Let's drop it. Stop it. I don't want to talk about the war any more."

But Spruance could not escape the war. Despite his general anonymity with the American public, he was a celebrity to the citizens of Monrovia. The Rotary Club asked him to speak at a luncheon and he reluctantly agreed, but he told Margaret he would not wear his uniform. Margaret scolded him that a sixteen-year-old neighborhood boy "just idolizes you as an admiral. When you appear up there in your worn old civilian clothes he'll think you're just another old man."

Spruance wore his uniform and gave a straightforward and impressive talk about the war against Japan.

Later the mayor asked him to meet a middle-aged invalid named Arthur Sproul, a self-taught intellectual who was revered by the local

FIFTEEN CENTS   JUNE 26, 1944

TIME

THE WEEKLY NEWSMAGAZINE

ADMIRAL SPRUANCE
After the Marianas, The Empire.
(World Battlefronts)

VOLUME XLIII   (REG. U. S. PAT. OFF.)   NUMBER 26

Spruance on *Time* cover, 26 June 1944

community. Spruance had no desire to meet anybody, but he politely assented. He entered a modest bungalow with walls covered with war maps and press clippings and met a unique man, whose body was crippled with arthritis, but whose mind was extraordinarily keen. Although Sproul had been confined at home for years, he was conversant with every aspect of war, strategy, and world politics. The two men's minds immediately meshed. They quickly became agreeable companions, and the admiral commanding the mightiest fleet in history devoted hours to the secluded Sproul, relishing their philosophical discourses in the quietude remote from war.

Spruance returned to Pearl Harbor to problems large and small. Among the small problems was the question of medals and decorations, which the Navy traditionally had been reluctant to award. Although America had been at war for two and a half years, no clear policy existed to handle the flood of meritorious recommendations generated by the Fifth Fleet's recent battles. "There is great need for some official 'norm' for each of the medals now authorized," wrote a harried Barber, "so that commanders originating recommendations will have some guidance as to the appropriate award. I know of no place where even the relative degree of all current medals is given! I obtained a list from the CINCPAC Awards officer who knew of no place the list was published as such. Thus Admiral Montgomery recommended 'reduction' for a number of awards in his GALVANIC Task Group from Silver Star to Legion of Merit, whereas in fact the Legion of Merit is the medal of higher degree."

Prodded by Barber's memorandum, Spruance established exacting standards for awarding medals, and the flag secretary developed a half-dozen form letters of approval and disapproval for the hundreds of recommendations that crossed his desk. By comparison with Spruance, many flag and general officers were profligate in awarding medals. In Spruance's view, an appropriate entry on a regular fitness report generally was adequate recognition of a commendable performance in battle. Acts regarded by many as "above and beyond the call of duty" usually were considered by Spruance as the expected norm of performance in war.

Spruance seemed indifferent to the medals that he received, an attitude reflected in an early 1945 letter to Margaret. "I knew nothing about a second gold star to my D.S.M. [Distinguished Service Medal] until yesterday," he wrote, "when several newspaper clippings turned up. Apparently, it was for my time as Chief of Staff to CINCPAC. The D.S.M. is the only medal I have from this war, and it is in my trunk at Pearl Harbor, along with all my other unnecessary belongings."

Spruance eventually received an impressive array of medals and awards, including the Navy Cross, the Navy's second highest award.

He stowed them unconcernedly in a cardboard box, and by his death in 1969 they were mouldered and tarnished.

A larger and ominous problem was that Kelly Turner had become an alcoholic. Turner later remarked, "When I came back from the Marshalls, I was dead tired. I stayed dead tired the rest of the war." Turner worked himself to exhaustion, and in the evenings he drank heavily. His liquor capacity was enormous. Although he was always alert and clearheaded the next day, his disposition was mean and intemperate. He riled even the normally tolerant Nimitz. Whenever Nimitz threatened to slap down Turner for his transgressions, Spruance would intervene. "Let me handle him," Spruance would say, and Nimitz would trust Spruance to smooth the stormy waters in Turner's wake.

Turner's drinking worsened as the war progressed. He was drunk during the flag-raising ceremony on Tinian in the Marianas, and following the Okinawa ordeal Spruance found him staggering drunk just before a dinner with Nimitz. Spruance personally sobered him before Nimitz arrived. Spruance felt that he usually was able to control his amphibious commander, and he served as a paternal buffer for Turner's frequent ill-considered outbursts. As long as Turner's performance did not degenerate because of his drinking, Spruance would protect his indispensable genius.

But Spruance's solicitude for Turner was based as much upon their solid friendship as upon the need to keep Turner in the war. In the prewar years theirs had been a warm and affectionate relationship. Turner and his wife were childless, and Turner compensated by seeking the company of his friends' children. He was particularly fond of Spruance's son and daughter, and young Margaret always remembered Kelly Turner as sweet, gentle, and kind, genuinely interested in what she was doing.

Furthermore, Spruance was resolutely loyal, not only to Turner, but to all his friends, and he forgave their trespasses. He appreciated, more than anyone, Turner's private torments and sufferings, and Spruance always treated him with tolerance, understanding, and sympathy.

As young Margaret once expressed Spruance's feelings toward Turner, "Dad was devoted to him."

Chapter 18

BATTLE OF THE PHILIPPINE SEA

THE Marianas campaign would be radically different from the earlier campaigns against the Gilberts and Marshalls. The latter are low-lying coral atolls with islands no larger than several hundred acres. In contrast, the Marianas objectives—Saipan, Guam, and Tinian—are large, rugged, vegetated islands, over three hundred square miles in total area. The American assault troops were accustomed to concentrated frontal attacks and restricted maneuver over the compact sand and coral islands. Now they would have to fight wide-ranging battles on mountains and farms, in sugarcane fields and well-developed towns. And this time civilian inhabitants would be heavily involved, because thousands of Japanese, Okinawans, and native Chamorros tilled the fields and operated the sugar refineries.

During early 1944 the Japanese had hastily reinforced the Marianas, sensing that they were the next logical American objective. But by June 1944 the fortifications were still incomplete, owing to a late start and to continual attacks upon supply convoys by American submarines. Yet the Marianas were formidable, defended by nearly 60,000 troops entrenched in rugged terrain and bolstered by more than 50 tanks and considerable artillery of many sizes.

Spruance commanded over 127,000 amphibious assault troops, transported and supported by over 600 ships. Turner and Holland

Smith directed the Northern Attack Force—the 2nd and 4th Marine Divisions with the 27th Infantry Division in reserve—which would seize Saipan on 15 June. Once Saipan was secured, they would assault adjacent Tinian. Rear Admiral Richard L. Conolly and Marine Major General Roy S. Geiger would lead the Southern Attack Force—the 3rd Marine Division and the 1st Marine Brigade—against Guam, whose D-Day tentatively was 18 June, although the ultimate date would hinge upon progress on Saipan. The 77th Infantry Division remained in reserve in Hawaii.

Many forces were dedicated to supporting the American assault troops. Hoover's land-based air forces in the Marshalls, assisted by MacArthur's air force in the Southwest Pacific, would suppress enemy air in the Caroline Islands. Mitscher's Task Force 58 would smother Japanese air power in the Mariana, Volcano, and Bonin Islands, and it would shield the amphibious forces from any attacks by the Japanese fleet. The Japanese fleet had avoided any major action since the Battle of Midway, two years before, allowing plenty of time to rearm and retrain its depleted carrier air groups. The Americans estimated that Japan had nine combat-ready carriers in the southern Philippines.

Opinions varied as to whether the enemy fleet would oppose the Americans in the Marianas. Nimitz and Spruance had discussed that possibility and concluded that the enemy fleet probably would not appear. Spruance assumed that the Japanese would seek a fleet action only when they believed they would have a good chance of success. Significantly, they had recently ignored a tempting opportunity to crush MacArthur's assault on Biak Island off northwestern New Guinea in late May. MacArthur, operating as usual without strong naval support, had been vulnerable to an attack by the Japanese fleet, but it had never appeared. If the Japanese would not attack MacArthur when they did have naval superiority, Spruance reasoned, then they were unlikely to attack the Fifth Fleet at the Marianas where they would be outnumbered. Eventually the Japanese would fight, Spruance thought, but their cause would not be helped by sacrificing their fleet in a one-sided sea battle off the Marianas. Nevertheless, he was prepared to fight the Japanese fleet if it unexpectedly appeared.

Spruance departed Pearl Harbor on 26 May in *Indianapolis* and headed for the Marshall Islands, where the Fifth Fleet had assembled in the lagoons of Majuro, Kwajalein, and Eniwetok. There Spruance conferred on final plans with his principal commanders: Turner, Smith, Mitscher, Hoover, and Conolly. He also inspected the base developments ashore and, as always, was impressed by the Seabees' industry. "The progress in four months in clearing away the wreckage and in building up from nothing again is phenomenal," he wrote Margaret. "We really are a great people. For example, I went over to Roi-Namur, which I had last seen as a terrible scene of devastation and dead Japs. Now it is neat and orderly, with no signs of wreckage remaining."

Anticipating long, confining weeks at sea, Spruance capitalized on his last opportunity to stretch his legs ashore. At Hoover's invitation he attended the opening ceremonies of the Eniwetok open-air officers' club. A group of Navy nurses, serving aboard a hospital ship, also were guests, and Spruance watched them with a discrimination born of experience. The nurses wore slacks and were not particularly attractive—except to the women-starved naval officers. (One appreciative South Pacific officer remarked, "They are the first white women I have seen in 20 months.") But Spruance, whose standards were more rigorous, wrote Margaret that "they should have worn their white uniforms which make any woman look her best."

As Spruance and *Indianapolis* moved from one lagoon to another, the news that the Allies had landed in Normandy swept the fleet. The military and industrial might of the United States never was more evident than at that moment, for America had successfully assembled two huge and powerful amphibious assault forces, a half-world apart, for simultaneous June offensives against the Axis powers. "I hope we get some of the [Normandy] news," Moore wrote home. "I would like to follow the campaign. However, in a very short time we will have our own hands full, and I rather expect we shall forget that there is a Europe."

On 9 June *Indianapolis* left Eniwetok and next day joined Task Force 58. Mitscher, responsible for eliminating the Japanese air threat in the Marianas before the amphibians arrived, proposed an afternoon strike on the airfields in lieu of the usual early-morning strikes, hoping to change the pattern of attack and to surprise the enemy. Spruance concurred. By now he fully trusted Mitscher and allowed Mitscher to remain OTC during the approach as well as during the attack.

The carrier preinvasion attacks against the Marianas on 11 and 12 June worked well, as Mitscher had hoped, and he estimated that his planes had destroyed 124 Japanese aircraft and had sunk or damaged 20 ships in a Japanese convoy escaping from Saipan. On the third day of the continual air strikes, the battleships under Vice Admiral Lee[1] hauled out toward Saipan to provide covering fire for the diminutive minesweepers clearing the approaches to the landing beaches. Spruance wanted a close look at Saipan, so *Indianapolis* accompanied Lee's battleships but did not join in the bombardment. The fast battleships, untrained in shooting at targets ashore, accomplished little of value. Fortunately, the Japanese did not bother the minesweepers, which in turn did not find any mines.

Late that night, with the Saipan landing scheduled to begin in less than thirty-six hours, the submarine *Bowfin* radioed a portentous message. She had sighted a Japanese force of 4 battleships, 6 cruisers, and 6 destroyers entering the Sulu Sea near the northeast tip of Borneo.

The Japanese fleet was on the move.

Spruance's reaction to the *Bowfin's* report would be the first of his many critical deliberations and decisions during the Marianas campaign, and he established a routine that would best aid his power to concentrate and reason. By day he haunted the *Indianapolis* forecastle, interminably walking, thinking aloud with whoever was with him. Often Gil Slonim, his Japanese language officer, would dash to the forecastle and fall in step with his admiral, and the two men would discuss Slonim's latest intercept of Japanese message traffic and its clues about the enemy's next move.

When Spruance was not walking, he read, and he resented disturbances. "Unless you had something really important to talk to him about, he just wouldn't talk," Moore recalled. "He would make a nasty face and look disgusted, and if he did listen he acted as if he were bored to death. He never was excited and never showed any great amount of emotion. He was probably more quiet than ever."

Yet Spruance concentrated intensely on those matters he thought important and conferred with his staff any hour of the day or night when he knew he had to make a decision. "He was thinking all the time," said Moore, "and when the time came for something to be done,

---

1. Vice Admiral Willis A. Lee commanded the battleships and cruisers in Task Force 58.

he usually anticipated me. He was ready to act on it before I was ready to present him with any proposals."

Spruance now turned his attention to the *Bowfin* report. Although it indicated the Japanese fleet might be headed for Saipan, the report was still inconclusive. Spruance decided to proceed with the Saipan landings on schedule and await further information about the Japanese movements. On the other hand, Spruance had to alert the Fifth Fleet to the implications of the *Bowfin* sighting, and he also had to establish preliminary contingency plans.

The implication was that the enemy fleet might assemble and attack the American amphibious forces at Saipan as early as D+2 Day (17 June). An attack before then was improbable owing to the long distance of the sighted force from Saipan. Spruance earlier had scheduled two fast carrier task groups to strike Iwo Jima on 16–17 June, and he now alerted them that he might recall them early. He next directed Hoover to send long-range seaplanes to Saipan as soon as practicable, in order to patrol the western approaches to Saipan where the enemy might appear. He was helped by Nimitz at Pearl Harbor, who arranged for intensified submarine and land-based air searches. Finally, Spruance revised his fueling schedule so that Task Force 58 would be topped off the day before the Japanese fleet could first reach Saipan. Meanwhile, Turner's amphibious forces continued their approach.

On D-1 Day *Indianapolis* joined a bombardment group of cruisers and old battleships. The ships' crews saw that Saipan was a large bucolic island, beautiful and green with an entire hillside swathed with red blossoms from indigenous flame trees. Peaceful villages dotted the countryside, and tall stacks marked the locations of sugar refineries. Then the dispassionate naval gunners methodically began to devastate the countryside. The Japanese replied with erratic cannon fire.

The Marines landed on 15 June. *Indianapolis* cruised just off the beaches, and the troops in the LVT's and landing craft waved as they passed close aboard, manifesting the enthusiasm that always seemed to be aroused by the awesome prelanding barrage. The Japanese replied with intense cannon and mortar fire, but by evening 20,000 Marines had advanced to their first day's objectives. Turner, apparently optimistic after the first day's success, recommended an 18 June D-Day for Guam. Despite the activity of the still-distant Japanese fleet, its intentions remained uncertain, so Spruance approved Turner's recommenda-

tion. If progress on Saipan slowed or if the Japanese fleet appeared, he
was prepared to reschedule the Guam landings.

That evening the tactical situation worsened. The submarine *Flying
Fish* reported that a powerful Japanese naval force, which included
carriers and battleships, had exited from San Bernardino Strait north of
Samar in the Philippines. It was headed westward at high speed into
the Philippine Sea and could reach Saipan within three days. Therefore
it could launch air strikes as early as the afternoon of the eighteenth,
which Spruance had just designated as D-Day for Guam. The prospect
was alarming.

Spruance decided to gather the scattered carrier task groups of Task
Force 58 near Saipan on the seventeenth, the day before the Japanese
fleet could possibly reach Saipan. In accordance with his earlier directive, two of his four task groups had departed for strikes against enemy
airfields in the Bonin and Volcano Islands, over seven hundred miles
northwest of Saipan. The first impulse would have been to recall them
immediately. Spruance, however, was not in a rush. He decided they
had time for an abbreviated mission before he might need them at
Saipan. Therefore he ordered the two task groups to limit their strikes
to one day only, the sixteenth; to return immediately in order to be
within range of Saipan by the seventeenth; and to rejoin Task Force 58
by the eighteenth. The Fifth Fleet commander was cutting it thin, but
he wanted to carry out as much of his original plan as possible before
repositioning his warships to meet the new threat.

On the morning of the sixteenth the submarine *Sea Horse* sighted
another enemy task force, this one two hundred miles northeast of
Mindanao, within two days' steaming of Saipan. The western half of
the Philippine Sea seemed to be crawling with Japanese ships headed
toward the Marianas. Spruance was now certain that the Japanese fleet
was seeking a fight and would risk everything in a determined attack
while the Americans were entangled in the early and critical part of a
large amphibious operation. The 18 June D-Day for Guam clearly was
not feasible, and he postponed the Guam landings.

The Saipan invasion could not be canceled, however, because it had
been underway for over a day. The American troops would be fighting
ashore when and if the Japanese fleet arrived; Spruance therefore scheduled an immediate war council with Turner and Smith. *Indianapolis*
bent on knots and shortly arrived alongside Turner's flagship *Rocky*

Mount, anchored off the Saipan landing beaches. As Spruance waited for a boat he surveyed the many fat, helpless transports, wallowing in the Saipan anchorage as they unloaded supplies and reinforcements for the troops ashore. Landing craft churned to and fro delivering cargo to the beaches. They were all so very vulnerable, mused Spruance—sitting ducks for an attack by the Japanese fleet.

"The Japs are coming after us," said Spruance when he met with Turner and Smith. He was deeply worried about the transports' safety and asked Turner if he could move them to a safer position to the east. Turner replied that the battle ashore was going badly. He was reluctant to evacuate the transports because the troops desperately needed the food and ammunition still in the ships' holds.

"Well," replied Spruance, "get everything that you don't absolutely need out of here to the eastward, and I will join up with Mitscher and Task Force 58 and try to keep the Japs off your neck." Turner's operations officer recalled years later that everyone present was confident that Spruance would keep his promise.

Returning to *Indianapolis,* Spruance broadcast messages to his forces to prepare them for the looming fleet action. Mitscher was to assemble and refuel Task Force 58 in order to be ready to fight by next day, the seventeenth. While they waited, his carriers were to neutralize the major airfields on Guam and Rota, which were another potential threat. Hoover was to send the long-range seaplanes to Saipan to begin immediate searches to the west. Turner simultaneously detached his heavy bombardment ships to augment Task Force 58 and began to move his excess transports to the safety of the east.

At sunup on the seventeenth, Spruance estimated that the Japanese fleet could be within striking distance of Saipan by that afternoon. His carrier aircraft scoured the western approaches throughout the morning but found nothing. Yet he was convinced that it was only a matter of time until the enemy appeared.

Spruance considered the possible Japanese tactics. *He assumed the Japanese were after Turner's transports.* Their attack probably would begin with long-range carrier aircraft strikes, followed by a surface engagement by their battleships, cruisers, and destroyers. The enemy might split their forces, turn Spruance's flank, and sneak behind Task Force 58 in order to fall upon Turner's transports off the Saipan beaches. The probability of a flank attack weighed upon Spruance's mind; just before leaving Pearl Harbor in late May he had received a translation of a captured Japanese document containing the enemy's current naval battle doctrine. The document recommended a feint at the center to draw the adversary's attention, followed by a flanking attack. Since the Japanese navy had split its forces at the battles of Coral Sea, Guadalcanal, and Midway, Spruance had compelling reasons to believe the Japanese would do the same at Saipan, as well.

The airfields on Guam and Rota were another threat, because they were within easy range of American forces near Saipan. Despite Mitscher's efforts to neutralize the airfields, the airfields could be continually reinforced by replacements flown in from the Caroline and Volcano islands. Furthermore, the enemy could return and refuel his carrier aircraft on those fields, then reattack without the planes having to return to their carriers. Therefore the Japanese carriers could launch their initial attacks at extreme range (far beyond the range of American aircraft) knowing their planes would be refueled ashore before returning.

Spruance pondered the best methods to employ Task Force 58 to meet these threats. His operation orders for all his amphibious campaigns contained a "Major Action Annex," which purported to describe how he intended to fight a fleet action. The annex envisioned that his main body of battleships and cruisers would form a battle line, and the carriers would operate to the rear. This plan, however, was flexible. Spruance never felt obligated to adhere to any of its provisions. Its primary purpose was to assemble his fast combatant ships in one body. From then on he would devise an extemporaneous battle plan based upon the tactical situation at the moment.

Throughout the morning of the seventeenth, Spruance and Moore discussed what that battle plan would be. *Spruance had firmly established in his mind that his primary mission was to protect Turner's amphibious shipping.* He wanted to sink the Japanese fleet if he could, but only if the opportunity arose without risk to Turner's ships.

By early afternoon their discussions were ended: the admiral had decided how he would fight the Japanese. Moore assumed that Spruance, as before, would want him to write the battle plan as a message order using the standard Naval War College format. To Moore's surprise, Spruance began to write the battle plan himself. The War College format was too cumbersome and stereotyped, Spruance felt, and it might not accurately convey his thoughts to his subordinates. He wanted Mitscher and Lee to understand precisely what he wanted done, so throughout the battle Spruance personally wrote his plans and orders in a simple language.

"Our air will first knock out enemy carriers as operating carriers," Spruance wrote, "then will attack enemy battleships and cruisers to slow or disable them. Lee's battle line will destroy enemy fleet either by fleet action if enemy elects to fight or by sinking slowed or crippled ships if enemy retreats. Action against the retreating enemy must be pushed vigorously by all hands to ensure complete destruction of his fleet. Destroyers running short of fuel may be returned to Saipan if necessary for refueling."

Spruance's conventional yet aggressive battle plan was based entirely upon one unstated assumption: his conviction that the Japanese intended to grapple at close quarters off Saipan. Should the Japanese be that obliging, Spruance could achieve the desirable twofold objective of the "complete destruction" of the enemy's fleet and the simultaneous protection of Turner's ships. But his battle plan was flawed. It was too brief, too simple, and it disregarded two other enemy capabilities.

• It did not allow for the possibility that the enemy might avoid a fleet action by limiting its attack to long-range carrier strikes beyond the shorter combat radius of the American carrier planes. In that event, Spruance would have to decide either to steam westward to close the range or to remain near Saipan and absorb the Japanese air strikes without being able to retaliate.

• It had no plan for a possible end run, a curious omission considering his preoccupation with that possible threat.

Spruance's plan would have to be revised if his assumption was wrong. And Mitscher, ignorant of Spruance's rationale in developing the battle plan, easily could misinterpret that plan—which indeed he did. Furthermore, Spruance's battle plan suffered because it was based upon the enemy's assumed intentions rather than the enemy's capabilities, in violation of sacrosanct Naval War College doctrine. Yet Spruance was well aware of the potential danger of plans based upon intentions rather than capabilities. Perhaps he felt he could easily revise his battle plan without jeopardy, should his original assumption be wrong—which it was and which he did.

Mitscher, upon receiving Spruance's battle plan, asked the senior admiral what he wanted Task Force 58 to do that night, indirectly raising the issue of who would be the OTC. In earlier operations Spruance sometimes had acted as OTC; at other times he had passed tactical command to Mitscher.

Spruance replied: "Desire you proceed at your discretion selecting dispositions and movements best calculated to meet the enemy under most advantageous conditions. I shall issue general directives when necessary and leave details to you and Admiral Lee."

Thus Spruance had given Mitscher broad—albeit somewhat ambiguous—discretionary authority to employ Task Force 58 against the enemy. Mitscher's authority, however, was governed and constrained by two directives: Spruance's battle plan, which, when paraphrased, simply said, "Sink the Japanese fleet"; and Spruance's basic operation order, which directed Task Force 58 to protect Turner's amphibious force. At this point—the afternoon of 17 June 1944—both missions seemed compatible. If Mitscher sank the Japanese fleet (which had always been the aviators' greatest ambition), he would simultaneously be fulfilling his obligation to protect Turner's transports.

But the battle would not be that simple, and as time passed the tactical situation would become obscured in the fog of war. Spruance and Mitscher soon would disagree on how Task Force 58 could best "meet the enemy under most advantageous conditions," and the two missions seemingly would become impossible to achieve simultaneously.

These problems came later. For the moment, Spruance had authorized Mitscher to select the tactics and formations that Task Force 58 would use against the Japanese fleet. In view of the aviators' continuing criticism of Spruance's use of the carriers, one might expect that Mitscher, a carrier admiral, would employ the task force in a different way from Spruance. But, in fact, Mitscher's own Major Action annexes were similar to Spruance's, which implied that the two admirals thought much alike in contemplating a fleet action. Mitscher formed a battle line under Lee and assigned Lee a carrier task group to provide close air support. He then positioned his other three carrier task groups behind the battle line, precisely as Spruance would have done.

The rationale for Mitscher's arrangement was threefold, and it assumed that the carriers would be the enemy's prime target. First, the battle line, being interposed between the enemy and the American carriers, would provide a barrier of antiaircraft fire against the enemy planes passing overhead toward the carriers in the rear. Second, the enemy aircraft, reaching the battle line first, would be tempted to attack the expendable battleships and cruisers rather than pressing on to the carriers. And third, if the enemy surface ships did manage to close Task Force 58, the battle line could engage them before they reached the thin-skinned carriers.

Aviators in earlier years had opposed the Naval War College doctrine of tethering the carriers to the battleships, because the prewar battleships, slow and unwieldy, restricted the carriers' speed and mobility. But the new battleships were as fast as the carriers and served as a moving shield. And that was how Mitscher intended to use them. Turner's plodding, obsolescent battleships from the bombardment group remained behind, just off the Saipan beaches, in order to protect the transports from any Japanese surface ships that might slip by Task Force 58.

The seventeenth of June wore on without further sign of the Japanese fleet. Turner returned from the east during the day with transports that landed troop reinforcements and supplies. He reported that the Saipan fighting was hot and heavy and that the enemy was strongly resisting. Over 1500 Americans had been killed and 4000 were wounded in the first three days of fighting. As evening fell, a handful of Japanese planes attacked and hit several amphibious ships, and Turner again withdrew his force to the east.

Spruance waited for more information on the location of the Japanese fleet. He received some coastwatchers' reports, but they were old and unreliable. When Spruance went to bed that evening, he still believed that the Japanese would bore in for a fleet action.

So did Nimitz. He made his expectations explicit in a message to Spruance. "On the eve of a possible fleet action," radioed the commander in chief, "you and the officers and men under your command have the confidence of the naval service and the country. We count on you to make the victory decisive."

Spruance's sleep was interrupted when Moore wakened him a few hours after midnight. The submarine *Cavalla* had sighted a fifteen-ship Japanese task force eight hundred miles west-southwest of Saipan.

Spruance and Moore reevaluated the Japanese movements, and new conclusions emerged from their analysis. Increased bogey activity indicated that the Japanese were shadowing Task Force 58, and it seemed that the Japanese fleet was not converging upon Saipan as rapidly as it could. It was as if the enemy, knowing where Spruance's carriers were located, was deliberately staying beyond the range of the American search planes. The enemy seemed to be probing and feinting, as if hoping to hit Turner while avoiding Task Force 58, perhaps by luring Spruance westward so they could sneak behind him. The latter gambit seemed possible, Spruance thought, because the Japanese fleet was scattered and not accounted for. Furthermore, the submarine sightings indicated to him that a separate task force might be creeping up from the south for a possible end run.

Spruance concluded that he had again misinterpreted the enemy's intentions. Before the Marianas operation he had believed that the enemy fleet would not oppose the invasion; then, on the basis of reported enemy movements in the Philippines, he had changed his mind and had assumed they would seek a fleet action. "For a second time it turned out I was wrong," he later wrote Nimitz. "Their attitude about risking their fleet had not changed. Their methods of operation had changed, in that they were using carriers again. They intended to use their fleet to exploit any advantages that their carrier air might gain. They had no intention of throwing everything at us by coming in to Saipan at high speed to fight it out."

Spruance now had to change his battle plan to adapt to the newly apparent Japanese tactics. *Until he knew the locations of all the major elements of the Japanese fleet, he felt he could not leave Saipan unprotected either to attack or to search for the enemy.* The Japanese alone would decide the time and the place that the fight would begin. They knew where Spruance was, but he did not know where they were. He would have to wait and let the enemy come to him.

Spruance's chances of winning a "decisive victory" for Nimitz were ebbing.

The sun rose and an early morning breeze swept across the dew-wet decks of the Fifth Fleet. The staff officers on *Indianapolis* watched Mitscher's nearby carriers turn into the easterly wind and launch the first search planes.

Damn that east wind. The enemy fleet lay to the west, but whenever Mitscher wanted to land or recover aircraft he had to steam eastward, away from the enemy and opening the range. The Japanese, however, by steaming eastward simultaneously could operate aircraft and close the range, an important tactical advantage.

Spruance's thoughts had drifted back to the Naval War College, and he recalled his study of the 1904 Russo-Japanese War. The Russian fleet had attempted to reinforce Vladivostok, and it had been opposed by a Japanese fleet commanded by Admiral Togo. Togo had elected to wait for the Russians and thereby had won a crushing victory. "The way Togo waited at Tsushima for the Russian fleet to come to him has always been on my mind," Spruance later wrote an historian. "We had somewhat the same situation, only it was modified by the long range striking power of the carriers."

Spruance had always admired Togo, whom he had once seen at a reception decades before, during the cruise of the Great White Fleet to Japan. As a Naval War College student in 1926, Spruance had written that Togo had allowed his subordinate commanders freedom of action and the exercise of initiative. Spruance had also been impressed by Togo's coolness, patience, and great presence of mind in the stress of battle. The Japanese admiral had successfully persevered in his original battle plan, wrote Spruance, and he had not yielded to thoughtless, impetuous actions.

Now Spruance found himself torn between a compulsion to seek out the enemy fleet and a constraint to remain near Turner at Saipan. "I believe that making war is a game that requires cold and careful calculation," he once said. "It might be a very serious thing if we turned the wrong way, just once."

At 0730 *Cavalla* radioed that she still was chasing the same Japanese force, which she had reported at midnight 800 miles southwest of Saipan. It now was 700 miles from Saipan and closing. Mitscher announced that he thought the *Cavalla's* contact was the main body of the Japanese fleet. In conformity with Spruance's battle plan of the day before, Mitscher said that he intended to steam southwest at high speed toward the enemy, to locate the enemy fleet with search planes in the afternoon, and to seek a surface engagement that night.

But Spruance had drastically changed his plans, and he quickly restrained his carrier commander by issuing new instructions. Spruance began by reminding Mitscher of his primary mission: "Task Force 58 must cover Saipan and our forces engaged in that operation." He disagreed with Mitscher's assumption that the Japanese fleet would come from the southwest and warned against diversionary attacks and end runs. Rather than racing to the southwest as Mitscher had proposed, Spruance intended to stay near Saipan, searching westward by day and retiring eastward toward Saipan at night to prevent the Japanese from passing them in the dark. Furthermore, neither Spruance nor Lee wanted a night surface engagement proposed by Mitscher. Spruance's numerical superiority made him stronger by day, while the hazards of a night melee favored the numerically weaker Japanese, who were better trained for night action.

Spruance's revised battle plan was wholly defensive in tone, with the exception of a contradictory closing sentence, ". . . earliest possible strike on enemy carriers is necessary." The sentence reflected wishful thinking; it would be almost impossible to achieve given the restrictions Spruance had imposed upon Task Force 58. Tied down to Saipan, the force would have scant opportunity to close the range in order to attack the skittish, evasive Japanese carriers.

Mitscher's searches to the west were fruitless throughout the day of the eighteenth. Yet bogies continued to shadow the task force, convincing Spruance, more than ever, that the enemy was monitoring his movements with long-range carrier and cruiser planes. The differing ranges of the opposing aircraft were a vital factor. The American planes could attack at ranges of 150 to 200 miles and could search out to 350 miles when extra gas replaced the ordnance load. The Japanese planes carried more gas because they were not weighted down with armor and self-sealing fuel tanks; thus they could attack at 300 miles and search to 560 miles. These ranges could be increased if they refueled at the Marianas airfields.

Spruance waited for more reports as he continued to pace the forecastle, frequently accompanied by Barber and Slonim. Although the two younger officers were not involved in operational planning, Spruance often discussed with them his intentions and his reasoning for his decisions, using them as sounding boards. He told them he had decided to proceed westward until midnight, and if he had not discovered the Japanese fleet by then, he would reverse course and return to Saipan.

Spruance signaled these intentions to Mitscher at dusk, and the aviator responded that he would prefer to continue westward past midnight. Spruance, respecting Mitscher's advice, reconsidered his decision with Moore and the staff, then reaffirmed to Mitscher that he still intended to reverse course at midnight unless they found the enemy.

Night fell, and the locations and intentions of the Japanese fleet remained a mystery. The staff continued to discuss the best course of action, and their opinions were divided. Some agreed with Spruance, while others supported Mitscher's desire to continue heading west. Spruance, perhaps weary of the debates, left flag plot and went to bed about 2100. The staff's arguments continued unabated after his departure.

Slonim and Barber drifted into the admiral's cabin, joined the watch officer on duty at the plotting board, and resumed their discussion of the tactical situation. Spruance suddenly appeared from his adjacent bedroom, perhaps disturbed by their voices, and he again explained his decision.

As he spoke, it became clear that his battle plan was based upon assumed Japanese intentions—he was trying to think like his enemy. "If I were the Japanese admiral in this situation," he said, "I would split my forces and hope that the ships remaining to the west were sighted in order to decoy the main forces of the American Fleet away from Saipan. Then I would slip behind with my separated strike force in order to get into Saipan and if possible destroy the transports." Spruance also explained that he assumed the Japanese admiral's mission "was to protect Saipan, and this could be most effectively done by destroying the transports and the support forces, the Japanese troops ashore being quite adequate against the Marines that already had been landed."

Having explained his reasoning, Spruance returned to bed.

Some years after the war, Spruance revealed his way of thinking when he fought the Japanese. Whenever he was in a tight situation he would say to himself, "Now what would I do if I were a Japanese with these capabilities in this position?" Spruance felt he understood the Japanese mind and character after his years of study and his personal friendship with Japanese naval officers before the war. Using this kind of logic, Spruance by midevening had convinced himself not only that the Japanese were *capable* of an end run in order to hit the transports, but that indeed they *would* do exactly that. *Apparently Spruance did not seriously believe that the Japanese admiral might have been after Mitscher's carriers rather than Turner's transports, using a concentrated naval force in one main body.*

If the Japanese admiral did not split his forces and sought carriers rather than transports, then Spruance's revised battle plan was potentially disastrous. It would expose his carriers to long-range air attack, and they would be unable to retaliate. In the long run, the potential losses and damage to his carriers might jeopardize the operations against the Marianas more than the loss of several transports. Furthermore, if he lost his own carriers without sinking Japanese carriers in return, the growing American preponderance in naval strength might well be abated, thereby handicapping or delaying future American offensives.

On the other hand, if Spruance changed his mission from covering Saipan to seeking out and destroying the Japanese fleet, the possible gain might be worth the increased risk. If he was successful, he would eliminate a major threat to future American operations and would possibly shorten the war. That kind of gain might well be worth the risk of losing a few transports and a concomitant delay in seizing Saipan. Nimitz's explicit message the day before, urging a decisive victory in the possible fleet action, was more than enough justification for Spruance to modify his original mission of covering Saipan regardless of the tactical situation.

The risk of leaving Saipan unguarded by Task Force 58 could be alleviated by other means. Spruance had stationed Turner's seven old battleships off the Saipan beaches to help guard against an enemy surface force. In addition to the fast carriers of Task Force 58, he had eleven escort carriers whose planes could provide limited protection at Saipan against Japanese ships and planes. These forces—the old battleships and escort carriers—could fight a delaying action against an end run (should it materialize) while Task Force 58 was fighting a fleet action to the westward. In that event, Task Force 58 could immediately return to Saipan at high speed, continually heading into the wind for air operations while quickly closing the range to Saipan, hopefully before a Japanese flanking force could inflict unacceptable damage. Mitscher claimed later that he favored this plan.

But this plan, too, had several drawbacks. Both the old battleships and the escort carriers were slow and could be easily outmaneuvered by the swifter Japanese combatants. The old battleships were armed primarily with high-explosive projectiles for shore fire bombardment; therefore they carried a limited supply of armor-piercing projectiles, which were best suited for surface engagements. Similarly, the escort carriers carried few if any torpedoes and armor-piercing bombs, their mission being to employ thin-skinned high-explosive bombs in support of the forces ashore.

There also was the possibility that the enemy fleet, if it was concentrated and did not plan an end run, would avoid battle by counter-marching in response to an advance westward by Task Force 58. In that event, the Japanese fleet would escape damage, but on the other hand, the enemy would not be able to attack the transports.

All these alternatives and more had been discussed, examined, and debated between Spruance and his staff throughout the day and early evening of the eighteenth. Spruance had to make the final decision, and when he went to bed about 2130 it was irrevocable: he would stay near Saipan and let the enemy come to him. He would risk his carriers before he would risk his transports.

Spruance had been in bed less than an hour when he received a message from Nimitz. CINCPAC radio interceptors had located the flagship of the Japanese commander in chief, estimated to be west-southwest of Task Force 58 at about three hundred and fifty miles. The watch officer plotted the position on the chart in Spruance's cabin. The position presumably was accurate to within a hundred miles, and it coincided with the estimated course and speed of the large Japanese task force twice sighted by *Cavalla* within the past twenty-four hours.

Moore, Forrestel, and others of the staff assembled with Spruance in the flag cabin to analyze the radio-intercept report. To some of them, it proved that a major portion of the Japanese fleet was closing at high speed and would attack in the morning. Again they urged Spruance to head westward in order to hit the Japanese carriers at dawn. But Spruance was dubious. Perhaps it was a fake transmission, he said, a decoy to draw Task Force 58 westward. And even if the transmission was genuine, it still did not eliminate the possibility of an end run.

A half hour before midnight, Mitscher sent Spruance a TBS message, which the staff watch officer copied and passed down to the flag cabin. In view of the CINCPAC radio intercept, Mitscher proposed to come west at 0130 in order to launch an attack against the enemy carriers at 0500. Did Spruance concur?

Mitscher's message renewed the controversy within the flag cabin. Then yet another report was received—the submarine *Stingray* was trying to transmit a message and the Japanese were jamming the radio frequency. *Stingray* was 135 miles south of the suspected Japanese main body; perhaps, said Spruance, she had discovered a flanking force and was being jammed to prevent a sighting report.

An answer to Mitscher's message was imperative, and an hour had passed since it had been received. Spruance summarized his estimate of the situation to the staff. Nothing was clear, he said. The Japanese fleet might be concentrated or it might be divided into two or more groups. The enemy might be advancing directly toward Saipan, he might be remaining at long range from Saipan, or he might be maneuvering for a flanking attack from the north, the south, or from both directions.

Spruance announced his decision: Task Force 58 would return to Saipan and would not head west as Mitscher had recommended. Had anyone anything else to say? he asked. All were silent.

Spruance picked up a pencil and wrote his reply to Mitscher: He did not agree with Mitscher's proposal. The *Stingray* jamming report was more significant than the CINCPAC radio intercept. Spruance still thought an end run was possible.[2]

Task Force 58 turned their sterns toward the advancing enemy and retired toward Saipan.

At dawn on 19 June Mitscher had filled the sky with search planes, but they found nothing. Japanese planes, however, began flying from the airfields on Guam, and Mitscher launched a fighter sweep. Just before 0900, Spruance received a delayed sighting message from a long-range seaplane based at Saipan. It had sighted a large enemy force at 0115 in the general vicinity of the CINCPAC radio intercept—the same force that Mitscher had wanted to advance upon and attack. Although annoyed that such an important sighting report had been delayed almost eight hours, Spruance would have returned to Saipan under any circumstances. Even that report did not preclude the possibility that other Japanese forces still were undiscovered. Nothing could change his certainty of an end run.

With Spruance in that frame of mind, the entire Japanese navy could have announced its presence on the western horizon, but Spruance would not have gone after it unless he was positive the enemy would not attack from either of his flanks. His freedom of action was thereby severely curtailed by his refusal to attack unless he knew the location of every Japanese naval force within range of Saipan. A decisive victory over the Japanese fleet seemed remote.

At 1000 hordes of Japanese aircraft approached the task force, some

---

2. Mitscher was puzzled by the explanation because he was unaware of the *Stingray* report.

from the enemy carriers to the west and others from the airfields on Guam and Rota. *Indianapolis* sounded general quarters but Spruance, pacing the forecastle, seemed not to notice. In exasperation, the *Indianapolis* commanding officer asked Moore to get Spruance inside so the ship could fire her forward antiaircraft guns. Eventually the admiral came to the flag bridge to watch the action. Mitscher was in charge, and Spruance quietly read in his chair during most of the ensuing battle.

It was a spectacular, one-sided battle. Mitscher's deployment of Task Force 58 worked precisely as envisaged. The enemy planes initially concentrated their attacks on Lee's battle line, stationed in front of the carriers and acting both as a magnet for the Japanese planes and buffer for the carriers in the rear. The surface ships belched smoke from their antiaircraft batteries, darkening the sky with black, bursting flak. The American carriers continually launched and recovered their aircraft, which when airborne climbed into the western sky toward the cloud of attacking Japanese planes.

Throughout the day the enemy tumbled into the sea from aloft, with long trails of smoke marking the path of their final descent. A few evaded the CAP and the battle line and bored into the cruiser-destroyer screen surrounding the carriers in the rear. One low-flying plane near *Indianapolis* simply disintegrated in flight; its torpedo fell lazily into the sea, and its wings and fuselage drifted apart, spiraled down, and splashed. Another plane swept over the flagship, and the *Indianapolis* gun crews poured a torrent of tracers skyward which eventually converged on the target. The plane jolted, faltered, and crashed, and the ship erupted with cheers and exultation.

But the Japanese carriers launching the planes still were undiscovered and remained immune from attack. Spruance had to find them. At mid-morning he ordered Harry Hill at Saipan to fly in as many seaplanes as he could handle and to resume long-range searches again that night. In the early afternoon Mitscher flew a search to the west. The American planes found no Japanese ships, but they did tangle in dogfights with Japanese carrier planes, while the Japanese carriers cleverly stayed just beyond the range of Mitscher's search planes. And Mitscher could not close the range owing to the easterly wind, which forced Task Force 58 gradually to move into the lee of Guam.

By midafternoon Spruance no longer feared an end run. The Japanese had lost several hundred planes during the day and few would remain for any attacks against the transports. Now eager for an aggressive search and attack westward, he sent new orders to Mitscher: "Desire to attack enemy tomorrow if we know his position with sufficient accuracy," adding that he wanted to go as far west as air operations and the fickle east wind would permit.

By early evening the last American plane landed, and Task Force 58 charged toward the Japanese fleet. Spruance now had reliable reports that an American submarine had torpedoed an enemy carrier about 375 miles west of Task Force 58, and he hoped to hit the crippled carrier next morning, as well as any attending escorts. Very likely Spruance had begun to doubt that he would find any healthy Japanese ships. They were probably in full retreat, he reasoned, given the heavy Japanese air losses during the day.

The Japanese losses were catastrophic—383 planes, Mitscher estimated. (The battle became informally known as "The Marianas Turkey Shoot.") By comparison, Mitscher lost only 25 planes and his carriers were untouched. One American battleship had been hit, but damage was slight. But the ships of the Japanese fleet were still unscathed (except for the torpedoed carrier), they were getting away, and as darkness fell on the nineteenth Spruance and Mitscher and Task Force 58 had embarked upon a belated tail chase.

By midmorning of the next day, the enemy's whereabouts still was unknown. Spruance told Mitscher to continue searching. If they had found nothing by the end of the day, the Americans would abandon the chase and return to Saipan. Mitscher concurred.

The day wore on without any sighting reports. Even the damaged carrier had disappeared, and the atmosphere in flag plot was tense. The nervous staff smoked often and fouled the air. The smell revolted Spruance, and finally he sternly forbade smoking in flag plot. As usual in such cases, the staff did not take him seriously. Spruance never would pressure his staff to change their personal habits—whether it was smoking or Moore's feet on the furniture—because he might hurt their feelings. The staff knew this and knew just how far they could circumvent Spruance's edicts. In this case, they simply smoked when the admiral was absent. Whenever he entered, the staff would elaborately extinguish their cigarettes, immediately relighting them after Spruance left. As Spruance frequently was in and out of flag plot, the ban on cigarettes became ludicrous.

Mitscher's search planes finally found the retreating Japanese fleet in midafternoon. It was like a reprieve. But the report was garbled, and Spruance, Moore, and Forrestel anxiously hovered over the sweating watch officer trying to decipher the information. Eventually the enemy position was plotted on the chart.

The enemy ships were at the extreme range of the American attack aircraft, and darkness was but a few hours away. If Task Force 58 launched that afternoon, the aviators would have to conserve their fuel, attack in dusk, and land at night with gas tanks nearly empty. The Americans might be able to wreak considerable damage upon the enemy, but a follow-up attack in the morning would be nearly impossible owing to the confusion and delay of a night recovery. Mitscher therefore told Spruance that the carriers "were firing their bolt," and that he wanted to attack immediately. Spruance concurred. Mitscher's planes roared aloft, were briefly silhouetted in the late-afternoon sun, then disappeared into the western sky.

Hours of waiting. Then the familiar argot of pilots in combat blared over the radios, pilots obviously fighting their way through Japanese fighters and naval gunfire in order to attack the enemy fleet. They reported they were hitting ships, but the darkness and the want of fuel prevented a sustained attack. Soon they began their return to the carriers. It was now night.

The ships turned on their lights and fired starshells and flares to guide the aircraft home. The returning planes plopped aboard any flight deck they could find. Many planes fell short, either from battle damage or fuel exhaustion, and destroyers rescued the pilots. The scene before Spruance was unreal: planes milling overhead and crashing in the water; the tired, strained voices of exhausted pilots on the radio; searchlight beams stabbing the sky as homing beacons, or sweeping the water in search of survivors; ghostly flares sputtering over the warm, calm waters fired by gallant pilots in life jackets waiting for rescue. To add to the confusion, an anonymous radio voice reported that a Japanese plane had tried to land on a carrier. Rattled voices ordered, "Commence fire," but the orders wisely were ignored.

When night ended, Task Force 58 was in disarray. Ships were scattered over the ocean, many still searching for survivors, and the carriers were sorting out the aircraft that had landed on the first available flight deck. Spruance and Mitscher reorganized the force and continued their pursuit and search westward, but by then they only could hope to find cripples. Search planes could see the Japanese fleet retreating to the northwest, but they were beyond range of attack. Spruance could not close the range; as before, the need to head into the east wind for flight operations restricted any significant advance north-westward towards the fleeing enemy, and the advance was further slowed by the need to refuel the destroyers.

At 2000 Spruance abandoned the chase, and Task Force 58 reversed toward Saipan, seven hundred miles away. The Battle of the Philippine Sea had ended.

"The enemy had escaped," wrote a disappointed Mitscher in his battle report. "He had been badly hurt by one aggressive carrier air strike, at the one time he was within range. His fleet was not sunk."

Mitscher's embittered conclusion typified the criticism and reproach directed against Spruance in the aftermath of the Battle of the Philippine Sea. "There will be a lot of kibitzing in Pearl Harbor and Washington about what we should have done," wrote Moore shortly after the battle, "by people who don't know the circumstances and won't wait to find them out." There was considerably more than kibitzing. Towers even then was demanding to Nimitz that Spruance be fired for mishandling Task Force 58 and for allowing the Japanese fleet to escape. Towers, of course, recommended himself as Spruance's replacement.

Naval writers, historians, and naval officers have all expressed their opinions of Spruance's decisions during the battle. Their judgments vary widely, reflecting the complexity of the problems that Spruance had to solve in the pressure of war.

The crux of a battle analysis revolves about Spruance's mission, which he steadfastly maintained was *to protect the transports at Saipan.* He accomplished that mission, but in so doing he risked extensive losses and damage to his carrier force. By not allowing Task Force 58 to hit the Japanese carriers on 19 June, Spruance forced the American carriers to absorb the full impact of the Japanese air attack. Furthermore, when Spruance returned to the Marianas on the night of 18–19 June, he denied the carriers the sea room they needed for prolonged flight operations. The carriers had to steam eastward toward Guam throughout the day while launching and recovering, and some ran out of both wind and room. More than one carrier had to delay flight operations in order to dodge around the islands.

Earlier in the war, these tactical handicaps would have been fatal to the Americans. But the Japanese aviators in June 1944 were poorly trained and inexperienced when compared to their predecessors of the 1942 era. They were no match for Mitscher's superb fighter pilots, who were able to crush the Japanese attacks and thereby prevent damage to Task Force 58. Spruance was very lucky that Mitscher's superior aviators were able to overcome his deliberately imposed hazards.

Could Spruance reasonably have modified his mission on the night of 18–19 June to include two objectives: to destroy the Japanese fleet and to cover Saipan? The answer is yes.

Spruance returned to Saipan that fateful night because he thought the transports would be needed there the next day. *But they were not needed.* Spruance could have ordered all the transports to safe haven in the east without unduly jeopardizing the troops ashore at Saipan. The looming fleet action would have been decided within a day. The troops could have held their own for that long, even if they had been forced temporarily to delay their offensive.

Recalling the situation on the eve of the sea battle, Holland Smith later wrote, "Our position ashore was not too bad. When I went ashore I had not the slightest apprehension. We had landed all our artillery and this partially compensated for the lack of naval gunfire. . . . The Marine has a winning philosophy. He feels that once he gets on the beach with his weapons, he can't be pushed off. And we were all too busy to worry a great deal about the departure of the fleet."

Yet Smith's optimism had not been made apparent to Spruance. When Spruance deliberated on the night of the eighteenth, he had heard nothing to modify Turner's original warning of the sixteenth that the troops were in trouble and that the transports were indispensable for their survival. In fact, Hill had radioed Turner on the night of the eighteenth that he would require the entire transport force at Saipan for unloading as early as practicable on the nineteenth, implying that the troops still were in deep trouble. Although Turner refused Hill's request and directed the transports to retire eastward on the night of 18–19 June, Spruance must have assumed that at least some would return to Saipan in the morning.

In reality, Hill's request had been triggered by Holland Smith's concern on the eighteenth that his stockpile of supplies might become dangerously low. Nevertheless the American troops were winning, the Japanese were staggering, and the official Marine Corps history states that "all in all, the situation looked as promising to American eyes as it seemed grave to the Japanese."

Thus, unknown to Spruance, the tactical situation on Saipan had greatly improved in the sixty hours since he had conferred with Turner and Smith on the forenoon of the sixteenth. It would appear that by the evening of the eighteenth every transport could have remained in the safety of the east for the next thirty-six hours without endangering the troops ashore. Yet Spruance continued to operate on the assumption that the transports still were vitally needed off the Saipan shores on the nineteenth.

In a swiftly moving battle, the tactical situation frequently changes. Plans must be modified to adapt to new situations, because original plans often are based upon assumptions which no longer are valid. In the military planning process, this step is known as the Supervision of the Planned Action.

When Spruance was deliberating whether to close the Japanese fleet on the night of 18–19 June, he would have been prudent to reconsider his original assumptions made two and a half days before. The relevant question that fateful night should have been whether all the transports could be moved eastward for twenty-four to thirty-six hours in order to free Task Force 58 for a decisive fleet action. Yet Spruance did not propose this to Turner, nor did Turner volunteer to clear to the east so Spruance could advance on the enemy. Rather everyone seemed to assume that it was essential that Turner return some of his transports to Saipan on the nineteenth. When no one thought to ask otherwise, Spruance returned to Saipan with Task Force 58 rather than advancing westward toward the enemy.

The Battle of the Philippine Sea could have been entirely different had Spruance asked Turner on the night of 18–19 June: "I propose to head west to meet the enemy in the morning. Can your troops dig in for 36 hours while you move all your transports east to safety, so that I can seek a decisive fleet engagement?" Knowing the personalities of Turner and Smith, the answer probably would have been yes.

The most ironical aspect of the battle is that Spruance thought he could read the mind of the Japanese admiral and made his decisions on that basis. But time and again Spruance was wrong in analyzing his opponent's intentions. Whereas the Japanese admiral, Misaburo Ozawa,[3] knew he would be fighting Spruance, and he correctly predicted both Spruance's state of mind and his intentions.

---

3. Spruance did not know Ozawa was in command. Perhaps he assumed most Japanese admirals thought alike.

Spruance assumed Ozawa would split his forces and attack Turner's transports. Ozawa did just the opposite: he concentrated his force in order to attack the American carriers. On the other hand, Ozawa assumed that Spruance, with his known caution, would remain near Saipan, thus allowing Ozawa to launch long-range air strikes without endangering the Japanese carriers. Although Ozawa had only 9 carriers as opposed to the 15 of Task Force 58, he counted upon help from Japanese land-based aircraft at Guam, Rota, and Yap. Ozawa's plan had two fatal flaws: his ill-trained pilots were devastated by Mitscher's fighter planes, and Mitscher had eliminated much of the land-based air forces before Ozawa arrived.

Spruance was lucky, and Ozawa was unlucky.

The Japanese suffered irreplaceable losses: 476 planes and 445 aviators. The Americans lost 130 planes and 43 aviators. American submarines sank two enemy carriers on the nineteenth, and Mitscher's aviators sank a third and damaged two others during the dusk attack on the twentieth. Although six Japanese carriers survived to steam another day, their overwhelming loss of planes and aviators emasculated their fighting strength for the remainder of the war. The Japanese carrier navy remained afloat but impotent.

The battle had many other long-range effects. The Japanese correctly assumed that in future battles the Americans would go hell-for-leather toward any Japanese carriers that threatened American amphibious operations. Thus during the Battle of Leyte Gulf, impetuous Halsey charged off after a decoy carrier force devoid of aircraft, exposing the transports off the Leyte beaches to a marauding Japanese surface force that had sneaked behind him.

Spruance's failure to meet the enemy fleet in decisive action would forever haunt him, and his postwar letters reflected his disappointment. "As a matter of tactics," he wrote to historian Morison, "I think that going out after the Japanese and knocking their carriers out would have been much better and more satisfactory than waiting for them to attack us; but we were at the start of a very important and large amphibious operation and we could not afford to gamble and place it in jeopardy."

To his death, Spruance clung to his belief that Turner's transports were needed off the Saipan beaches during the Battle of the Philippine Sea.

Chapter 19

THE MARIANAS CAMPAIGN

THE Battle of the Philippine Sea was over, and Spruance could shift his attention to the land warfare on Saipan. Reports from Turner indicated that the fighting was heavy but that the American troops were making steady progress. The 27th Infantry Division (which had been in reserve) had landed to reinforce the 2nd and 4th Marine Divisions. By 22 June, the day following the sea battle, Holland Smith's forces had seized the southern half of the island and were advancing northward.

Spruance returned to Saipan on 23 June and conferred with Turner on the status ashore. Spruance's principal concern was selecting dates for the invasions of Tinian and Guam, because both dates depended upon the progress on Saipan. Turner reported that a major offensive was underway with the 27th Division in the center and the Marine divisions on either flank. They were attacking the enemy's main line of resistance, a rugged terrain of forests, caves, ravines, and steep mountains. But many days of fighting remained, Turner said, and he could not predict a date for the final seizure of Saipan. Spruance arranged to meet with Turner and Smith the next morning. Then *Indianapolis* got under way for the night—a common naval practice that allowed sea room against nighttime enemy air and submarine attacks.

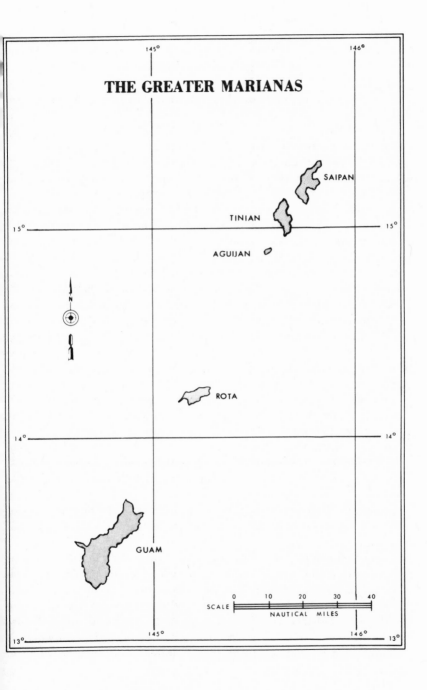

THE GREATER MARIANAS

Next morning the flagship anchored in the transport area off Saipan to await Turner and Smith. They brought bad news.

Holland Smith wanted to fire Major General Ralph C. Smith, the Army general commanding the 27th Infantry Division. He explained his drastic request. The 27th Division had failed to advance up the center of the island during the major assault the day before, imperiling the inboard flanks of the two Marine divisions moving up the east and west sides of the island. As a result the offensive was stalled. Smith felt that the Army division had failed him and would continue to impede progress for the remainder of the Saipan campaign.

Ralph Smith had been in command for twenty months and had been unable to improve the division's fighting ability to Holland Smith's satisfaction. The Marine general, impatient and intolerant, now asked Spruance to replace Ralph Smith with Major General Sanderford Jarman, an Army officer then on Saipan, who would become the island commander when the island was secured. Jarman had agreed that the 27th's performance was unsatisfactory, and, according to Holland Smith, Jarman had vowed that he could make the division fight if he were given command.

Holland Smith thus forced Spruance to make a distasteful decision with potentially explosive repercussions. Although there was ample precedent for removing flag and general officers who failed in combat, such officers traditionally were relieved (discreetly if possible) by their own superiors within their own service. Spruance was contemplating the open firing of an Army general by a Navy admiral upon the recommendation of a Marine Corps general. The Army would be humiliated and infuriated. The Army–Marine Corps relationship, at best tenuous, could suddenly disintegrate into a permanent estrangement that would impair the future Pacific war effort. And giving Jarman command was no guarantee that the division would improve in the next few weeks' fighting on Saipan; its problems were too deeply ingrained to permit any immediate remedy.

Had Holland Smith possessed a modicum of forbearance, had he promoted harmony rather than provoked antagonism, perhaps the crisis would have been averted. But the inflammatory general—Spruance's personal choice to lead his troops—finally had precipitated an imbroglio that Spruance could no longer evade or smooth over. Unless Spruance could find an alternative solution, he had to support his Marine general and to accept the unpleasant consequences. Holland

Smith was the commander responsible for the fighting ashore and presumably was best able to judge the ways and means necessary to seize Saipan. Furthermore, Kelly Turner supported Smith's recommendation. Yet all three officers, recognizing the gravity of the moment, groped about for a tactful way to fire Ralph Smith. They all liked him personally and knew they were about to ruin his career and reputation. Their discussion, according to Carl Moore, "bid fair to be rather endless." The chief of staff, hoping to end their soul-searching, drafted a terse, straightforward dispatch for Spruance's signature. All three parties read the draft, agreed with the wording, and Spruance signed the orders that relieved Ralph Smith and placed Jarman in command of the 27th Division.

Jarman accomplished little. For the next five days the soldiers tried unsuccessfully to dislodge the Japanese embedded in positions with the macabre names of Death Valley, Purple Heart Ridge, and Hell's Pocket. It was a futile task. Jarman cashiered a regimental commander, other unit commanders were killed in combat, and the 27th suffered demoralizing casualties. On 28 June, Major General George W. Griner relieved Jarman. (Jarman's command had been on an interim basis owing to his previously assigned duties as an island garrison commander.) By the end of the month the division finally overran the opposition and regained contact with the Marine divisions on either flank. Central Saipan was at last under American control, and the three divisions once more were a united front for the final drive against the remaining Japanese in the northern third of the island.

The dismissal of Ralph Smith had failed to vitalize the 27th Division, yet Spruance had no apparent regrets. On 4 July the fighting on Saipan was nearly over, and Spruance justified what he had done in a personal letter to Nimitz. "The relief of Ralph Smith from command of the 27th Division was regrettable but necessary," wrote Spruance. "He has been in command of that division for a long time and cannot avoid being held responsible for its fighting efficiency or lack thereof."

Spruance never publicly doubted the wisdom of his decision. The inevitable controversies raged both during and after the war, and although Spruance readily acknowledged full responsibility, he received little criticism. Instead, Holland Smith was the focus of the Army's wrath, and Spruance was spared from the acrimonious charges and accusations that reverberated over the years.

Saipan, 14–15 June 1944

The ships' crews saw that Saipan was a large bucolic island, beautiful and green with an entire hillside swathed with red blossoms from indigenous flame trees.

Then the dispassionate naval gunners methodically began to devastate the countryside.

The Marines landed on 15 June . . . the troops in the LVT's and landing craft waved as they passed close aboard. . . .

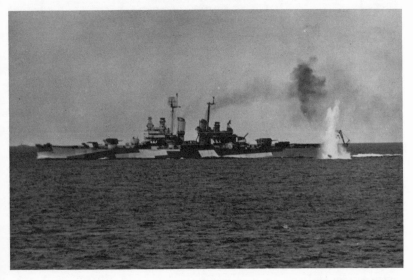

The Japanese replied with intense cannon and mortar fire. . . .USS Birmingham takes near miss.

Vice Admirals Marc A. Mitscher, left, and Willis A. Lee, right

The selection of dates for the seizure of Tinian and Guam continued to perplex the Americans. Nimitz, Spruance, and Turner were anxious to begin the amphibious assaults as soon as possible. The bad weather season was approaching, the Japanese daily were strengthening their defensive fortifications, and the schedule for later invasions in the Pacific theater depended upon the timely capture of the Marianas.

Holland Smith was cautious and conservative. Impressed by the tenacious Japanese defense of Saipan, he predicted similarly tough fighting on Tinian and Guam. Therefore Smith wanted as many troops as he could get. The III Marine Amphibious Corps originally was scheduled for Guam, but Spruance's generals said that they were not enough and requested reinforcements from the 77th Infantry Division, 3500 miles away in Honolulu.

The only troops available for Tinian were the 2nd and 4th Marine Divisions and the 27th Infantry Division, still fighting on Saipan. Those divisions would be battered and weary after weeks of combat, and no one could predict when they would be ready for an assault against Tinian. But no decisions were possible until Saipan was secured.

Spruance was forced to wait on *Indianapolis,* which either was anchored off Saipan or was providing gunfire support to the troops ashore. The sounds of war rolled across the water. Spruance could watch the entire battlefield panorama from his flagship bridge. Occasionally he went ashore to see the fighting at close hand, but Smith, nervous about the danger of Japanese snipers, surrounded Spruance with a Marine bodyguard and would not allow him near the front lines. "All of which is understandable," wrote Spruance to Margaret, "but prevents me going around and satisfying my curiosity as I would like to."[1]

"The Admiral caused me many anxious moments," Smith later wrote. "He refused to wear a steel helmet or green dungarees. Instead, he came ashore in a conspicuous khaki uniform which made him a first-class target for a Japanese sniper." Describing how he asked Spruance to accept an armed escort, Smith wrote, "Being above all a reasonable man, Spruance agreed, and his keen interest in the landing forces and his inspection trips provided him with a much more accurate and comprehensive picture of the battle than he would have had otherwise."

Smith also fondly recalled that "Spruance repaid his visits ashore by a princely largesse of ice cream, which was a cause for celebration at Corps Headquarters. The Admiral would send a Filipino mess steward ashore with a five-gallon drum of ice cream as a present for me."

At Smith's insistence, Spruance viewed the fighting from a mountaintop observation post. "We had a grandstand view of a modern land battle," he wrote Margaret. "With good glasses we could see our tanks in action, troops on foot moving up in support, other troops coming in trucks from rear areas, and we could hear our shells passing overhead and see them exploding in enemy territory. Our ships off-shore were bombarding. Our planes in the air were bombing and strafing the Japs.

"Conquering one of these islands is a slow and costly process. There are believed to have been over 20,000[2] Japanese troops, practically all

1. Harry A. Gailey's *"Howlin' Mad" versus the Army: Conflict in Command Saipan 1944* (Novato, California, 1986) makes a stong case for Ralph Smith and the 27th Division.

2. There actually were almost 32,000 Japanese defenders.

of whom have to be killed. Once we get our beachhead cleared, we have the advantage because we push our troops and guns and supplies ashore and we have complete control of the air. The Japs get more and more disorganized, some of their artillery gets knocked out each day, they lose men and gradually get weaker. Up to the last gasp, however, they fight tenaciously and fanatically, asking only to die.

"This has been, and probably will continue to be, a most interesting operation, but long drawn out."

On 3 July the Saipan campaign was nearing an end, and Spruance finally could meet with his amphibious commanders to select the long-deferred landing date for Tinian and Guam. Their mood was somber. The casualties on Saipan had been heavy, over 11,000 out of the 71,000 troops that had landed. (The final total was 14,111, or 20 percent of the troops committed, the same percentage as at Tarawa.) The admirals and generals had a new-found respect for the stoutness and endurance of the Japanese defenses. The battles would no longer be short and decisive as they had been in the Gilberts and Marshalls. Saipan had proven that battles henceforth would be long and expensive, and the amphibious commanders wanted the entire 77th Infantry Division to augment the III Amphibious Corps on Guam. That division was in Honolulu and could not reach the Marianas until 25 July, so Spruance recommended that date to Nimitz as D-Day for Guam. D-Day for Tinian remained undecided because it was uncertain when the exhausted American troops on Saipan would be rehabilitated and ready for a new assault.

Nimitz quickly replied by message that Spruance's proposals were "not acceptable," unless there were compelling reasons of which he was unaware. The entire 77th Division was unnecessary, argued Nimitz, and he wanted a 15 July D-Day. At least some of the 77th would be available by then—in his view enough to augment the III Corps. The original date for Guam had been 18 June, and any further delay would slow the entire war effort against Japan. "You are directed," said Nimitz, "to reexamine the question with a view to finding ways and means of meeting an earlier date."

Spruance responded with indignation. The Marine generals had reexamined the situation, wired the Fifth Fleet commander, and affirmed the need for the entire 77th Division. "If the views of the military commanders as to the military forces needed are to be overruled," warned

Spruance, "the decision should be made by higher authority on the basis of the effect of the delay upon the conduct of future operations."

Spruance's uncompromising message finally forced Nimitz to accede to a 21 July D-Day.[3]

Spruance resigned himself to more waiting. The Americans squeezed the Japanese into the northern tip of Saipan, the remaining defenders made their final banzai attack, and on 9 July the battle was over. Spruance was delighted to receive information about one dead Japanese in particular. "One thing that has appealed to me most in this operation was the end of the Saipan commander, Vice Admiral Nagumo," wrote Spruance. "He is the gentleman who commanded the Jap Fleet on December 7th, 1941 and again at Midway. After Midway he went ashore to Sasebo and then came here in May. Three strikes and out."

Spruance and Moore went ashore for the flag-raising ceremony outside Holland Smith's headquarters on Saipan. Two enlisted Marines were stationed at the base of a crude flagpole, flag in hand. A long row of admirals and generals stood at attention, then saluted in unison as a band began to play the National Anthem.

The halyard jammed and the Marines could not hoist the flag. The Marine generals squirmed with embarrassment. Some hissed orders at the flustered enlisted men and others could scarcely restrain themselves from breaking ranks to hoist the flag themselves. Spruance was impassive, and the flag eventually was raised without the generals' help.

Ashore, Spruance surveyed the Saipan civilians, a polyglot group of Japanese, Koreans, and native Chamorros. Thousands had been trapped in the battlefield crossfire and had suffered terribly. Warned by the Japanese that the Americans would torture and kill them if captured, the civilians had hidden in the caves and hills among the Japanese soldiers, and American weapons unknowingly had killed many of the noncombatants. Hundreds of civilians committed suicide, but many thousands—diseased, wounded, starving, and homeless—chose to surrender. The Americans gathered them in internment camps where they became the flotsam of war.

Spruance, imbued with his theories of racial characteristics, wrote

3. Additional transports allowed the 77th Division to expedite their transit, and D-Day advanced from 25 July to 21 July.

Lighthouse
The destruction of war on Saipan

Margaret that the Japanese and Korean civilians were "very woebegone looking but stolid and uncomplaining. They are miserable looking specimens of humanity." When he later visited the interned civilians on Tinian, he wrote that "as human material, most of them are very low grade. We should get them out of the Marianas after peace is made and populate the island with Chamorros, who are a fine people."

Later he also inspected the children's ward of the internment camp hospital on Tinian. "Most of these were orphans," he wrote Margaret, "and they ranged from small babies on up. There were only two or three mothers there with their children. One of them sat cross-legged on the end of her child's cot just staring at it. She paid absolutely no attention to anything else, never even glanced up at our party. I wondered what, if anything, was going on in her mind.

"Some of the wounded children in this war were pitiful cases. There were two small boys, each of whom had lost an eye. Others, recent arrivals, would be mere bags of bones, in the last stages of starvation when brought in, and utterly without animation or energy."

After exposure to the civilian war victims on Saipan, Spruance worried about the safety of the Chamorros on Guam. They were friends and wards of the American government after the many years that Guam had been an American possession. While waiting for the 77th Division to arrive, Spruance's naval forces began a systematic, protracted destruction of Japanese fortifications on the island. In order to avoid killing the Chamorros, Spruance warned Conolly (who would command the Guam invasion forces) not to bombard the island indiscriminately. On another occasion Mitscher ordered his surface ships to bombard the towns on Guam during the nights. Spruance promptly countermanded Mitscher and told him to bombard the airfields only.

But Spruance regarded the killing of Japanese soldiers with dispassion and detachment. Many of the enemy remained hidden and dangerous in the caves and jungles of the islands, months after the main battles had ended. "There will be the usual man hunt for a long period before all the Japs have been eliminated," he wrote Margaret. "On Saipan we continue to kill from 50 to 100 of them a day. If they would only surrender when licked, a lot of lives would be saved; but, if they did, we would have the bother of guarding, feeding, and transporting a lot of POW's, most of whom would contribute little of value in the intelligence line. That is really the only legitimate military reason for taking POWs."

Enemy soldiers, dead

With Saipan captured, Turner could finally set an invasion date for
Tinian. He chose 24 July, thereby allowing the fatigued soldiers and
Marines two weeks to recuperate. But a visit by Harry Hill brought
unsettling news to Spruance.

Hill revealed that he and Holland Smith disagreed with Turner on
the most suitable landing beaches on Tinian. Hill and the Marines
wanted to land on two small beaches on the northwestern tip of the
island, identified as the White beaches. The Marines had reconnoitered
the beaches at night, wearing two-toed Japanese shoes so their foot-
prints would not betray the Americans' interest in the beaches. They
reported that the beach gradient was favorable and that the beaches had
few natural or man-made obstructions. Another advantage was that the
beaches were undefended and within range of American artillery on
Saipan. Their disadvantages were their narrow widths—fifty and one

Enemy soldier, alive

hundred yards each—and the absence of substantial egress routes inland—routes needed to clear men and equipment rapidly from the landing area.

These very disadvantages were the bases for Turner's objection to their use. Turner had ordered Hill to plan for a landing at Tinian Town in the southwest corner of the island, whose wide beaches were more suitable for a major amphibious landing. But an American landing there would be hotly opposed and costly. The Japanese, who had reasoned like Turner, had concluded that the Tinian Town beaches were the most likely to be used, and there they had concentrated their defenses.

Hill was distressed because Turner was in a black and vituperative mood and had violently refused even to consider the White beaches.

Rear Admiral Harry W. Hill, who argued with Kelly Turner about the
Tinian landing beaches

Thus in desperation Hill had bypassed Turner in order to plead his case
with Spruance. Spruance tended to agree with Hill, but he was reluctant
to overrule Turner, whom everyone regarded with awe as the Navy's
supreme authority on amphibious warfare. Furthermore, Spruance had
always treated Turner with deference because he believed that Turner
was his intellectual superior. But Turner could be wrong, and if he was
wrong, many Americans would die unnecessarily.

Spruance quickly convened a conference with Turner and his amphibious commanders. The others were nervous owing to Turner's
intransigence and the acrimony that had preceded the meeting. Following military custom, Spruance solicited their recommendations, beginning with the junior officer. (This procedure presumably encourages
frankness by a junior, as he might be inhibited by his senior's views if
the senior spoke first.) Five generals and admirals voted for the White
beaches. Spruance turned to Turner.

Turner quietly said that he approved the White beaches.

Everyone in the room was relieved that Turner's acquiescence had avoided a showdown. Spruance would have overruled his friend if he had persisted with his objections, but Turner had avoided that disagreeable prospect.

After the meeting Spruance asked Hill if he needed any special assistance at Tinian. Hill said the only thing that bothered him were possible heavy waves at the beaches, churned up by fierce seasonal storms west of the Marianas. Spruance assured Hill that he would provide additional long-range search planes that would maintain a careful weather watch to the west. The younger admiral was encouraged by Spruance's readiness to support the Tinian operation in every possible way.

After deciding upon the White beaches, Spruance had to wait two more weeks before the assaults could begin upon Tinian and Guam. Meanwhile he received a number of visitors, who came from varying missions.

One was Lieutenant General Robert C. Richardson, the senior Army general in the Central Pacific and Holland Smith's perpetual antagonist. Richardson, in a misguided effort to invigorate the morale of the 27th Division, arrived from Pearl Harbor on 12 July. While Spruance, Turner, and the amphibious commanders were aboard *Indianapolis* debating the merits of the Tinian beaches, Richardson was ashore ostentatiously distributing medals to the soldiers. His actions violated military etiquette; the 27th Division was not under his command and he had no authority to assemble and decorate the troops while they were in a combat zone outside his jurisdiction.

Hoping to prevent a hostile confrontation, Spruance urged his fiery Marine general not to argue with the Army general, regardless of the provocations—such as the relief of Ralph Smith. Suprisingly, Holland Smith complied. Spruance himself was indifferent to Richardson's activities ashore.

Turner, however, could not tolerate Richardson. Physically and mentally tired, still smoldering from the aftermath of the Tinian beaches debate, Turner was furious with Richardson for meddling with the Army troops. He called Moore to his flagship on the morning of the 14th and announced that he personally intended to castigate the lieutenant general. Moore was appalled and pleaded in vain with Turner to reconsider in the interest of interservice harmony. When Richardson

arrived on board *Rocky Mount,* Turner unleashed his fulminous wrath
upon the Army general before Moore's horrified eyes. Richardson
turned white with anger but retained his self-control; he quickly left
the ship, accompanied by a flustered and apologetic Moore.

Richardson went directly to *Indianapolis,* while Moore tried to disas-
sociate Spruance and the staff from Turner's actions. But Richardson
said nothing until he met with Spruance, whereupon he angrily denounced Turner's "insulting" behavior. Spruance tried to make light of
the episode. "That's just Kelly Turner's way," he said, "and no one
takes him seriously," implying that Richardson should have disregarded Turner's outburst as a minor incident. But Richardson was not
mollified, and interservice relations reached a new low.

Turner's fury did not abate. He sent a letter to Nimitz via Spruance
entitled, "Reporting unwarranted assumption of command authority
by Lieutenant General R. C. Richardson, Jr., USA," and Spruance's
endorsement generally confirmed Turner's charges. Nimitz, sick of the
squabbling, ignored the letter. In Spruance's later report of the Marianas campaign, Nimitz deleted all mention of Ralph Smith's relief by
crossing out Spruance's pertinent sentences with a wide-tipped black
pen.

On 17 July King and Nimitz landed at Saipan to inspect the island,
and Spruance went ashore to meet them. When the CNO stepped off
his plane, his first words to Spruance concerned the recent Battle of the
Philippine Sea. "Spruance, you did a damn fine job there," said King.
"No matter what other people tell you, your decision was correct."

King, Nimitz, Spruance, and the principal amphibious commanders
piled into a landing craft and chugged out to *Indianapolis.* The OOD
had not been forewarned and was startled to see King's head pop up at
deck edge from the Jacob's ladder, followed by Nimitz, Spruance, and
a galaxy of star-encrusted uniforms. For the remainder of the day and
night, recalled the OOD, everyone "tippy-toed" about the ship.

Moore met the group at the gangway. Still bitter at King for denying his promotion, Moore greeted the Navy's top admiral coldly yet
correctly, then deliberately welcomed Nimitz with effusive warmth.
The guests went below to freshen up and later assembled for dinner in
Spruance's flag mess.

The meal was a fiasco, owing to gigantic swarms of enormous black
flies that inundated the flagship. Carl Moore remembered them viv-

idly. "It was the kind of fly that you couldn't scare off," he recalled. "You had to push it. It would light on your nose and you'd have to practically pick it off . . . at mealtimes it was a horror, because it would be in your food and under your spectacles and into your ears. You kept thinking that the flies had all been eating dead Japs and were coming out to the ship for a little fresh air."

Spruance as the host sat at the head of the table with King at his right and Nimitz at his left. The remainder of the flag and general officers were arrayed by descending seniority on either side of the linen-covered table. The flies attacked, and the besieged diners began swatting and swinging in self-defense. An errant swipe splattered a glass of water, and Harry Hill knocked his ice cream upon the table. The guests excused themselves as soon as possible, in full retreat from the onslaught. The Japanese would have been pleased that something could rout the Americans.

"Otherwise," recalled Moore, "it was a pleasant occasion."

The visitors spoke on many subjects during their business meetings, the most important being future strategy against Japan. King asked for Spruance's recommendation for the next objective.

"Okinawa," responded Spruance.

"Can you take it?" asked King.

"I think so," said Spruance, "if we can find a way to transfer heavy ammunition at sea." Spruance explained that the fast carriers would have to remain at sea in order to "run interference" between Okinawa and Japan during the invasion. In the past, ships replenished ammunition while at anchor alongside a supply ship in a protected lagoon. Normally those anchorages were hundreds or thousands of miles away from the scene of action, and ships wasted many days in transit.

But off Okinawa Spruance could not afford to send his combatant ships to a rear area. They would have to remain on the front lines for months and would require underway replenishment. Nimitz promised to pass the problem on to Vice Admiral Calhoun, Commander Service Force at Pearl Harbor. (The Service Force proceeded successfully to devise a method for rearming and provisioning ships at sea that was used at Iwo Jima and Okinawa.)

Spruance also tried to resolve Moore's future. King and Nimitz had remained overnight aboard *Indianapolis,* and the next morning Spruance and King sat together at breakfast. Spruance reaffirmed that he needed Moore and wanted to keep him on his staff. He asked King

Lieutenant General Robert C. Richardson,
who argued with Spruance
about Kelly Turner

either to promote Moore to rear admiral and allow him to remain as
chief of staff, or, if King would not promote Moore, to allow him to
remain as assistant chief of staff.

King refused to answer Spruance. The subject was closed, as far as
King was concerned. Nevertheless Spruance pressed for a decision on
Moore's future, particularly since Vice Admiral Randall Jacobs, the
Chief of Naval Personnel, was in King's party. When King and Nimitz
departed *Indianapolis* on the morning of the eighteenth to return to
Pearl, Moore again deliberately was cool toward King and warm toward
Nimitz, which hardly helped his case.

That evening the staff assembled in the flag mess for dinner, and
Spruance asked Moore to sit next to him. Spruance was ill at ease as he
began to speak. He explained to Moore that he, Jacobs, and Savvy
Cooke (King's chief of staff) had convinced King and Nimitz to reas-

sign Moore as chief of staff to Vice Admiral McCain, who would rotate command of Task Force 58 with Mitscher. Their general feeling was that McCain, although competent, was impulsive, and presumably Moore could keep McCain "out of trouble." Would Moore accept the new job?

"I blew up immediately," Moore later recalled, "and told Spruance it was the most outrageous thing I'd ever heard of, that I wouldn't think of doing it, that it was quite obvious that they were putting me in the most embarrassing position, where if anything went right McCain would get all the glory for it, and if anything went wrong at all, I would be responsible for it. . . . I said, 'I haven't any influence on him.' . . . I could tell that his ideas were screwball in a great many ways, and I wouldn't have agreed with him on practically anything that he wanted to do. . . . And then this ridiculous idea of making me responsible for the commander of Task Force 38, to keep him on the track and keep him from doing foolish things! I said, 'Make *me* the commander of Task Force 38 and let me take responsibility for it and that's fine, but don't put me in a position of that sort!'

"Well, I got to speaking louder and louder and more and more indignant as I went along, and Spruance said, 'Keep quiet! Keep quiet! Not so loud!' So I tried to calm down, but I was simply sputtering and furious. I said that I wouldn't do it under any circumstances. He didn't try to persuade me, because I think he realized he had made an awful mistake in approaching me that way. If they had wanted me to do it, that was no way to persuade me."

The remainder of July passed with an exchange of messages and letters between *Indianapolis* and Washington. Although Arthur Davis soon would arrive to relieve Moore, Moore's future remained unresolved, which further nettled the dispositions of both Spruance and Moore.

The stifling July heat, the tension of the fighting ashore, and the uncertainty of Moore's future all created continuing conflicts and disagreements between Spruance and Moore. They argued incessantly and rarely attempted to be pleasant to each other. Moore's most frequent gripe was that Spruance allowed his subordinate commanders *too much* freedom, to the point that Spruance would not countermand their orders that obviously were wrong. For example, Spruance ordered Mitscher to raid Palau in late July in order to cover the landings on Guam and Tinian. Mitscher subsequently ordered his antiaircraft cruis-

The chiefs visit Saipan.
Left to right, Chester W. Nimitz, Ernest J. King, and Spruance

ers, whose largest guns were 5-inch, to bombard Palau, which was defended by 8-inch guns. Moore respected the superior range and accuracy of the Japanese guns and told Spruance that Mitscher was needlessly hazarding the light-gunned cruisers. Spruance stubbornly refused to intercede. Moore loudly persisted until Spruance finally told Mitscher to change his plans.

At the same time, Rear Admiral J. J. (Jocko) Clark, commanding one of Mitscher's carrier task groups, proposed to raid Woleai in the western Carolines on his return from Palau. Moore objected because Woleai was in MacArthur's theater, and his B-17 Army bombers attacked it frequently. "All hell could break loose," argued Moore, "if Clark's carrier planes and MacArthur's bombers arrived over Woleai at the same time without their being aware of the other's presence. Besides making MacArthur furious for our interfering in his territory, those planes could shoot at each other and it could be a disaster." Spruance ordered Clark to cancel the raid.

"That's the sort of thing that would keep popping up," Moore later recalled. "And there were other things that I would object to and think that he should do something about, and sometimes he would, sometimes he wouldn't. He was usually right and usually didn't pay any attention to me, but I insisted on his knowing what I was talking about. Spruance often intimated to me and directly said many times that the reason that he wanted me there was because I wasn't a yes-man and didn't simply agree with what he had to say. He was quite sure that if I disagreed, I'd make my disagreement known, and that's what he valued. That's what he really wanted. But it was very painful, many times, to keep on arguing and trying to make him understand what I was trying to say. He would interrupt and interfere and try to push me aside, and I simply had to hang on and insist on being heard."

As D-Day approached, the artillery ashore and the naval guns afloat increased the tempo of their systematic destruction of targets on Tinian and Guam. Japanese defenders on Tinian had watched the assault on Saipan only three miles away, and for weeks both the Tinian and the Guam garrisons apprehensively had observed Spruance's Fifth Fleet cruising offshore, gradually shifting its attention from Saipan toward these last two islands. The Japanese knew it was only a matter of time until they, too, would die like their comrades on Saipan. "I sometimes wonder what the state of mind of these Japs is," Spruance wrote Margaret, "when they know that they are just waiting to be killed off."

The Americans had discovered a new way to kill Japanese, a firebomb consisting of gasoline and napalm (a material originally used to waterproof motor vehicles). It could incinerate people over an area the size of a football field. Two days before the landing on Tinian, Spruance and his amphibious commanders boarded a destroyer to watch a demonstration as guests of Harry Hill.

A P-51 Army fighter swooped low over Tinian, and a gasoline wing tank tumbled from its belly toward the ground. "The effect was awe-inspiring," remembered Hill. "A burst of flame rose 100 feet or more into the air, and then the flame just seemed to flow along the ground." Everyone agreed the napalm bomb would be ideal to use against the

Lieutenant General Roy S. Geiger, U.S. Marine Corps. Commanded the Marines at Guam and Okinawa. Admired by Spruance for his "natural fearlessness."

foxholes and dugouts located behind the White beaches. Tinian was the first place that napalm bombs ever were used in war, and the Americans unhesitatingly employed their new weapon against the Japanese for the remainder of the war.

Spruance was willing to use any weapon that could kill Japanese quickly and efficiently. It was his conviction that they would never surrender, that only by killing them could islands be captured and the war eventually ended. Later, when planning the invasion of Iwo Jima and Okinawa, Spruance saw an Army film that demonstrated a new poison gas that could penetrate the standard Japanese gas mask. "After viewing the picture," Spruance later wrote, "I remarked that if we could be allowed to use this new gas at Iwo Jima, we would save a lot of American lives. The Japanese defenders of Iwo would die anyway, and there was no civilian population. Being killed quickly by gas was at least as merciful as being killed by flame throwers, bullets, bombs, and shells. For the Okinawa operation we could have used this gas with benefit from the standpoint of the military, but there was a large civilian population that had to be considered, so gas was hardly to be considered seriously." (The Americans never used poison gas in the Pacific War.)

To Spruance, the overriding concerns of the American commanders were "the efforts of our men out here to kill Japs without themselves getting killed in the process."

The long-postponed landings went off on schedule. As expected, the Japanese on Tinian were surprised and demoralized when the Americans landed on the White beaches, and in eight days the fight on that island was over. Spruance always considered that the Tinian assault was the most brilliantly conceived and executed of all the amphibious landings he commanded, and one of the few in which he achieved total surprise.

On Guam, Smith used the entire 77th Division to augment the III Amphibious Corps, also as expected. The pattern of fighting was repeated. The terrain was rugged, the days were hot and soggy, and the Japanese, masters of concealment, had to be dug out of their jungle caves, one by one. By 10 August General Geiger declared Guam secured, although the hunt for Japanese survivors would continue for months.

Moore wanted to raise the American flag on Guam for sentimental reasons. In 1899 his father, a naval officer in command of a detachment of sailors, had landed on Guam to take possession of the island for the United States from Spain and personally had raised the first American flag on Guam. Turner and Smith thought it appropriate for his son to raise the flag when the United States again took possession of the island, this time from Japan. Unfortunately, they did not inform Geiger, and his Marines raised the flag before Moore came ashore. Moore wrote ruefully to his wife, "Thus my last chance for distinction, even borrowed, has passed along the way."

Spruance remained at Saipan until late August in order to coordinate base and harbor developments; then Halsey relieved him. The Spruance-Halsey interchange was the beginning of the new strategy to keep pressure on Japan. King and Nimitz wanted to continue pounding the enemy and to allow them no respite between amphibious assaults. Thus after Spruance had captured his objective he would return to Pearl Harbor to plan the next amphibious operation, while Halsey assumed command of the fleet in order to resume raids on Japanese bases. Spruance's Fifth Fleet then became Halsey's Third Fleet, but the ships remained the same.

Art Davis reported aboard *Indianapolis* at Saipan in mid-August, and he was greeted warmly by both Spruance and Moore. During the long return passage to Pearl Harbor, Moore relaxed and allowed Davis quickly to assume the duties of chief of staff. There was little to do; the next objective after the Marianas was unknown, so neither Spruance nor the staff had any responsibilities. When *Indianapolis* arrived in Pearl Harbor, Moore prepared to leave for the States. He had finally received his orders, for an unspecified job in Washington.

During the return trip Spruance wrote a letter recommending that Moore receive the Distinguished Service Medal. The DSM was the Navy's third highest decoration, ranking just below the Medal of Honor and the Navy Cross. King, however, was peeved at Moore for refusing to become chief of staff to McCain. At King's direction, someone in Washington disapproved the recommendation, rewrote Spruance's citation, and eventually awarded Moore the Legion of Merit, the next inferior decoration.

"You certainly earned a Distinguished Service Medal," Spruance later wrote Moore. "However, under the circumstances I believe I would only be batting my head against a stone wall if I tried to get the matter reopened and other action taken. I have seen too many instances of Admiral King's determination in such things to have any illusions."[4]

But Spruance did what he could by ending Moore's final fitness report with the statement, "I have twice recommended Captain Moore for promotion to rear admiral, and these recommendations are now repeated." Although Moore was grateful for Spruance's endorsement, he never would receive that promotion while on active duty.

Moore described their parting in Pearl Harbor in early September 1944. "Admiral Spruance saw me off," said Moore, "and he expressed appreciation and affection as best he could without being sentimental or emotional. He spoke of what a good time we'd had together, and how we'd played ball and worked together with such success and such pleasant relations. He spoke of my being free and willing to express my views, and that's what he wanted. We parted in the greatest good

4. Moore eventually received a DSM.

spirits, and nothing difficult, either emotionally or sentimentally, nothing unpleasant, a very pleasant affair."

Spruance's forces had fought continuously for three months. When the campaign was over some 5,000 Americans had died capturing the Marianas, while 60,000 Japanese had died defending them.

With a wife's intuition, Margaret wrote her husband that she was worried about his health and state of mind during the prolonged, grueling series of battles.

"You appear to be bothering yourself excessively about my health, weight and exercising," he replied. "I can assure you that you can place your mind at rest. . . . On board ship I walk on the forecastle in bathing trunks for two hours every afternoon, when nothing interferes. This is mild and not violent exercise, and I have to do it to keep feeling well. If I don't exercise, I don't feel as well and I get nervous and mentally depressed. I know what my system requires, especially in the tropics. I don't enjoy the tropical heat as you know [a Spruance euphemism; he suffered terribly in hot weather], but I am in tip top condition and intend to stay that way in order to do my job, which, after all, is an important one.

"I am glad things went off as well as they have," Spruance continued, "for we have acquired some valuable real estate and cleared the Japs out of a considerable area of ocean. I want to finish this war and then I shall be ready to go as President of the Naval War College any time they want to send me. In the meantime your job is to get Margaret cured, take care of yourself, and don't worry about me.

"I would not have any other job in the world in preference to my present one at this time. It is very interesting and pleasant, as we have a fine team out here that works harmoniously and efficiently together. Nimitz, Halsey, and I all appear to bear up fairly well under the war."

Then Spruance told Margaret about the commanding officer of a cruiser, whom they both knew, who had a mental breakdown and killed himself. "Some people can't take a war," Spruance remarked, "and others thrive on it."

Chapter 20

PLANNING FOR IWO JIMA AND OKINAWA

THE war against Japan gathered momentum in the fall of 1944. American B-29's from the Marianas airfields began to bomb the Japanese homeland. Halsey assaulted Peleliu Island in the Palau group on 15 September 1944, and MacArthur returned to the Philippines by invading Leyte on 17 October 1944.

But plans for 1945 were uncertain. When Spruance returned to Pearl Harbor from the Marianas in early September, he did not know his next assignment. As *Indianapolis* entered the inner harbor, the signal station flashed its customary congratulatory message from Nimitz. The flagship moored, and Spruance went ashore to the CINCPAC headquarters to talk of the future with his commander in chief.

"The next operation is going to be Formosa and Amoy," said Nimitz. "You just hop in a plane, go back to California to see your family, and be back here in a couple of weeks."

"I don't like Formosa," said Spruance.

"What would you rather do?" asked Nimitz.

"I would prefer taking Iwo Jima and Okinawa."

"Well," said Nimitz, "it's going to be Formosa."

King had long advocated seizing Formosa in order to sever Japanese lines of communication to the Philippines, Indonesia, and Southeast

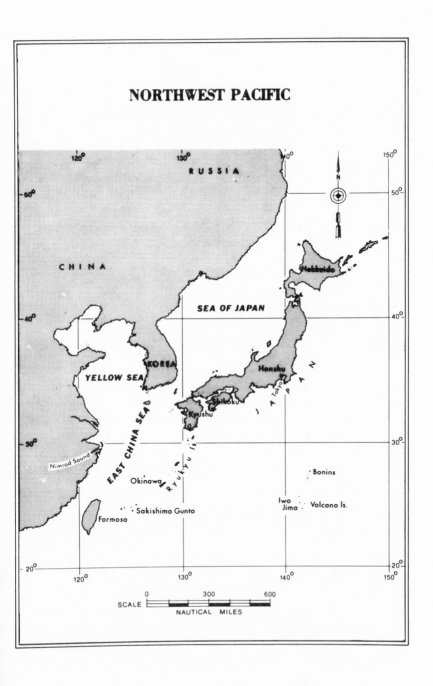

NORTHWEST PACIFIC

Asia—Japan's primary sources of oil, rice, and raw materials. Furthermore, King believed, Formosa could be used as a base for an invasion of China, which would be the last step in the blockade of Japan, a blockade that would force her surrender without the need to invade the Japanese home islands. King had influenced the JCS by the fall of 1944 to tentatively accept his Formosa strategy, but the merits of Formosa were still being debated both in Washington and in the high commands in the Pacific.

When Spruance told Nimitz he preferred Iwo Jima and Okinawa to Formosa, his answer, although unhesitating, was not impulsive. Rather it was based upon weeks of intensive study while he was at sea capturing the Marianas. During lulls in the fighting, he had frequently asked the fleet navigator to bring charts to the flag cabin, but he never looked at the chart of Formosa. Instead Spruance constantly studied two specific areas, the China coast and the Ryukyu Islands.

Spruance once confided to a friend that he made no claims for himself as a tactician, but that he tried to be a good strategist. He considered that geography and lines of communication were the essence of strategy.[1] Interior lines could be protected, while exterior lines were vulnerable to enemy attack. For example, he reasoned that the Marianas were located on the focus of an arc that extended from Tokyo through Kyushu, the Ryukyu Islands, Formosa, the Philippine Islands, and New Guinea. By seizing the Marianas the Americans had obtained interior lines of communication which would allow them to advance from the Marianas toward any of those Japanese-held positions.

Similarly, Spruance envisioned Iwo Jima as the focus of an arc through Tokyo, Kyushu, and the Ryukyus. He wanted Iwo Jima primarily as an air base because it was interposed halfway between Tokyo and the Marianas. It could provide air support throughout the Tokyo-Ryukyus-Okinawa arc when the fleet began to operate within aircraft range of Japan—as they soon would. The Japanese had hoarded thousands of aircraft on the home islands, and the carriers could not protect the fleet indefinitely. An American air base on Iwo Jima to augment the carriers would be a big help.

Spruance also was aware that Iwo Jima could provide an emergency airfield for damaged B-29's returning to the Marianas from raids

---

1. *Lines of communication* are the seaways, airways, roadways, railways, and their terminals, upon which pass a nation's commerce and military forces.

against Japan, and that it could be a fighter base for Air Force P-51 fighters escorting the bombers attacking Japan. Another bonus was that it would eliminate the Japanese use of Iwo Jima as an early warning outpost for incoming B-29 flights. *But Iwo Jima's value to the Air Force B-29 campaign was not Spruance's initial rationale for seizing that island.*

Okinawa, in turn, was a center from which the Americans could control the East China Sea. Spruance was more impressed with Okinawa for that reason than for its possible use as a base to invade Japan. Spruance did not want to land American troops on Japanese soil. Instead he wanted to blockade Japan and starve the enemy into submission. So did King. King, however, wanted to blockade from Formosa, while Spruance wanted Okinawa. In mid-August 1944 Nimitz and Forrest Sherman visited Spruance at Guam and reaffirmed that King did not want Okinawa and was advocating Formosa. Sherman opposed King's position. Apparently the CNO wanted Formosa *before* the Philippines, an illogical move because the Japanese forces in the Philippines could then imperil the southern flank of any American forces attempting to invade Formosa. Sherman was therefore preparing the plans under duress. The concept was "so ridiculous and so impossible" that he hoped the plans he had prepared "would be so obviously bad that they would cancel the idea."

A few days after Nimitz and Sherman had returned to Pearl Harbor, Moore brought two large volumes to the breakfast table and placed them next to Spruance. Moore explained that they contained the JCS study that recommended the seizure of Formosa in early 1945 *after* the Philippines had been seized. Spruance's only comment was that if anyone went to Formosa, it wouldn't be he. Yet when he returned to Pearl Harbor from the Marianas campaign, Nimitz affirmed that Spruance would indeed be taking Formosa. Spruance still could not take the plan seriously, and he suspected that the concept would be killed at a King-Nimitz conference scheduled for San Francisco in late September. In the meantime he told his staff to take leave—there was no reason to waste time working on a Formosa plan.

While Washington and Pearl Harbor continued to argue Formosa's merits, Spruance and many of his staff flew from Pearl Harbor to the mainland for a short vacation. Spruance arrived at Monrovia in mid-September, seeking rest and seclusion. When the local newspaper asked for an interview, Spruance tried to avoid it by saying he was under orders not to comment on the war against Japan. His only public appearances were at two service club luncheons, which he reluctantly attended.

Following one of his speeches, he was asked whether he thought the Japanese-Americans should be allowed to return to their homes from their concentration camps after the war. It was a loaded question because most Californians were hostile toward the Japanese-Americans. Spruance responded vigorously and firmly that he condemned their illegal and unconstitutional deportation. They were not disloyal, he said, and as American citizens they had been deprived of their legal rights. "That reply was not what they were expecting," his daughter recalled. "It caused a great deal of headlines. I was rather shocked at him, because in those days one simply did not come out in favor of anything for the Japanese or the Japanese-Americans. Of course, however, he was right."

During his vacation, Spruance made two significant comments on the war to his wife and daughter. One concerned his misgivings about the fact that the Royal Navy soon would be operating with the Fifth Fleet. Under pressure from Churchill, King had reluctantly agreed to allow the British fleet to integrate with the Pacific Fleet. King had opposed Churchill's offer because the British ships were not accustomed to the American way of doing things, and they might hinder rather than help. For example, the British ships had limited endurance and rarely ventured far from fixed bases. By contrast, the American Navy had developed a sophisticated logistical support system that allowed American ships to remain at sea for months. Furthermore, Spruance's fleet would be using a new and untried system for underway replenishment of ammunition and supplies, for which the British would be unprepared. Thus Spruance believed that the British would impose many unwanted problems upon him and his staff.

Fortunately, Spruance was wrong. The logistical problem was solved when the Americans told the British they would have to provide their own supply ships as a prerequisite to joining the Fifth Fleet. Tactical problems were minimized by having the British operate as an independent task force in separate geographical areas. Their contributions were invaluable and will be covered in later chapters.

Spruance's other reaction to the war was his sadness and disappointment about Moore. "Raymond is heartsick over losing Carl," wrote

Margaret to Moore's wife. "I have never seen Raymond so upset. Raymond feels that if he himself had had more pull with the powers that be, that it would have been a different story. Young Margaret feels very bitter."

Just before Spruance was scheduled to leave Monrovia, he received a telegram from Nimitz ordering him to extend his vacation and to meet with Nimitz and King in San Francisco on 29 September. Spruance made the most of his additional days with Margaret, then flew to San Francisco for the conference. The staffs who had accompanied their chiefs gathered for small talk before the meeting began.

Sherman handed Spruance a paper. "Read it carefully," said Sherman, "and tell me what you think of it." The paper was a CINCPAC staff study that recommended abandoning the plan to seize Formosa. The study contained sound strategic reasoning, but its most telling argument was that Nimitz did not have enough troops for seizing Formosa and that the JCS could not provide any reinforcements. The paper noted that Nimitz *did* have enough men to capture Iwo Jima and Okinawa, and Nimitz recommended their seizure in lieu of Formosa.

Spruance returned the paper to Sherman. "I wouldn't change a word of it," said Spruance.

The meeting convened, Nimitz presented the paper to King, and a protracted debate began. King stubbornly clung to his Formosa plan, and Spruance wondered why he persisted in a concept that made so little sense. Throughout the conference Spruance rarely spoke, and at one point King asked why he remained silent. Wasn't Spruance a persistent advocate of Okinawa over Formosa? he asked. Spruance replied that Nimitz and Sherman were presenting the case so well that he had nothing to add.

King eventually agreed to cancel Formosa and to recommend Iwo Jima and Okinawa to the JCS.

The Army and the Air Force had provided the arguments that Nimitz had used in finally convincing King to drop Formosa and to substitute Okinawa. Yet, ironically, Spruance and the other two services wanted Okinawa for widely differing reasons. Spruance envisioned Okinawa as a base for an eventual landing in China and for air attacks against Japanese lines of communication, which would isolate Japan and force her to "die on the vine." The Army—and MacArthur in particular—advocated an eventual invasion of Kyushu in southern Japan, reasoning that the Japanese never would surrender until the home islands were captured. Therefore, the Army wanted Okinawa as a staging base for the final assault against Japan. Finally, the Air Force wanted Okinawa as an air base for bombing strategic targets in the Japanese homeland, whereas Spruance foresaw Okinawa as an air base for bombing tactical targets.[2] Thus the the selection of Okinawa (as with the Marianas) was governed by the self-interests of each service rather than a unified national strategy. If the services could agree upon a physical objective (a major task in itself), perhaps they reasoned they could argue about how they would use it after it was captured.

Spruance quickly discovered that the conference was to be a social affair as well as a working session. Many wives had accompanied their husbands, so he phoned Margaret to join him in San Francisco. Margaret hesitated to leave her daughter, still recuperating from tuberculosis; but Spruance insisted, and Margaret came. The admirals and generals and their wives congregated at the St. Francis Hotel, and Spruance and Margaret were given a sumptuous suite of rooms.

"How much is this going to cost us?" muttered Spruance, before he learned that the rooms were free. And in truth, Spruance's parsimony was more pronounced than ever. At the time, he had accumulated thousands of dollars in back pay which he had never drawn. He later wrote Moore that Margaret "found nothing to buy in the shops—at least nothing that she told me about—so everything was OK."

For three glorious days the Spruances attended dinners, parties, and receptions. Margaret reveled in the excitement of being with her husband among good friends in the magnificent city. She sensed that her husband had been "fighting for something" and that he was cheerful because he had won. Indeed, all the men were ebullient—even stern Ernie King was jovial. Their mood was contagious. It was as if no war existed.

Yet the war was inescapable. Uniformed men jammed the streets, and great transports steamed to sea beneath the Golden Gate Bridge. The city hummed with tension, and Margaret mentioned to her husband that something certainly was going on. Spruance looked severely

2. For the purposes of this book alone, the following definitions are used: *Strategic* targets are cities and industries whose destruction weakens the enemy's ability to wage war. *Tactical* targets are the armed forces that oppose one's own armed forces.

at his wife as if she had disclosed a military secret, and he asked why she had made that remark.

"Well, it's perfectly obvious," replied Margaret. "Look at all these mothers and fathers walking the streets with their sons in uniform."

Margaret could have added, "And wives and lovers with their men in uniform." San Francisco was the port of embarkation for all points west, and there throughout the war privates and seamen and generals and admirals experienced bittersweet last moments and farewells.

Next morning the transports had left and the streets were deserted. The city's somber mood was a painful reminder of the imminent separation of Raymond and Margaret Spruance after their brief and joyous interlude in San Francisco, away from the war in the Pacific and the tedium of Monrovia. On their last night Spruance took Margaret to the train station, they parted, and the good times were over. Remembers Margaret, "I felt very alone and forlorn."

Spruance went directly to the airport the same night, joined Nimitz, and their plane returned to Pearl Harbor. Spruance wrote to Margaret shortly after he arrived. "Needless to say, I do miss you," he wrote, "but so far I do not feel as low about it as I did last May—why I don't know. We certainly had a fine leave together, not to mention the three days in San Francisco. I hope young Margaret learned something of the noble art of cooking during your absence and was not too lonesome. I have an idea that she got along all right."

Having returned to Pearl Harbor, Spruance attacked the piles of accumulated paperwork, then fled for the beach. "We had a long walk," he wrote Moore, "and not so long a swim, as my swimming muscles are soft. We missed you, as the beach, air and water were perfect." Spruance and Moore always had enjoyed watching pretty girls in bathing suits during their past excursions to the beach. This time, however, Spruance noted that "gals were scarce."

The two men also had enjoyed watching pretty Micronesian girls without bathing suits. In another letter to Moore, Spruance dwelled in statesmanlike tones on the postwar development of the Marshall, Mariana, and Caroline Islands. "Christianizing the natives will tend to bind them to us and to separate them from Japan, as will teaching them English," he concluded. Then he added a footnote, "Please don't think, however, that I am trying to put undershirts on any native belles who are not accustomed to wearing them."

Spruance had few demands in his office that kept him away from the beaches in October. Many of his staff were on leave and the atmosphere was relaxed, allowing Spruance and his new chief of staff plentiful time to establish their professional and personal relationship.

Thrice-married Arthur Davis was a lean, rough, aggressive fifty-one-year-old rear admiral with extensive planning experience both in Washington and in Pearl Harbor. He was an authoritarian who viewed problems in terms of black and white, and he acted and moved decisively and intelligently. Davis would have preferred command of a fast carrier task group, but he and Forrest Sherman disliked one another, and Davis felt that Sherman could and would block any chance of his getting command.

The intent of relieving Moore with aviator Davis presumably was to ensure that aviation considerations were properly incorporated within Fifth Fleet planning. Yet the new chief of staff caused hardly a ripple. Nothing changed. The staff—battle-tested, smooth, and efficient—continued as before, and Davis made no attempt to change what he recognized as a superb organization inherited from Carl Moore. The staff, in turn, was relieved to be able to work free from Moore's unrelenting pressure. Davis, therefore, saw no need to work Moore's man-killing hours, and he always was available and willing to accompany Spruance on hikes and beach excursions. Spruance and Davis had known each other before and were good friends. They continued to get on well together.

Davis idolized Spruance. He was awed by Spruance's intellect and regarded the admiral as modest, shy, unassuming, and unconceited. "Spruance was a genuine super-ability," Davis later wrote, "to be guarded against all minor distractions. I made up my mind that I would do all in my power to keep his mind free of all the deadening inconsequentialities that can waste time and take attention from the things that really matter. Without any discussion of the subject, we had an understanding that I would handle the nits and lice, as it were, and that he would be brought into the ring only on matters of importance."

Spruance always acted quickly and decisively on any problems that Davis referred to him, and in Davis's admiring eyes, Spruance invariably was right.

Their few disagreements were trivial. For example, Davis objected to the raw onions that Spruance insisted accompany each meal, because their smell made him ill. Davis also tried—without success—to intro-

Rear Admiral Arthur C. Davis

duce fish, chicken, lamb, and pork into the flag mess menu in order to add variety. Davis's wife tried to help. She mailed over five hundred recipes for use by the cook. Spruance still preferred beef.

Spruance had fixed ideas on the proper food for himself and his staff. His own food intake was so carefully regulated that he would not indulge in ice cream for dessert unless he had used an equivalent number of calories by walking in the afternoon. Lunch invariably was soup and salad. When the stewards served the salad to guests, Spruance would admonish, "That's all you're going to get, so you had better take a generous helping."

A reserve lieutenant from Arkansas, Cyrus R. (Cy) Huie, became Spruance's flag lieutenant in January 1945. Among other duties, Huie supervised the stewards and the menu for the flag mess. The hungry mess members soon urged him to provide solid food for the luncheon menu. The naïve Huie and the chief steward consented and produced a superb meal: soup, salad, meat, potatoes, and dessert. Spruance ate without comment. Afterwards the other mess members praised the offering and thanked Huie for the inspired meal.

That afternoon Spruance and his flag lieutenant were walking, and Spruance tactfully commented, "Huie, about that meal."

"Yes, sir?"

"It was rather heavy," said Spruance.

"Yes sir," replied Huie, "but several members of the staff have complained that soup and salad don't stay with them very long."

Spruance listened politely but insisted that heavy food at lunch induced lethargy. "I want my staff to be alert during the afternoon," he said, "and besides, I prefer soup and salad."

The luncheon menu remained soup and salad forever more.

Holland Smith did not want to invade Iwo Jima. "It will be the toughest place we have had to take," he told Spruance. "I don't know what anybody wants it for, but I'll take it."

Smith's pessimism worried Spruance. His Marine generals incessantly reminded their fleet commander of the hazards and the enormous loss of life that would be inevitable when the Marines landed on Iwo Jima. Spruance began to doubt whether the costs of taking the island would be worth the gains, and the uncertainty troubled him throughout the three-month planning period from October through December 1944.

Smith's apprehension was justified. Iwo Jima was an island four and a half miles long and two and a half miles wide, dominated by a 550-foot extinct volcano on the southern end, Mount Suribachi. A deep, black volcanic ash covered the barren slopes, and plumes of steam revealed still active deposits of hot sulphur. Desolate, remote, and austere, the island was useful to the Japanese only as an air base, and American carriers frequently had attacked its airfields during mid-1944 to cover the landing operations in the Marianas.

When the United States first began to seize Pacific islands from the Japanese in 1943 and 1944, the Americans could choose their objectives from many possibilities. The Japanese defenses were thinly spread over hundreds of atolls and millions of square miles of ocean, and the Japanese usually were unable to guess the Americans' next objective until the landings began. They often were surprised and unprepared, and the battles, although fierce, were short. But by mid-1944 the Japanese occupied fewer and fewer outlying islands. After the Marianas fell the next American objectives were as obvious to the Japanese as they were to the Americans.

The Japanese therefore correctly guessed that Iwo Jima was destined for an eventual American invasion, and they began to fortify the island. They had many months to prepare. Men and equipment poured in, and the Japanese transformed Iwo Jima into a fortress. Mount Suribachi was infested with caves, tunnels, and ravines containing artillery, machine guns, and mortars that commanded the only possible landing beaches, which were located at the base of the volcano. The flat part of the island was defended by blockhouses, pillboxes, and trenches that were connected by tunnels and caves protected by thick layers of steel, concrete, and dirt. Food, water, and ammunition were stowed deep inside the bowels of Suribachi. The entire island was an armored honeycomb impervious to bombs and shells. Some 20,000 Japanese troops, commanded by a skillful and determined general named Kuribayashi, were ready to do battle with Holland Smith's Marines.

In the past the Americans had tried to seize an important objective before the Japanese could get dug in, but the assault on Iwo Jima had to wait. All the Navy's resources were committed to supporting MacArthur's cherished return to the Philippines in the last months of 1944, and the enemy used the time continually to reinforce and strengthen the Iwo defenses. Air Force B-24's from the Marianas constantly raided Iwo, but their bombs were ineffective against the well-protected fortifications and served primarily to encourage the Japanese to dig deeper. Nimitz and Spruance urged that the Air Force bombers lower their altitude in order to improve their accuracy, particularly against the ships that were supplying the island. But the Air Force refused, protesting that they were untrained for antishipping missions. Thus the Air Force bombers flew in high and level, the Japanese ships easily evaded their bombs, and the flow of reinforcements and war material into Iwo continued unabated.

Spruance damned the entire massive effort of the Air Force against Iwo Jima, for it had done little to soften the island's defenses despite six months of raids. The Japanese were even able to launch successful air strikes from Iwo Jima against the B-29's on Saipan. The Americans responded with intensified attacks on Iwo airfields with both Air Force planes and naval guns. But sturdy Iwo Jima grew stronger each day, and her airfields were quickly restored to operation for more counterattacks against Saipan.

Holland Smith had an elemental solution for reducing the Iwo defenses before his Marines landed: ten days of naval gunfire bombardment. "Impossible," said Turner, and his objections were many. Bombardment ships were not available, he argued, because they had to remain in the Philippines until the last moment to support MacArthur. And even if the ships were available, they would exhaust their ammunition before the landings could begin. Fifth Fleet ammunition resources were limited. Although underway replenishment ships would be available for rearming Task Force 58 in the waters off Iwo, that method was experimental and could not help the bombardment ships. Many combatants would still have to steam over nine hundred miles to Ulithi Atoll (a newly acquired fleet anchorage in the Carolines) in order to replenish at anchor, or to the inadequate anchorages in the Marianas six hundred and fifty miles south-southwest of Iwo. Finally, said Turner, ten days of bombardment would herald the imminent invasion and thereby forfeit any chance for surprise.

Turner's counterproposal was three days of intensive pre-D-Day bombardment. Marine Major General Harry Schmidt, who would be in tactical command of the landing force, thought about Turner's plan for three weeks, then replied. Schmidt agreed in principle with Turner, but he asked that the bombardment be given four days rather than three, in order to provide slower and more deliberate fire. Turner forwarded Schmidt's proposal to Spruance for a decision.

Spruance appreciated the Marines' legitimate concern over the Iwo defenses and their desire for a thorough prelanding bombardment. But the admiral had other overriding considerations, primarily the threat of thousands of enemy aircraft based in Japan, only seven hundred and fifty miles away from Iwo. Spruance had to suppress the enemy air during the first critical days of the landing and intended to strike the menacing airfields with Task Force 58 simultaneously with the prelanding bombardments on Iwo. If the bombardment began before the carrier strikes, he reasoned, the Japanese would be forewarned and Task Force 58 would lose the advantage of surprise. The alerted Japanese either could attack Task Force 58 or they could disperse and hoard their aircraft for attacks against the Iwo transports—or both.

Spruance therefore overruled the Marine generals' expert recommendations for a four-day bombardment, even though he knew they had considered that period as an irreducible compromise from their original request for ten days. Spruance told them to expect a three-day bombardment only, and he carefully explained his reasoning.

"The initial surface bombardment must be simultaneous with the initial carrier attack upon the Tokyo area," Spruance wrote. "The carrier attacks will be continued there for three days if practicable, but it may prove desirable or necessary to discontinue attacks after two days or less. If the attacks were made on D minus 4 and D minus 3 days, time would then be available to the enemy for recovery and reinforcement early enough to initiate threatening air operations at the objective by D-Day."

Spruance then reinforced Turner's prediction on the shortage of bombardment ammunition. He first explained that prelanding naval gunfire would not be accurate enough to eliminate the well-camouflaged and well-protected trenches and pillboxes that would defend the landing beaches. They would have to be taken by the troops ashore, who would be able to discover and pinpoint their locations and then direct naval gunfire precisely to the target. The Marines would need an immense volume of naval gun ammunition on D-Day. "There will be no early opportunity for replacement of naval ammunition," wrote Spruance, "a large proportion of which must be saved for support on D-Day. There is a limit to the quantity of ammunition which can be made available for pre-D-Day bombardment and no advantage is seen in delivering that quantity in four days rather than in three."

Finally, Spruance noted, the Air Force would have been bombing

Iwo for six months. Although he privately disparaged the results, he told the Marines that the total effort certainly was the equivalent of the extra day's ship bombardment recommended by the Marines. Spruance did, however, hedge his decision to the extent that he authorized a fourth day of bombardment *once the shooting started,* if the commanders at Iwo Jima at that time thought the additional day was necessary.

Spruance's decision culminated two months of discussion, study, and correspondence between the Navy and the Marine Corps. It became the basis for bitter recriminations by critics—mostly Marines— who later charged that the heavy Marine casualties on Iwo would have been lessened had Spruance allowed more days for bombardment, as initially recommended by the Marine generals. The soundness of that decision will be assessed in the following chapter.

MacArthur's Philippines campaign in late 1944 absorbed both time and resources, so much so that the D-Days for Iwo Jima and Okinawa were slipped a month, to 19 February and 1 April 1945 respectively. Spruance worried about the beating his ships were taking in the Philippines, and he wrote to Hoover that "we may not have anything like the forces we originally counted on when we start doing business." But ready or not, the two Iwo-Okinawa dates now were inviolate. The typhoon season likely would begin about the first of May, and the troops had to be firmly established ashore before the expected storms began to thrash Okinawa.

Spruance worried also about the Japanese air threat. When the first kamikaze attacks began in the Philippines in late 1944, Spruance viewed their use as "very sound and economical war and a form especially suited to the Japanese temperament." Spruance at that time did not feel that the suicide planes would be used extensively against his forces at Iwo and Okinawa. But he was disturbed by intelligence reports that Japanese aircraft production was thriving despite the B-29 raids, thereby increasing the numbers of conventional aircraft which he was certain would hit his fleet during the Iwo-Okinawa amphibious assaults.

By November 1944 Spruance began to consider ways and means permanently to attenuate the looming air threat. "Perhaps we should stop fighting the products of the Jap aircraft factories on the perimeter," he wrote to a friend, "and take our carrier air in to the center to knock out the factories themselves. We cannot afford to await the outcome of bombing 'with precision instruments' from 30,000 feet, often through solid overcast. That may work for large areas, but it is too slow and inaccurate to take out specific targets. Our Iwo operation will benefit by a precision carrier strike, provided we have enough ships by that time to do the job."

Spruance's letter was prompted by the poor bombing results against Japan by Saipan-based B-29 bombers in late November. Two separate strikes of 110 and 81 bombers each had tried to hit vital aircraft factories on 24 and 27 November. The bombers had flown over Japan at altitudes ranging from 27,000 to 33,000 feet in order to avoid antiaircraft fire, and an undercast had almost completely obscured the targets. Only 24 bombers on the 24 November strike had even attempted to bomb the aircraft factories; the remaining planes on both strikes had unloaded against secondary targets.

The B-29 effort did not improve during December. Although aircraft factories were their primary targets, the B-29's were thwarted by a number of factors: bad weather continued to hide the targets; radar bombing techniques were ineffective; weather forecasts were inaccurate owing to faulty reports from Russia and China; jet streams aloft moving at velocities up to 180 knots further degraded bombing accuracy; many bombers never located the target area owing to navigational errors; many other bombers had to abort their missions owing to the numerous mechanical defects that plagued the bomber; and crews lacked adequate training.

It was apparent to Spruance that the B-29's would not be able to eliminate the factories—the source of the Japanese air threat. The only solution was for the Navy to encroach on the Air Force's strategic bombing domain. Accordingly, he ordered Mitscher to have Task Force 58 strike aircraft factories as well as airfields and aircraft during the covering attack against Japan. "We would use our accuracy to attack military targets," Spruance later remarked, "and would leave attacks on the civilian population to the Army Air Force."

"I am getting restless to get on with the war," wrote Spruance to Margaret. He had been marking time in Pearl Harbor for two months, and two and a half months remained before D-Day on Iwo Jima. "The trouble now is that I do not have enough work thrust on me to keep me busy, and I am too lazy to dig up work for myself. Hence, I wish the time would come to start moving again. On board ship, if there is not much to do, I can sit down and read a book, but here I feel more or less obliged to keep office hours and reading a book during office hours does not look well."

Chuck Barber invited his future wife to dinner in the flag mess one evening, and the attractive woman sat next to Spruance at the head of the table. The conversation turned to the subject of submerged sea mountains in the Pacific. A lively discussion ensued, but Spruance remained silent.

The young woman turned to the taciturn, dignified admiral. "Certainly you must know something about these sea mountains," she said brightly. "You're an old sea dog."

Spruance could not resist the temptation.

"Woof, woof," said the fleet commander.

The usual Honolulu social activities occupied much of Spruance's time. "I am getting to be a regular social butterfly," he wrote Margaret, "and it is high time that I got out and did some more fighting before I get too soft. This place is getting much too frequented and civilized."

His new schnauzer, Peter, was a pleasant diversion. "He is a very nice dog," wrote Spruance, "quiet, friendly, and well behaved, but still full of life. I take him out for a walk every morning. He enjoys it and it improves my appetite."

Spruance wanted to send Peter home to Margaret, but she was reluctant because Spruance's earlier schnauzer had been a terror. "I wish I could send Peter to you when I leave," he coaxed, "for he is a very nice young dog and you would enjoy him. He might keep you from getting so bored with life. He has a singing voice that improves day by day. You will like him very much."

Margaret was unconvinced, and Peter remained in Pearl Harbor until Spruance brought him home after the war.

The Battle of the Philippine Sea always would haunt him, and when he read the Japanese version three months after the battle, he commented to Margaret, "Either their intelligence is terrible or else they are bigger liars than even I gave them credit for being."

With his own past battle in mind, he followed Halsey's trials in the Battle of Leyte Gulf in October 1944 with great interest. Halsey, reacting to Spruance's experience, had been determined not to allow the Japanese fleet to escape should it appear in the Philippines. The Japanese, however, cleverly reasoned that Halsey, aggressive and impulsive, would be susceptible to a decoy during the landings at Leyte. The Japanese successfully lured Halsey, along with his fast carriers and battleships, away from the Leyte beaches, and Japanese battleships and cruisers sneaked behind Halsey through the San Bernardino Strait. MacArthur's transports survived only through the bravery and sacrifice of a weak covering force of American escort carriers and destroyers.

"What happened during this whole Leyte action," Spruance wrote Margaret, "was just what I was expecting off Saipan and was trying to prevent—being drawn off to the westward while part of the Jap fleet came in around our flank and hit the amphibious force at Saipan." Understanding the predicaments plaguing a fleet commander during a battle at sea, Spruance did not criticize Halsey and simply commented that "Bill Halsey did a fine job on the outfit that came down from Japan [the decoy force of carriers]."

On the last day of 1944, Spruance sent his wife a melancholy, introspective letter. "Yesterday was our 30th wedding anniversary," he wrote. "That sounds like a long time in the abstract, but actually the time has gone by very quickly. This war has used up one tenth of it, and we may be separated most of the time for the next two or three years. I can see no predictable end at present, but the next six months [the Iwo Jima–Okinawa campaign] will give us a much better idea of how long it is going to take. However long this war may last, you and I have had a very happy life together (except on Christmas Eves) and we should have many years more later on."

Just before leaving Pearl Harbor in January 1945 for the long haul to Iwo Jima, he summarized his attitude on the war in another letter to Margaret. "I am certainly happy with my job," he wrote. "I would not trade it for any other the Navy has to offer now. We have some tough fighting ahead, and make no mistake, the Japs are still far from licked. But if we get away with it, and we must and will, the war will be pushed along toward a successful conclusion."

Chapter 21

IWO JIMA

SPRUANCE resumed making war against the Japanese in mid-January 1945. The *Indianapolis* signalmen again broke his flag at the truck, and Spruance and the staff moved aboard. Several new officers had joined the staff, in addition to Davis, because a number of the original senior staff officers had asked for commands before the war ended. Spruance had approved their transfer, but he retained the most important people: Forrestel, Biggs, Armstrong, McCormick, and Barber.

On 14 January *Indianapolis* got underway in Pearl Harbor, steamed past the sunken *Arizona* and the antisubmarine nets guarding the harbor entrance, and began her journey toward Iwo Jima, 3600 miles to the west. D-Day was slightly more than a month away. Spruance's first destination was Ulithi in the eastern Carolines, where he would take command of the fleet from Halsey.

The tranquil passage to Ulithi required eleven days. Spruance resumed his familiar at-sea practice of reading, exercising, and listening to classical music on the ship's loudspeakers in the early afternoon. "When there is no excitement going on, a daily routine like this keeps you in shape and helps to pass the time," he wrote Margaret. "I must say that, except for the heat and humidity, I enjoy a spell at sea. I am also glad to be getting out where we shall be accomplishing something once more."

Indianapolis entered Ulithi lagoon on the morning of 25 January and slowly eased among the great fleet of gray warships assembled in the anchorage. The staff watched from the flag bridge, and they could hear the navigator's voice drifting from the ship's pilothouse nearby, calling out the distance to the *Indianapolis* anchorage berth. "Let go the anchor!" ordered the captain, and on the forecastle a boatswain's mate swung his sledgehammer and whacked open the pelican hook. The huge anchor plunged into the bottom of the lagoon in a cascade of spray, followed by a roaring anchor chain shedding a cloud of rust. The jack on the forecastle and the ensign on the fantail were raised and two-blocked. *Indianapolis* was properly anchored.

In the afternoon the long and graceful silhouette of the *New Jersey* emerged over the horizon, and the great battleship steamed majestically into the lagoon and anchored near the venerable *Indianapolis*. Halsey had arrived. Spruance and the staff piled into a boat and made their way to *New Jersey* to pay their respects and to relieve the watch.

Halsey had been at sea for five months. In that period his Third Fleet had captured Palau, supported MacArthur's invasion of the Philippines, fought the Battle of Leyte Gulf, and had been ravaged by a December typhoon. Its carriers, roaming the Western Pacific, had destroyed over 7000 Japanese planes and had sunk 90 warships and over 550 merchantmen totaling over a million tons of shipping. Now Halsey and his staff would return to the States for a breather, but his tired and ragged ships would remain at war. When Spruance took command, the Third Fleet again would become the Fifth Fleet.

Halsey greeted his old friend at the quarterdeck, and the two senior admirals retired to the flag cabin. Halsey seemed in good spirits, but he was anxious to return to Pearl Harbor and to the United States. The two men chatted at length about their families, and Halsey proudly showed Spruance pictures of his son's recent wedding. Meanwhile the staff officers met with their opposite numbers, and Barber exchanged information with Halsey's flag secretary, a Minnesota politician named Harold Stassen.

Two days later Spruance relieved Halsey.

Spruance had been unable to dispel his concern about the costs of taking Iwo Jima, because he felt he had been largely responsible for influencing the ultimate decision to seize the island. He knew it would be valuable as a base for projecting land-based air power against the enemy. But would it be worth the thousands of American lives that inevitably would be lost? Lives for which Spruance felt responsible? Although there was no turning back from the American commitment to seize Iwo, Spruance wanted assurance that he had been correct in advocating the invasion.

He sought that assurance from Major General Curtis E. LeMay, commander of the XXI Bomber Command, the B-29 force based in the Marianas. LeMay came aboard *Indianapolis* at Ulithi on 28 January to discuss how the Air Force would support the Iwo landings. Spruance's first question reflected his uneasiness.

"What do you think about the value of Iwo Jima?" asked the admiral.

"It's going to be a tremendous value to me," the general responded immediately. "Without Iwo Jima I couldn't bomb Japan effectively."

LeMay had commanded the XXI Bomber Command less than ten days. A young, aggressive general, he was an exponent of using long-range bombers against strategic targets, and he had earned a reputation as a strategic bombing expert in the air war against Germany. The air war against Japan had been going badly for many months, and the Air Force had sent in LeMay in order to improve the B-29 performance. Thus LeMay was anxious to acquire Iwo Jima, primarily as a refueling and emergency landing field for the B-29's, but also as a base for long-range fighter escorts that would protect his bombers from Japanese interceptors.

LeMay had confirmed Spruance's opinion of Iwo's strategic value. "This took a load off my mind," Spruance said later. "LeMay's opinion was reassuring to me."

Following LeMay's visit, the Fourth Cruiser Squadron arrived at Ulithi as the vanguard of the Royal Navy's contribution to the Pacific war. The squadron commander, Rear Admiral E. J. P. Brind, requested permission to call on Spruance. Brind's visit, added to the respect many Americans felt for the Royal Navy, had its effect upon the *Indianapolis* executive officer, who was a stickler for enforcing naval regulations. Wanting to observe peacetime naval protocol, he planned an elaborate welcoming ceremony with full honors, including the Marine Guard as well as the ship's band playing ruffles and flourishes. Spruance quashed the exec's scheme and directed the same procedure that was used for visiting American flag officers. When the British admiral later struggled up the *Indianapolis*'s sea ladder, he was honored by a lone boatswain's mate in dungarees trilling his pipe.

The Royal Navy task group was but a small element of the Fifth Fleet force that would seize Iwo Jima. Spruance commanded more than 900 ships, over 100,000 troops, and more than 250,000 total Marines, soldiers, sailors, and airmen. A corps of three Marine divisions would assault the island, under the immediate command of Major General Harry Schmidt and supported by an amphibious force under Harry Hill. Both Turner and Smith would be in overall command of the Joint Expeditionary Force, but the assault was so vast and complex that their subordinates increasingly controlled the detailed operations.

Spruance commanded a platoon of flag and Marine general officers within the Fifth Fleet organization: 5 vice admirals, 31 rear admirals, 7 commodores, 1 lieutenant general, 4 major generals, and 3 brigadier generals. Many called upon their fleet commander as *Indianapolis* swung on her anchor at Ulithi. "I have been very busy," Spruance wrote home, "mostly seeing people, which I enjoy in not too large doses."

Flag officers were not the only ones who wanted to see Spruance. War correspondents were sprinkled throughout the ships jammed into the Ulithi anchorage. Anxious and curious to meet the admiral who commanded the massive armada, they repeatedly asked for a press conference before the fleet sailed. Spruance initially refused but finally relented. This would be his first press conference of the war. It would not be what the correspondents expected.

Spruance decided to restrict the conference to no more than an affirmation of his refusal to radio press copy during the Tokyo raid. He had thought the question had been settled weeks before at Pearl Harbor. "Everything went along very smoothly at Pearl this time," he had written Moore, "except that I had to do some arguing with the public relations people to make them understand that we were fighting a war and I would not break radio silence just to satisfy a lot of newspaper correspondents. There may be some complaints from the latter, but I intend to have Task Force 58 keep radio silence and lots of it, just as we did going to Truk and to Palau. They can send all they want from the landing objective."

The anticipated complaints had materialized. The newsmen were excited at the prospects of the Task Force 58 raid on Japan, the first naval attack on the home islands since the Doolittle raid two years before. The upcoming raid would be big news. When the "press conference" convened, the reporters again clamored for permission to radio the results from the carriers at the earliest possible moment. Spruance responded by repeating his restrictions to the disgruntled newsmen. He discussed nothing else, and the conference abruptly ended.

"The first carrier strike on Tokyo had been planned by Admiral Nimitz for several months," Spruance later wrote to an historian. "It made good publicity, but I can assure you it did not enter into the reasons for making it, in so far as I was concerned."

The problems of the prelanding bombardment had not abated, even as Spruance made his final plans at Ulithi. MacArthur's prolonged offensive in the Philippines had continued to divert resources that Spruance needed for Iwo Jima. The general had retained many of the old battleships for gunfire support in Luzon, and kamikazes had damaged others. Consequently, of the seven old battleships that supposedly would bombard Iwo, only two ultimately were available. Nimitz scraped together four other old battleships for a total of six, but of these six, four were the oldest in commission. All had been built before World War I, and their guns were either 14-inch or 12-inch caliber.

Turner wanted more 16-inch guns to blast the Japanese defenses. Without Spruance's knowledge, he arbitrarily requisitioned two fast battleships, *Washington* and *North Carolina*, from Task Force 58. Spruance did not discover Turner's action until he read Turner's operation order, which he quickly countermanded for two reasons. The two battleships had a limited supply of bombardment ammunition, because they carried a large quantity of armor-piercing projectiles for a possible fleet action. The other reason was that Spruance wanted the two battleships to accompany Task Force 58 to Japan, because their antiaircraft batteries were essential for defending the task force against the expected heavy enemy air attacks. Spruance did promise, however, to have *Washington* and *North Carolina* available for bombardment on D-Day, as well as any other Task Force 58 ships that Turner needed.

Some historians claim that Spruance "stole" the two fast battleships from Turner and upset Turner's bombardment plans. However, the ships never were assigned to Turner in the beginning, and he had no right to assume that he could use them.

By the first week in February the ships of Task Force 58 had assembled en masse within the Ulithi anchorage. The force was weary from the Philippines campaign, and it rested, made repairs, and replenished from the attending oilers, tenders, and supply ships. Ulithi Atoll now encompassed American naval power at its zenith. Mitscher commanded five carrier task groups, totaling 16 carriers, 8 fast battleships, 1 battle cruiser, 16 cruisers, 81 destroyers, and over 1200 airplanes.

After a brief visit with Nimitz, Spruance left Ulithi on the afternoon of 8 February, leaving Task Force 58 behind to complete preparations for the Tokyo strike. Two days later the flagship anchored off Saipan, where Turner and Smith soon would arrive with their Joint Expeditionary Force to conduct final rehearsals.

On the afternoon of 11 February, the huge invasion fleet arrived at Saipan, and Spruance went to the *Eldorado* to visit Turner in order "to clear up some last minute matters." When he arrived on Turner's flagship, he discovered that Turner was asleep in bed—ill with a high fever, said a staff officer.

But Turner had more than a fever. He was a sick man and was in danger of missing the Iwo invasion. A bad back caused considerable pain, and a heavy brace was little help. Overwork had weakened his physical resistance to virus infection, and he was threatened with pneumonia. Harry Hill, Turner's second in command, was deeply worried, for he never had seen Turner so debilitated. It was less than three weeks before the Iwo invasion. Without Turner the invasion would be jeopardized.

Spruance did not waken Turner, realizing that rest was vital to restoring his health. He returned to *Indianapolis* and next day left Saipan without having seen Turner. Spruance's concern for Turner— both as his friend and as his indispensable man for capturing Iwo Jima—must have been extreme. Providentially, Turner recovered before D-Day.

The key to the success of the Tokyo raid was *surprise,* and Spruance had adopted uncompromising measures to avoid alerting the enemy. He had forbidden naval gunfire bombardment of Iwo before the Tokyo strike; submarines, destroyers, and B-29's[1] would seek and destroy Japanese picket boats in the task force path of advance; carrier planes would knock down Japanese search planes and sink Japanese submarines before they could discover the American carriers; and, finally, the

---

1. Spruance had persuaded LeMay to fly his B-29's at 3000 feet at twelve-mile intervals on an "anti-picket boat sweep." The B-29's found plenty of small ships, but it is doubtful that they tried to sink any, or even that they could have if they had tried.

task force would silence their radios and radars to avoid betraying their location.

Of equal concern to Spruance was the weather. It was wintertime in Japan, a period of vile and unpredictable storms which had defeated the efforts of the B-29's during their earlier high-altitude bombing attacks. Spruance realized that weather would largely predicate the outcome of the carrier raid, and he and his staff meteorologist, Commander M. C. Burns, had made elaborate preparations for forecasting during the Iwo Jima and Okinawa operations. Three staff radiomen operated two radio receivers which were tuned exclusively to weather report broadcasts, providing Spruance with continuous weather data. Mitscher's radio equipment operated poorly, however, and deprived him of information needed for his own forecasts. He was almost entirely dependent upon Spruance for predictions of the weather over the targets at Tokyo.

Burns predicted good weather over Tokyo, basing his estimate primarily upon weather reports that originated in Russia and China. Spruance wanted clear skies over Tokyo; if the targets were hidden beneath low-lying clouds, the carrier aircraft would have the same difficulties in finding and hitting targets that had plagued the B-29's. And although bad weather might help the task force by masking its approach to Japan, it also could prevent flight operations altogether.

Two days after leaving Saipan, 13 February, *Indianapolis* made rendezvous with Task Force 58, 500 miles southeast of Iwo Jima and 1200 miles from Tokyo.

It was a day for refueling. The fat, squat oilers plodded into the sea, the fast combatants sped hither and yon awaiting their turn to come alongside, and carrier and battleship skippers conned their huge ships with the verve of destroyermen. The ships at times seemed to be dashing about at random. Yet there was reason and order to their activity, and task group commanders directed their movements with signal flags and flashing lights.

One by one, men-o'-war large and small approached the oilers at high speed from astern, then decelerated to fall in precisely alongside the oiler. Shot lines snapped across the narrow stretch of water separating the ships, followed by messenger lines, span wires, and inhaul lines. Then sweating, straining sailors in kapok life jackets yanked across the snake-like fuel-oil hoses, and boatswain's mates wrestled the nozzles into the receiving trunks. Finally the oilers regurgitated their thick, slimy cargo into the bellies of warships. The interval from approach to hookup usually was a matter of minutes, but the pumping could last for several hours. During that time the crews could relax, the larger ships' bands would entertain the oilers' crews, and signalmen would gossip between ships by flicking their hands in an abbreviated semaphore.

When the refueling was completed, oilers recovered their hoses, and the combatants, tanks topped off, rang up flank speed and charged off. Their adroit seamanship during a major replenishment was always a pleasure to watch.

The dull and sluggish oilers lacked the grace and élan of the fast combatants, their work was drudgery, and naval officers preferred to serve on glamorous warships rather than tedious oilers. Yet the oilers were indispensable to Spruance. They provided the superb logistical support that allowed the Fifth Fleet to roam the oceans for endless weeks, thousands of miles from American bases.

By sunset the refueling was not completed, so Mitscher adjourned for the night and headed north on a track that would pass five hundred miles east of Iwo Jima. Next morning, the fourteenth, refueling resumed. Before noon Task Force 58 had drunk its fill, and the nearly-empty oilers rode high in the water. With Mitscher acting as OTC, the carriers and their screens shaped course for Tokyo, and the oilers drifted from view over the horizon astern.

The weather forecasts, based upon special weather reports from the B-29's and submarines near Tokyo, continued to be optimistic. Burns predicted a weather front and rain in the morning, but Spruance felt it would not hinder the raid. Search planes reported that most of the picket boats were well to the west of the approach track. All was going well. That evening the task force was eight hundred miles from Tokyo. In thirty-six hours Mitscher would launch his attack.

At first light on the fifteenth the task force was drenched in rain, as predicted. The sky was overcast, visibility was halved, yet the sea was calm. Spruance told Mitscher that he still believed the weather would be good over Tokyo next morning.

A destroyer scouting group moved ahead and out of sight, under orders to screen the main body by sinking picket boats and by warning of air and surface threats. A CAP circled above the destroyers to assist. Before day's end the destroyer-CAP team had discovered and destroyed a small Japanese patrol boat and a search plane, and Spruance had reason to hope that the Japanese were still unaware of his approach.

The weather worsened on the eve of the strike. A strong wind blew from the northeast, and darkness came swiftly in the murk and gloom of the gathering storm. On Spruance's suggestion Mitscher imposed absolute silence on the TBS and the radars, and the task force—tense, silent, and excited—raced into the night at 20 knots. Sleepless commanding officers sailed blindly in the rain-swept darkness, and through faith alone they hoped to avoid colliding with adjacent ships. The laboring destroyers slammed into the heavy seas as they strained to keep pace with the larger ships, which were less affected by the wind and waves. Below decks the destroyer crewmen could hear and feel their ships groan and shudder from the tons of water pounding overhead.

Burns hovered over his weather maps throughout the night, analyzing messages from weather-reporting stations across the Western Pacific. Occasionally he received messages from unidentified stations, which he discarded with frustration. On the weather decks the sodden, shivering lookouts noticed that the rain that slapped their faces now was mixed with snow. *Indianapolis* rolled and pitched in the angry sea, and Spruance, standing alongside Burns in the swaying, stuffy compartment, had to fight down the nausea that always came with heavy weather. ("I am enjoying the cool weather," he later wrote Margaret, "but I could do without the storms we had up north.")

An hour or so past midnight, Burns announced his prediction for the coming day: low ceiling and restricted visibility at the launching area, and clouds over the target. Spruance passed the information to Mitscher. Despite the bad weather, nothing could deter Mitscher from predicting the "greatest air victory of the war for carrier aviation." The strike was on.

At the first faint light of dawn the task force was 125 miles from Tokyo in what Spruance later described as the "damndest, rottenest weather I could think of." But Mitscher's planes flew, thundering down the rain-lashed decks and disappearing into the low-level, dark, and turbulent overcast. Spruance and Davis entered flag plot to monitor the reports from the aviators and the carriers.

Radio Tokyo had been broadcasting continuously, evoking a general feeling that the enemy was unaware that Task Force 58 was nearby. At the predicted time for the first wave of aircraft to cross the coast, Radio Tokyo abruptly went silent. Surprise was complete.

Spruance listened to the aviators' welter of words pouring into flag plot through the radio loudspeakers, words distorted by blasts of static and garbled by simultaneous transmissions. Barber described the atmosphere. "The Admiral and the Chief of Staff were both about, popping a question every other minute," he wrote. "Who is that? How many planes are in the air now? Did ——— get the fighter sweep up? Have you heard from ———? What's our course now? Have we had any reports of weather over the target?"

The gist of the reports was that clouds covered many of the targets, and at noon Mitscher advised that the southern half of Tokyo was "weathered out." That was the area that contained the primary targets—the aircraft engine factories. Nevertheless, Mitscher's aircraft rampaged over Tokyo throughout the day, hitting whatever targets they could find and meeting little opposition from enemy gunfire or interceptors. Surprisingly, the Japanese were not defending their capital, and the American aircraft had to contend primarily with weather.

By early evening Mitscher had recovered his aircraft, having lost 32 during the day. He reported to Spruance that Task Force 58 had destroyed 350 aircraft, had damaged airfield installations, and had sunk or damaged 33 small ships. Only one aircraft factory had been "effectively" hit by two small strikes; the weather had shielded the other factories.

The unharmed factories were primary targets, and they lay virtually over the horizon at the mercy of Spruance's fleet. Spruance had to get them. Burns predicted improved weather over Tokyo next day, so Task Force 58 cruised unmolested in Japanese home waters, preparing for renewed attacks in the morning. The only casualties to the task force ships were two destroyers whose luck had run out when they collided during the night.

Dawn on the seventeenth revealed more miserable weather, although the wind had abated. Mitscher relentlessly pressed on and resumed his launching. When the planes were airborne, Burns predicted even worsening weather, forcing Spruance to decide whether to remain off Tokyo or to return to Iwo Jima to support the landings, which would begin in forty-eight hours. He was concerned that Mitscher would be reluctant to admit that his aircraft could not cope with the weather and thereby might continue flight operations against his better judgment. "No subordinate likes to tell his boss that he is afraid to do something," Spruance commented to a staff officer.

Spruance himself decided it was time to quit. An hour before noon he signaled Mitscher that the weather forecast "made launching of further sweeps inadvisable." Mitscher ended his flight operations but allowed the airborne strikes to complete their missions before returning. Despite the storms over Japan, his aircraft managed to bomb two aircraft engine factories, sink a light carrier at her moorings, and destroy additional aircraft and airfield installations. By late afternoon the task force retired toward Iwo Jima.

"I promised to return and finish what we had started," Spruance said years later, and he sent a message of praise and congratulations to the task force. He also asked Mitscher for recommendations for future Task Force 58 operations during the Iwo assault. Mitscher, in consonance with Spruance's own thoughts, responded that he wanted to hit Japan again, then Okinawa. "Approved," replied Spruance. "Make your plans accordingly."

Perhaps Spruance now sympathized with the Air Force, for the weather had thwarted his carrier planes almost as effectively as it had the B-29 bombers. The weather data he had received from Russia and China—the breeding ground for Japanese weather—were "absolutely no good. They were telling us things that never existed," said Spruance. He condemned the Russian weather data as "worthless" and asked Nimitz to "invite the attention of Commodore Miles [Commander, Naval Group China, a naval guerrilla force] to the importance of his reports indicating the movement of cold fronts over Asia." Spruance also asked for intensified weather reports from American submarines near Japan and Okinawa.

The passiveness of the Japanese air interceptors had been unexpected. None had attacked the task force, and those over Japan had not been aggressive and had avoided combat. Many planes on the Tokyo airfields had not attempted to become airborne, suggesting a shortage of pilots or fuel—or both.

Or perhaps the Japanese were conserving their aircraft to attack the American invasion forces at Iwo Jima and Okinawa.

With the landings due in thirty-six hours, *Indianapolis* hurried toward Iwo Jima, accompanied by two carrier task groups and the battleships that would join in the D-Day bombardment. Spruance also directed a minor strike on Chichi Jima and Haha Jima, near Iwo, on the eighteenth, and Mitscher reassigned his carrier task groups accordingly.

Spruance could now concentrate upon matters at Iwo Jima. Rear

Admiral W. H. P. Blandy's advance bombardment force of battleships and cruisers had been shelling Iwo Jima since the sixteenth, simultaneously with Spruance's Tokyo strike. Spruance and Turner had based their decision for a three-day prelanding bombardment (overruling the Marines' request for ten days) on the hope that Blandy's force could effectively reduce the island's defenses in the shorter period of time. In the quiet of his cabin, Spruance read Blandy's analysis of the first two days' bombardment to determine if he and Turner had been right.

The reports were discouraging. Bad weather had degraded the first day's bombardment, reported Blandy, and at the end of the second day, the seventeenth, the majority of the known defensive installations remained apparently intact. Enemy shore batteries had damaged one cruiser and had severely damaged almost a dozen rocket-launching craft that had been supporting the underwater demolition teams (UDT) surveying the landing beaches. Their hazardous mission had been to check beach and surf conditions and to look for and destroy underwater obstacles while under the guns of the enemy. Fortunately, the UDT's had been able to do their job, and their report was heartening: the beaches were suitable for landing.

Spruance hoped for the best. Blandy would continue his bombardment on the third day, but the first forty-eight hours of bombardment apparently had not dented Iwo's defenses. Only one day remained before the landing, and it was likely that Blandy would request the optional fourth day (allowing an extra twenty-four hours of prelanding bombardment) that Spruance had authorized.

On D-1 Day *Indianapolis* continued to close Iwo Jima. Spruance had reluctantly agreed to forward the news correspondents' press copy of the Tokyo strike using an untried contraption that would allow airborne pickup from ships at sea. Two helium-filled balloons, tethered by a long line to the *Indianapolis,* would hoist the mailbag aloft, where presumably it would be snagged and retrieved by an Air Force bomber flying low overhead. Spruance grumbled about the unnecessary rush to deliver information to the newspapers and resented distracting his ships and staff for the convenience of the newsmen.

At high noon the balloons soared aloft, their heavy burden swaying and bouncing precariously beneath them in the turbulent air. The bomber roared overhead and hooked the bag, but the bag fell loose and tumbled into the water astern.

"So much for that nonsense," snorted Spruance.

On D-Day a seaplane arrived at Iwo Jima to take the press copy, but it bashed its tail upon landing and was immobilized. A relief plane finally flew out the material a day later.

On the eve of the invasion Spruance waited for Blandy's report on the day's bombardment, which would determine whether the Marines could land in the morning. Blandy's first message arrived in midevening. "The principal defense installations in the landing area were either destroyed or heavily damaged," reported Blandy. Certain targets, however, would have to receive special attention by the bombardment ships on D-Day. But Blandy left unanswered whether he wanted an extra day's bombardment or whether he would recommend that the landing proceed as scheduled on the nineteenth.

At midnight he provided that answer in a message to Turner. "Though weather has not permitted complete expenditure of entire ammunition allowance," advised Blandy, "and more installations can be found and destroyed, I believe landing can be accomplished tomorrow as scheduled, if necessary."

In the darkness, *Indianapolis* cautiously threaded through the hundreds of ships surrounding Iwo Jima and took station several thousand yards seaward of the landing beaches. The island stronghold was first dimly seen as an indistinct mass at daybreak; then the image sharpened as the sun rose behind the flagship in a clear, bright sky. A cool, refreshing northern breeze blew soft, scattered clouds above a tranquil ocean. It would be a beautiful day.

Iwo Jima was a fortress besieged. For six months American ships and planes had cannonaded Iwo's rocky, barren slopes and plateau. Its 20,000 stoic Japanese defenders had burrowed ever more deeply into the island's bowels, awaiting the inevitable invasion. Now the siege was over and the assault begun.

The final attack began with a massive barrage at daylight, the first of more than 38,000 rounds that would pound Iwo that D-Day. *Indianapolis* joined in the bombardment, and Spruance had an unimpeded view of the developing battle.

The amphibious assault was a twentieth-century version of a medieval army storming some ancient citadel, the attackers in disciplined, symmetrical military formations advancing resolutely toward the ramparts. Thousands of Marines, the vanguard of the seventy-thousand-man corps, descended into landing craft which formed ranks and columns of great precision. "Land the landing force," ordered Kelly Turner, and the unflinching waves of infantry-laden craft surged toward the beach. It was a brave and inspiring spectacle, and one almost expected to hear the sounds of drums and trumpets urging the warriors onward beneath flying banners.

But the perfection and order of their advance through the water collapsed into chaos and terror on the landing beaches. The soft, black volcanic ash immobilized men and machines, and they lay naked and exposed beneath the fire and thunder of Japanese weapons that were no longer concealed.

The fight was on.

The battle for Iwo Jima lasted more than a month. Spruance was a patient observer and quietly waited for the Marines to finish. "The Japs have 20,000 men on this small island," he wrote Margaret, "all dug into the ground. They have to be cleaned out foot by foot, but the job is proceeding and eventually it will be done."

The fighting ashore was but one aspect of the total campaign which Spruance commanded. Weighing heavily on his mind was the imminent landing on Okinawa, eight hundred miles westward, on 1 April, just six weeks after D-Day on Iwo Jima. He and the staff had the intricate task of providing continuing naval support at Iwo Jima; attacking Tokyo with Task Force 58 in late February; withdrawing ships from Iwo Jima for repairs and replenishment; and reassembling the mightiest fleet in the history of the world for the invasion of Okinawa.

The complex matrix of ship employments was constantly disarranged by casualties to individual ships caused by enemy airplanes, collisions, groundings, and equipment failures. For example, the propeller blades of the archaic battleship *New York* fell off as the result of metal fatigue, reflecting the fact that many of the Navy's older ships were dilapidated and had been pressed into fighting a war for which they were obsolete. And the collisions and groundings, which removed a ship from action as surely as an enemy bomb, manifested that even the newer ships were weary and that their crews were both tired and inexperienced. This grinding attrition continued on a scale never before experienced by Spruance's fleet. It was only a forerunner of worse things to come at Okinawa.

While Forrestel shuffled ships about the ocean and Biggs worried

*The amphibious assault was a twentieth-century version of a medieval army storming
some ancient citadel, the attackers in disciplined, symmetrical military formations
advancing resolutely toward the ramparts.* D-Day at Iwo Jima (Official U.S.
Navy photo, National Archives)

about ammunition and fuel for the fleet, Spruance daily paced the
forecastle on the disengaged side of the 8-inch gun turrets. Absorbed in
thought, he was oblivious to the ear-shattering roar of the *Indianapolis*
guns just a few yards away, pounding at Iwo Jima from the opposite
side of the forecastle. If the flagship reversed course, Spruance simply
moved to the other side of the forecastle so he could remain at the rear
of the turrets. His companions either were guests like his old friend and
classmate R. C. (Sunny Jim) Parker, or the less busy staff officers such
as Commander Michael LeFanu, the Royal Navy liaison officer.

During the period of the Iwo Jima battle, Spruance often reflected on the personal publicity associated with high military commanders. He recently had read an article about him in *Argosy* magazine entitled "Ice Water Admiral," and his response on the routing slip was a terse "much hooey." And when young Margaret wrote her father and voiced her disapproval of personal publicity in war, Spruance responded by promising, "I shall answer it in due course (I hope) and shall explain my ideas on the subject of the evils of officers being bitten by the publicity bug in time of war. It is bad business, and I have watched a lot of it."

Spruance unexpectedly expressed his "ideas on the subject" to a friend while the two men were marching about the forecastle, occasionally chatting about inconsequential things. The Iwo Jima battle raged about them, and the friend later remarked that the sound and fury must have stimulated Spruance's adrenaline, because he broke his usual silence and his talk began to flow.

"Personal publicity in war can be a drawback," he said, "because it may affect a man's thinking. A commander may not have sought it; it may have been forced upon him by zealous subordinates or imaginative war correspondents. Once started, however, it is hard to keep in check. In the early days of the war, when little about the various commanders is known to the public, and some admiral does a good or spectacular job, he gets a head-start in publicity. Anything he does thereafter tends toward greater headline value than the same things done by others, following the journalistic rule that 'names make news.' Thus his reputation snowballs; and soon, probably against his will, he has become a colorful figure, credited with fabulous characteristics over and above the competence in war command for which he has been conditioning himself all his life.

"His fame may not have gone to his head, but there is nevertheless danger in this. Should he get to identifying himself with the figure as publicized, he may subconsciously start thinking in terms of what this reputation calls for, rather than of how best to meet the action problem confronting him. A man's judgment is best when he can forget himself and any reputation he may have acquired, and can concentrate wholly on making the right decisions. Hence if he seems to give interviewers and publicity men the brush-off, it is not through ungraciousness but to keep himself impersonal and realistic in his thinking."

Spruance had Halsey in mind—among others—because Halsey recently had given an interview that was more flamboyant than usual. "I did not think much of Bill Halsey's interview," he wrote Margaret. "In the first place, I do not think we should call our enemies a lot of names the way Bill does. In the second place to belittle their resistance and fighting qualities is no way in which to prepare the country for the hard and perhaps long war that still lies ahead of us. There is still a sizable portion of the Jap fleet left, and I have every expectation that they will come out to sink or be sunk when they consider that the time is most propitious for them.

"Except for their defense of Iwo Jima, the Japs have done very little against us this time. If their reaction is equally as poor next time, I shall begin to agree with Bill and think that they have shot their bolt. Until that occurs, however, I prefer to remain on the basis that they are conserving their strength, training their people, and getting ready to let us have the works.

"Bill's attitude seems to be—the Japs are low rats, whom I have already licked, and there is not much more to be done to finish them off.

"Our Marines on Iwo certainly do not feel that way about them."

The Japanese, in turn, had plenty to say publicly about their American enemies—Spruance and Turner—in a Tokyo broadcast to the people of Japan on the day after the landing. "According to reports issued by the enemy," said the broadcast, "the man who commands the enemy American amphibious forces which effected landings on our Iwo Island is Vice Admiral Richmond Turner. He is the right-hand man to Commander in Chief Spruance of the enemy Fifth Fleet."

After castigating Turner as a "devil man" and an "alligator," the broadcast concluded that "Spruance, with a powerful offensive spirit and Turner, with excellent determinative power, have led their men to a point where they are indeed close to the mainland, but they find themselves in a dilemma, as they are unable either to advance or retreat.

"This man Turner, who has been responsible for the death of so many of our precious men, shall not return home alive—he must not, and will not. This is one of the many things we can do to rest at ease the many souls of those who have paid the supreme sacrifice."

Spruance was amused by the Japanese propaganda broadcast. "Please note that I am not marked for execution," he wrote Margaret.

On the fifth day of the battle a small group of Marines struggled toward the summit of Mount Suribachi. Tens of thousands of Americans afloat and ashore watched expectantly from afar. At midmorning the summit was conquered, and the American flag unfurled in the breeze. Triumphant cheers swept the field of battle.

Spruance sent Margaret a copy of the famous photograph of that flag-raising, calling it the "finest photograph this war has given us to date. When we settle down, I want to have this picture framed. Some first class sculptor should do this in bronze, it is so perfect."

Years later, the sculptor Felix deWeldon fulfilled Spruance's prophecy by creating the heroic bronze monument at Arlington National Cemetery. It was also deWeldon who sculpted the bust of Spruance that is now at the Naval War College.

Despite the flag-raising, the battle was far from over. While it raged, Spruance and Mitscher struck again at Japan with Task Force 58 in late February. Although the predictions again were optimistic, the weather was worse than before. Destroyers crashed into heavy seas trying to keep pace with the carriers, and many of the small ships suffered storm damage. Somehow Mitscher's aviators found targets beneath the clouds and hit enemy aircraft, airfields, and aircraft engine plants, but with limited results. Spruance had been thwarted again.

"I have come to the conclusion the Jap weather in winter is bad most of the time and almost unpredictable all the time," he wrote Margaret afterwards. "One storm followed another with scarcely any good weather in between. This time again the Japs made no attempt whatsoever to attack us, either while we were there or on the run out. This is very different from the way they used to be, when they threw everything at you they could as long as they could reach you."

In a rueful comment on his seasickness during the stormy expedition, he informed Margaret, "Sunny Jim Parker's stomach can stand more punishment than mine, but not his hind legs."

Two weeks after the first Marines had landed, Spruance went ashore at Iwo Jima for his first visit. His arrival was unceremonious, for he rode in an unpretentious landing craft carrying supplies to the troops ashore. "When she beached," he wrote, "we made a run for it over her ramp, but most of us got wet half way to our knees." He walked up the steep slopes from the beach, his sodden feet sinking into the disabling volcanic ash.

The battlefield scene was familiar. It was a relatively quiet day. The Marines were resting and regrouping for a renewed attack the next morning against the Japanese that were still entrenched in the northern end of the island.

Spruance and Art Davis inspected some wrecked Japanese ships that were stranded on the beach. One was inhabited by a group of Marines, who, wrote Spruance, "had moved on board with a very smart and happy yellow dog, and all were having a good time, cooking and eating their dinner, washing themselves and their clothes."

Spruance chatted amiably with the Marines, who gazed in wonderment at the lean, spare anonymous man wearing four stars on his collar. Just before Spruance and Davis left, one of the bolder Marines asked "very politely" if the admirals would please identify themselves. "When I did so," wrote Spruance, "he said he thought he had recognized me from my photograph. These men had at first been most friendly and polite, but they became even more so and expressed themselves as highly gratified that we had paid them a visit."

Spruance also visited his Marine generals. As he was leaving, a messenger reported that one of their leading officers had just had his head blown off.

As always, Spruance visited the wounded. "Seeing our badly wounded," he wrote Margaret, "especially the men who will suffer some permanent disability, takes a lot of the pleasure out of a successful operation."

Spruance scrutinized the ingenious Japanese fortifications and concluded that only a Marine with a rifle and flamethrower ultimately could eradicate the enemy soldiers on Iwo, regardless of the amount of air and naval gunfire. He was convinced that his decision for a three-day bombardment was correct, and that he had been justified in overruling the Marines' request for ten days.

Whether Spruance was right or wrong never will be satisfactorily answered. The official Marine Corps history of Iwo Jima, published in 1971, best expresses the impasse. "This dispute still simmers more than 25 years after the event," state the Marine historians, "and it appears doubtful that it will ever be completely resolved to the satisfaction of all concerned. . . . It would serve no useful purpose at this time to rekindle the barely submerged passions that have occasionally popped to the surface regarding this subject. Even minute inspection of all available data does not lead to concrete and infallible conclusions that would stand up to prolonged investigation. Thus the controversy simply becomes one of the vantage point occupied by each of the participants at the time of the operation. "

In early March Spruance and Turner left Iwo Jima and returned to Ulithi to prepare for the Okinawa invasion. Harry Hill remained behind to finish the job. The Americans had suffered over 14,000 casualties, including 2500 men killed in action. Over 6000 were killed before Iwo Jima was secured.

Spruance was a sensitive man. The deaths of thousands of Americans under his command were his responsibility. Unquestionably, Spruance grieved. Yet death was inevitable, he accepted it as a part of war, and he sought to avoid unnecessary casualties. His mixed emotions were reflected in a letter to Margaret as the campaign came to a close.

"I understand some of our sob fraternity back home have been raising the devil about our casualties on Iwo," he wrote. "I would have thought by this time they would have learned that you can't make war on a tough, fanatical enemy like the Japs without our people getting hurt and killed. I recommended both Iwo and our next operation [Okinawa], and I have never had any doubt as to how tough the next one is going to be. It is going to be very expensive to us, but the results should be of the greatest value in pushing the war along. "

As he wrote the letter, Spruance probably assumed that the Air Force "would push the war along" by using Iwo Jima to help attack Japanese aircraft factories. In Spruance's mind they were legitimate military targets, and the Air Force had acknowledged they were first priority. But Air Force priorities quickly changed after Iwo Jima was in American hands. General LeMay became disillusioned with high-altitude, daylight attacks using "precision" bombing against aircraft factories, because the B-29's could not overcome the handicaps imposed by the persistent bad weather that shielded Japan. Therefore, in early March, LeMay began his devastating fire raids with the approval of the Air Force command in Washington. The hope was that B-29 area bombing would be more profitable than precision bombing.

Thus Spruance's role in choosing and seizing Iwo Jima ultimately served a purpose which he opposed. He had hoped that Iwo Jima would be used to project American air power against Japanese military forces,

Marine graves on Iwo Jima. Mount Suribachi is in the distance.

lines of communication, and—his most immediate concern—against enemy aircraft factories in order to reduce the air threat to his forces that would be attacking Okinawa. In the end, however, Iwo Jima supported the Air Force incendiary raids that cremated hundreds of thousands of civilians. Whatever their effects on the Japanese will to fight, the fire raids did not prevent the Japanese from throwing thousands of kamikazes and conventional aircraft against the Okinawa invasion forces.

Spruance's opinion of the firebombing was contained in a postwar letter to a military writer. "I may say," Spruance wrote, "that during World War II I was old fashioned enough to be opposed to unlimited destruction of the civilian population and of non-military targets, and I wanted to confine our attacks to military targets. [Most senior naval officers felt the same way.] Even with these, the civilian population suffered enough to make them lose what appetite they might have had for the war."

But it is unclear how Spruance "opposed" the unlimited destruction policies of the Air Force. Iwo Jima certainly contributed to the kind of

Japanese dead on Iwo Jima

devastation to which Spruance objected, *yet after the war he always emphatically justified its seizure and its use by the B-29's.* Perhaps he recognized that the B-29 raids were inevitable regardless of his personal disapproval of their bombing policy against Japanese cities. At least Iwo Jima's emergency landing fields saved the lives of thousands of crewmen who otherwise might never have been able to reach the Marianas in their crippled B-29's.

It is also possible that Spruance's objection to the mass destruction of cities was military rather than moral. At no time did he show any remorse or pity for the Japanese civilians when he later viewed their wretched lot in the first months of the postwar occupation. Rather,

Spruance's objection may have been the diversion of the B-29's from their raids against "legitimate" military targets to their area bombing against cities, which Spruance probably viewed as an unprofitable use of American military resources.

One other possibility remains to explain Spruance's curious inconsistency. Over 6000 Americans died in the Iwo Jima campaign, deaths for which Spruance felt responsible by having recommended the seizure of that infernal island. It is not inconceivable that, being entirely human, he would hesitate publicly to admit that they had died in vain. Indeed, he hardly could be expected to proclaim that the seizure of Iwo Jima was a mistake. Although the Air Force never used Iwo for the purposes Spruance had envisioned, he still could justify the American deaths by the fact that Iwo Jima was used for a purpose that was generally approved by the American public. The B-29 bombing of Japan, to this day, is viewed as a major contribution to the defeat of Japan. Even if Spruance was disappointed in the way that Iwo Jima ultimately was used, his nature never would allow him to precipitate a postwar controversy.

No, it would be better simply to say that the value of the island had been worth its terrible cost in blood. Perhaps he had found solace in the knowledge that history had confirmed the strategic value of Iwo Jima to the ultimate American victory in the Pacific.

Chapter 22

OKINAWA

THE invasion of Okinawa was equivalent in magnitude to the invasion of Normandy. Raymond Spruance commanded 1500 ships, the largest and most powerful fleet in the history of the world. It never again will be duplicated, for fleets never again will be as large as those of World War II. The amphibious force comprised 1200 of these ships, which transported and supported the 182,000 assault troops of the Tenth Army, containing five infantry divisions and three Marine divisions. Lieutenant General Simon Bolivar Buckner, U.S. Army, commanded all the ground forces, replacing Holland Smith, who had returned to the United States, a tired, embittered old warrior.

Spruance's objective was Okinawa, a narrow island 60 miles long with an area of 465 square miles, as well as several smaller adjacent islands suitable for anchorages and airfields. Most of Okinawa's half-million population lived in the southern half of the island, where the gently rolling terrain was extensively cultivated. The northern half of the island was rugged and mountainous, not unlike Saipan.

The Americans intended to land upon Okinawa's southwestern shores on 1 April. They expected heavy opposition from about 77,000 enemy troops. These troops were Buckner's concern; Spruance's primary concern was the Japanese air threat.

Spruance always had placed top priority on gaining local air superiority over the objective area before the amphibious forces began to land. During the 1943–1944 Central Pacific campaigns, Task Force 58 had demolished Japanese land-based air power in a matter of days. Okinawa was a different matter. It was within easy flying distance of Japanese airfields located on the home islands and on Formosa. MacArthur's air force on Luzon would try to suppress Japanese air strength on Formosa, but Task Force 58 would have to shield the amphibious forces from the thousands of Japanese planes on the Japanese mainland, 350 miles north of Okinawa.

Neither Spruance's carrier raids in February nor the concurrent B-29 raids had significantly reduced those dangerous aircraft, so carefully hoarded were they by the Japanese for eventual use against the Okinawa invasion fleet. Spruance was determined to diminish that threat. In early March he directed Mitscher to plan yet another raid on Kyushu for mid-March. Surprise would be essential. In the past the Japanese had dispersed and hidden their aircraft just before Task Force 58 arrived off the Japanese shores.

On 9 March *Indianapolis* anchored in crowded Ulithi lagoon, in the midst of Task Force 58 preparing for battle. Mitscher and Lee called on Spruance, and they agreed that the carriers would hit Kyushu on 18 and 19 March, followed by continual air strikes on Okinawa beginning on 23 March through D-Day.

The lagoon churned with activity day and night, and the tightly packed ships were an irresistible target. As a prelude of things to come, a flight of kamikazes fell upon the immobilized task force early one evening, hitting the heavy carrier *Randolph* and removing her from action for at least a month. Spruance belatedly issued orders to bolster the lagoon's security.

Spruance sent Margaret one last letter before getting under way for his final campaign. "Before you receive this letter of mine," he wrote, "you will probably know by the news that we are on the move again. Our next operation should be a climax to everything we have done so far. It will be a long, tough party, and we must expect heavy casualties."

On 14 March *Indianapolis* weighed anchor at Ulithi, made rendezvous with Mitscher and Task Force 58, and the 16 carriers and their escorting battleships, cruisers, and destroyers set sail for Kyushu, 1700 miles to the north. The force refueled on the sixteenth and began their final run-in.

In addition to the Kyushu airfields, Spruance also wanted to hit the Japanese naval base at Kure in southern Honshu. The Japanese fleet, although battered, was still dangerous, and Spruance feared it might try a last, desperate foray against the Okinawa invasion forces on D-Day. Although he did not expect to destroy the enemy fleet, he hoped at least to disrupt its preparations and thereby delay any attacks the Japanese may have planned for the critical, early stages of the landing.

Nimitz had placed one specific target off limits: the Emperor's palace. Nimitz's directive explained that the Emperor at present was not a liability and later might be an asset.

The weather forecasts were good, but Spruance's luck was bad. On the eve of the strike bogies were shadowing the force and reporting its approach. Spruance's hoped-for surprise was lost, and he could visualize the Japanese again dispersing and camouflaging their aircraft before his arrival.

Next morning Mitscher's planes roared over Japan in beautiful weather. The enemy retaliated, no longer supine as during the February raids. Japanese aircraft hit three American heavy carriers, causing moderate damage. The carriers patched their wounds and continued flight operations throughout the day. By noon Mitscher reported that all scheduled airfields had been hit and that a hundred Japanese aircraft were destroyed.

The most promising news was that Mitscher's aircraft had discovered the super battleship *Yamato* and three cruisers at Kure. Enticed by that alluring target, Mitscher proposed wrapping up the Kyushu airfield strikes so he could hurry north overnight and permit his torpedo planes to attack *Yamato* next morning.

Spruance feared *Yamato* would escape by then. "Can you attack and disable her this afternoon?" asked Spruance. "No," replied Mitscher, "all my attack aircraft are airborne." An attack on *Yamato* would have to wait until morning.

Yamato escaped.

Spruance sat in his bridge chair next morning while Mitscher's planes swarmed upon the Japanese ships that had remained behind at Kure. About 0700 he saw a massive column of smoke erupt from an American carrier in a nearby task group. The smoke roiled thousands of feet skyward like a volcanic discharge, and huge explosions periodically reddened the base of the towering black column.

It was the heavy carrier *Franklin,* hit by a Japanese bomber that had swooped out of the overcast. After years of apparent invulnerability, five of Spruance's largest and most powerful carriers had been hit within a week. *Franklin,* the worst damaged, seemed unlikely to survive.

The *Franklin*'s fiery agony symbolized the beginning of the war's final cataclysm. The desperate Japanese were fighting for their nation's survival, because the fall of Okinawa would doom the Japanese Empire. The Japanese had decided that the time had come to hurl their remaining air and naval resources against the American invaders.

The Japanese military position was critical. Their merchant fleet was devastated, and the home islands were nearly isolated. The people had little food, and their war industries were denied the raw material needed for munitions. Fire storms from B-29 incendiary raids had reduced cities and their populations to ashes and rubble. The armed forces were shattered remnants of their former might. Yet the Japanese fighting spirit would not allow a sense of hopelessness or defeat. Japan was a wild, dangerous enemy—wounded, weakened, cornered, yet still powerful—convulsively lashing at Spruance's forces with reckless fury.

The *Franklin,* unbelievably, would not sink, and Spruance had to decide whether to abandon or to salvage the stricken carrier. She was a burning, ravaged hulk, helplessly wallowing with a sickening list less than a hundred miles from the Japanese mainland. The weather had cleared and she was dead in the water. If Spruance decided to salvage *Franklin,* Task Force 58 would have to remain nearby as protection. The gain of saving the carrier and her men trapped below had to be weighed against the danger of exposing Task Force 58 to prolonged air attacks. A crippled carrier would attract enemy aircraft and submarines as a crippled animal attracted scavengers.

Spruance withheld a decision and watched developments. Cruisers and destroyers encircled *Franklin* to rescue her crewmen and to fight her fires, disregarding the threat of lurking submarines. (A very real threat. During the Battle of Midway, a Japanese submarine sank the crippled *Yorktown* and her salvor, destroyer *Hammann.*) By late morning the fires seemed under control, and a cruiser prepared to tow the carrier. It began to appear that she could survive.

At noon Spruance decided to salvage *Franklin* and committed Task Force 58 to stay with her until she returned to safe waters. The Americans began their withdrawal. Gradually *Franklin* restored her ability to steam. The skies remained clear, and the Japanese planes continued to pursue and attack for three days. The CAP brawled overhead protecting the task force, but several enemy planes broke through and bombed two more American carriers. Providentially, they controlled the damage and later resumed flight operations.

By the twenty-second the attacks had subsided, and Spruance took stock. Three of his carriers—*Franklin, Enterprise,* and *Wasp*—were so badly mauled that he sent them back to Ulithi to join the *Randolph,* damaged a week before. Service Squadron 10 could repair all but *Franklin,* which would have to return to the States. Thus, within the first week of the Okinawa campaign, four of Spruance's eleven large carriers were out of action. In all his raids and battles from Tarawa to Iwo Jima, his large carriers never had been seriously hurt. Okinawa would be different—and much more expensive. Three carriers returned within time, but on the eve of the Okinawa invasion Spruance must have been thankful for the five Royal Navy carriers that would join the Fifth Fleet.

The damage that Task Force 58 inflicted upon the enemy was some compensation. Mitscher estimated that his aviators had destroyed over 550 planes and probably had destroyed or damaged another 175. At least 17 naval ships and 40 merchantmen had been damaged. Unfortunately the Americans had been unable to find most of the cleverly concealed planes that were dispersed before the attack, but they had raised havoc with their alternate targets, such as airfields, factories, fuel depots, and power stations.

Although Mitscher had weakened the enemy air threat against the Okinawa invasion force, thousands of Japanese planes remained. Yet Spruance's public evaluation of the Kyushu strikes was optimistic. Whatever his personal doubts about the future, he knew that Mitscher's carriers had accomplished all that reasonably could have been expected of them. The carriers were essential to victory in Okinawa and the aviators needed all the encouragement they could get for their looming ordeal ahead. So Spruance sent an appropriate message of commendation and appreciation to Mitscher and Task Force 58. "This has been an auspicious beginning for the operations immediately ahead," said Spruance. "I am proud to have operated with you again."

Mitscher reorganized his remaining seven heavy carriers and six light carriers into three task groups, then refueled and prepared to begin preinvasion air strikes against Okinawa. The longest, most grueling air battle of the Pacific war had begun, and Task Force 58 now had fewer carriers than at the Battle of the Philippine Sea, nine months before. As Spruance later wrote Margaret, "The weather was perfect and the Japs did everything they could to make up for their lack of cordiality the two times off Tokyo."

The final days of March were devoted to preparations for D-Day. Minesweepers swept the approaches to the Okinawa beaches, Mitscher's carriers pounded Okinawa airfields and fortifications, and surface ships bombarded targets ashore. The invasion force converged upon the island.

On 26 March the 77th Infantry Division landed on the islands of the Kerama Retto, located twenty miles west of the southern tip of Okinawa. The island group would provide sheltered anchorages for the repair and replenishment of the Fifth Fleet. By then the Japanese surely knew that the Americans would invade Okinawa, and Spruance waited for the enemy's reaction. Spruance's operation order predicted a "violent enemy air reaction" from enemy air bases and carriers, and that "enemy surface forces will oppose to the limits of their capabilities."

On D-4 Day, 28 March, Spruance received a report that the Japanese fleet was in the Inland Sea, heading down the east coast of Kyushu toward Okinawa. The report was a false alarm. Mitscher charged north but did not find the fleet. Since he was in the area, he bombed some Kyushu airfields and merchantmen before returning to Okinawa.

Surprisingly, the Japanese did not oppose the offshore operations of the underwater demolition teams, the minesweepers, and the bombardment ships. Instead Okinawa was strangely quiet and passive as D-Day approached. American ships and planes in close support near and over Okinawa were unmolested by Japanese guns.

While awaiting D-Day, Spruance perused other message reports that would affect the invasion. . . . The East China Sea was infested with heavy minefields, and Spruance ordered his fleet to stand clear of that area, a decision that unavoidably would restrict the movements of Task Force 58. . . . A typhoon was raging a thousand miles south, and Spruance warned his commanders that it might possibly head toward Okinawa. . . . Nimitz advised that escort carriers would be scarce, and Spruance pondered anew whether his naval air strength would be adequate to neutralize the enemy air threat. . . . Japanese planes were flying off Okinawa airfields at night and attacking his amphibious ships in fits and starts. Heavier and more brutal air attacks were sure to follow.

In the midst of making war, Spruance received a whimsical operation order from Nimitz that seemed conceived in fantasy. Someone in high authority feared that Japanese carriers would attack the west coast of the United States in order to divert American forces off Japan. In that event, Spruance was to "designate two fast carrier groups and logistic support ships from the Fifth Fleet to intercept and destroy retiring enemy raiding forces." Spruance's reaction must have been a moment's amusement before contemptuously dismissing the matter from his mind.

Spruance, always the good administrator, used the lulls in the war at sea to attend to omnipresent paperwork. He frequently annotated pungent comments upon documents that had caught his attention for one reason or another. If Spruance was dubious about signing letters prepared for his signature, he would refer it to flag secretary Barber with a note, "Please see if this is in due form and technically correct." On one occasion he noted, "It is evident that the writer of this excellent report lacked the benefits of a classical education—or else it did not take."

Spruance insisted upon exacting standards of style and vocabulary for his official correspondence, but he compromised occasionally. In a note to Barber attached to a letter Spruance had drafted, the admiral wrote, "Please note that I have violated a vow never to 'strongly recommend' anything. This is done in a worthy cause, but does not constitute a precedent."

As D-Day approached, Spruance became suspicious of the Japanese defenders' unexpected silence, and he became concerned that Turner's invasion force would become careless and overconfident. On D-2 Day he cautioned Blandy (who again commanded the bombardment ships and escort carriers that provided close support to the assault troops) that he "hoped our pilots would expect a more cordial reception on D-Day than they have received to date and would govern themselves accordingly." Blandy also wanted to avoid complacency, and he warned his forces that "the present passive attitude of the enemy could not be permitted to induce the opinion that enemy defenses had been destroyed."

Meanwhile the mammoth invasion fleet approached silent, menacing Okinawa.

*   *   *

The kamikaze hit *Indianapolis* at 0710 on the morning before the invasion.

It was a cloudy day, and the flagship was standing in to resume shore bombardment. An aircraft emerged through the clouds, rolled over, and dived. *Indianapolis* managed to fire one gun before the suicide plane crashed into the fantail. The plane's bomb tore through the hull and exploded beneath the ship. The plane itself disintegrated against the ship.

Everyone knew the flagship was hurt. The shock had knocked people off their feet, and the explosion had been deafening. Now clouds of acrid smoke engulfed the ship. Men's voices rose above the sounds of the roaring fire, some yelling orders, others in pain and calling for help. One thought was on everyone's mind. Save the ship.

Spruance's first reaction was to give his flag lieutenant two orders: ascertain the ship's damage from the commanding officer, and determine whether the kamikaze carried a code book. The flag lieutenant departed and upon his return reported that the ship's propellers and propeller shafts had been damaged and that the after compartments were flooded. No code book had been found.

The crew extinguished the fires and temporarily repaired the structural damage. *Indianapolis* cautiously spun her starboard propellers and limped into the recently captured anchorage at nearby Kerama Retto. A salvage ship moored alongside, divers inspected the flagship's wounds, and they reported severe damage. That evening Spruance had to inform Turner that *Indianapolis* would not participate in the D-Day bombardment.

Earlier in the day Blandy had evaluated the bombardment by his amphibious support forces in the prolonged preparation of the landing beaches. After conferring with his weatherman, he announced to Spruance and Turner that the Tenth Army could land next day as scheduled.

The landing was unopposed. It was as if the Japanese had abandoned Okinawa. Never before had the Japanese failed to fight at the beaches, but on D-Day the Okinawa invasion was a matter of peacefully wading ashore and walking inland. Over 75,000 troops landed on the first day and extended the beachhead depth inward as far as two and a half miles.

The unexpected absence of opposition was welcomed by the astonished invaders, who speculated on the enemy's whereabouts and intentions. Where were the fanatical Japanese soldiers? Where was the furious battle that had been predicted? "We feared the worst," Spruance later wrote, "and were both surprised and relieved when we went ashore unopposed." For the next several days the troops pushed steadily ahead with only occasional skirmishes. Spruance knew that a large-scale land war was inevitable. But he still misjudged the eventual magnitude of the kamikaze attacks, even though they were increasing in intensity, especially at night when the American ships were most vulnerable.

"Our landings on Okinawa have gone better than our wildest dreams could have led us to expect," Spruance wrote Margaret on the fifth day. "The Japs pulled out of the entire landing area, so we got our beaches, two airfields and right through to the eastern side of the island almost without resistance. Up to today the fighting has been minor in nature, but it will not continue so, as there are many thousands of Jap troops on Okinawa and undoubtedly they will put up a stiff fight and have to be killed.

"We have had a fairly steady dribble of Jap air attacks, from dusk through the moonlight nights to daybreak, against our ships. It is annoying and ships get hit, but nothing they have been able to do so far is sufficient to affect the final result of this operation.

"We are in process of taking a most valuable island away from the Japs, and their officials admit to their own people the seriousness of their predicament."

Meanwhile, *Indianapolis* remained immobilized at anchor out of sight of the battle. The crew of the salvage ship hoped to remove and repair her damaged propeller while afloat, and Spruance paced the wrecked fantail while divers struggled underwater with their strenuous task. The chief salvage officer, his face crestfallen, approached the admiral. "Sorry to report, sir," he said, "my men have dropped the propeller off and it is at the bottom of the harbor." The officer expected a torrent of reproof, but Spruance quietly replied, "That's too bad," and resumed walking.

Indianapolis all too obviously needed shipyard repairs, so on 5 April Spruance shifted his flag to the elderly battleship *New Mexico*, chosen because she had flag facilities but did not have an admiral aboard. A sister ship of the *Mississippi* (Spruance's 1938 command), *New Mexico* was limited to a speed of 21 knots, but Spruance apparently did not need the mobility provided by *Indianapolis*. Instead, Spruance intended to remain near Okinawa—where *New Mexico* was gainfully employed in providing naval gunfire support—so that he could follow closely the fighting ashore.

Fifth Fleet under air attack at Okinawa
(Official U.S. Navy photo, National Archives)

New Mexico and the other battleships of her generation had once been the premier ships of the Navy, but, handicapped with slow speed and old equipment, they could not compete with the fast new carriers and battleships. Thus their missions were almost exclusively confined to naval gunfire support, a role with much drudgery and little glory, even though their huge guns were beloved by the assault troops.

Despite her diminished status, *New Mexico* was a happy ship with a first-rate performance record. Her radar operators, despite inferior equipment, always were among the first in the fleet to detect incoming enemy planes, and in many other respects the crew were inspired to get the most out of their less modern weaponry. The crew welcomed Spruance's staff because of the prestige and excitement associated with a

USS *Hazelwood* after hits by kamikazes
(Official U.S. Navy photo, National Archives)

flagship of a fleet commander, and the staff-crew relationship was instantly cordial. As Chuck Barber fondly recalled, "For an old ship, it was a very pleasant place to serve."[1]

Indianapolis departed for the United States for repairs. Spruance insisted that she quickly return and again serve as his flagship. But she never again flew his flag. Following shipyard repairs, *Indianapolis* trans-

1. USS *New Mexico* (BB 40), displacement 32,000 tons, main battery twelve 14-inch guns, commissioned 20 May 1918. The *New Mexico* was with the Atlantic Fleet when Pearl Harbor was attacked in 1941, but soon redeployed to the Pacific. Her primary mission during World War II was shore bombardments, and she earned six battle stars in the process. Decommissioned 19 July 1946, she was scrapped the next year.

USS *New Mexico* struck by kamikaze, 12 May 1945

ported the components for the Nagasaki and Hiroshima atomic bombs to the Air Force at Tinian in late July. Having delivered her lethal cargo, she sailed for the Philippines for refresher training before returning to Okinawa. On 29 July 1945, two weeks before the end of the war, a Japanese submarine torpedoed *Indianapolis,* and she quickly sank.[2]

Many crewmen who survived the actual sinking later unnecessarily died through prolonged exposure at sea. Through a series of errors the Navy was unaware she had sunk until a plane on a routine patrol stumbled upon the wretched survivors, who had been adrift on the hostile ocean for three and a half days. Rescue ships then belatedly

2. Spruance was aware of the ship's poor design and instability. He remarked to his staff at Iwo Jima that, if *Indianapolis* ever was hit cleanly by a torpedo, she would quickly capsize and sink.

arrived on the scene and pulled hundreds of bodies—alive, dead, and nearly dead—from the water. Only 316 crewmen eventually survived. From 350 to 400 had gone down with the ship; almost 500 perished afterward in the water.

Spruance and his staff were ashore on Guam when the *Indianapolis* commanding officer, Captain Charles B. McVay, was admitted to the hospital. The admiral immediately visited his former flag captain and expressed his sympathy and hopes for a full recovery. But McVay received no sympathy from the Navy, which decided to make him the scapegoat to still the public uproar caused by the fiasco. The Navy expediently court-martialed the captain for losing his ship to enemy action, the first time the Navy had so acted in a hundred years.[3]

The first massive enemy air attack began on 6 April, the day after Spruance had shifted to *New Mexico*. Over 700 Japanese planes, half of them kamikazes, flung themselves against the Fifth Fleet surrounding Okinawa. Task Force 58 CAP claimed 233 bogies, ships' antiaircraft fire reportedly downed 35 more, but 22 kamikazes evaded the American defenses and crashed into Spruance's ships. By nightfall the enemy had sunk three destroyers, one tank landing ship, and two ammunition ships. Ten other ships—mostly destroyers in the nakedly exposed radar picket stations—were damaged. The attack continued through the seventh, hitting a carrier, a battleship, and two more radar picket destroyers.

Spruance suspected that the remnants of the Japanese fleet might sortie from the home islands and attack the Okinawa transports simultaneously with the 6 April air attacks. Accordingly he ordered intensified air searches, and the submarines off Japan increased their vigilance. His suspicions were confirmed by submarine contact reports during the night of 6 April. Two large Japanese ships with many escorts were proceeding down the east coast of Kyushu, 400 miles northwest of Okinawa.

Spruance assumed that enemy aircraft would accompany the ships in any attack on Okinawa. He decided that Task Force 58 would concen-

---

3. A recent book, Raymond B. Lech's *All the Drowned Sailors* (New York, 1982), asserts that Spruance had asked Captain McVay for a ride to Leyte, but changed his mind at the last minute. Lech also shows that Captain McVay was not informed of Japanese submarine activity on his intended route to Leyte.

trate exclusively on countering the expected air threat and that the old battleships and the cruisers of the bombardment group would handle the enemy ships in surface action. Shortly after midnight Spruance ordered Mitscher to allow the enemy "fleet" to proceed south and alerted Rear Admiral M. L. Deyo, commanding the bombardment group, to prepare for surface action.

It is not certain when Spruance discovered that the enemy task force contained the super-battleship *Yamato*, whose 18.1-inch guns and 28-knot speed made her superior to the old American battleships, which included *New Mexico*. But Deyo's force was numerically superior and could defeat the *Yamato* should she appear, even though some of Deyo's staff were apprehensive. Furthermore, any battleship captain worth his salt yearned for a chance to fight an enemy battleship, however powerful, as a respite from months of unexciting shore fire support. Spruance would allow his beloved old dreadnoughts one final opportunity to fight the classic surface action that always had been denied them—and him.

By early morning of the seventh, reports indicated that the enemy task force was turning away from Okinawa. Spruance feared that the enemy, rather than pressing its attack, might be escaping to a safe haven in Kyushu. In that event, Task Force 58 was the only force in position to reach the enemy. Spruance was worried because he did not know Mitscher's location or whether he was within range of the evasive *Yamato*. To Spruance's relief, Mitscher's search planes found the Japanese battleship.

"Will you take them or shall I?" asked Mitscher.

Spruance quickly wrote his reply on a radio message blank. "You take them."

Mitscher's carrier planes sank the *Yamato* that afternoon, as well as one cruiser and four destroyers. Spruance's last chance for a surface action went down with the Japanese battleship.

The Okinawa campaign became a savage war of attrition. The Tenth Army finally collided with the Japanese main line of resistance, and Buckner's daily battle reports to Spruance were dismaying. The enemy defenders were entrenched in almost impenetrable terrain, and they fought ferociously. Rain and mud inhibited battlefield maneuver. In an island 60 miles long the daily progress ashore was measured in hundreds of yards. Frequently there was no advance at all. Although it was inevitable that the American troops would conquer the island, the battle would be months long and would exact enormous casualties ashore.

During that prolonged period, the Fifth Fleet had to remain off the shores of Okinawa in order to support the Tenth Army. The Japanese continued to attack with thousands of aircraft, both conventional and kamikaze. The campaign lasted three months, and continual, relentless enemy air attacks eventually sank 30 ships and damaged 368, killed 4900 sailors, and wounded 4800 more.

Spruance and Nimitz tried everything in their power to eliminate or mitigate the enemy air threat in order to reduce the appalling damage to the fleet. Their efforts were belated. "Looking back over our Central Pacific operations," Spruance later wrote, "I have thought that we might have saved a lot of smaller ships damaged or sunk on the picket line off Okinawa, if our plans had called for seizing some of the small islands lying northward of Okinawa, and then had established on them radars and fighter director groups. None of us, however, foresaw the suicide plane threat while we were making our plans for Okinawa. . . . We tried hard during the fighting on Okinawa to get some troops to occupy the large island [Kumei?] that lies to the westward of southern Okinawa, so that we could use it with a radar and fighter directors to stop the suicide planes starting from Formosa. The Army always had some reason why they could not do this."

Nimitz turned to the Air Force for help. He asked that the Mariana-based B-29's hit Kyushu and that MacArthur's 5th Air Force in Luzon suppress the enemy air on Formosa. LeMay, commanding the B-29's, objected to using his bombers for "tactical" missions, believing that the big planes best could help the war effort by fire raids on Japanese cities. But Nimitz insisted on help during the initial stages of the Okinawa campaign, and in response LeMay's forces bombed the Kyushu air-fields. Unfortunately, the B-29's did little more than to crater runways, which quickly were repaired. The Air Force could not stop the Japanese from launching air raids against the Fifth Fleet. It was futile to continue, and in mid-May Nimitz released LeMay to resume destroying Japanese cities and mining Japanese waters. The Kyushu airfields continued to launch aircraft against the Fifth Fleet.

Nimitz also requested that Air Force long-range P-51 fighters, based on Iwo Jima, hit the Kyushu airfields. But these attacks were equally unsuccessful. The Air Force fighters could not navigate over open water or find the well-hidden targets on Kyushu.

To compound Spruance's problems, the B-24 bombers of the 5th Air Force, flying out of Luzon, were ineffectual against Formosa. Although the bombers dumped tons of bombs upon airdromes, they were unable to destroy the well-dispersed enemy aircraft, and Formosa consequently provided 20 percent of the kamikazes that attacked the Fifth Fleet. The Navy and Air Force argued heatedly about the tactics to use against Formosa, because neither service could agree on just how many enemy planes were based on the island. The Air Force maintained that few remained and wanted to concentrate on more "profitable" targets. The Navy insisted that Formosa was crawling with kamikazes and demanded renewed attacks against the airfields.

Spruance, his fleet ravaged by land-based Japanese aircraft, was embittered by what he considered to be the worst performance ever by the Air Force in support of the Navy. When Halsey relieved Spruance in late May, he asked Spruance how well the 5th Air Force had aided him.

"They've destroyed a great many sugar mills, railroad trains, and other equipment," Spruance caustically replied.

With the Air Force unable materially to reduce the kamikaze threat, Spruance tried, whenever possible, to hit Kyushu with Task Force 58, but he rarely had enough carriers available for that purpose. Mitscher's carriers usually were needed for CAP duties off Okinawa, task groups had to be released for periodic rest and replenishment in Ulithi, and kamikaze damage to the carriers further limited the numbers of carriers available for Kyushu strikes.

One bright spot was the splendid performance of Task Force 57, the carriers of the Royal Navy, under the command of Vice Admiral Sir H. B. Rawlings. Although Spruance initially had opposed their use with the Fifth Fleet, the British carriers justified themselves by successfully neutralizing Japanese airfields in the Sakishima Gunto island groups, 250 miles southwest of Okinawa, and by frequently hitting Formosa as well.

Spruance congratulated Rawlings by message; then, after the war, he expressed his gratitude before a distinguished British military audience in London. "In spite of the fact that Admiral Rawlings and I had no chance for a personal conference before the operation," said Spruance, "Task Force 57 did its work to my complete satisfaction and fully lived up to the traditions of the Royal Navy. I remember my chief of staff remarking one day that, if Admiral Rawlings and I had known each other for twenty years, things could not have gone more smoothly."

When the British withdrew to rest and replenish, Turner's escort carriers competently filled the gap.

Nimitz pressed Spruance to establish airfields ashore on Okinawa as soon as possible so that shore-based fighters could assist Task Force 58. But airfield construction was handicapped by lack of building material—especially coral—and by bad weather. Once the fields were operational, they, too, often were attacked by Japanese aircraft. On one bizarre night the Japanese landed a transport plane on an American airfield, and 22 Japanese commandos galloped out and proceeded to destroy 7 parked aircraft and 70,000 gallons of aviation gasoline.

But the airfields did get built, and their aircraft were able to share the load with the carrier aircraft.

The Okinawa campaign was entirely different from the earlier battles in the Gilberts and Marshalls, the kind of war that Spruance would have preferred. "I like the idea of isolation, death or capture, which our small island positions have permitted," he wrote Margaret in late 1944. "It is final and conclusive, like the end of Hamlet."

As the Okinawa battle dragged on Spruance despaired of an early victory, and after the seventh week he expressed his gloomy feelings in a letter to Carl Moore. "The suicide plane is a very effective weapon, which we must not underestimate," he wrote. "I do not believe any one who has not been around within its area of operations can realize its potentialities against ships. It is the opposite extreme of a lot of our Army heavy bombers who bomb safely and ineffectively from the upper atmosphere.

"I doubt if the Army slow, methodical method of fighting really saves any lives in the long run. It merely spreads the casualties over a longer period. The longer period greatly increases the naval casualties when Jap air attacks on ships is a continuing factor. However, I do not think the Army is at all allergic to losses of naval ships and personnel.

"There are times when I get impatient for some of Holland Smith's drive, but there is nothing we can do about it."

Whether Holland Smith with an all-Marine force could have seized Okinawa more rapidly is doubtful, because rugged Iwo Jima had required more than a month for the Marines to capture. The size, terrain, and fortifications on Okinawa required different tactics from those the Marines had used on the coral islets. The struggle for Okinawa was more suitable to the Army method. Spruance's deprecation of the Army was unfair and was motivated by his growing impatience and his concern over his continuing loss of ships. Wisely, he never expressed his feelings in public on the Army's performance at Okinawa.

On the evening of 12 May, New Mexico had finished replenishing ammunition and was approaching her anchorage for the night. The day had been quiet and peaceful. Suddenly, two low-flying kamikazes appeared at sunset and streaked toward the flagship. The ship's antiaircraft fire got one, but the other smashed into the side of the ship abaft the bridge. A huge fire roared from a gaping hole amidships. The carnage was horrible: the blast had killed 50 men and wounded more than a hundred.

Spruance was missing, having last been seen in his cabin aft. The staff frantically searched the ship, fearing for his safety. They found him manning a fire hose. His instructions were the same as they had been before on Indianapolis: ascertain the damage and check for code books.

Spruance later described his narrow escape from death. "I had just started for the bridge when the AA batteries opened up," he wrote Moore, "so I remained under cover while going forward on the second deck. We were hit before I got very far, which was fortunate for me as the two routes to the bridge lead right through the area where the plane and bomb hit."

New Mexico remained at anchor for the next two weeks and repaired her damage. Savvy Forrestel wondered why the Japanese continually ignored such an obvious and important target immobilized in the center of the anchorage. "We laid at anchor for weeks and brought a repair barge alongside to repair the damage," he later recalled. "And we knew that this photographic plane was coming over every morning, and we knew they must have spotted this battleship down there, day after day in the same place. We didn't know when they were going to come in after us, but whenever they came in we'd have smokers out, and the whole anchorage would be under smoke. Why they just didn't drop torpedoes into that smoke cloud, I don't know. They could not have missed hitting a few ships in there."

By then the staff was physically and mentally exhausted from the continual strain of the incessant kamikaze attacks. The Japanese preferred to strike at dusk and dawn and during moonlit nights, robbing the staff of sleep and increasing their fatigue.

Spruance, however, usually slept despite the attacks and the ship's gunfire. Sometimes *New Mexico* shot at aircraft, other times at targets ashore. "I have gotten very good at sleeping through 5 and 14 inch gunfire and Jap hecklers at night," he wrote. "I manage to sleep through most of that provided the firing is at regular intervals. Sometimes there is a long lull and then a number of rounds are fired, which tends to be disturbing.

"The moon is a remarkable institution," he observed to Margaret. "When you are using the moon to walk abroad under with your best girl in the evening, it is remarkable how little of it there is. When the Jap is using it for his planes to attack you with, it is remarkable what a large proportion of the month you have moonlight. Last night was about full moon. We had visitations off and on most of the night—not that I staid up for them, however."

Spruance occasionally visited ashore, and he told Margaret of his impressions of the land he was trying to capture. "This is a beautiful and fertile island," he wrote. "The natives live very close to the soil and are excellent farmers and producers of offspring, but otherwise low grade, dirty, and docile. The dirt must come from the Chinese influence.

"It is reported that the women do all the work, but of this I can not be sure, as the Japs have left behind no men and few women of working ages. The people we have are mostly old men and women, mothers and young children. In all of these islands the poor natives are generally innocent bystanders who have no interest in the quarrel and who suffer most from it."

The battle had its absurd moments. Shortly after the landings began in early April, the flagship was swinging peacefully at anchor off Okinawa. Just before taps the crew was jolted into a frenzy by the public address system blaring, "Turn on all lights, search all compartments! There may be a Jap aboard!"

The Marines doubled their guard on Spruance while the staff tried to discover the reason for the alarm. They soon learned that a Marine sentry on the main deck had been assaulted by a mysterious figure whom he had discovered coming aboard along the boat boom. His assailant never was found. "That's the variety and excitement that keeps life interesting," wrote Barber to his parents.

Spruance and the staff retained their sense of humor as the battle progressed, and Spruance often played practical jokes on his subordinates. His medical officer reported that Major General Roy Geiger, commanding the Marines ashore, was afflicted with the mumps. Although a mild childhood disease, it could sterilize an adult. Geiger, said the doctor, was mortified and wanted to conceal his embarrassing predicament. Spruance said nothing, but a week later he asked the doctor to give Geiger a package. When Geiger opened the package he found a well-shaped diaper and a safety pin. The Marine general roared with laughter. "Tell Spruance," he directed the doctor, "that I will keep this in my private archives along with my most treasured battle flags and trophies."

Vice Admiral Johnny Hoover had been a Spruance guest during the Iwo Jima invasion, and he had complained when the American ships had destroyed some Japanese boats (which were hiding snipers) during the bombardment. Hoover had planned to establish his headquarters on Iwo, and he wanted to use one of the boats for fishing.

The Americans later captured a handsome Japanese boat at Okinawa, intended to be used, with hundreds of others, as a suicide craft. Spruance arranged for the *Indianapolis* to deliver the boat to Hoover while en route to the States to repair the kamikaze damage. He told Barber to compose an appropriate letter of transmittal.

The staff had become proficient at writing comic poetry to one another as a form of amusement. The most talented poet was the British naval liaison officer, Mike LeFanu, later an Admiral of the Fleet, Chief of Naval Staff and First Sea Lord. His doggerels became fondly known as "Limey Rhymes." With a precedent established, Barber decided that a poem was appropriate and composed a sixteen-stanza piece entitled "A Boat for King Johnny," quoted below in part.

> Our brave soldiers they captured a new kind of boat,
> Meant to sink our great ships as a matter of rote.
> "Hold your fire," Ray commanded when dynamite charge
> Was placed on the frame of this just captured barge.

He remembered the tears of King John at CENPAC,
He remembered the story of thwarted attack
On the king of the sea off the reef in the lee.
He remembered "no boat" was the gist of his plea.

In the Indian Maru[4] by the enemy smote,
He provided a place for this just-captured boat.
"Quick now take it," commanded the Admiral then,
"To King Johnny of CENPAC, that prince among men."

Nimitz realized the strain imposed on his high commanders and their staffs at Okinawa, a strain that could lower his commanders' efficiency and harm their health. They needed a rest, and he ordered Halsey, Hill, and McCain to relieve Spruance, Turner, and Mitscher, respectively, in late May. Even though the battle was not over, victory at Okinawa was only a matter of time. Spruance and his commanders would recuperate and then begin planning for the invasion of Japan.

Halsey arrived in his flagship *Missouri* on 26 May, and the staffs began the familiar turnover procedure. Spruance would have preferred to remain at Okinawa to finish the fight, but his haggard staff were happy to be relieved. A Halsey staff officer, initially shocked by the exhaustion of Spruance's officers, was amazed at Spruance's contrasting serenity and composure. Spruance, however, had been under extreme tension, and he commented years later to Margaret, "No one knew of the butterflies in my stomach."

Despite the prolonged and intimate contact between Spruance and his staff, they had been aware only of his apparent stoicism and stamina throughout the four months of continual combat at Iwo Jima and Okinawa. In early 1945, Secretary of the Navy James V. Forrestal, concerned about the health of his fleet commanders, had assigned a senior naval doctor, M. D. Willcutts, to serve as Fifth Fleet Medical Officer in title, but as personal physician to Spruance in reality. Not once did Willcutts detect physical or mental fatigue in Spruance, nor did Spruance ever require medication, not even aspirin.

Spruance reportedly lost his temper but once during the Okinawa ordeal. A task force commander had requested permission to take his ships to sea to drill them in preparation for a possible enemy threat.

4. USS *Indianapolis*. "Maru" is a Japanese suffix that designates a merchant ship.

"The dispatch was essentially foolish," Art Davis later related. "But Spruance was a wholly dedicated man and the dispatch struck a John Paul Jones nerve. It was John Paul Jones who said, 'Show me the man who refuses duty and I'll have him flogged so goddamned quick it will make his head spin.' Spruance was in a complete fury. He thought the force commander was implying that, without opportunity for drilling, he wouldn't do his job. Spruance was about to relieve him of his command. But he finally saw that the dispatch was merely poorly written, that it was puerile rather than insubordinate; so he contented himself with sending for the force commander and explaining carefully that two plus two equals four."

Halsey relieved Spruance at midnight, 27 May 1945, in the midst of one of the heaviest and most prolonged Japanese air attacks of the campaign. Over 150 enemy planes, in 56 separate raids lasting more than twenty-four hours, sank or damaged 14 American ships.

Chuck Barber vividly described the wild, sleepless night of Spruance's last hours at Okinawa, which typified the tempo of the fighting throughout the two-month ordeal. "It started at dinner," he wrote to his parents. "I had just started my ice cream when air defense sounded. I was off to the bridge. Three or four planes were coming in from the north. . . . By 2200 they were still coming in. . . . Shortly things quieted down. The admirals turned in for some shuteye. . . . Got back to Flag Plot about 10 minutes 'till midnight. Jap planes were still in the vicinity. The near full moon cast an eerie light through the haze.

"It was about 12:30 PM when the next big raid came in. Pretty soon we heard the heavy AA from the beach—then the boom boom of lighter guns aboard ships near us. We did not fire in as much as we thought the Japs had not seen us. We could hear the drone of the motors overhead. I stepped outside—and as I searched the sky it was as though I were looking for witches riding their broomsticks across the harvest moon. . . ."

New Mexico got underway for Guam early next morning. A bogey was reported closing the anchorage, and anxious gunners with sleepy eyes scanned the predawn gloom. The staff on the flag bridge at first could not see the kamikaze, but tracers from the adjacent ships began to converge on the still invisible incoming plane. Suddenly the staff saw the plane—then it exploded in a huge ball of fire. Spangles and streams of sparks glittered in the sky, glowing fragments of the aircraft, which drifted down into the water.

Halsey relieves Spruance at Okinawa, 26 May 1945

"I was reminded of the finale of the great fireworks displays—Niagara Falls on fire," wrote Barber. "A beautiful four star finale to an exciting night."

As Barber watched the glorious sunrise, Spruance joined him briefly. "That's one to write about," the admiral commented. On the forecastle the boatswain mates housed the anchor, and the sturdy old battleship steamed through the anchorage and made her way to sea. Two destroyers took station on either bow, and *New Mexico* sailed away from Okinawa.

The war was over for Raymond Spruance.

Chapter 23

VICTORY AND OCCUPATION

O N 1 June 1945 Spruance shifted his flag from USS *New Mexico* to headquarters ashore on Guam. There he joined Nimitz, who had moved his staff to Guam in order to be nearer to the fighting. Pearl Harbor was too far to the rear.

Guam was a welcomed haven after the rigors of Iwo Jima and Okinawa. Flag quarters consisted of large, airy four-bedroom bungalows on a mountaintop, and the elevation above sea level corresponded to the occupants' seniority. At six hundred feet, Spruance's quarters were cool and comfortable. "The climate is much superior to that ashore at sea level," wrote an appreciative Spruance, "and beyond comparison with the heat below on board ship. The land in front of the house drops steeply off with a dense mass of jungle vegetation on the slope. It is rumored that a Jap or Japs live down in there, but I don't vouch for this or lie awake at nights on account of it."

Spruance's task in Guam was to plan for the next American offensive against Japan. Military leaders differed about what that step should be and had been debating for months about American strategy following the seizure of Okinawa. Many hoped to defeat Japan through a blockade, while others believed that Japan would not surrender until the Americans invaded the home islands.

Spruance opposed any invasion of Japan and wanted instead to seize the waters and adjacent land areas of Nimrod Sound, located on the China coast a hundred miles south of Shanghai. This would provide both an excellent fleet anchorage and good airfield sites and would allow the supply and reinforcement of the Chinese army. Once strengthened, that Army then could clear the Japanese army out of south and central China, and eventually northern China. While the Chinese fought the Japanese, argued Spruance, American air power would operate from Nimrod Sound, the Philippines, Okinawa, Iwo Jima, and the Marianas, and would sever all lines of communication leading into the Japanese home islands. Eventually Japan could be starved into surrender.

Spruance was willing to wait as long as necessary. "In war the time element is often an important consideration," he later wrote. "Sometimes, time is working for the enemy, and we ought to push the fighting. Sometimes, time is working for us, and then we can slow down the fighting. In the case of World War II, toward the end, time was decidedly on our side. Japan was cut off and could well have been permitted to 'die on the vine,' as we had done with the by-passed islands in the Pacific."

Spruance's reasoning overlooked three important factors. First, time was not "decidedly on our side." Rather, it was working against the United States. The American public was war-weary, and it was questionable whether the government could persuade the American people to accept a prolonging of the war. Very likely the public would not have tolerated an indefinite and inconclusive blockade, especially since the Japanese had never before surrendered any military position during the war, regardless of the hopelessness of their position. Americans are impatient. They want action and movement. A war by blockade would have been politically unacceptable if it did not achieve a rapid victory.

The second questionable Spruance argument was that a beachhead at Nimrod Sound would have invigorated the Chinese army. Many factors suggested otherwise. For example, Spruance knew in 1945 that Chiang Kai-shek was more interested in fighting Mao Tse-tung than the Japanese, and the inept performance of the Chinese army throughout the war was common knowledge. Still, years after the war, he continued to argue (unconvincingly) that an American base on the China coast would somehow have motivated Chiang to do what he had never done before. Furthermore, there was no reason to tackle the formidable Japanese army in China—it was more sensible to bypass the army. The territory it occupied had no strategic value to the United States, nor did it threaten American forces in the Pacific. *The Japanese army in China* was therefore the logical force to let "die on the vine."

And there was a third factor that Spruance overlooked: he did not envision an active role for the American ground forces, other than the limited task of seizing and defending a beachhead in Nimrod Sound. Millions of American men were under arms in the Army and Marine Corps, and if they were not used against the Japanese army, how would they be used? It would have been unthinkable to demobilize the ground forces while Japan was still at war. On the other hand, it would have been equally unthinkable to allow millions of men to remain idle while waiting—perhaps months, perhaps years—for Japan to surrender because of the blockade.

Why, then, did Spruance advocate taking the war to China? The probable answer is that he was dismayed with the killing and destruction and horror of war. He regarded the Okinawa campaign, with its appalling loss of American lives and damage to his fleet, as a "bloody, hellish prelude to the invasion of Japan." Spruance could not accept the enormous casualties that would be inevitable when the Americans landed on Japanese soil, so he sought alternatives which might defeat Japan with a minimum loss of American lives.

Nimitz had first asked Spruance for his post-Okinawa recommendations in the fall of 1944, and Spruance at that time had recommended Nimrod Sound. Spruance next pressed for China during the first week of the Okinawa invasion by recommending to Nimitz that some of the Okinawa objectives be deleted and that the CINCPOA forces land in Nimrod Sound instead. But his views were never accepted, even though at one time both King and Nimitz had also advocated a China invasion. Generals Marshall and MacArthur consistently opposed the Navy and insisted upon an invasion of Japan. The Army generals finally convinced President Truman, who approved the concept in June 1945. Nimitz met with King and Secretary Forrestal in San Francisco in late June, and King announced the President's decision.

Spruance had hitched a ride that June to the mainland with Nimitz for a week's leave in Monrovia. He must have been disturbed. During his visit he told his wife and daughter that Japan was the next objective and that he preferred China. Young Margaret was surprised that he would confide what was obviously a military secret. He returned to Guam and sadly began plans to implement the President's decision.

The Fifth Fleet would land General Kruger's Sixth Army on Kyushu on 1 November 1945, followed by Halsey's Third Fleet landing General Eichelberger's Eighth Army on the Tokyo plains. Spruance dreaded the prospect. His son Edward, commanding a Guam-based submarine, became aware of his father's foreboding. One day the admiral confessed his grave concern for the death and damage that the kamikazes were inflicting on the fleet off Okinawa. Far worse destruction was inevitable off Japan. "He seemed more worried," Edward remembered, "than I had ever seen him before."

Spruance's staff was in transition. Most of his key officers were leaving for new assignments: Forrestel to command a battleship, Biggs to assume a logistics post in Washington, and Davis to command a carrier division. Only Chuck Barber and the two communicators—Armstrong and McCormick—remained of the staff that first had assembled two years before to plan for Tarawa.

Armstrong had not mellowed with time. One day in the Guam headquarters office, when the dial phone went dead, Armstrong's frustrations came to a boil. With a sound that reverberated through the whole building and language to match, he tore the instrument from the wall. Spruance seemed not to notice.

Spruance's enlisted staff were harassed by the Nimitz staff, who frequently placed Spruance's men on report for minor infractions such as improper dress and failure to salute. Cy Huie was the enlisted men's division officer. He attempted to remedy the situation through the power of suggestion by reading "Rocks and Shoals" (the predecessor to the *Uniform Code of Military Justice)* while the sailors were assembled at quarters.

A day or so later Spruance remarked to his zealous aide that men who had been through an operation like Okinawa were entitled to relax while ashore. The minor infractions reported by Nimitz's staff—who were ashore all the time—might well be viewed very leniently. Spruance never mentioned the "Rocks and Shoals" reading nor did he imply any criticism towards his flag lieutenant. But, as the young officer recalled, "I got the message."

On 26 July the Allied Powers issued the Potsdam Declaration, a document that publicized the conditions for Japan's surrender. Two days later Japan rejected the declaration, yet an air of expectancy permeated the Guam headquarters, an expectancy that Japan would surrender or collapse at any moment. Nimitz's staff began planning for the occupation rather than the invasion of Japan.

One day in early August Spruance assembled his staff in his office and read them a top secret dispatch: within a few days the United States would drop an atomic bomb on Japan. Barber, for one, could not visualize the bomb, but Spruance seemed to know about it. (How much he knew is uncertain.) The admiral hoped that the bomb would shock Japan into surrender, and no one expressed any moral reservations about its use.

Spruance later admitted to mixed emotions on the use of nuclear weapons. In August 1945 he was brooding that the Japan invasion "would have been a terribly bloody, unnecessary proposition. I was very glad in a sense when, finally, the two atomic bombs that we dropped over Hiroshima and Nagasaki decided the Japanese to surrender. It is impossible to know how long the war would have lasted, but it is certain that the bomb shortened it by a great length."

He would not have used the bombs if his China strategy had been approved. In considering a nuclear war of the future, Spruance later wrote, "I am still opposed to the idea of war being conducted by mass destruction of civilian targets by long range missiles armed with nuclear warheads. I recognize that, if our enemy has them, we must be prepared to counter an attack and probably to retaliate in kind. I hope that the responsible governments of the world will be successful in their negotiations to prevent such a situation from ever coming to pass."

The bombs destroyed the two Japanese cities on 6 and 9 August, and the radio reported peace overtures by Japan. Nimitz warned his forces to remain vigilant against Japanese treachery.

A major controversy arose among the Allies as they awaited Japan's decision in early August whether to surrender. The hotly debated issue was whether the Emperor should be allowed to remain in office after the war. Many wanted him removed, and some advocated his execution as a war criminal. Others maintained that Hirohito was essential to a stable postwar government. Spruance expressed his opinion to Margaret in a letter of 12 August, written just after the American government had assured Japan that Hirohito could remain.

"This morning's press carried our full reply, which I think is very sensible," he wrote. "If the Japanese want an emperor of great honor and sanctity, that is their business. Our business is to see that they are left in no position to run amok again and not to tell them that they must have some kind of government they are not used to and don't want. If they accept in reasonable terms, the war will be over shortly; if not, it will continue until they have been beaten some more. I think they will accept.

"If they do, I shall probably be headed north in a few days. Don't get excited about my coming back at an early date, for it is going to take a considerable time to get Japan in hand and to wind up the war out here. I assume that the people who are already out here will have these jobs to do."

On 14 August Nimitz issued his plan for the occupation of Japan. Spruance and the Fifth Fleet would land Kruger's Sixth Army in western Honshu, Kyushu, and Shikoku. Halsey and his Third Fleet would land Eichelberger's Eighth Army in eastern Honshu. Nimitz warned everyone to be prepared to execute the plan on short notice.

The next day, 15 August, Spruance and Edward were walking together, and as they passed by a group of Quonset huts they heard a great shout from the people inside. They entered one of the huts and asked what had happened.

The excited men replied that the radio had just reported Japan's surrender.

Spruance expressed quiet satisfaction. Then the father and son resumed their walk. Spruance showed no visible signs of emotion.

Spruance was absent from the surrender ceremonies aboard USS *Missouri* in Tokyo Bay. MacArthur had invited him to attend, but Spruance had declined, saying that if Nimitz had wanted him there, Nimitz would have told him so.

Obviously Nimitz did not want Spruance in Tokyo. Spruance's orders were to plan for the occupation of Japan. When the Japanese signed the surrender documents on 2 September, Spruance was aboard his flagship *New Jersey* in Buckner Bay, Okinawa. One can speculate that Spruance was not in Tokyo Bay so that he could take command of the Pacific Fleet should the Japanese, rather than surrendering, treacherously attack the *Missouri* and kill the high-ranking Americans aboard. Although the staff wondered aloud why Spruance had not been invited to witness the ceremony, the admiral did not seem disappointed. Barber later recalled only that the Fifth Fleet commander was eager to repatriate the American prisoners in Japan.

*   *   *

On 21 August, Spruance and *New Jersey* arrived in Manila Bay. Planning conferences began, and two days later Spruance called on MacArthur. Spruance had never before met MacArthur and was extremely nervous as he left his flagship. The hostility between MacArthur and the Navy was well known. But MacArthur and his wife charmed and disarmed Spruance with gracious hospitality, and Spruance quickly discovered that he and the general were of one mind. Spruance returned to *New Jersey* that afternoon and commented, "He's not so bad." Spruance's distrust and dislike of the general dissolved and were replaced with admiration and respect. The two senior officers shared a common attitude toward Japan.

Five years later Spruance staunchly defended MacArthur's controversial actions in the Korean War. "When the Korean war broke out," wrote Spruance in 1964, "and [MacArthur] proposed to Washington that they take the wraps off of it and allow him to win it, I agreed with him entirely. Had he been permitted to carry out his plans, I think the trouble we are now in in South East Asia would not have occurred."

His support of MacArthur is curious. Spruance regarded the President's orders as Commander in Chief to be inviolable, yet MacArthur had been relieved for actively opposing President Truman. Carl Moore has suggested the best explanation. "I never undertook to discuss [with Spruance] MacArthur's performance in Korea," said Moore. "I never tried to argue that with Spruance, because he was sold on MacArthur from the minute he met him in Manila."

"MacArthur is a very able man and, I think, is handling this occupation job in a very dignified and far sighted manner," wrote Spruance to Moore just before the Japanese surrender ceremony. "He is correct and formal with the Japanese, impressed them with our power and authority, but, at the same time, does not humiliate them and accedes to their reasonable requests. On their part, the Japanese seem to be doing everything within their power to get and keep their people under control and to comply with our orders. The Japanese people are an excitable race, but they are accustomed to obeying orders and are well disciplined in the mass. Time has been given by our plans for the Government to impose its will on all elements, and this has been very wise and has avoided a lot of unnecessary trouble and bloodshed."

Then Spruance discussed his defeated enemy. "I have no sympathy with that element of our home population who insisted on the overthrow of the Emperor," he wrote, "regardless of the fact that this would have meant the continuance of the war and much more bloodshed. So long as the Japanese people want an emperor, they will continue to have one, and foreign opposition will only strengthen their determination. If we want to change them, the best way to do it—now that we have beaten hell out of them and they have surrendered and are giving up all of their territorial gains of the past fifty years—is to set them an example of what we hope they will be like. We shall get nowhere if, by our treatment of them, we make them hate us as their treatment of the occupied countries has made the inhabitants of these countries hate the Japanese.

"Our peace terms are, and should be, such as to prevent the Japanese from ever going on a rampage again, but we should enforce these terms in a civilized manner. If we should adopt Japanese methods, we would merely be bringing ourselves down to their level. This does not mean that we should not punish individual war criminals, provided we get our hands on them and get the evidence to convict them.

"There is nothing to indicate any feeling of war guilt on the part of either the Germans or the Japanese—only a feeling of regret at having lost. I think the most we can ever expect from them is an admission that they made a bad mistake in starting the war. I never heard of a Southerner feeling that the South was in the wrong in starting our Civil War."

China, Manchuria, and Korea were in anarchy and chaos. There were many causes: the warfare between the forces of Chiang Kai-shek and Mao Tse-tung; the territorial acquisitiveness of the Soviet Union; and the presence of an organized Japanese army on the China mainland. Spruance foresaw the potential problems in the same letter to Moore. "Affairs in China and Korea appear to contain plenty of possibilities for further trouble and bloodshed," he wrote, "but I hope we shall be able to get the Japanese part of the mess untangled and clear. What the Chinese will do with their domestic squabbles remains to be seen. From brief items in this morning's press it looks as if the Russians had made a deal with Chungking [Chiang Kai-shek's wartime capital] before they came in, to take back what they had to give up to the Japanese in 1905.[1] They will undoubtedly dominate the government of both Man-

---

1. Spruance guessed wrong. Truman, not Chiang, gave Stalin the Chinese territorial concessions at the Yalta Conference, in exchange for Russia's entry into the war against Japan.

churia and Korea, whatever the nominal status of those governments to China and to the rest of the world may be. Russia is going to be a very powerful country, with all its territory in one bloc and no control by international trusteeship, and with a very strong influence over most of its near neighbors."

Spruance then summarized his tasks of occupying Japan and concluded, "This should be an interesting time for the next couple of months, and I hope and shall endeavor to see that everything goes smoothly."

In late August, at about the same time as his late August 1945 letter to Moore, Spruance consented to a press conference (his second of the war) with the American and foreign correspondents then in Manila. Spruance's remarks, as reported by the press, reflected his enlightened attitude toward Japan, but they also included two other main points that shocked the Navy Department.

First, he maintained that the United States should not occupy bases on or near the eastern coast of Asia, such as Formosa and Okinawa, in order not to offend Russia and China. "It would be a sore point with us if a foreign power held a string of islands blockading our coasts," Spruance was quoted by the Associated Press. "In political terms, we want to do everything we can to leave no sore spots in international relations." The Associated Press continued that Spruance viewed Okinawa as extremely valuable strategically but potentially explosive internationally, and that diplomats would have to determine its ultimate disposition.

Spruance's other sensational remark was that the American Navy should be drastically reduced in size, because the United States now had no enemy naval powers, and the cost of retaining a large American fleet was unjustified.

Spruance's published views evoked mixed reactions in the United States. The Navy Department was furious. It was fighting a political war in Washington against influential critics who advocated armed services unification, the ascendency of air power over naval power, and an immediate demobilization of the American fleet. The Department regarded Spruance's views as ill-timed and as detrimental to the best interests of the Navy, and Spruance's knuckles were vigorously rapped by his superiors in Washington.

In contrast, important newspapers published editorials that praised

Spruance's statesmanship. "Admiral Raymond A. Spruance's words of seasoned wisdom about the United States postwar naval policy sweep in as a refreshing breeze from the Far Pacific," the Washington *Post* editorialized. "They are all the more arresting because of the contrast with the imperialistic jargon so often heard from Admiral Halsey and other fire-eaters among our naval commanders. We had been looking earnestly for evidence of statesmanship in the Navy. This particular example of it is especially heartening because it coincides with the start of the colossal assignment of demilitarizing Japan and preparing the way for lasting peace in the Far East."

Whether Spruance's remarks were appropriate at that time and under those circumstances can be debated both ways. There are perplexing ethical questions. For example, when should an influential military officer (which Spruance was) reveal his true feelings on a subject, and when should he be silent? If Spruance's policy was to avoid controversy, he missed the mark by a wide margin during the press conference. His blunt yet well-intentioned intrusion into delicate matters of State and Navy Department policy suggests naïveté in dealing with the press, and he apparently did not realize the potential impact of his honest and forthright statements. His letter to Margaret immediately following the press conference manifests his ingenuousness.

"It lasted about an hour," he wrote Margaret, "during which I talked to them about the war and tried to answer a lot of questions. I rather enjoyed the experience. From what Comdr. Paul Smith said later, I must have made a reasonably favorable impression, as their writeups were friendly.[2] I hope Margaret approves. Now that the war is over, the situation about publicity is greatly changed, and I recognize it."

The editorial's phrase, "colossal assignment," was no exaggeration. Spruance's first priority was the speedy repatriation of thousands of Allied prisoners of war who were imprisoned on the Japanese mainland, an enterprise codenamed Operation REAMPS (Recovered Allied Military Personnel). Mines and typhoons had obstructed American rescue ships and disrupted transportation and communications ashore. Yet when Spruance first arrived in Japan on 15 September 1945, he found

---

2. Smith was a public affairs specialist assigned to Spruance's staff in 1945, despite Spruance's objections. One wonders if Smith was candid in his analysis of the conference results.

Edward Spruance shows a captured Japanese submarine to his father.

that REAMPS was progressing well. *New Jersey's* first stop was the port of Wakayama, located on the eastern entrance to the Inland Sea, where more than 1300 POW's were being received aboard the hospital ship *Sanctuary* and two small transports.

Spruance inspected the evacuation organization and was impressed with its smooth and efficient performance. The POW's were given haircuts, bathed, deloused, and clothed, then moved aboard ship and assigned wards appropriate to their physical condition. The admiral moved among the men, talked to many, and was disturbed by their poor physical condition, which he attributed to inadequate food. The *Sanctuary,* her decks lined with jubilant POW's, later steamed by the *New Jersey* and the two ships exchanged salutes. Barber later recalled the event as a very emotional and satisfying experience for the entire staff, and one wonders if Spruance still believed that the only legitimate military reason for taking prisoners was to gain intelligence information.[3]

Before *Sanctuary* departed, Spruance had received his first reports of Japanese brutality against the POW's which eventually changed his attitude toward some of his former enemies. Spruance insisted upon a thorough investigation of all maltreatment allegations, and in some cases he found that POW's had disobeyed strict camp rules and had not been punished unfairly. And he leniently regarded the POWs' malnutrition as a result of the general food shortage in Japan caused by the American air and naval blockade.

On the other hand, he became convinced that many of the atrocity charges were true. He advocated speedy executions of convicted war criminals, both as retribution for their crimes and as an expedient method to rid the Japanese nation of people who exerted an evil and corrupting influence. In a vengeful mood, he wrote Carl Moore, "Those responsible for the maltreatment of our POWs will get what is coming to them." After he and Halsey had viewed alleged war criminals imprisoned in Yokohama, he described them to Margaret as "brutes and thugs," and one in particular as a "fat slob and bully" whose execution would "rid the earth of vermin." Perhaps Spruance was influenced that day by Halsey, who in his autobiography devoted two pages to describe the hate and contempt that he felt when he saw and talked with those accused of treason and war crimes. In particular, both admirals vividly recorded their loathing of the German Weisenger, a Nazi known as the "Butcher of Warsaw." In prison he was reduced to a frightened, groveling coward.

Yet Spruance would contradict himself on the subject of war crimes. When Edward remarked that every Japanese officer guilty of atrocities should be shot, Spruance rebuked him. "Military men should not be subjected to such treatment," he said. "Look at what would have happened to us if we had lost the war with Japan and such a policy had been adopted."

Spruance first stepped upon Japanese soil after leaving the hospital ship. He walked and rode unarmed, curious and inquisitive about the people and the country he had helped to conquer. This set the pattern

3. See chapter 19.

for his frequent exploratory expeditions ashore during the following weeks.

The city of Wakayama had been destroyed by a B-29 raid, but Spruance expressed neither remorse nor regret about the destruction to that or to any other Japanese cities that he later visited. His first impression of the Japanese civilians was that they were stolid and emotionless, with no sign of humor or laughter—except for the children, always irrepressible regardless of nationality and circumstances.

But he shortly came to appreciate the Japanese people's cooperation with the occupation forces—and their tenacity. "The more I see and hear of this country," he wrote Moore, "the more I am impressed with the fact that Japan fought to the last ditch." His only criticism seemed to be that they were not making much effort to repair and rebuild their ruined cities, whose rubble he found revolting. The Japanese ships and buildings, he wrote, were replete with "rats, vermin and general muck and corruption." Yet the disagreeable conditions, combined with the continual rotten weather, had one advantage. "It looks as if the tourist experts will descend on us," he wrote Margaret. "I think they will be so thoroughly uncomfortable in Japan that their reports may keep down further influxes."

After Spruance had returned to the United States and had reflected upon the war and the Japanese nation, he wrote a letter in December 1946 to Tsuneo Sakano, then a retired Japanese admiral, with whom he had been friends in the late 1920's. Sakano had opposed war with America, and the Japanese navy had forced him to retire in disgrace once war began. Spruance's letter eloquently expressed his ultimate attitude about war and about his former enemies.

"Japan put up a fine fight during this war," Spruance began. Then after discussing the future of Japan, he wrote, "The brutal treatment accorded our prisoners of war by the Japanese military caused many of our people to hate the Japanese. From my observations in Japan last year I never had the feeling that the mass of the Japanese people were in any way cruel or brutal. Their treatment of animals and children was quite the contrary. My only explanation was that cruelty and brutality were deliberately fostered in the Army, and to some extent in the Navy, as a matter of high policy with the idea of producing tougher fighting men.

"There are always enough brutes in any population and enough of the brute in each individual to make this easy. The difficult thing in war is for the high command to restrain the brutal instincts which fighting tends to rouse in many individuals, while at the same time conducting relentlessly the operations which the war requires. For my own part I never found that I had to develop in myself a hatred of the Japanese as a race, in order to make what I hoped would be a good war against them.

"If militarism in Japan and a desire for conquest abroad do not come to life again, I see no reason why the Japanese and American peoples should not once more be on friendly and helpful terms with each other, each with a tolerant recognition of the essential differences and an appreciation of the fine qualities of the other."

Three admirals—Spruance, Halsey, and Frank Jack Fletcher—were initially responsible for repatriating POW's in their assigned sectors of Japan. Within two weeks of the surrender ceremony, however, Spruance prepared to relieve the other two and to assume duties as Commander Naval Forces, Japan. His primary mission would be to land and support MacArthur's occupation army, and, equally important, to sweep the thousands of American and Japanese mines in the waters surrounding Japan.

New Jersey entered Yokosuka in Tokyo Bay on 17 September, and Spruance began conferences with Halsey. The next evening the two comrades and their staffs were entertained by Vice Admiral Rawlings, commander of the redoubtable British Task Force 57 during the Okinawa campaign. The officers gathered aboard Rawlings's flagship, HMS *King George V,* which, as with all Royal Navy ships, was well stocked with liquor. "It was quite a celebration," wrote Spruance to Margaret, "and, as Bill was having a thoroughly good time and feeling no pain whatever, it was 1:30 a.m. before we got back to our ships."

On Halsey's final night in Japan, the officers of the Third Fleet gave a farewell party in the officers' club at the Yokosuka Navy Yard. "I left early," wrote Spruance, "but I judge that the party lasted well into the night, with Bill the life of the party and again feeling no pain."

The next day Halsey left for the United States to begin a five-week publicity and speaking tour, during which he would receive a hero's welcome and the adulation of America. Nimitz also returned to the United States for a similar reception.

Spruance was not disappointed that he would miss the parades and public acclaim. "I am very glad to be out here at this time," he wrote

Margaret. "What is going on is extremely interesting. Also, we are escaping the Navy Day Reviews and most of the headaches of demobilization. Can't you imagine my having to go through what is just ahead of Nimitz? I certainly would suffer."

The problems of landing MacArthur's occupation army were complex, owing principally to the pressures to return ships and men to the United States at the earliest moment. Most Navy men were civilians in uniform, tired of war and eager to return to their families. Demobilization proceeded helter-skelter with gathering momentum. Spruance sympathetically expedited the veterans' return to the States, even though this policy evoked protests by commanding officers whose ships were being stripped of experienced personnel.

Despite efforts to maintain order and discipline ashore, the American sailors and Marines in Yokosuka were raising hell while on liberty. Rape, venereal disease, drunkenness, and minor crimes were increasing, and Dr. Willcutts, the fleet medical officer, proposed a solution to Spruance.

Willcutts recommended that Spruance authorize a house of prostitution under naval control, supervised by naval medical personnel to ensure both sanitation and prostitutes free of VD. Spruance agreed, and Willcutts made the necessary arrangements with the appropriate Japanese officials. When the preparations were complete, Spruance personally inspected the premises, which after the war he quaintly described as "the places of business of the ladies of negotiable virtue." The house passed inspection, and business began. "Everything was working according to plan," recalled Spruance's flag lieutenant. "The rate of venereal infection was low, reports of drunkenness and rape at a minimum, the shore patrol having no difficulty, and the men were happy."

A Navy chaplain, however, wrote his congressman that the Navy was sanctioning and abetting prostitution in Yokosuka. In short order the Navy Department ordered Spruance to cease operations forthwith.

Spruance's reaction was that "it was none of Washington's business," but he dutifully obeyed his orders. "Supervision was withdrawn," said the flag lieutenant, "the house closed, crime and VD rates climbed, and that was the end of that."

"The following is confidential and you are not to pass it on to anyone else." So began a letter to Margaret on 30 September 1945 that prefaced Spruance's speculation on his future duty. Flag officer assignments were in flux. Some, like King and Halsey, were retiring. The aviator admirals were pressing for influential positions in the postwar Navy, and the greatest debate was who would replace King as CNO. Nimitz wanted the job, but Secretary Forrestal was balking.

Spruance wanted to remain at sea as long as possible and hoped to replace Nimitz as CINCPAC. When and if he went ashore, Spruance wanted only to be President of the Naval War College, and under no circumstances would he go to Washington. Nimitz promised to do everything in his power to get Spruance to the War College when the time came.

"Needless to say, I should be very happy to be CINCPAC," he wrote Margaret. "This will be my last cruise and I like sea duty. Don't ask me where I would have my headquarters, or what I would be able to do about you, for I don't know as yet. I am in favor of our high command getting back on board ship during peace, so as not to lose touch with the fleet.[4] You know well enough that wherever I may be, I want to have my family near me. I know you must be disappointed over this, but you know my feeling that a line officer must be willing and anxious to go to sea and to remain at sea. So just be patient for a while longer and wait to see what happens."

Weeks passed, and the future of both Nimitz and Spruance remained in limbo while the infighting continued at the Navy Department. In early November Towers relieved Spruance as Commander Fifth Fleet, and Spruance returned to Pearl Harbor to sweat out the future with Nimitz. In answer to Margaret's requests for definite plans, he responded, "As I told you, I will never ask to go ashore from sea duty, and, as long as I remain on the active list, I shall do everything I can to benefit the Navy." But he had no word on his future.

Margaret also was worried about the status of both his health and his wardrobe. "If and when I come home," he replied, "I shall wear a good looking blue uniform, so you need not worry about that. I shall, however, continue to take such exercise as my system requires. My exercise since last April has been approved and participated in by Dr. Willcutts, who is one of the best medical officers I have ever run into. It is just possible that he knows more about the subject than you do. So please let's stop arguing about that subject."

4. Spruance earlier had denied a request from his staff to move ashore at Yokosuka into Halsey's recently vacated quarters, apparently to isolate his staff from the temptations of wine, women, and song during working hours.

Change of command on USS *New Jersey*. Admiral John H. Towers relieves
Spruance as Commander Fifth Fleet, Tokyo Bay, 8 November 1945.

Then soothingly he added, "Personally, I shall be very happy if my
orders to the War College come through soon, and I think there is a
50–50 chance that they will. You and I have been mostly separated too
long, and you have been living around from pillar to post for eight
years, less about four months. You deserve to get our household effects
collected and about you once more."

Two weeks later the orders finally arrived, and Spruance relieved
Nimitz as Commander in Chief Pacific Fleet and Pacific Ocean Areas.
He held that position for only ten weeks. On 1 February 1946, Towers

again relieved him, for Spruance had received orders as President of the Naval War College.

And so Spruance returned home from the war. He had served in the Pacific theater for nearly four and a half years. There were no cheering crowds to welcome him home, only his wife and daughter, who were the only people he wanted to see. Spruance and Margaret left Monrovia in his old car with worn-out tires, and they began their long cross-country trip to Newport, Rhode Island.

III

After the War

Chapter 24

PRESIDENT, NAVAL WAR COLLEGE

RAYMOND SPRUANCE became the twenty-sixth president of the Naval War College on 1 March 1946.[1] The war had been over for a half-year, and the Navy was in turmoil owing to a stampeding demobilization. Hundreds of ships were being scrapped or placed in mothballs, shore installations were being reduced in size or totally shut down, and hundreds of thousands of officers and men were returning to civilian life. The demobilization had acquired a disorderly momentum, and no one could confidently predict the future composition and missions of the United States Navy.

The Naval War College reflected the Navy's predicament. During the war it had lost its normal student body of senior professional naval officers, who were occupied in fighting Germany and Japan. In the interim the college had taught short courses in naval planning to officers (more than half were reservists) who later would serve on naval staffs. The War College staff had been small, mostly senior officers who, for various reasons, could not serve in combat.

Thus at war's end the War College was little more than a specialized

---

1. For a general history of the Naval War College with specific details of Spruance's tenure as president, see John B. Hattendorf, *Sailors and Scholars: The Centennial History of the U.S. Naval War College* (Newport, 1984), especially chapter 8.

training facility. It no longer was educating senior naval officers in the art of naval warfare, its traditional mission in the years before World War II. Now, with the war ended, both the college and the Navy had to plan for the future, however nebulous.

Chester Nimitz always had championed the Naval War College, which he credited with developing the strategy and tactics that the Navy used to defeat Japan. He had kept the War College in operation during the war,[2] and he wanted to restore its prestige once war was over. Nimitz was CNO when Spruance became the college president. He gave Spruance two directives: revitalize the War College and "get as near a new deal as possible." With these broad guidelines, Spruance set about to make the college responsive to the needs of the postwar Navy.

His problems would be enormous, his tasks exacting. For example, money was scarce. Spruance, scrupulously honest, insisted upon a stringent budget. He overrode the protests of his staff, who predicted that the budget request would be reduced in Washington. They argued for a "buffer" that would compensate for the inevitable cut, but Spruance was resolute. He would not request one penny more than he thought was the necessary minimum. The budget went to Washington and was reviewed by a Navy captain and two civilian assistants in the Bureau of Naval Personnel. As predicted, they arbitrarily cut the college operating funds even further.

The greatest problem, however, was the proper curriculum. Naval officers rarely agree on what that curriculum should be; the subject always has been controversial. In 1946 the ideal postwar War College education was particularly difficult to define, owing to the uncertainties about the role of the postwar Navy.

Thus the presidency would demand hard work and energy, things that Spruance had not devoted to the War College in the prewar years, when he had regarded shore duty as a time to relax and to recuperate from the rigors of sea duty. Now both he and Margaret were ready to slow down and rest after a long war and long separations. For the first time in their lives they would live in government quarters. The spacious President's House would be staffed by enlisted servants, and the Spruances would enjoy the prestige accorded to a distinguished senior

---

2. As Chief of the Bureau of Navigation just before the war, he discovered that the Bureau intended to close the college in the event of war. Nimitz changed the plans forthwith.

admiral. These amenities had not been overlooked when Spruance had told Nimitz that he wanted the job.

Would Spruance, then, be willing to exert the effort that was necessary to invigorate the War College? He had been neither reformer nor innovator while a College staff officer during the thirties. After the war he returned to Newport as an illustrious naval hero. Had he chosen, he could have lived in dignified leisure at Newport until he reached the mandatory retirement age of sixty-two in the summer of 1948. As it turned out, Spruance was able both to revitalize the War College and to relax while doing it, owing to his ability to get other people to do the work for him.

Spruance decreed that the primary mission of the Naval War College was to broaden the intellect, to enhance the professional judgment, and to stimulate the sound reasoning of professional naval officers in order to prepare them for higher command. He regarded the human mind as an officer's most valuable asset. It could best be developed by strenuous mental exercise. Realizing that all naval minds were not alike, Spruance sought an appropriate War College education that would develop every student's mental power to its full potential, whatever that might be. He did not blame a person for being dull or slow-thinking for want of mental ability, but he scorned anyone who had a good brain and didn't use it.

Spruance classified the naval mind into three categories. "I have come to the conclusion," he once said, "that imagination and reasoning power are deficient in many individuals. When these qualities are lacking, no amount of study or training will cause them to appear and grow. An officer of this type may be a fine officer on the bridge of a ship, but he is unable to solve satisfactorily intricate problems whose solution is not obvious."

He regarded officers in this category as "tactical types." Next were those who had "the energy and industry to grasp the ideas that some more creative mind has produced," yet who were not themselves creative.

The third and highest level was the inventive intellect. "If imagination, tempered and guided by common sense and reason, is the scarce and valuable quality which I believe it to be," said Spruance, "it behooves us to recognize the individuals who possess this disciplined imagination, to encourage and make full use of them."

Deep thinkers, which he called the "strategical type," sometimes hesitated to make early decisions in a tight situation. Nevertheless, he maintained, both types—tactical and strategical—were needed by the Navy. But the ability to think was not enough. The commander also needed a "willingness to take responsibility and to fight," he asserted, a "sine qua non for command in time of war." He esteemed the fighter with the creative mind, regarding Kelly Turner as the finest example.

The War College could not instill fighting spirit. It could seek and develop the thinkers. That became Spruance's goal as Naval War College president in his last two years of active duty.

The Naval Service regarded its Naval War College with mixed emotions. Ever since its inception in 1884, many naval officers had questioned its usefulness. An Army War College education was a requisite for general rank in the Army, yet many naval officers became admirals without having attended the Naval War College. The naval criticism of the college is too complicated to relate herein, but it was a festering problem that Spruance had to address. He believed in the value of a War College education, and he undertook to evangelize those who did not.

Shortly after assuming the presidency, Spruance assembled the staff. He told them that the prestige of the college depended upon a difficult curriculum which would require the student "to concentrate and put forth effort near his maximum capabilities." The curriculum, then, was the essence of the War College education. Spruance was well qualified to guide its development. He had been closely associated with the prewar curriculum; during World War II he had put college theory into practice and had discovered its strengths and defects; now as president he could apply his wartime experience to the postwar curriculum. "I tried to make the courses practical," he later wrote, "and not, as Hanson Baldwin [New York *Times* military specialist] called them in the 30's, so pedantic."

The greatest failure of the prewar curriculum was that it had concentrated on surface warfare and had slighted the techniques and weapons that later were decisive in winning World War II. It had stubbornly clung to the concept that the United States would defeat Japan through a series of naval engagements culminating in a fleet action between battleships. In order to avoid the same kind of mistake, Spruance decreed that the postwar college would concentrate on *future naval warfare*. Students would study recent technological discoveries in atomic energy, guided missiles, and electronics. Based upon his war experiences, Spruance introduced studies that illuminated the influence of intelligence and meteorology on naval planning and operations. Carriers, submarines, logistics, and amphibious warfare all had important places in Spruance's new curriculum.

Spruance believed that the compleat naval officer needed a familiarity with world affairs, foreign policy problems, international relations, and national government. These formed the "liberal education" portion of the curriculum, included not necessarily to enhance the officers' professional expertise but rather to make them better-informed citizens. A number of distinguished visitors, experts in these fields, delivered lectures before the students in hopes of expanding their horizons beyond the technical aspects of war at sea. In later years, these kinds of subject became known as "national security affairs" and took precedence over the study of naval warfare, a change of emphasis which Spruance had not intended.

Spruance knew that battleship-oriented officers had dominated the prewar college, that naval aviators had shunned the college, and that this separateness had generated a hostility between the two branches that had hurt the Navy during the war. Furthermore, he recognized that the frequent lack of understanding and cooperation between the Army, Navy, Air Force, and Marine Corps often had hampered the American war effort. Now an acrimonious debate had begun in Washington on the unification and the future role of the armed forces. Spruance hoped that a Naval War College education for officers of all services (including the State Department) would promote the kind of harmony and team spirit that he viewed as essential to winning future wars. ("It is a great help to us," he had written Margaret during the war, "to deal with Army officers who have been around our War College.")

He emphasized this philosophy while speaking before an interservice audience at the National War College in 1947. "I am a great believer in personal contact between people so they can get confidence in each other and get to know the other man's problems," he said. "I think with joint staffs we can lick any of these things. In other words, we have to pull together and have the best brains we can get to work on the problems, and I think we will get the solutions. I don't believe there are any of these things that can't be licked one way or the other."

But there was no interservice harmony in Washington. The Navy and the Air Force were fiercely debating the merits of carrier aviation versus long-range Air Force bombers carrying atomic bombs. Feeling ran high, and the Air Force students at the Naval War College felt they were in hostile territory. Spruance called them into his office upon their arrival. "Don't be afraid to speak up," he urged, "or else you won't have any fun."

Spruance had expressed the fundamental tradition of the Naval War College education: *academic freedom*. Students had always been encouraged to express their uninhibited views. There was never a "right answer" or a "school solution" to any problem. Examinations, grades, and class standings never were used, and students were expected to think for themselves. Hot and spirited debates were the rule, regardless of rank and seniority.

"The Naval War College advocates no dogma, nor doctrine, nor any fixed set of rules by which campaigns can be conducted or battles won," Spruance declared. "There are no such rules. But it can and does endeavor to show that there are certain fundamentals, the understanding of which assists a commander in the orderly thinking and planning necessary to solve a military problem."

Spruance once explained the benefits of this tradition in a 1948 commencement address at a civilian university. "During the war I was always impressed with the necessity of keeping an open mind and of being receptive to the ideas of others," he said. "We study military history for the lessons it has to teach us, but we must not expect necessarily to obtain from history the correct answers to future problems. Situations rarely repeat themselves, and preconceived solutions, which result in fitting the situation to the solution and not the solution to the situation, are apt to be dangerous or costly. No one of us can be highly competent in all fields. It behooves us to recognize this fact and to take advantage of the superior knowledge and capabilities of others in their respective fields. Don't insist upon making a lot of the decisions yourself which your subordinates can make better than you can.

"The larger the organization over which you are placed," he continued, "the less proportionately becomes the share which your own output as an individual can contribute to it, and the more important becomes your power to guide and to direct, to encourage and to use the ideas of your subordinates. There are some persons who seem to feel that to recognize and use the ideas of others is an admission of their own inferiority. Persons of this mentality do not fit well very far up in an organization.

"In using the ideas of others, a generous recognition of their origin is always in order," he concluded. "The Navy has a saying that, to have loyalty up, there must be loyalty down. A selfish, self-centered individual, who uses his subordinates for his own personal advancement and fails to appreciate their contributions and to look out for their interests, is not apt to have a very high degree of loyalty among his subordinates. We can either drive men through fear of punishment—as we see being done in large portions of the world today—or else we can lead them by obtaining their friendship and loyalty and encouraging them to exercise their individual initiative. Punishment of recalcitrant individuals is required occasionally, but with intelligent Americans the other way is much the best."

Spruance charged his staff in March 1946 to develop a new curriculum in time for the first postwar class that would arrive in July. Of immediate concern were the naval planning problems and the war games, which Spruance held to be the most important part of the entire curriculum.

One of his first acts as president was to replace Kalbfus's *Sound Military Decision,* the controversial naval planning manual that had precipitated the showdown between Spruance and Wilcox in the late thirties at the War College. In its place—and with Nimitz's blessing—Spruance set about to create a permanent manual that would be affirmed by the CNO, used throughout the naval service, and would not be changed at the whim of each new college president. Under Spruance's direction, the staff produced the genesis for the planning guide used by the Navy today.

The war games needed an opponent for the United States, and for decades Japan had played that role. But with Japan defeated, Spruance needed a new potential enemy. He chose Russia because that country "seemed the logical, and about the only, candidate." At the time Spruance regarded the Soviet Union as no more than a theoretical enemy, because he could not conceive any potential conflicts between the two great powers. When Spruance was CINCPAC in Pearl Harbor in December 1945, he was visited by the Soviet Consul General from San Francisco. The Russian had asked what Spruance thought about the future relations of their two countries. Spruance replied that they should be good; both were "have" countries, well separated and with a history of friendly relations in the past.

He amplified this line of reasoning to his daughter while he was college president. World War II had been the first truly global conflict in which all the great powers had suffered. No one in his right mind would want another war, he maintained. Furthermore, the only two reasons for war were religion and economics. The days of religious wars were over, and there was no foreseeable economic conflict between the Soviet Union and the United States. Therefore, Spruance concluded, the threat of global war was over.

The deteriorating relations between the two countries after the war convinced Spruance that his reasoning was faulty. He began to read every book he could find on communism and quickly changed his thinking. He came to regard communism as a new kind of religion; a future "war of religion" with Russia was a real possibility. He became a militant anticommunist, but he was not anti-Russian.

Should an American-Soviet war ever erupt, Spruance did not believe that it could be won by long-range bombers dropping atomic bombs on Russian cities. He wanted to defeat Russia by convincing the Russian people that the United States was friendly and by inducing them to overthrow their communist government. "In this connection," he wryly noted, "I doubt if unrestricted bombing of non-military objectives in Russia would be a good way to cultivate civilian friendship."

How would he fight Russia? Not by an invasion of the homeland, which history showed had always been a "tremendous undertaking" and which usually served to unite the Russian people. He visualized fighting Russia on her perimeter, giving the Western Powers shorter lines of communication to the battlefront. The Navy would support that kind of war by providing sea lines of communication to European bases. "Victories should be exploited," he wrote, "by our propaganda to impress the people of the U.S.S.R. that they are being defeated and to make them lose confidence in their government. No 'unconditional surrender' business."

Spruance enlisted an old friend, Commodore Penn L. Carroll, to develop the strategic problems and war games. Carroll at first glance would have seemed an unwise choice. A heart-attack victim (perhaps from overwork), he was a sixty-year-old battleship officer with years of War College staff experience. He could not be identified as an officer of the "new Navy," but Spruance did not select Carroll because they were cronies. Rather, Spruance respected Carroll's intellect, his willingness to work, and his knowledge of strategy.

Carroll met Spruance's expectations. He envisioned that the most likely wars against Russia would be in the North Atlantic and the Mediterranean, and his scenarios contained the tactics and weapons of the future: atomic warheads, air warfare, submarine-launched strategic missiles, mine warfare, and extensive use of radar and electronic countermeasures. Although Russia did not possess long-range bombers, atomic weapons, or a large modern navy at the time, Spruance and Carroll assumed that capability was inevitable. In the meantime, the Russia of the war games used American bombers, ships, and weapons so the students could plan for the future.

The students prepared for Carroll's naval warfare problems through lectures and readings in strategy, atomic energy, tactics, and weapons. During his second year Spruance began a separate course in logistics under Captain Henry E. Eccles in recognition of the importance of logistics during the war. Vice Admiral Robert B. Carney, Halsey's former chief of staff and a future CNO, provided moral and financial support from Washington. Everything emphasized the future. The Naval War College was being revitalized.

And it grew in size. The staff and student body doubled its prewar numbers, and the college acquired a former enlisted men's barrack to provide a building for more room. Spruance improved the quality of the student body by insisting that a formal board select only the best qualified officers as prospective students. In the past, students had been randomly chosen and many had been mediocre. He also wanted top officers for his staff, including plenty of naval aviators. Unfortunately, a 1946 Navy "plucking board" forced many of his senior staff officers to retire, and competent replacements were hard to find.

Spruance worried that a flag officer without a War College education would be handicapped. In 1948 he noted that only one of the recent 53 flag selectees had attended the senior course of the college. He urged the Chief of Naval Operations to send all the selectees to the War College to remedy the gap in their education. His suggestion was not accepted.

Spruance constantly publicized the college through articles in magazines and journals, and, despite his aversion to publicity, he consented to interviews if they would advance the cause of the War College. He disliked and avoided speeches but felt obligated to accept a limited number of invitations. He was a poor public speaker because his quiet voice did not project, and his texts lacked humor and informality. He wrote his own speeches because his staff could not satisfy his requirements, and he practiced with Margaret as his audience. Margaret tried to improve his delivery, as Carl Moore had tried in earlier times. (Following a well-received speech before a British military audience in 1946, Spruance wrote Moore, "I took your advice and tried to put a little more life in my talk than in what I had written.")

His speeches usually refought the war in the Pacific, regardless of the audience or the occasion. The military audiences might have been interested, but the civilians probably were bored and baffled. One speech, however, concerned the Revolutionary War, with unexpected results.

The Secretary of the Navy had ordered Spruance to give a 1946 Independence Day speech at Newburgh, New York, commemorating the town that had once been Washington's headquarters. The peremptory orders ruined previous holiday plans, and Margaret was sorely disappointed. Spruance, however, dutifully composed a long speech that recited Newburgh's historical significance in the Revolutionary War, and he practiced long and hard with Margaret.

On the fourth of July Spruance and Margaret drove into the quiet little town and to its park festooned with flags and bunting. Spruance mounted the bandstand and delivered his speech. He had an audience of two people: his wife and one old gentleman.

Spruance, undeterred, said what he had come to say. "I was sitting there seething," Margaret later recalled, "and nobody was interested. They didn't know who Spruance was; the name meant nothing to them. There he stood!"

His only comment afterwards to Margaret was, "I was certainly roped in." He later wrote Moore that the "celebration was a very minor one."

Spruance's interviews were not always successful, either. Fletcher Pratt wrote a 1946 *Harper's* article about Spruance that was inaccurate and distorted. "I thought he wanted background and information for his historical articles on the war," wrote Spruance to Moore. "He does not take any notes and trusts to memory for his impressions, which results in what, to us, are numerous inaccuracies.

"I don't believe there is anything to be gained by trying to correct such inaccuracies in a magazine article. The reading public does not get much more out of such articles than a general impression, which, itself, usually is soon forgotten."

Another series of articles that Spruance would not respond to were written by Holland Smith and published in the *Saturday Evening Post* in 1948. Smith's articles reflected his tempestuous personality. He denounced those with whom he had clashed during the war, opening old wounds and renewing old controversies. Although he wrote admiringly of Spruance, Smith asserted that the seizure of both Tarawa and Iwo Jima had been unnecessary, implying that Marines had died in vain and that Spruance had been wrong in advocating the capture of the two objectives.

Spruance would not publicly dispute Smith's accusations because he wished to avoid any open strife, but he privately expressed his feelings to a fellow naval officer. "Holland Smith was a first class fighting man," wrote Spruance, "and he did a brilliant job for all of us. However, I think I know more about the basic strategy of the Central Pacific than he does, just as he knows a lot more than I do about amphibious landings and subsequent operations on shore. His memory may not always be too accurate, however."

Other articles attacked Spruance directly. Admiral Frederick C. Sherman, who had been a carrier task group commander during the war, wrote several newspaper articles charging that Spruance had made bad decisions both at the Battle of Midway and at the Battle of the Philippine Sea. Spruance remained silent.

But from time to time Spruance reacted to articles or editorial policies which he believed damaged the Navy's reputation through unfairness or inaccuracy. For example, a large Rhode Island newspaper published a series of anti-Navy articles which prompted Spruance to invite its officials to the War College. He tactfully protested the paper's apparent bias and lack of objectivity. The paper's representatives responded to his quiet persuasion by promising to give a more balanced viewpoint in the future. Later they ran a full-page spread that complimented Spruance and the activities of the War College.

Only once did Spruance allow himself to be drawn into a public quarrel. A reporter named Gill Robb Wilson wrote a column for the New York *Herald Tribune* called "The Air World," and in early 1948 he denounced the Navy's stand in the aircraft carrier versus B-36 bomber dispute. Spruance responded with a long letter to the editor that defended naval aviation and contradicted most of Wilson's assertions.

In his letter's last paragraph, Spruance digressed from facts and analyses to a personal slap at Wilson, probably the only time that

Spruance ever publicly criticized anyone by name. "I suggest that if Mr. Wilson wishes to write on naval aviation or sea power," wrote Spruance, "he first consult with some student of sea power who can enlighten him on these subjects. Some of the prophets of air power have been wide of the mark in the past when they turned their attention to naval matters, and they appear to be equally far off today."

Wilson retaliated by writing that he needed "no instruction on his viewpoint from Admiral Spruance or anybody who may write the admiral's letters for him." He concluded, "A word of reciprocal advice to Admiral Spruance might concern a check-up on who writes his letters to the editors. They left a fine man and a great officer as wide open as the sea he sails."

Wilson insinuated in his rebuttal that Spruance was either incapable of writing his own letters, or that Spruance would injudiciously sign a controversial letter prepared by a subordinate. The style of the letter, however, is definitely Spruance. And even if it had been written by a subordinate, it still would have had to be approved by Spruance. The letter, therefore, expressed Spruance's beliefs, not those of a subordinate.

Spruance's uncharacteristic verbal battle with a combative columnist was an offshoot of the desperate struggle in Washington over the future missions of the armed services. Each was competing for the dwindling dollars in the contracted defense budget. In Spruance's eyes, the Air Force was arguing that the B-36 bomber could win future wars by dropping atomic bombs on enemy cities. It seemed to him that the Air Force wanted the lion's share of the defense budget, with little remaining for the Army and the Navy.

Spruance opposed the Air Force arguments at every opportunity and spurned their theories. "No great war has ever been won in the past merely by blows struck from a great distance," he said before the National War College in 1947. "I doubt if one will be won by this means in the future. If not, then we must get close enough to any distant enemy to come to grips with him and to hit him with decisive blows."

Spruance advocated sea power and amphibious operations "in order," he said, "to advance our national strength as rapidly as possible toward objectives which are vital to the prosecution of the war. If we use our sea power to push the war toward the enemy, we shall be both protecting our home territory and getting in a better position to inflict damage on the enemy."

Yet Spruance did not suggest that sea power alone could defeat a potential enemy, and as always he advocated teamwork among all the services. "In making war," he said to the same National War College audience, "we have to use all the arms and weapons and everything we have that the problem needs. That means teamwork by the ground troops, the air forces, the surface ships, and everybody. When you come to do an operation you take everything you can lay your hands on, and you find very little that can't be used to do the job that you have to do."

But future war raised questions that Spruance could not answer, such as the influence of nuclear weapons. He conceded that an atomic bomb would demolish a large naval concentration, especially during an amphibious assault. While he advocated amphibious warfare in the future, he did not know what new tactics would be necessary to reduce the vulnerability to nuclear attack. That dilemma would have to be solved by his successors, perhaps by his college students, to whom he gave the task of writing a thesis, "The Influence of the Atomic Bomb on Future Naval Warfare."

He also foresaw revolutionary changes in naval warfare because of technological developments in nuclear ship propulsion, submarines, and guided missiles, but he could not predict the end results. He was nearing retirement. Others would have to solve the problems of the future.

But of one thing he was certain. The Navy would endure. "I can see plenty of changes in weapons, methods, and procedures in naval warfare brought about by technical developments," he said just before his retirement, "but I can see no change in the future role of our Navy from what it has been for ages past for the Navy of a dominant sea power—to gain and exercise the control of the sea that its country requires to win the war, and to prevent its opponent from using the sea for its purposes. This will continue so long as geography makes the United States an insular power and so long as the surface of the sea remains the great highway connecting the nations of the world."

The office of college president permitted many pleasant social activities that gave respite from official duties. Spruance enjoyed entertaining the distinguished lecturers: public officials, journalists, educators, jurists, and the military. He had lengthy conversations with such luminaries as President Truman, George Kennan, and Walter Lippmann. Staff and students attended luncheons with the guests, and young Margaret recalled that they made life "very exciting." Many became permanent friends.

One frequent visitor, however, caused problems. He was a high government official whose wife was an alcoholic. The Spruances dreaded his visits because of his wife's prolonged, embarrassing drunkenness. The official further irritated Spruance by trying to steal his Marine chauffeur for his own use in Washington. (The official was unsuccessful.)

The college president was automatically invited to the dinners, parties, and teas of the wealthy socialites who lived in the stupendous mansions on Bellevue Avenue. Most of these events were sumptuous but boring, and the Spruances and the Newporters had little in common. A matriarch of one of America's richest families was particularly wearisome. One day she called at the President's House for a visit, and Margaret fled out the back door to avoid seeing her.

The War College itself bustled with social activity. "It was the end of the war," said young Margaret, "and there were many unmarried officers and unmarried girls. It was a very happy, exciting social life as a consequence, with picnics, sailing, dancing, and many other activities." Acting as an intermediary, young Margaret persuaded her father to eliminate Saturday classes to allow the students longer weekends.

Many became married, including young Margaret. Her wedding to Commander Gerard S. Bogart, a naval aviator who was a college student, took place in the President's House. Not knowing that Bogart was his prospective son-in-law, Spruance earlier had counseled him to seek duty in Warsaw as a naval attaché in order to learn more about communism. He regretted that advice when he learned that his daughter's first home with her new husband would be in that war-ravaged, desolate city.

Retirement was approaching. In the fall of 1947 Spruance journeyed to California for a Navy Day speech, with an understanding with Margaret that he would "look around and see if there was anything worth buying." When he returned several days later, Margaret asked if he had found any place that had appealed to him. Spruance answered evasively, arousing Margaret's suspicions. "He began looking kind of funny," she recalled.

Suddenly it dawned on Margaret what her husband had done.

"You've bought a house!"

"Yes," he replied.

"That's too bad," said Margaret, "because I've bought one in Newport." (Margaret later said that her reply was unpremeditated and impulsive.)

Spruance was stunned. Margaret thought he might faint. "I'm only joking," she quickly reassured him.

Margaret recalled her feelings about her husband's audacity. "I was dazzled and overcome by what he had done," she said. "Our friends were shocked that Raymond had bought the house without my seeing it and asked me what I was going to do."

There was nothing she could do, except to hope her husband had made a good choice. It was the first house they had ever owned in their thirty-three years of marriage. She would not see it until they moved to California.

Margaret loved it.

Spruance would retire on the first of July 1948. The last few months had been busy. He had received many honorary degrees from universities and colleges and had spoken at a number of graduation exercises at both civilian and military schools. Rhode Island philanthropist John Nicholas Brown invited the Spruances for a cruise aboard the three-masted barque *Sea Cloud*. It was the same kind of ship that had taken Spruance on his first cruise at sea as a midshipman forty-five years before. The final cruise of his career would be under sail as well. The voyage from Annapolis to Newport was among the happiest times that Spruance and Margaret spent together.

Brown was then Assistant Secretary of the Navy for Air. Several weeks before, the Secretary of the Navy had appointed him to speak at the War College graduation ceremonies. He had been surprised to discover that the Navy Department had no plans for a public tribute to Spruance upon his retirement. Spruance was being officially ignored. Brown considered it to be shabby treatment by the Navy toward one of its greatest officers, so he included special praise for Spruance in his graduation address in an effort to compensate for the Department's silence. The cruise on the *Sea Cloud* followed.

Raymond A. Spruance in retirement

On the day of his retirement, 1 July 1948, Spruance hoped to slip away quietly. Dressed in civilian clothes, he joined Margaret in their car and drove down the hill from the President's House toward the main gate on Coaster's Harbor Island. There had been a few quiet farewell parties in the days before, but no one from Washington had come to Newport. There had been no retirement ceremony. But then, perhaps Spruance wanted it that way.

As the Spruances approached the gate they came upon the War College staff, a Marine Guard, and a naval band, all standing in ranks on either side of the road. The band played ruffles and flourishes and the "Admiral's March," the Marine Guard presented arms, and the staff saluted. Spruance got out of his car and moved among those who had come to honor him.

His face was rigid as he tried to suppress the emotions surging inside him. As he drove away his staff waved and cheered. Margaret told him he ought to smile at them, but he could not.

"I think they all understood," said Margaret afterward.

Chapter 25

AMBASSADOR TO THE PHILIPPINES

NAVAL officers view retirement with mixed emotions. The more active seek a second career, and admirals and generals frequently become highly paid corporate executives or directors. Others write memoirs. Some travel. More than a few are unable to make a happy transition from an active naval career to a less active civilian life.

Spruance was none of these. He had received job offers but none interested him. He and Margaret had lived a nomadic life. Now they were ready to settle in their new home in order to enjoy their remaining years in comfort and leisure.

Their years of retirement were idyllic. Their Spanish-style home was located in Pebble Beach on the Monterey Peninsula in California. The area's greatest virtue to Spruance was its consistently cool and moderate weather, but it had many other attractions: dramatic ocean beaches and cliffs, tall trees, abundant wildlife, and handsome homes in pastoral settings. Spruance was enraptured. "How privileged we are to live here," he would exclaim to Margaret.

At first they were strangers, and initially they preferred solitude in order to adjust to their new life. Their house occupied a three-quarter-acre lot, and the grounds were overgrown and disorderly. Spruance worked energetically to improve the landscaping. He soon became an avid gardener, although he never before had been interested in horticulture. With the aid of a hired man, Spruance planted shrubbery and flowers, installed a brick terrace and a sprinkling system, built a greenhouse, and began a compost pile that was his particular pride.

Margaret, meanwhile, learned how to cook and keep house, for she was without domestic help for the first time in her life. The Spruances easily could have afforded a full-time maid, but Margaret preferred to go it alone. Stores were minutes away when she needed to shop, and San Francisco was but a few hours' journey by train.

Margaret was an ardent golfer and made frequent use of the nearby country club. Golf bored Spruance, but while he was president of the Naval War College he had accompanied Margaret to please her and keep her company. His shots usually went awry. Mostly he searched for his ball, found many others, and debated with nearby golfers as to who owned which ball. One day he came to Margaret, beaming because he had found his ball. She was exasperated. "If you don't start taking the game seriously," she said, "I prefer playing alone."

"I've been waiting for you to say that," he replied. "Now I'm through playing this game."

He did not change his mind upon retirement and explained why in a 1948 letter to Moore. "I still have sufficient projects mapped out ahead," he wrote, "to keep me busy for a long time without bothering about the whereabouts of the little white ball. If I ever get caught up with all the jobs I want to do and with the other things (such as letter writing) that I don't like but ought to do, and if then I get bored with life, perhaps I shall buy a set of golf clubs and make another start at the game."

Spruance was a model citizen. He involved himself in community affairs and was a volunteer executive in many local charitable activities. One of his proudest accomplishments was the Institute of Foreign Languages in Monterey, which he helped establish with Dr. Remsen Bird, a retired president of Occidental College.

He occasionally traveled about the country in response to requests for his assistance. In October 1949 he was one of many retired flag officers who testified before the House Armed Services Committee during the climax of the "Revolt of the Admirals." The internecine dispute had been exacerbated by the cancellation of the construction of the carrier *United States* in favor of the continuing procurement of the B-36 bomber. The Navy unlimbered its heaviest guns to protect its diminished role in the nation's defense. Spruance's testimony reflected his earlier views on a future war with Russia and generally supported the opinions expressed by other senior naval officers.

But trips beyond his beloved forest were infrequent, and Spruance preferred to remain at home. Navy friends frequently visited, liked what they saw, and many remained to buy homes nearby. Thus a retired naval community began to develop with the Spruances as the nucleus. Their happiness grew and grew.

Their life changed dramatically in early January 1952.

The Secretary of the Navy phoned from Los Angeles and asked Spruance to accompany him to Washington. He gave no explanation. Margaret bubbled with excitement and speculated happily on the reason for the summons. "This must be something very important," she exclaimed.

"Why do you think that?" he responded.

"Maybe you are going to be recalled to Washington," said Margaret. She later remembered that she was "raring to go." Life in retirement had become too quiet, and she was restless for a change.

Spruance packed his bags, the two drove south to the airport, and Spruance boarded the Secretary's plane and flew away. Margaret returned home next day in a heavy rain and saw the local paper lying on the flooded lawn. She debated whether it was worth retrieving, then staggered out beneath her umbrella into the downpour. The headlines were in bold, black letters.

ADMIRAL SPRUANCE HAS BEEN NOMINATED AS AMBAS-SADOR TO THE PHILIPPINES.

Margaret was stunned. She stared uncomprehendingly at the words, then returned to the house in an exhilarated daze. The phone began ringing with calls from excited well-wishers.

Next day she received a letter from her husband. "Dear Margaret," it began. "Keep this absolutely quiet. This is completely hush hush. I have been asked to go as Ambassador to the Philippines and of course we're going, because anything the President wants I shall do."

When he returned from Washington, Margaret asked him why he had been chosen for the job. He replied that the Philippines were in a dangerous situation, the communists were at the very door, and that the State Department felt it needed a military man to handle the situation. He suspected there were other reasons, as well, but he never knew what they were.

An analysis twenty years after the fact does suggest a number of logical possibilities. The Philippine political situation in early 1952 was critical. The government was corrupt, the general population were poor and exploited, and Hukbalahap (Huk) insurgents were threatening to seize the country by violent revolution.

The Huks had originated in early 1942 as a communist-led guerrilla organization pledged to fight the Japanese occupation army in the Philippines. At war's end the Huk leaders had refused to disband. The Philippines became an independent nation on 4 July 1946, and another war—the Huk Rebellion—began. It gained in scope and ferocity during the next six years. When Spruance became ambassador, it was still being fought between government troops and the insurgents. In the eyes of the Americans, the Huks were a communist organization that was trying to overthrow the Philippine government by force.

The threat of communism dominated American foreign policy in the Far East. China had been lost, a bitter war was being fought in Korea, and the United States was waging an ideological battle with international communism throughout Asia. Americans wanted Asians to choose democracy as their way of life. They hoped that the Philippines would display that democracy, rather than communism, worked best for Asians. Thus it was deemed imperative that the Philippines have a strong, thriving democratic government.

The Truman administration needed an ambassador with special talents. Senator Joseph McCarthy and his supporters had devastated the State Department with charges of communist influence, so the prospective ambassador had to be acknowledged as a strong anticommunist in order to ensure Senate confirmation. Another factor was that the State Department—especially in the early fifties—wanted ambassadors to solve their own problems and to make their own decisions without bucking their troubles back to Washington.

Spruance fitted these requirements. As War College president he had entertained many important people (including President Truman) who were impressed by his integrity, his wisdom, and by his knowledge of foreign affairs, government, and economics. John Carter Vincent, a foreign service officer and a close associate of Secretary of State Dean Acheson, was a frequent visitor. A specialist in Far East affairs, he recommended Spruance to Acheson. Others probably echoed similar praise. [1]

Acheson later wrote, "The President asked me for the recommendation of an ambassador whose presence might strengthen the Philippine government. I was and had been a great admirer of Admiral Spruance and, knowing the high regard in which he was held in the Philippines, I thought that his appointment would be ideal. The President agreed and it was made."

Spruance's nomination was acclaimed by the press. The Washington *Post* called him "one of the most distinguished Americans of his generation" and editorialized, "His presence at Manila will add strength to our diplomatic personnel in the Far East. Most of our diplomats out there are punch-drunk under the impact of the loyalty program, and factual reporting and true independence of judgment are fast disappearing. Neither of these virtues can ever be squeezed out of Admiral Spruance."

The first task of the new ambassador was to analyze the Philippine domestic situation. He talked with knowledgeable people. He read books and reports. He visited the countryside. What he found was the classic situation described by his favorite economic philosopher, Henry George. Wealthy, privileged landowners were exploiting the peasants, Spruance believed, and were causing most of the political and economic problems besetting the Philippines.

In June 1952, Spruance had been in the Philippines four months. He sent young Margaret a letter containing his first impressions of the country. "I am sure," he wrote, "that the basic difficulties of the Philippines stem from the Spanish and from them back to feudalism. When we came here in 1898, the land paid no taxes. The proper investment for wealthy Filipinos was then, and is now for most of them, land. There is little venture capital."

Spruance then explained that land taxes were ridiculously low and frequently unpaid. "Business, on the other hand, is burdened with numerous taxes, all of which have to be passed on and thus increase the cost of living," he continued. "Land prices are sky high. Land use, both in the country and in the towns and cities, is very poor. For example,

1. Vincent was later fired by Secretary Dulles, because Vincent's forthright views on China had infuriated Senator McCarthy and his supporters. Vincent has since been vindicated posthumously.

most rice land produces one instead of two crops of rice a year. This is due to a general lack of irrigation during the dry season. There are many large landed estates, with the owners living in Manila and doing little to improve things."

Spruance concluded his letter by deploring the fact that homesteaders could not get titles for their property, after speculators had encouraged them to clear land and plant crops. The speculators either would evict them or would force them to pay exorbitant rents for the small farms they had created through their own labors. The Huks capitalized on both the peasants' discontent and on urban labor unrest caused by low wages and unemployment. Until these grievances were eliminated, the Huks would be a constant threat to the nominally democratic government.

Spruance's sense of justice was outraged. He was the kind of man for whom Henry George had dedicated *Progress and Poverty:* "who, seeing the vice and misery that spring from the unequal distribution of wealth and privilege, feels the possibility of a higher social state and would strive for its attainment." Land reform was essential if the Philippines were to be saved, but achieving it was nearly impossible. Spruance tried.

"All we can do out here," he wrote young Margaret, "is to point out what we think is wrong and the remedies, and hope to get enough honest and patriotic Filipinos in the Government to correct conditions. We can bring pressure to bear on the Government to pass the laws we think are necessary, but we cannot get the laws enforced against the wealthy minority who are now in control . . . all this is discouraging, but still it is interesting."

Private diplomacy was Spruance's forte as an ambassador. He was unusually adept at achieving agreements and understanding with quiet conversations. Whether dealing with Americans or Filipinos, he spoke logically and frankly, and his reasoning and suggestions were usually persuasive.

There were exceptions. He found that talking to the President of the Philippines, Elpidio Quirino, was futile. Quirino's government was corrupt, and the president either could not or would not redress the evils that were debilitating his country. Spruance therefore tried to gain through other means what he could not achieve through private exchanges.

Throughout the summer and fall of 1952, he suspected that Washington officials were being deceived by the Quirino administration and were ignoring his own official reports. Spruance was a tough negotiator and felt that the United States too often compromised with the Philippine government. In his mind, American negotiators frequently dealt in wishful thinking rather than reality. The Philippines were receiving extensive American economic aid, and Spruance wanted to use American money as a lever for government reform. "If we can persuade the Filipinos to remedy the basic conditions which are wrong," he wrote young Margaret, "then I am in favor of our {financial} assistance. If not, what we are doing will be a shot in the arm but of little permanent value. If we want to get something, we have to have something to offer in trade. So far, Washington seems not to recognize this oriental—and perhaps universal—characteristic."

In late October 1952 a number of important Washington officials arrived in Manila for a well-publicized conference on mutual defense. "Many of them are important to us," Spruance wrote a friend, "as we are able to present the local situation to them and clear up certain misconceptions which prevail in Washington thinking and which we are unable to change by telegrams or writing. Once an idea becomes firmly imbedded in the minds of the lower bureaucracy, nothing seems to penetrate. It is only when we can talk personally out here with the higher-ups that we can make any impression. After they get back home, we hope there will be a change in some aspects of the Washington attitude. Manila is a very difficult place, at the best, in which to do business. When you have to fight Washington at the same time, it is almost a hopeless undertaking to expect to get anything accomplished."

Spruance warned his Washington visitors not to be tricked by Quirino's affable hospitality. He stressed that the Filipino president had made no attempt at land reform despite a written pledge to the United States that he would do so in return for economic aid. Spruance wanted Quirino's obstructionism on public record, so he deliberately stage-managed a confrontation at the final meeting. The room was packed with American representatives, Filipino officials, and the press. By skillful maneuvering Spruance had arranged for Quirino's political opponents to attend as well.

"The last thing in the afternoon," Spruance later related, "I carefully introduced two topics—free elections and land reform—which were not received by Quirino with any enthusiasm whatsoever. I have been told that Quirino was furious with me about this." Spruance had

Ramón Magsaysay and Ambassador Spruance

achieved his objective of exposing Quirino's intransigence to the glare of worldwide publicity. He hoped that the Washington visitors no longer had illusions about Quirino's intentions.

The stormy meeting provoked the final break between the Quirino administration and the embassy. Spruance believed there was no hope for the Philippines as long as Quirino remained as president. The two men became bitter enemies. One would have to go.

An undeclared war had begun. "If the shackles of the landed aristocracy are not loosened," wrote Spruance to young Margaret in late 1952, "there will be a revolution in the Philippines when we get off the lid— and it will not be a peaceful and bloodless one. Our best hope is for a free election in 1953 and a candidate who wants to effect the much needed reforms and who has a Congress that will cooperate with him in doing so."

Elpidio Quirino

That candidate was Ramón Magsaysay. He was a forty-five-year-old national hero—handsome, robust, fearless, intelligent, a rousing leader. Having fought the Japanese as a guerrilla during the war, he later became a politician. He was overwhelmingly supported by the common Filipino owing to his empathy with the masses. By 1952 he was Secretary of Defense and had managed temporarily to suppress the Huk rebellion through a program of military force tempered with humanitarian treatment.

His integrity and honesty made him a rarity among Filipino politicians. Deeply troubled by his country's economic plight, he was a zealous reformer who sought to save his country. He, almost alone among Filipino leaders, seemed equipped by temperament and experience to be the savior of the Philippines.

But many obstacles impeded his possible ascendency to the presidency. He belonged to Quirino's Liberal Party, and Quirino intended to seek reelection in November 1953. The opposition Nacionalista Party had many aspiring candidates of its own, should Magsaysay consider crossing party lines. Furthermore, popular politicians did not always win. Philippine elections were ruthless, unlawful, and bloody. They more often were stolen than won. "Political assassination is by no means uncommon in the Philippines," wrote Spruance, "so you can see to what extremes the rougher breeds of politicians will go in order to keep or gain power."

Magsaysay had many important American friends who urged him to run for president in 1953, for it was clearly in the best interests of the United States government to see Magsaysay elected. Magsaysay's closest advisor and confidant was an American Air Force officer, Colonel Edward G. Lansdale, an agent of the Central Intelligence Agency. Lansdale had fought beside Magsaysay in the mountains against the Huks and had smoothed his way to meet influential Americans in the United States. Despite American entreaties to seek the presidency, Magsaysay remained undecided.

Lansdale returned to the United States for leave in the winter of 1953, and in his absence Magsaysay visited Spruance. The two men frequently had met and had established a rapport. Magsaysay wanted advice. Several Nacionalista senators had asked him to sign an agreement, said Magsaysay, that he resign as Secretary of Defense and join their party. In return, they would exert their "best efforts" to secure his nomination for president. If nominated, however, he would have no control over selecting the other candidates or the members of his cabinet. Spruance had advised Magsaysay to seek the presidency, but he opposed his signing any document. The "agreement" would not guarantee the nomination, argued Spruance, and a president had to choose his own cabinet.

Unknown to Spruance, Magsaysay already had signed the agreement the previous November. Lansdale was horrified when he returned from leave and found out. He feared it might be used to blackmail Magsaysay, and he was correct. He retrieved the document from the backyard of one of the signers and took it to Spruance in a sealed envelope. Without revealing its contents, Lansdale emphasized the envelope's importance and asked Spruance to hold it for safekeeping. Spruance affixed several wax seals on the flap, said he did not trust the embassy safe, then stowed it in his bedroom safe.

Rumors about the signed agreement grew in intensity, and newspapers asked Spruance if he knew about it. He avoided a direct answer, but after many months it became too hot to handle. He returned it to Lansdale, who hid the envelope beneath the floor of a house. "It's still there today, as far as I know," said Lansdale recently.

Intense political maneuvering continued, and Magsaysay's intentions were a source of daily speculation. Finally he broke with Quirino and the Liberals. In early 1953, Ramón Magsaysay became the Nacionalista presidential candidate. The battle had begun.

Spruance had been ambassador for more than a year. He was as laconic with newsmen as ever. Shortly after he had arrived in Manila, a persistent journalist had asked, "Sir, how does it feel to have been one of the world's greatest admirals and now to be a senior ambassador?"

Spruance paused for at least ten seconds before speaking.

"Different," he finally replied.

The ambassador's residence was a stately old Spanish-style house with large, well-furnished rooms. "It had a beautiful, spacious drawing room," remembers Margaret, "and a handsome spiral stairway that made you feel like a queen coming down the steps." They inherited a retinue of smiling Filipino servants, including Chaquita, a personal maid for Margaret.

"What in the world am I going to do with a personal maid?" asked Margaret.

"It won't take you long to find out," Spruance answered.

When they later returned to Pebble Beach and their home without servants, Margaret would call out "Chaquita" and her husband would appear to zip the back of her dress.

State Department officers and employees are accustomed to serving noncareer ambassadors, so the embassy staff did not resent Spruance's naval background. They had recognized Spruance's stature and reputation even before he had arrived. They had greeted him warmly, and he quickly won their loyalty. He allowed the deputy chief of mission to act as a chief of staff and to supervise the daily affairs of the embassy. His deputy during most of his tenure—and during the crucial 1953 presidential campaign—was William S. B. Lacy, a fiery, emotional, and unconventional foreign service officer. Their personalities clashed, they argued often, and Spruance did not trust Lacy's impulsive judgment. Despite their differences, however, the two men established an effective working relationship.

The first months had been exciting for the Spruances, who were unaccustomed to the pomp and splendor of the diplomatic world in which they were the monarchy. Spruance wanted to be treated simply and unobtrusively. Both as admiral and ambassador, he disliked pretentious behavior and elaborate ceremony. He could not escape it in the Philippines. Lavish parties, receptions, and dinners followed one after the other, interspersed with official functions of every nature. Government leaders and wealthy Filipino civilians—whom Spruance later would oppose—entertained the Spruances with an extravagance that belied the poverty of the majority of the population. The wealthy Filipino women, for example, had a predilection for ostentatious evening gowns, costing many hundreds of dollars, which they would wear once and discard.

The social demands were wearing. At first the Spruances accepted the majority of the invitations. Later they became more judicious, went to fewer activities, and left as soon as possible.

Margaret once was asked what her principal task was as the ambassador's wife.

"Smiling," she responded.

Margaret smiled and much more besides. Her grace and charm compensated for her husband's shyness and reserve. She was in charge of all entertaining, one of the most vital embassy functions.

Sometimes the guests were distinguished Americans—Vice President and Mrs. Nixon, Mrs. Eleanor Roosevelt, Adlai Stevenson, Associate Justice William Douglas, Secretary of State and Mrs. Dulles, Cardinal Spellman, and Joseph Alsop. The diplomatic corps were frequent guests, and the Spruances especially liked the Nationalist Chinese ambassador and his wife. The Filipinos, however, were difficult to entertain. Invitation lists and seating arrangements were carefully planned by Margaret and the embassy staff. One had to weigh the seniority and precedence of each potential guest while guarding against gaffes such as seating feuding politicians alongside one another. The Filipinos, however, were unconcerned about these matters, for they frequently arrived early—or did not arrive at all—forcing the harried protocol officer to rearrange place cards hurriedly as dinnertime approached. Margaret finally abandoned formal seating arrangements when her guests were predominantly Filipino.

Margaret was essential to her husband's success. One of Spruance's deputies later wrote admiringly of "the splendid performance of his

Margaret Spruance entertains a distinguished guest at the embassy.

distinguished, beautiful, and intelligent wife, Margaret. A great Ambassador is only as great as his wife will help him be."
Everyone at the embassy would agree.

Spruance had established his authority and personality shortly after arriving in Manila. He preferred being addressed as "Admiral" rather than "Mr. Ambassador," and his style of leadership was unchanged from World War II. Although Spruance's theoretical jurisdiction was restricted to the embassy, he nevertheless exercised de facto authority over local American military commanders and other government agencies. The Filipinos were sensitive about their newly acquired independence and were easily offended by infringements against their sovereignty. Spruance was acutely aware of their feelings and would not tolerate the discourteous American behavior that was a holdover from the days of colonialism.

The United States Air Force ran a mail truck between Clark Field and Manila, a sixty-mile trip over congested roads. The truck displayed a large sign, "U.S. Mail. Do Not Delay" and drove at high speed with wailing siren. Before World War II this kind of procedure was commonplace, but now it enraged the Filipinos. Spruance did not ask, but ordered the Air Force to cease the practice immediately. The Air Force obeyed.

Spruance planned and implemented American policy through the Embassy Country Team, whose members included the embassy staff, the heads of the economic aid and military assistance groups, and local military commanders. They met often, everyone was heard, and loud arguments were frequent. Spruance, unperturbed and uninvolved, remained aloof from the torrents of words. He would quietly pace the room while the discussions ensued.

"Gentlemen," Spruance finally would say, "I thank you very much for your views and your comments. I've thought this over, and this is what I think we'll do."

"They fell right in line," recalled one participant. "I think we all respected him, and he earned that respect. We all admired him so much, and his views were always so damned sound, that when he got through telling us what he wanted, the answer was 'yes sir.' "

One government agency, however, did not attend the Country Team conferences. Shortly after Spruance became ambassador, a soft-spoken retired Army brigadier general introduced himself as Ralph B. Lovett.

He explained that he was the head of the CIA in the Philippines. All CIA agents—including Lansdale—reported to him. Spruance and Lovett (who had similar personalities) soon became close friends. Lovett had been ordered not to divulge CIA activities to the State Department, but he made one exception. He kept Spruance fully informed.

Spruance's paramount concern was the 1953 Philippine presidential elections. He first made himself familiar with the earlier campaigns by directing his embassy staff to study the methods and practices that had been used before. Their report on Quirino's victory in 1949 was chilling. Armed thugs, hired by the Liberals, had surrounded the polls to frighten away opposition voters. Later, the ballot boxes had been stuffed with phony ballots while in transit from the distant regions to Manila, where they were counted. These and other fraudulent techniques revealed that Philippine elections had been savage affairs. Rumors flew that the Liberals planned a repeat performance. Many felt that another illegal victory by Quirino would provoke a bloody revolution—led by Magsaysay. Democracy in the Philippines was in name only. Brute force, not votes, had been the deciding factor in past elections.

The Philippines in anarchy was an appalling prospect to the United States government. America had an emotional involvement with the Philippines owing to a half-century of close association. Thousands of Americans had died liberating the country from Japan in World War II. Hundreds of millions of American dollars had later poured into the Philippines to help rebuild the country from the ravages of war. The Philippine government had been established in 1946 under American guidance as the "showcase of democracy" in the Far East. In an Asia threatened by communism, the Philippines were "proof" to other Asians that democracy could work for them as well. Thus few Americans wanted to see the Philippines lost, first to violent revolution and chaos, then probably to communism. Magsaysay, reasoned most Americans, had to win if the Republic of the Philippines was to survive.

The question was whether Magsaysay could win without American help. Despite Magsaysay's potential plurality, Quirino was in power and was fully capable of stealing the election as before. Assuming that Magsaysay could not win by himself, would the United States be justified to give him support, either moral or material? The United States had condemned the Soviet Union for interfering in the political processes of other countries. Would not American support of Magsaysay be the equivalent? Would not the United States then be interfering in the political processes of the Republic of the Philippines?

In any question concerning foreign policy, a country must—in the last analysis—decide what is best for its vital interests. Some would argue that it was a vital interest to the United States that the Philippines have a stable, democratic government. Others would argue—contrarily—that it was also a vital interest to the United States that it lawfully conduct its international affairs with the same code of ethics and morality that it expected of other nations. It seemed impossible to serve both interests in the Philippines. These dilemmas were faced by Americans both in Washington and Manila.

In the end, expediency supplanted ideology. The decisions reached in Washington are unclear and will be addressed later. What is clear, however, is that Spruance committed himself and the embassy to assist Magsaysay in the 1953 presidential elections. He also decided that his assistance would be surreptitious ("circumspect" in Spruance's words) to avoid charges of American interference. If American involvement became known, it might lose the election for Magsaysay as well as discrediting the United States in the eyes of the world community.

Once Spruance had made his decision, he devised ways and means to help Magsaysay. He wanted the Filipino to win legally, so Spruance's primary objective was to ensure free and honest elections. If the electorate could express themselves at the polls without fear of fraud or intimidation, Magsaysay seemed a sure winner.

The role of the embassy and the Country Team became one of giving advice and encouragement to Magsaysay and the Nacionalistas. The CIA in the Philippines was also fully committed to the Magsaysay cause and provided its support through covert operations. Both Lovett and Lansdale kept Spruance informed so that the embassy and the CIA efforts were coordinated and harmonious. The ambassador was more interested in results than details of how they were achieved.

The embassy's deliberate involvement in the election campaign was dangerous. The newspapers reported every move and every statement by the American community. Quirino desperately sought to implicate Spruance and the embassy for meddling in Philippine national affairs. He knew what the Americans were doing but couldn't prove it. As the election campaign progressed, Quirino's accusations gained in shrillness and intensity. Spruance responded with a stony silence.

His silence was a deliberate policy, first expressed in a public statement on 13 March 1953, seven months before the presidential elections. "In order to avoid any possible interference on the part of American citizens residing in the Philippines in the coming political campaign, and the coming election," he proclaimed, "I am, as American Ambassador to the Philippines, issuing a warning to all American residents here to refrain scrupulously from any kind of participation in the election."

Spruance's Counselor of Embassy for Economic Affairs, Daniel M. Braddock, wired the State Department in order to explain Spruance's proclamation. Braddock reported it had been in response to appeals by local American businessmen who were being pressured by Filipino political fund raisers. Spruance's policy statement would give the Americans justification for refusing to donate their money. He left unsaid that it was also a subterfuge.

Secretary of State John Foster Dulles replied to Spruance by dispatch the following day. "Department most pleased at press reports that Ambassador warned Americans living in Philippines to refrain from taking part in coming Presidential campaign," wired Dulles. "Department completely agrees that Philippine politics are exclusively concern of Philippine people and that Americans residing in Philippines should maintain same attitude of strict non-involvement observed by their government. U.S. government is confident that observance of fundamental principle upon which both Philippine and U.S. governments based, that of right of people freely to choose their leaders, will characterize forthcoming elections and U.S. government looks forward to continuing full cooperation with any administration elected on basis that fundamental principle."

The Dulles dispatch was unclassified and obviously intended for public disclosure. Throughout the election campaign, the State Department and the embassy frequently would quote the dispatch as the official United States policy. For example, Senator Langer, on the floor of the United States Senate on 20 May 1953, demanded that the Eisenhower administration investigate charges of embassy interference in Philippine politics. The State Department responded by citing the Dulles dispatch and a 30 March policy statement by Spruance.

The latter Spruance statement was precipitated by a visit by Adlai Stevenson to the Philippines in late March. Quirino had entertained Stevenson and Spruance at a luncheon in Baguio on 30 March. Stevenson spoke at the luncheon and expressed the hope that the November elections would be "free and honest." Whether deliberate or unintentional, Stevenson's statement must have infuriated Quirino.

Quirino held a press conference after the Americans had left the luncheon. He became visibly angry and excoriated Spruance and the embassy. The United States was actively supporting Magsaysay, he charged. His proof was a dinner that Spruance had held for Stevenson several nights earlier. Only one Liberal Party official had been invited, said Quirino, while Magsaysay and many Nacionalista Party representatives had been present. "Blatant favoritism!" said an agitated Quirino.

Quirino then challenged Spruance through the press to answer two inflammatory accusations. First, did the Ambassador have the Magsaysay–Nacionalista Party agreement in an embassy safe? (He did.) Second, would the Ambassador deny that the United States favored Magsaysay in the coming election?

The newspapers carried Quirino's tirade in screaming headlines. Spruance was under intense pressure to respond. American-Philippine international relations were at stake. He later told the State Department that he consulted "with my staff and experienced American observers in Manila" before releasing a policy statement from which he never would deviate.

Spruance addressed Quirino's charges following a press conference for Stevenson at the embassy. It was a classic of equivocation. "I wish to state now," said Spruance, "that the United States Embassy will observe strict neutrality in the course of the coming campaign and the election. For this reason, I do not propose to comment upon, to confirm, or deny charges of the sort that have appeared in the public press recently, as to do so would be tantamount to intervention in Philippine politics."

In other words, Spruance could cleverly avoid answering any and all charges of interference on the grounds that any reply on his part would be interference. Quirino was speechless, although some of his more vocal supporters still called for Spruance's expulsion because of his "favoritism" shown at the Stevenson dinner. But that pretense vanished when it was discovered that Spruance had invited an equal number of representatives from each party. In true Filipino fashion, some of the Liberals had simply failed to show up.

Stevenson later apologized to Spruance for the rumpus he had caused. "I've been worrying about your 'trouble,' " wrote Stevenson, "and I hope and pray that my visit did not aggravate it. . . . I suppose it's not unlikely that we are destined to see more and more of this sort of political tactic to capitalize the nationalistic impulses of the people. But it would seem to me that for the Department to yield to it would only invite more and more of the same in the future."

Spruance's statements were deliberate falsehoods designed to disguise the embassy-CIA involvement. Lovett later explained Spruance's motivations. "He had no qualms about misrepresenting the United States policy in the Philippines," said Lovett, "because the end justified the means. For example, Americans believed it was wrong to kill, but it was not wrong to kill in war. The election campaign was just like a war, and the forces were good against evil, democracy against communism. At no time did Spruance give any indication that he felt he was compromising his integrity with his public pronouncements of United States and embassy policies."

The campaign developed into another brawling, tempestuous, emotional affair typical of the past, replete with rumors, intrigue, espionage, and violence by both parties. Eventually Spruance told Magsaysay not to visit the embassy, to preclude possible charges of American influence, but they occasionally met clandestinely. Lansdale continued as Magsaysay's constant companion, although he remained out of the public eye on Spruance's orders. Magsaysay and his party gained strength and confidence from their American allies, who provided both moral and material support. His popularity soared while Quirino's correspondingly declined. Spruance's bland statements of America's neutrality and his hope for "free and honest elections" drove Quirino wild. Spruance thoroughly enjoyed the battle. He was winning.

The heat of Manila, however, was an enemy that Spruance could not overcome. He and Margaret fled at every opportunity to the mountain resort at Baguio so that Spruance could recuperate in its cool, refreshing climate. One day in late summer Spruance was summoned to the phone at his Baguio residence. He returned and spoke to Margaret. "He was smiling like an imp," Margaret recalled.

"Well, are you ready to go home?" he asked.

"Yes, I am," said Margaret impulsively. Upset by Quirino's vilification of her husband, she had begun to fear for his life.

"The embassy just told me," he said, "that Quirino is about to declare me persona non grata."

Spruance seemed amused despite the sober realization that they would have to leave the country immediately if the report was true. "My feelings were that it was all right with me," said Margaret, "because things were in such a mess at the time. I was also worried because Raymond was suffering so much from the heat. Although he was well and did not look tired, I still knew that the heat was bothering him terribly."

Quirino did not follow through (perhaps in fear of economic retaliation by the United States government), but there could be no doubt in Washington that Spruance was unwelcome in Manila. A month before the elections, he returned to the United States for "routine consultations." Before leaving Manila he spoke with Lovett. "What am I supposed to know about the CIA operations in the Philippines," he asked, "and what am I not supposed to know?" He was half serious and half joking. Arriving in Washington, he conferred with President Eisenhower, Secretary of State John Foster Dulles, Assistant Secretary Walter Robertson, and CIA Director Allen Dulles. There is no record of their conversations in the State Department or Eisenhower archives, although Spruance later wrote that they all "were generally familiar with the situation out there."

Speculation mounted in the Philippines whether Spruance would return. On 20 October the speculation ended when Spruance arrived at the Manila airport. Reporters surrounded the ambassador and barraged him with questions. No, he said, he would not comment on matters discussed in Washington. But he did make one statement: the United States was vitally interested in the November tenth elections but it would remain strictly neutral. When he next saw Lovett, he assured the CIA head he had not "given anything away" in Washington.

Next day President Eisenhower announced that Spruance would remain as Ambassador to the Philippines.

A Manila newspaper editorial reflected the significance of Spruance's return. "We are afraid President Quirino and his Liberals will have to put up with the presence here of Ambassador Raymond A. Spruance, whether they like it or not," said the editorial, "for President Eisenhower has decided to retain him in his present position. There is no more eloquent indication that Washington is fully satisfied with Ambassador Spruance's work. . . . Ambassador Spruance has never been guilty of any act which can be utilized by the Liberals as fodder for their current anti-Embassy campaign. Indeed, the Ambassador has comported himself with such exasperating decorum as to render the Liberals completely helpless."

As the election approached, nerves stretched to the breaking point. All eyes were upon the Philippine Constabulary, a branch of the armed forces who would police the polls and deliver the sealed ballot boxes. A free election depended upon the honesty and integrity of the Constabulary commanders. Major General Calixto Duque, the Army chief of staff, began recalling the scrupulous commanders and replacing them with Quirino henchmen. Quirino started purging the armed forces of high-ranking officers suspected of favoring Magsaysay, and he "pardoned" a large number of thugs and gunmen from prison several weeks before the election.

The newspapers publicized Quirino's crude power plays, convincing Magsaysay and his Nacionalista followers that Quirino would steal the election. Magsaysay vowed that if Quirino won he would take to the hills and overthrow Quirino by force.

"I told him not to talk this way," said Spruance afterward, "as Quirino was informed of everything he said and did. There was no writ of habeas corpus for cases of sedition, and Quirino would have it in his power to clap him in prison before the election and keep him there. Right up to a couple of days before the election, important officials of the Nacionalista Party were convinced that the election was going to be stolen from them. If it had been stolen, I am convinced that there would have been serious bloodshed in the country."

Major General Robert M. Cannon, U.S. Army, proposed a solution to neutralize the Quirino strong-arm tactics. Cannon was chief of the Joint U.S. Military Advisory Group in the Philippines, an organization of about a hundred American military personnel who served as military and naval advisors to the Philippine armed forces. The United States was then providing vast quantities of military equipment to the Philippines, primarily to enable the Filipinos to "maintain internal peace and order," i.e., to fight Huks.

Cannon approached Spruance and explained that his Army superiors in Washington had ordered him to stand clear of Philippine political matters. Nevertheless, Cannon proposed organizing his advisors into small teams and sending them into the countryside to observe the elections. With the Americans present, the Quirino thugs could not openly intimidate the Magsaysay supporters at the polling places. Cannon could publicly justify his actions because his advisory group was authorized by law to observe how the Filipino Constabulary used the equipment given them by the Americans. On election day they would simply be observing how it was used at the polling places.

Cannon's scheme was brazen yet ingenious. On the other hand, if it backfired it could cost the election or rupture United States–Philippine relations.

Spruance approved the plan. "I think you're entirely within your charter," said Spruance. "You're doing what is proper and you have my support."

The operation nearly went awry. Cannon unwisely instructed his men in writing, and a copy of his orders fell into Quirino's hands. After the election Quirino threatened to expel Cannon and the entire United States Military Advisory Group. It appeared that he finally had proof of American interference. Spruance was unperturbed. He went before the press and coolly backed the general. "I am entirely familiar with General Cannon's instructions," he said. "What he did was to ensure so far as he could that the elections would be held in a free and honest manner, and without intimidation. Also, what he did was with my knowledge and approval."

Deputy Chief of Mission Lacy was in Tokyo with Vice President Nixon, who apparently was concerned over the publicity surrounding Cannon. Spruance wired assurances to Lacy. "You are authorized inform Vice President I do not regard this matter as serious," advised Spruance. "I believe Cannon's order entirely within scope of his responsibility and duty. I am convinced release of text Cannon's order will take care of this matter."

Spruance was right. The matter died. His forthright response marked the end of Quirino's last convulsive effort to discredit the United States.

The embassy also had arranged for numerous foreign journalists to disperse throughout the country on election day. Quirino's thugs were at the polling places, but they dared not move under the scrutiny of the outside observers.

It was a free and honest election.

Magsaysay was elected by an overwhelming majority.

Spruance's role in influencing the election of Ramón Magsaysay poses profound moral and ethical questions. The crux of the matter is whether Spruance was justified in aiding and abetting the Filipino's candidacy.

One possible assumption is that Spruance acted independently and violated the noninvolvement policy stated by Secretary Dulles. If this assumption is correct, then Spruance was unjustified in his actions. This assumption is improbable, however, for Dulles must have known what Spruance was doing. Furthermore, President Eisenhower asked Spruance to extend his tour as ambassador after the 1953 elections. It is unlikely that this request would have been made had Spruance disobeyed either the President or the Secretary of State.

It is probable that the Eisenhower administration authorized Spruance surreptitiously to support Magsaysay, and that Spruance enthusiastically carried out his orders without qualms or moral reservations. If this is the case—and the author believes it is—then the Eisenhower administration and Raymond Spruance must stand together in judgment for their actions.

The Republic of the Philippines was a sovereign state. It had been granted its independence by the United States and had the absolute right to choose its own form of government and its own leaders, however imperfect their elective processes might be. If the United States could interfere in the Philippines under the guise of ensuring political stability, then the United States *and any other power* could also interfere in the governmental processes of any other country in the world. No responsible government would publicly condone that dangerous and unlawful precedent.

Thus the United States had neither authority nor justification to interfere with the 1953 presidential campaign. Furthermore, both the United States government and Spruance deliberately deceived the American people with false statements of neutrality, when in fact the government was anything but neutral. Again, there is no justification for lying to the American people.

A case might be made that the political stability of the Philippines was a vital interest to the United States, and that extreme measures were therefore necessary. In other words, the loss of the Philippines to an unfriendly government after a period of political instability would jeopardize the national security of the United States. Three arguments might be made to support this thesis.

First, the Philippines were necessary for strategic reasons, principally for their air, military, and naval bases. However, if the United

States had to abandon those bases, other bases remained throughout the western Pacific such as Taiwan, Okinawa, and Japan. Spruance himself later became impatient with the Filipinos in a series of squabbles over American base rights. He was more than ready to pull out of the Philippines and use the facilities in the American Trust Territories of Micronesia. Thus this first argument is unconvincing.

Second, the Philippines were necessary to prove that democracy would work in Asia. This argument is cynical. Within the embassy, at least, many Americans felt that the Filipinos were not "ready" for democracy. One high official believed that the Philippines needed a benevolent dictator—Magsaysay. This same official believed it was wrong to force the American form of government on the Philippines because it simply didn't work there. Another high official felt that the Philippines were not ready for independence and that they should have remained an American colony. One needs only to look at the Philippines today to see that its government has little resemblance to the American concept of democracy. Thus the election of Magsaysay did not prove that democracy is the best form of government for Asians.

The third argument is that a victory by Quirino would have triggered a bloody revolution that Magsaysay had promised would follow. It is a telling argument that many Filipino lives may have been saved by American altruism. On the other hand, one could also argue that Magsaysay used the specter of revolution to coerce the Americans into increasing their support. "If I don't win," Magsaysay seemed to be saying, "then I will start a revolution, and you, the government of the United States, certainly don't want me to do that." There is no way of knowing how much of Magsaysay's threat was genuine and how much was bluff. Thus the *possibility* of a revolution was not justification for American interference. There are revolutions, loss of life, and political instability in countries throughout the world, year after year, in which the United States has never become involved.

One concludes in retrospect that the presidential campaign in the Philippines was not a vital issue to the United States.

Could Magsaysay have become president without American support? The answer is probably yes, if not in 1953, at least by 1957. Magsaysay was a robust young man; Quirino was old and tired and sick. Magsaysay was a power within the Philippine government as Secretary of Defense, and a power within the Liberal Party as a popular politician with overwhelming support within the electorate. Had the embassy remained neutral, and had the United States told Magsaysay he was on his own, surely Magsaysay still would have been capable of eventually displacing Quirino and gaining the presidency. Meanwhile he would still have been a strong influence within the Quirino administration, in a position to urge reforms and to bring good men into his camp. A wait of several years also would have allowed him to gain experience in dealing with politicians and the bureaucracy, one of his weaknesses after he became president.

As it was, Magsaysay became president thanks to American support rather than to any permanent improvement in the Philippine electoral processes. A short-range goal of expediency was achieved, but there were no long-range benefits for the people of the Philippines. Until they themselves could straighten out their government by their own efforts, American-backed Filipinos like Magsaysay were on shaky ground. Interestingly enough, many Americans—such as Lansdale—truly wanted the Filipinos to help themselves to achieve political maturity. Nevertheless, Magsaysay was elected largely through direct, clandestine American support.

Once elected, Magsaysay proved to be a well-intentioned but not particularly effective president. Although he remained immensely popular with the electorate, the intricate, overwhelming problems of government were beyond his grasp. He was more at ease fighting Huks in the jungles or electioneering in the provinces than he was at coping with obstinate politicians in the presidential palace in Manila.

Magsaysay died in an airplane crash in March 1957. What few reforms he had managed to achieve died with him. The Filipino people now revere him as a national hero. It was his only legacy to his country.

By 1959 Spruance despaired of progress in the Philippines. "The situation in the Philippines," he wrote a friend, "from all that I read and what I hear from men recently from out there, is very bad. Corruption is reported to be worse than under Quirino. Garcia [the incumbent president] said that they had to stop the work which Magsaysay had started on land settlement and on the subdivision of big estates, because of lack of funds. This is a standard Filipino excuse for not doing something which they should do, but do not want to do. It sounds to me as if the old landed interests are in control of the government again."

It was a bitter admission that perhaps his efforts as ambassador had been in vain.

* * *

In retrospect, then, Spruance was wrong in supporting Ramón Magsaysay. Not only were Spruance's actions contrary to the lawful relations between two sovereign states, he also deceived the American people and the world through his false and misleading statements of American neutrality. How much more fitting it would have been had he resigned as ambassador rather than to compromise his integrity that hitherto had been unblemished over a lifetime.

Yet, however others may judge him, Spruance believed he was acting in the best interests of both the United States and the Filipinos. He felt particular compassion for the wretched peasants, and he hated Quirino and everything Quirino represented. For once, perhaps, Spruance allowed emotion to affect his judgment. In Spruance's eyes, Magsaysay was the only solution for political and economic stability in the Philippines. Spruance was proud of what he had done and regarded his performance as ambassador with satisfaction. "I think the most important things that were accomplished while I was out there," he wrote a friend, "were to have an honest election and to allow Magsaysay, the overwhelming choice of the Filipino people, elected as their President."

Spruance wanted to retire following the 1953 elections, but President Eisenhower—a fervent admirer—persuaded him to remain another year. As always, the President's wish was his command. Spruance dreaded telling Margaret, and he confided to his daughter, "I promised your mother that I wouldn't. I wonder how she is going to take this."

He became involved in many other matters during his tenure, such as the Japanese-Philippine Peace Treaty and mutual defense and economic aid agreements between the United States and the Philippines. But they were anticlimactic.

Spruance retired as ambassador in the spring of 1955. The Philippine newspapers praised him, American and Philippine government leaders thanked and congratulated him, and his embassy associates expressed their admiration and gratitude. There has never been one word of reproach from these contemporaries, which indicates that Spruance was not alone in believing that the United States had acted correctly in the Philippine presidential campaign.

"The producer is at his best in the economic field," wrote Plato, "the warrior is at his best in battle; they are both at their worst in public office; and in their crude hands politics submerges statesmanship. For statesmanship is a science and an art; one must have lived for it and been long prepared."

Military scholar and historian Michael Howard has a different view of statesmanship. "The term 'statesman' is vague," Howard has written. "I shall use it to indicate the professional groups whose function is to preserve and if necessary exercise the power and the authority of the state: politicians, civil servants, police, diplomats, soldiers. They are groups which sometimes have a bad press in academic circles. Younger members of society tend to be suspicious of them, find it hard to identify with them, see them often as sinister or at best as grotesque. Some of them are. I can think of some students and not a few dons who are as well. With these exceptions we need not concern ourselves. Most of the people of whom I speak are men of good will and exceptional ability, doing their best, among conditions of great difficulty, to make the right decisions. The options open to them are likely to be far more limited than is generally realised. Where the decisions have moral implications they are likely to be complex and obscure. Seldom is a statesman fortunate enough to have a clear-cut choice between an obviously 'good' or innocuous course of action and one equally obviously bad. His choice is likely always to be one between two evils. And for those with whom ultimate powers of direction and decision rest in great modern states, the implications of their decision may well be vast; not only for their own peoples and their descendants, but for the whole of the world."

Chapter 26

THE FINAL YEARS

SPRUANCE began his second retirement at the age of sixty-nine, resuming his gardening and his pleasant way of life in Pebble Beach. He and Margaret periodically visited Edward and young Margaret and their families. Otherwise they did little traveling.

He retained his intellectual curiosity and was still intrigued by new discoveries. By chance he began reading Darwin. He was fascinated. "Listen to this," he would say to his family, and then he would read aloud the passages that had captured his interest.

He was willing to talk about the experiences of his naval career, but he was reticent when his son-in-law asked his opinion on current Navy policies and trends. "It's not my problem now," he would reply. "There's nothing I can do about it. I've done my share."

He corresponded with writers and historians who sought information about his activities in World War II. He apologized for a poor memory, but the data he provided usually was accurate. Publishers provided quantities of books about World War II which he acknowledged but seldom read; he preferred working outside, and failing eyesight limited his reading. Spruance stubbornly refused to write an autobiography or to record his memoirs, and he discouraged any attempts by others to write his biography. Carl Moore and the Director of Naval History finally convinced Spruance to allow Savvy Forrestel to write a "study in command." Spruance cooperated with his former operations officer, and the result was an abbreviated biography published by the Government Printing Office in 1966.

Kelly Turner lived nearby with his wife, and the Spruances visited them often. Turner had become a total alcoholic and was in failing health. When Mrs. Turner died in the early sixties, Spruance feared that Turner would drink himself to death. He arranged with Turner to phone at seven each morning to reassure himself that Turner was up and around. One Sunday afternoon in 1961 Spruance received a call that Turner was dead. He had died of a heart attack.

The Spruances visited the Nimitzes from time to time in San Francisco and reminisced of days past. Chester Nimitz died in 1966. Spruance went alone to his funeral; Margaret was ill and stayed at home.

Nimitz had arranged with the Navy Department that he, Spruance, and Turner would be buried alongside one another at a military cemetery overlooking San Francisco Bay. The day of Nimitz's funeral was cold and blustery. Everyone wore overcoats. Except Spruance. Dressed only in his admiral's uniform, he stood rigidly throughout the service while the wind whipped his spare and aging body, which had been weakened by a recent siege of influenza. When Margaret later learned of his behavior, she chastened him for endangering his health. The admiral was unrepentant. He had forced himself to endure physical discomfort since he was a teenager, and he would not change now.

Slowly his constitution began to fail. He required corrective hernia surgery, and cataracts dimmed his vision. He was eighty years old and regarded his illnesses with a detached curiosity. The new experiences in the hospital would be "interesting." Surgeons removed the cataracts, and he spent long days at home with his eyes bandaged, dependent upon Margaret for his reading and writing. When the bandages were removed, he wrote his first impressions to a friend.

"The final result is not as good as nature originally endowed me," he wrote, "but it is a lot better than it was a year ago. The changes in colors have been most interesting. The various shades of blue, which were blocked off by the cataracts, now come through. Colors are changed and more brilliant, which particularly appeals to a gardener in the spring of the year."

Contact lenses aided his vision. "Margaret is getting quite the expert in taking care of the lenses and in putting them in," he wrote. "I am getting rather good in flipping them out in the evening."

By then, however, another disease had attacked that doctors could never cure. Arteriosclerosis had thickened and hardened his arteries. Its most pronounced effect was the degradation of his memory and mental powers.

He knew he was slipping. He went to Newport for the last time in 1967 to see his daughter's family. The admiral could not recall familiar places and past events. During his visit he and Margaret called upon a couple who were lifelong friends.

"I just don't remember them," insisted Spruance during the ride to the friends' home.

"I am sure you will once you see them," Margaret assured.

The Spruances and their friends had a pleasant and relaxed reunion. They chatted amicably and everything seemed well. Afterwards Spruance became dejected.

"What is wrong?" asked Margaret.

"I still don't remember them," he said.

Yet he retained his sense of humor. During a tea party his hostess suggested that they move to another room and take their tea with them. Spruance's hands were weak and shaking. "I will," he said, "but not in a cup."

Edward had retired from the Navy as a captain after thirty years' service. His father had encouraged him to become an intelligence specialist after the war. Edward had followed the advice, but his postwar naval career was full of disappointments. Spruance wrote several letters of encouragement in an effort to buoy his son's spirits. Following retirement, Edward and his family moved to nearby San Rafael. Father and son grew very close, in contrast to their earlier lack of rapport. As Spruance's health worsened he became dependent upon his son, and Edward assumed increasing responsibility for his father's affairs. Finally Spruance wrote Edward a pathetic letter that awkwardly expressed his longing for his son.

"Early this morning I had a bright idea about your future," he wrote. "This your mother and I have been discussing and cogitating over at intervals all day. . . . My idea was that at our age it would

The final years

mean a great deal to us to have you settled very near us. . . . If you were settled in the Country Club area we would get you a golfing membership, and you would have two golf courses to play on. That would give you ample opportunity to meet people and make friends among your contemporaries. My third lot would be available to build a house on, if you wished.

"There would be no trouble about our financing this scheme."

Edward did not accept the offer, but he nevertheless visited his parents often and was a tower of strength to the failing admiral.

In the spring of 1969 Edward was severely injured in an automobile accident. He was rushed to a hospital and was near death.

Margaret dreaded telling her husband.

"Edward has been in a very bad accident," she said.

"Oh, yes?" he responded quietly.

"Yes! Raymond, this is very, very serious," she said. "This is very terrible news."

Spruance turned away from his wife. "Let's take a walk," he said. They walked slowly and silently. Then his wife spoke again.

"Young Margaret is coming over this afternoon."

"And why is she coming?" asked the admiral. Margaret felt he still hadn't understood what she had been saying.

"Edward has been terribly hurt," Margaret said emphatically. "He may not live."

Spruance refused to speak. Two weeks later Edward died. Spruance never talked again about his son, regardless of Margaret's efforts.

He was dazed during Edward's funeral and seemed oblivious to everything about him. Still his sardonic humor persisted. Afterwards he listened to a cantankerous old woman complain about her illness.

"You've had a stroke, haven't you?" asked Spruance.

"I've had three strokes," she snapped.

"Three strokes and you're out," said Spruance.

Spruance worsened after Edward's death, becoming lost in silent, overwhelming grief for his son. He rarely spoke and withdrew from the world. His body weakened, he lost weight, and he became so feeble that he was confined to bed. "Almost like a baby," said young Margaret, "he would lift his face to be kissed."

Margaret would not allow him to be taken to a hospital. His remaining days would be in the home he loved, and she hired nurses to attend his needs. He remained gentle and considerate and always thanked them for their help.

One evening he motioned to the nurse with his hand to come near him. His voice was so weak she could hardly hear him.

"I want to say goodnight to my wife," he whispered.

It was his last coherent sentence. He died on 13 December 1969.

The Navy buried him with full military honors alongside Chester Nimitz and Kelly Turner.

Acknowledgments

A WORK of this scope would not be possible without the help and cooperation of a great many people. I have been almost entirely dependent upon the good will of others in gathering my research material. Some were those who knew Spruance and provided information through letters and interviews. Others were those who are the custodians of material pertaining to Spruance and who allowed me access to what I needed. Still others provided advice and encouragement throughout my research and writing. I cannot acknowledge them all by name but I do thank them all collectively. There are some people, however, to whom I do wish to give a special thanks.

Mrs. Raymond A. Spruance and her daughter Margaret (Mrs. Gerard S. Bogart) were kind, courteous, and cooperative. Through these two gracious and delightful ladies, I discovered Raymond Spruance as only a wife and daughter would know him. Rear Admiral Charles J. Moore, USN (Ret.), allowed me to use and quote his invaluable oral history, and he promptly answered my many letters requesting additional details. (I shall always remember Carl Moore's repeated admonitions for objectivity. "Don't put Spruance on a pedestal," said Carl. "Remember that he was very human.") Captain Robert J. Oliver, USN (Ret.), was meticulous and conscientious in describing Spruance's role at the Battle of Midway, as well as other important periods of Spruance's career. Vice Admiral Emmet P. Forrestel, USN (Ret.), loaned his extensive research files containing data that was otherwise unobtainable. Similar thanks go to Professor E. B. Potter of the Naval Academy and to Mr. Arthur Sproul for loaning their Spruance correspondence files. Mr. Charles F. Barber provided revealing accounts of Spruance and the staff from the viewpoint of an inquisitive young reserve officer who was intensely interested in watching professional officers make war. I am also grateful to Generals Robert M. Cannon, Edward G. Lansdale, and Ralph B. Lovett, and to Ambassador William S. B. Lacy for allowing me to interview them concerning Spruance's role as Ambassador to the Philippines.

Mr. Anthony S. Nicolosi, Curator of the Naval Historical Collection, Naval War College, has been my ally throughout this project. Regardless of the complexity or difficulty in locating needed research material, Tony Nicolosi always found it. His spirit of service to the writer and researcher could be a model for all curators and archivists. Dr. Dean C. Allard of the Naval History Division, Navy Department, is another custodian of naval records to whom I am indebted.

Rear Admiral Henry E. Eccles, USN (Ret.), has been a valued advisor from the very beginning. Admiral Richard G. Colbert, USN, former president of the Naval War College, gave me moral support when I needed it the most. Vice Admiral Stansfield Turner, USN, the current college president, continued that moral support. The Naval War College Foundation, a private organization, provided financial assistance for the considerable expenses associated with my research and writing.

I should like to thank Mr. Josiah Bunting, III, for his good offices at a crucial time.

I am particularly grateful to Mr. Herman Wouk and to Rear Admiral Eccles for reading and commenting upon my manuscript.

An author needs a good editor. I have had two. Commander Robert M. Laske, USN, editor of the *Naval War College Review,* helped me in the writing of the Spruance monograph and encouraged me to write the admiral's biography. Mr. Llewellyn Howland, III, my editor at Little, Brown, has an abiding respect and a deep love for the English language, a capacity for sound advice, and an ability to help an author achieve his full potential. I cannot thank him adequately for all he has done for me.

Finally, I thank my wife Marilyn. She has typed every page of the thousands of pages of various drafts of the manuscript. She cheerfully accepted Raymond Spruance as a member of our family. I respect her opinion and seek her approval above all others. This book has been a joint venture. Without Marilyn to help me, it would not have been written.

Thomas B. Buell
Newport, Rhode Island
September, 1973

Appendixes

APPENDIX I

FIVE STARS

THE Congress during World War II created a limited number of five-star ranks for the Army and the Navy, designated General of the Army and Fleet Admiral. The Navy by law was authorized four Fleet Admirals. Three were easily chosen: Ernest J. King, Chester W. Nimitz, and William S. Leahy, chief of staff to President Roosevelt. The choice for the fourth was between Halsey and Spruance.

Secretary of the Navy Forrestal told King that he would have to decide between the two. It was a difficult task, because Halsey and Spruance both had influential supporters in Washington. The most powerful was Representative Carl Vinson, Chairman of the House Armed Services Committee, who had publicly endorsed Halsey. The Navy did not like to oppose Vinson on anything.

King put off the decision for several months, then sent a memorandum to Forrestal summarizing the pros and cons of each candidate. There were many things in Halsey's favor. He was the senior admiral, he had been at sea since 1938, his performance in the South Pacific in the dark days of 1942–1943 had been brilliant, and his raids against the Japanese empire in late 1944 had been spectacular and devastating. Against him, wrote King, were his errors in judgment in not evading two typhoons that severely damaged his fleet in the latter part of the war. King said little about Halsey's questionable decisions at the Battle of Leyte Gulf.

King then turned to Spruance, whom he would have endorsed for CNO had it not been for Spruance's mandatory retirement age. "As to brains," wrote King, "the best man in every way." His record in the Pacific was self-evident. The only argument against Spruance was that he had held relatively subordinate commands during the early part of the war.

Halsey eventually received the five-star rank. The Congress, in an effort to compensate Spruance and to acknowledge his wartime achievements, authorized full pay for life as a four-star admiral, whereas all other naval officers received reduced pay upon retirement. A controversy has continued ever since, the gist being that Halsey's publicity had won his fifth star, and that Spruance had been at a disadvantage because he had avoided publicity. Many efforts were subsequently made to promote Spruance to Fleet Admiral, all reportedly thwarted by Vinson. After Vinson retired, still more attempts were made, but the Navy has been unwilling to reopen the case. The Navy's reasoning is that Spruance was the only World War II naval officer who retired on full pay by a special act of Congress, and thereby he had been appropriately recognized and honored by the people of America.

Spruance expressed his personal feelings on the matter in a 1965 letter to Professor E. B. Potter of the United States Naval Academy. "So far as my getting five star rank is concerned," wrote Spruance, "if I could have had it along with Bill Halsey, that would have been fine; but, if I had received it instead of Bill Halsey, I would have been very unhappy over it. The present situation is that World War II will have been over twenty years next August, which is a long time. Also, the central and western parts of the Pacific Ocean are a long way from Washington."

APPENDIX II

DEFINITION OF AN ADMIRAL

WILLIAM FALCONER of London in 1776 published *An Universal Dictionary of the Marine*, which contained a "copious explanation" of the technical terms and phrases associated with ships and the Royal Navy. One of his subjects concerned the duties and responsibilities of an admiral. His treatise is as appropriate for mid-twentieth-century admirals as it was for those of the eighteenth century. Portions of Falconer's definition are quoted herewith.

"The ADMIRAL, or commander in chief of a fleet," wrote Falconer, "being frequently invested with a great charge, on which the fate of a kingdom may depend, ought certainly to be possessed of abilities equal to so important a station and so extensive a command. His fleet is unavoidably exposed to a variety of perplexing situations in a precarious element. A train of dangerous incidents necessarily arise from those situations. The health, order and discipline of his people, are not less the objects of his consideration, than the condition and qualities of his ships. A sudden change of climate, a rank and infectious air, a scarcity, or unwholesomeness of provisions, may be as pernicious to the former, as tempestuous weather or dangerous navigation to the latter. A lee-shore, an injudicious engagement with an enemy greatly superior, may be equally fatal to both. He ought to have sufficient experience to anticipate all the probable events that may happen to his fleet during an expedition or cruise, and, by consequence, to provide against them. His skill should be able to counteract the various disasters which his fleet may suffer from different causes. His vigilance and presence of mind are necessary to seize every favourable opportunity that his situation may offer to prosecute his principal design; to extricate himself from any difficulty or distress; to check unfortunate events in the beginning, and retard the progress of any great calamity. He should be imbued with resolution and fortitude to animate his officers by the force of example, and promote a sense of emulation in those who are under his command, as well as to improve any advantage, as to frustrate or defeat the efforts of his ill fortune.

"The most essential part of his duty, however, appears to be military conduct. As soon as the fleet under his command puts to sea, he is to form it into the proper order of battle, called the LINE. In this arrangement, he is to make a judicious distribution of strength from the van to the rear, throwing the principal force into the center, to resist the impression of the enemy's fleet; which might otherwise, at some favorable opportunity, break through his line, and throw the van and rear into confusion.

"A competent knowledge of the seas, weather, and reigning winds, of the coast or region where he is stationed, is also requisite, as it will greatly facilitate his plans on the enemy. It will enable him to avoid being improperly embayed, where he might be surprised in a disadvantageous situation; and to judge whether it will be most expedient to attack his adversary, or lie prepared to receive his assault. When his fleet is forced by stress of weather or otherwise to take shelter in a road or bay, it will likewise suggest the necessary conduct of keeping a sufficient number of cruisers at sea, to bring him early intelligence, that they may be ready to cut or slip the cables when they are too much hurried to weigh their anchors. . . .

"When the admiral intends a descent on an enemy's coast, or other attack which may be attended with complicated or unforeseen incidents, his orders should be delivered or drawn up with the greatest accuracy and precision: they should be simple, perspicuous, direct, and comprehensive; they should collect a number of objects into one point of view, and, foreseeing the effects of success or defeat, appoint the proper measures to be adopted in consequence thereof. History and experience confirm the necessity of this observation, and present us with a variety of disasters that have happened on such occasions, merely by a deficiency in this material article. In the commanding officer, inattention, barrenness of expedient, or a circumscribed view of the necessary effects of his enterprise, may be equally pernicious. And general orders ought to be utterly free from pedantry and perplexity, which always betray a false taste and confused imagination, besides the probability of producing many fatal consequences.

"When an admiral conquers in battle, he should endeavor to improve his victory, by pushing the advantages he has acquired as far as prudence directs; a conduct which merits his attention as much as any in the action! When he is defeated, he ought to embrace every opportunity of saving as many of his ships as possible, and endeavor principally to assist those which are disabled. In short, it is his duty to avail himself of every practicable expedient rather than sink under his misfortune, and suffer himself to become an easy prey to the enemy.

"He should be sufficiently acquainted with civil law, to judge with propriety of the proceedings of courts-martial, and to correct the errors, and restrain the abuses which may happen therein by mistake, or ignorance, or inattention. . . .

"Much more might be observed on this occasion. It appears however by the general outline which we have sketched, that the office and duty of an admiral requires greater skill and more comprehensive abilities than is generally supposed necessary to the command of a naval armament. And that he ought to be qualified, at least in this kingdom, to assist at the councils of his sovereign, and enter into the enlarged system of protecting his country from an invasion by sea, or of meditating a descent on an enemy's coast; as well as to improve navigation and open new channels of commerce. . . ."

APPENDIX III

Decorations and Awards of Admiral Spruance

Navy Cross
Distinguished Service Medal
Gold Star in lieu of Second Distinguished Service Medal
Gold Star in lieu of Third Distinguished Service Medal
Army Distinguished Service Medal
Navy Commendation Medal
Presidential Unit Citation
Cuban Pacification Medal
World War I Victory Medal with "Overseas" Clasp
American Defense Service Medal with "Fleet" Clasp
Asiatic-Pacific Campaign Medal
Navy Occupation Service Medal with "Asia" Clasp
Gold Cross of the Chevalier of the Order of the Savior, by Greece
Honorary Companion of the Bath (Military), by Great Britain
Grand Officer of the Order of Leopold with Palm, by Belgium
Croix de Guerre with Palm, by Belgium

Colleges and Universities Awarding Honorary Degrees to Admiral Spruance

Brown University
Central Philippine College (Ilo Ilo)
Rhode Island State College
Occidental College
Worcester Polytechnic Institute
Williams College
Yale University

BIBLIOGRAPHY

THE research material for this biography was obtained largely from unpublished primary sources such as letters, interviews, official reports, and oral histories. Much of this material has never before been used. Secondary sources were used sparingly, and the bibliography is restricted to a general description of the sources associated with each chapter. A fully annotated copy of the manuscript is available in the Naval Historical Collection at the Naval War College for those interested in the specific sources for each chapter.

The planning and battle narratives emphasize those aspects that were important to Spruance at the time. The details that would not have interested him, or that he would have entrusted to his subordinates, are not included in the text. Some readers may desire additional information on these omitted details and will be referred to appropriate official histories from time to time within the bibliography.

Spruance's letters to his wife sometimes rambled and frequently changed subjects from one sentence to the next. In order to enhance clarity, and without sacrificing the letters' phraseology or intent, the author occasionally has edited and paraphrased some of them in lieu of using distracting ellipses and brackets. This editing is indicated in the annotated manuscript at the Naval War College.

Following his retirement, Spruance was without a yeoman to assist in the paperwork which he so intensely disliked. He could not type, so all his letters were in longhand. In most cases Spruance first drafted his letters in pencil on any available sheet or scrap of paper, then transcribed the letter in pen upon stationery. His filing system was haphazard. His penciled drafts—as well as other correspondence, pictures, and memorabilia—were stored in random locations throughout his home, such as cardboard boxes and drawers. Mrs. Spruance was indispensable in locating and identifying the disorganized mass of family papers. Thanks to her wonderful cooperation, the Spruance papers are now in safekeeping in the Naval Historical Collection at the Naval War College for use by future historians.

The research material used in this biography is identified below.

PRIMARY UNPUBLISHED SOURCES

Author's Collection

This collection primarily contains correspondence and interviews between the author and Spruance's family, friends, and former shipmates. Interviews with Mrs. Spruance spanned the admiral's entire life. In addition, Mrs. Spruance generously loaned the author all the admiral's personal letters to her during World War II, a collection of hundreds of family photographs, and a number of family letters concerning Spruance's ancestry and boyhood years. All the photographs and copies of the letters have been retained in the collection.

The admiral's daughter Margaret (Mrs. Gerard S. Bogart) lives near the author in Middletown, Rhode Island. Numerous and continuing interviews and conversations with Mrs. Bogart provided an unusually perceptive insight into her father's career, personality, and family life.

The author wrote to nearly every living naval officer who had ever served with Spruance ashore or afloat before or during the war. Over one hundred responded, providing an abundance of useful information. The author also interviewed former World War II staff officers Charles J. Moore, Charles F. Barber, Emmet P. Forrestel, Robert J. Oliver, and William H. Buracker; former Naval War College staff officer Thomas H. Robbins, Jr.; former Tenth Naval District staff officers Rufus King and Robert S. Chew; and former Philippine associates Robert M. Cannon, William S. B. Lacy, Edward G. Lansdale, and Ralph B. Lovett.

Mr. Arthur Sproul loaned the author a large number of letters written to him by Spruance following World War II. Copies have been retained.

Dr. Walter Muir Whitehill kindly loaned the author a number of important papers from his files on Fleet Admiral King.

The Author's Collection is in the custody of the Curator, Naval Historical Collection, Naval War College, and is available to qualified scholars upon request.

Naval Historical Collection

Mrs. Spruance donated the bulk of her husband's papers to the Naval Historical Collection (NHC) of the Naval War College. These papers include personal correspondence between Spruance and other flag officers during World War II, penciled drafts of Spruance's postwar correspondence, Spruance's order file for his entire career (naval officers were required to retain every written order they ever received, as well as all endorsements), scrapbooks, hundreds of pictures of his World War II campaigns, and memorabilia such as medals, awards, diplomas, citations, and uniform accessories.

The NHC also holds the Naval War College administrative archives, which includes detailed records of each year's curriculum. These files were the primary source of information for re-creating Spruance's four tours of duty at Newport. They were initially used for the author's monograph, *Admiral Raymond A. Spruance and the Naval War College,* published by the *Naval War College Review* in the spring of 1971.

Another vital source of information at the college is the microfilm records of all World War II naval war diaries, major operation orders, and battle reports. The quality of these records varies with the competence and motivation of the harried World War II officers who wrote them. Chuck Barber was responsible for the Fifth Fleet War Diary, and Carl Moore wanted it to be extremely accurate. Barber's first attempts at recording the events at Tarawa drew severe criticism from Moore. The flag secretary's response typifies the difficulties of writing an accurate record in the heat of battle.

"The following items," wrote Barber, "explain in part inaccuracies which have appeared in the drafts submitted to the Chief of Staff:

"(a) At *no* place are *all* dispatches available to the writers.

"(b) The writers must occasionally guess in order to piece together the fragmentary information. This has been done assuming that inaccuracies, when occurring, would be corrected by officers having a full understanding of events and the reason therefor.

"(c) It has been assumed that it was more important to get a framework to the Chief of Staff than to delay for the time required to check all items to source. Considerable reliance has been placed on briefs prepared by the plotters.

"(d) It has been deemed desirable to get a few reasons into the diary. This has led the writers to record what seemed to them plausible reasons, in the belief that if inaccurate they would be corrected.

"(e) The writers have felt that it was essential to tell a consistent story. This has necessitated, in several instances, selecting one of two or more consistent reports.

"(f) The source material itself contained inaccuracies which have not been apparent to the writers.

"(g) In order to simplify the story, and in accordance with the policy to omit minor tactical matters from the diary, the full story of events has occasionally not been given. Thus in several cases where an order has been cancelled or modified before execution, only the final situation has been noted.

"(h) The diary has been prepared as a part time job by three officers. Each one has assumed that the facts recorded by the others have been in accordance with reports received. No one has had time to do the whole job himself. Since D-Day the Aviation Officer has averaged one hour, the Flag Secretary six hours, and the Plotting Officer four hours each day on this job."

Moore continued to insist upon accurate, well-written war diaries, and the author regarded them as a reliable source of information on the daily thoughts and activities of Spruance and the staff.

Forrestel Collection

Vice Admiral Emmet P. Forrestel, USN (Ret.), devoted several years in the early 1960's to gathering research material for his abbreviated biography of Spruance, in great measure by writing to Spruance or to former Spruance associates. Fortunately for the author, Forrestel's correspondence dated back to the years when important people were still alive and when the memories of all were still intact. Years later, many were either dead or had forgotten too much to be of help to the author. Admiral Forrestel generously loaned his entire correspondence file to the author. A complete copy of this file has been retained in the Author's Collection.

Of greatest value were the many letters from Spruance explaining his decisions and reasoning during the Pacific campaigns. Spruance's letters, however, usually disguised or understated his emotions and personal feelings. For example, his wife and daughter recalled his acute mental distress upon first seeing Pearl Harbor the day after the December seventh attack. His own recollection to Forrestel is entirely different. "I knew the war was on," he wrote, "but it was no great surprise. What was a surprise was the great extent of the damage to the ships and installations inside Pearl Harbor when we entered on the forenoon of 8 December."

Forrestel constantly asked Spruance to reveal his feelings during the most important moments of his career. Spruance never would. He wrote Forrestel that, having won the Battle of Midway, "I was pleased with the success of the operation, but sorry about the aviators we lost. I had enjoyed having the command, and I do not remember being tired." He could have been writing about a peacetime training cruise.

Potter Collection

E. B. Potter is a professor of history at the United States Naval Academy and the co-editor of the naval history textbook *Sea Power*. Professor Potter corresponded with Spruance while preparing his book, prompting the admiral to explain the background of many of his Pacific campaigns. In that Potter was in the business of educating midshipmen, Spruance expressed his feelings about his days at the Academy and about educating naval officers in general. Professor Potter kindly arranged for the author to receive copies of all these letters, which provided a wealth of information. The copies are now in the Author's Collection.

Navy Department Files

There is only fragmentary Spruance material in the Operational Archives of the Naval History Division in Washington. The material includes a handful of useful letters from Spruance to Samuel Eliot Morison and to the Director of Naval History. The magazine *Paris-Match* donated a 1965 taped interview with Spruance, in which he reminisced about the war in the Pacific. (A copy of the transcription is in the NHC.) The only other item of interest is a tape recording of a conversation between Spruance and several of his old friends long after World War II. It was arranged by Carl Moore in hopes of encouraging Spruance to comment about events during the war. Spruance was uncooperative and turned off the tape recorder whenever the subject became the least bit controversial. The only value of this tape is that it reveals Spruance's low-voiced, deliberate way of speaking. (One other taped interview with Spruance, conducted by G. F. McCauley in 1965, is available at the United States Naval Institute in Annapolis. Its only value is its expression of Spruance's political beliefs.)

The official Fifth Fleet files are contained in five cardboard boxes. They are mostly administrative material of little value. The secret and top-secret files are apparently missing.

The Commandant, Tenth Naval District, files are contained in forty-two cardboard boxes. They, too, are largely administrative and of little value.

Spruance's service record was moderately helpful, particularly his fitness reports, which revealed how Spruance fared in the eyes of his superiors. Copies of the fitness reports have been retained in the Author's Collection.

Columbia University Oral History Collection

Under the sponsorship of the Navy Department, Columbia University has acquired the oral histories of a large number of retired naval officers. Spruance steadfastly refused to participate in this program. Among other reasons, he was extremely uncomfortable when speaking into a tape recorder and was never satisfied with what he said or how he said it. The Director of Naval History, Rear Admiral E. M. Eller, USN (Ret.), asked Carl Moore to act as Spruance's alter ego so that some kind of record could be preserved of Spruance's naval career. Moore agreed and became Spruance's Boswell and the Navy's Pepys. His subsequent oral history comprises five volumes totaling 1245 pages. It is articulate, frank, and accurate, spanning Moore's career, his intimate relationship with Spruance, and his view of the Navy in the first fifty years of the twentieth century. It was indispensable to the author.

To a much lesser extent, the author also used the oral histories of Admirals Harry W. Hill, John H. Hoover, Richard L. Conolly, H. Kent Hewitt, and J. J. Clark.

It should be noted in passing that the United States Naval Institute has undertaken an extensive oral history program under Dr. John T. Mason, which will be of great value to naval scholars in the future.

Hoover Institution Collection

Spruance donated a small number of letters to the Hoover Institution on War, Revolution, and Peace at Stanford University. Its most important contents are Spruance's letters to Jeter A. Isely and Philip A. Crowl, authors of *The U.S. Marines and Amphibious War*.

SOURCES

Secondary Published Sources

The books listed below were used in varying degrees by the author. The list is not intended to include all published works which may pertain to the subject matter of this biography. Abbreviations in brackets indicate references in the bibliographical summaries for each chapter, below.

Abueva, José V. *Ramón Magsaysay; A Political Biography*. Manila: Solidaridad Publishing House, 1971. [*Abueva*]

Appleman, Roy E., James M. Burns, Russel A. Gugeler, and John Stevens. *Okinawa: The Last Battle*. The United States Army in World War II. Washington: Department of the Army, 1948. [*Appleman*]

Benjamin, Park. *The United States Naval Academy*. New York: Putnam's, 1900. [*Benjamin*]

Craven, W. F., and J. L. Cate, eds. *The Pacific: Matterhorn to Nagasaki June 1944 to August 1945*. The Army Air Forces in World War II, vol. V. Chicago: University of Chicago Press, 1953. [*Craven*]

Crowl, Philip A. *Campaign in the Marianas*. The United States Army in World War II. Washington: Department of the Army, 1960. [*Crowl*]

————, and Edmund G. Love. *Seizure of the Gilberts and the Marshalls*. The United States Army in World War II. Washington: Department of the Army, 1955. [*Crowl and Love*]

Dyer, George C. *The Amphibians Came to Conquer: The Story of Admiral Richmond Kelly Turner.* Washington: Government Printing Office, 1972. [*Dyer*]

Forrestel, E. P. *Admiral Raymond A. Spruance, USN: A Study in Command.* Washington: Government Printing Office, 1966. [*Forrestel*]

Frank, Benis M., and Henry I. Shaw, Jr. *Victory and Occupation.* History of U.S. Marine Corps Operations in World War II, vol. V. Washington: Government Printing Office, 1968. [*Frank*]

Garand, George W., and Truman R. Strobridge. *Western Pacific Operations.* History of U.S. Marine Corps Operations in World War II, vol. IV. Washington: Government Printing Office, 1971. [*Garand*]

George, Henry. *Progress and Poverty.* Garden City: Garden City Publishing Company, 1926. [*George*]

Halsey, William F., and J. Bryan, III. *Admiral Halsey's Story.* New York: McGraw-Hill, 1947. [*Halsey*]

Hart, Robert A. *The Great White Fleet.* Boston: Little, Brown, 1965. [*Hart*]

Karsten, Peter D. *The Naval Aristocracy: The Golden Age of Annapolis and the Emergence of Modern American Navalism.* New York: Free Press, 1972. [*Karsten*]

King, Ernest J., and Walter M. Whitehill. *Fleet Admiral King: A Naval Record.* New York: Norton, 1952. [*King*]

Lansdale, Edward G. *In the Midst of Wars.* New York: Harper & Row, 1972. [*Lansdale*]

LeMay, Curtis E., and MacKinlay Kantor. *My Story: Mission with LeMay.* Garden City: Doubleday, 1965. [*LeMay*]

Morison, Samuel Eliot. *The Rising Sun in the Pacific: 1931–April 1942.* History of United States Naval Operations in World War II, vol. III. Boston: Atlantic-Little, Brown, 1948. [*Morison III*]

———. *Coral Sea, Midway and Submarine Actions: May 1942–August 1942.* History of United States Naval Operations in World War II, vol. IV. Boston: Atlantic-Little, Brown, 1950. [*Morison IV*]

———. *Aleutians, Gilberts, and Marshalls: June 1942–April 1944.* History of United States Naval Operations in World War II, vol. VII. Boston: Atlantic-Little, Brown, 1951. [*Morison VII*]

———. *New Guinea and the Marianas: March 1944–August 1944.* History of United States Naval Operations in World War II, vol. VIII. Boston: Atlantic-Little, Brown, 1953. [*Morison VIII*]

———. *Victory in the Pacific.* History of United States Naval Operations in World War II, vol. XIV. Boston: Atlantic-Little, Brown, 1960. [*Morison XIV*]

Potter, E. B., and C. W. Nimitz, eds. *Sea Power.* Englewood Cliffs: Prentice-Hall, 1960. [*Potter*]

Shaw, Henry I., Jr., Bernard C. Nalty, and Edwin T. Turnbladh. *Central*

Pacific Drive. History of U.S. Marine Corps Operations in World War II, vol. III. Washington: Government Printing Office, 1966. [*Shaw*]

Smith, Holland M., and Percy Finch. *Coral and Brass*. New York: Scribner's, 1949. [*Smith*]

Taylor, Theodore. *The Magnificent Mitscher*. New York: Norton, 1954. [*Taylor*]

U.S. Congress. House Committee on Armed Services. *The National Defense Program—Unification and Strategy*. Hearings before the Committee on Armed Services, House of Representatives, 81st Cong., 1st sess., 1949. [*HASC*]

U.S. Naval Academy. *Regulations of the United States Naval Academy: Interior Discipline and Government*. Washington: Government Printing Office, 1907. [*Regulations*]

U.S. Navy Department. *Annual Reports of the Navy Department* (Various years from 1900 to 1940). Washington: Government Printing Office, various years. [*SECNAV Reports*]

Secondary Unpublished Sources

Barde, Robert E. "The Battle of Midway: A Study in Command." Unpublished Ph.D. dissertation, University of Maryland, 1971. [*Barde*]

Snow, Hugh B., Jr. "United States Policy and the 1953 Philippines Presidential Election." Unpublished M.A. thesis, The American University, 1968. [*Snow*]

U.S. Naval Academy. "Lucky Bag 1907." U.S. Naval Academy Yearbook. [*Lucky Bag*]

U.S. Naval War College. "The Battle of Midway Including the Aleutian Phase: June 3 to June 14, 1942." Unpublished strategical and tactical analysis, Naval War College, 1948. [*Midway Study*]

BIBLIOGRAPHICAL NOTES

Chapter 1: Heritage

SPRUANCE was much aware of his genealogy through his mother and his aunts. His papers contain records and correspondence concerning both his paternal and maternal ancestors. The author reconstructed the Ames family tree by using Annie Spruance's application for membership in the D.A.R. and her brother's application for membership in the S.A.R. An undated, unsigned document entitled "Family record," written in a feminine hand by someone who apparently knew the Ames history, supplemented the membership applications. Typed excerpts from *Cyclopaedia of Methodism* and *Methodist Bishops* yielded important information about Bishop Edward Raymond Ames, the most illustrious member of the clan. Spruance's interest in the bishop was described by both his wife and his daughter.

Bessie Hiss wrote an undated, unsigned four-page history of the Hiss family and drew her family tree, which the author used to reconstruct the background of Spruance's maternal grandfather.

Spruance's paternal ancestors are less well documented. A forty-year-old Delaware newspaper clipping told of the Spruance ancestral home in Smyrna, Delaware, and gave a résumé of the family history in that community. A copy of the will of John Spruance, the family progenitor, established that the Spruances first settled in Delaware in the mid-eighteenth century. Two letters from family cousins also provided some family information.

The author visited Smyrna in the spring of 1972 in what proved to be an unsuccessful search for more facts. Spruances no longer live in the sleepy, isolated rural town, although a few older residents remembered the name and recalled some of the admiral's relatives. No one questioned by the author had ever heard of the admiral himself.

Bessie Hiss, a self-appointed family historian, wrote a voluminous letter to young Margaret in 1950, in order to explain why Annie Spruance had abandoned Raymond as a boy. In it, Bessie related Annie's childhood and marriage, Raymond's boyhood, and the relationship between Raymond and his parents. Bessie also had written an earlier letter in 1944—when Spruance was promoted to admiral—which recalled how he had acquired his appointment to the Naval Academy. Mrs. Spruance and Mrs. Bogart provided additional information about Spruance's early years.

Mrs. Spruance also loaned the author several letters written by Spruance as a boy, which apparently had been retained by Bessie Hiss. Only one boyhood poem has survived, and through it one can sense young Raymond's sensitivity and imagination.

A fringe of black comes o'er the northern sky;
It grows and deepens till at last the sun
grows dim and disappears. The frightened cry
Of birds is heard that would the tempest shun.

The gloomy vault above grows blacker yet,
And all except the faintly rustling trees
Is quiet now. The dark clouds' fiery pet
The lightning silent plays about their knees.

But hark! The storm approaches and the rain
In the far distance may be seen. A sound
Of rushing wind, a thunderclap contain
A warning to be off the tempest's ground.

Spruance wrote and said little about his midshipman days, other than comments in letters to Potter and to Morison. He congratulated Morison on the biography of John Paul Jones and recalled his own participation in Jones's interment ceremony at the Naval Academy in

1906. Spruance also recounted his summer midshipman cruises in the same letter. His wife and daughter confirmed the admiral's personal feelings about the Academy.

Benjamin provided an assessment of the Academy at the turn of the century. *Potter* reviewed the status of the Navy in general during the same period. An analysis of the 1900-era Navy, naval officers, and midshipmen that was critical yet credible was contained in *Karsten.* *SECNAV Reports, Regulations,* and the Naval Academy "Register of Alumni" were useful, as well.

In that Spruance's personal experiences were largely unknown, the author turned to other accounts of the Naval Academy in the early 1900's and inferred that Spruance lived essentially the same life as that recorded and remembered by his contemporaries. *Lucky Bag* was the starting point in discovering the fortunes of the Class of 1907. The oral histories of Carl Moore, H. Kent Hewitt, and John H. Hoover recounted their midshipman days. Captain Rufus King and Admiral Hewitt (both classmates of Spruance) provided oral accounts to the author of their midshipman experiences. *King, Halsey,* and the autobiography of Harold G. Bowen were helpful.

Midshipman Ernest J. Small published an article, "The U.S. Naval Academy: An Undergraduate's Point of View," in the December 1912 issue of the *U.S. Naval Institute Proceedings.* It provided a critical analysis of the defects of the Academy curriculum.

The Branch-Meriwether scandal was well publicized in the New York *Times.* The midshipmen's view was expressed in *Lucky Bag* and orally to the author by King and Hewitt. Curiously, the scandal was not mentioned in the many Columbia University oral histories read by the author. Perhaps it was too painful a memory for those that survived it.

Chapter 2: The Apprentice

The status of the Navy when Spruance was a junior officer was derived from *Potter,* and *SECNAV Reports.* Statistics on ships in this and all subsequent chapters are contained in the appropriate editions of *Jane's Fighting Ships. Hart* describes the cruise of the Great White Fleet, and Spruance's scrapbook reflects his activities during that cruise. Spruance's experiences with Bill Rush and the *Connecticut* are recorded in memoranda in Spruance's order file. The order file and his service record provided details of duty on *Iowa, Cincinnati,* and at the General Electric plant. His command of the *Bainbridge* is vividly described in

Moore's oral history, and in letters from Moore and Haxton to Forrestel. Mrs. Spruance related their courtship in conversations with the author.

Chapter 3: Marriage

This chapter is based almost entirely upon conversations with Mrs. Spruance and Mrs. Bogart. Spruance's political, social, and economic beliefs are largely expressed in postwar letters to Arthur Sproul and in the McCauley tape, although these same concepts often were reflected in his World War II letters to Mrs. Spruance. Letters from former shipmates and from Edward often commented upon Spruance's reactionary conservatism. As expected, many of Spruance's beliefs closely resembled the theories espoused in *George*. His catholic intellectual interests are best summarized in his commencement address at Worcester Polytechnic Institute in June 1948.

Chapter 4: Peace

The general description of the Navy during the 1920's was derived from *Potter, SECNAV Reports,* from a research paper by Captain Robert J. Oliver, USN (Ret.), and from the Columbia University oral histories. *Halsey* describes the activities of Destroyer Division 32 in San Diego during the early 1920's. Mrs. Spruance recounted the social life ashore.

Duty in Washington and with Vice Admiral Philip Andrews in the Mediterranean is from Mrs. Spruance. Former shipmates wrote about Spruance's performance as commanding officer of *Dale* and *Osborne*.

The 1926–1927 Naval War College period is based upon the author's 1971 monograph, the research material having been obtained from the college archives and from letters from former staff and students. Duty at ONI was described by Mrs. Spruance, Mrs. Bogart, and in a letter from Edward Spruance to Forrestel. Spruance's duty on *Mississippi* is largely from letters from former shipmates to the author.

Chapter 5: Prelude to War

Spruance's duty at the Naval War College in the 1930's was extracted from the author's 1971 monograph, and from the author's article on Admiral Kalbfus and his *Sound Military Decision,* published in the *Naval War College Review,* May–June 1973. Of particular value was the author's interview with the late Rear Admiral Thomas H. Robbins,

Jr., USN (Ret.), who served on the War College staff in the late 1930's and as college president in the mid-1950's.

Command of the *Mississippi* and duty on Admiral Watson's staff is largely from letters from shipmates to the author. The activities of the fleet are again based upon *SECNAV Reports* and the Columbia University oral histories. Duty as Commandant, Tenth Naval District, is described in letters from retired naval civil engineer officers, in official district records for 1940–1941, and in interviews with former staff officers Robert Chew and Rufus King. Mrs. Spruance and Mrs. Bogart provided data on Spruance's personal life during this period.

Chapter 6: Cruiser Division Commander

Spruance's trip to Pearl Harbor and his premonitions about war are from Mrs. Spruance and Mrs. Bogart. His misconception about Japanese torpedoes is from a Spruance letter to Forrestel. The general status of the fleet in the last days of peace is described in *Halsey, Morison III,* and a 1960 lecture by Admiral Nimitz at the Naval War College. The relationship between Spruance and his staff is related in a letter from Victor D. Long to the author. The activities of Cruiser Division 5 are in the Naval War College World War II microfilm records (*NWC mf*).

Chapter 7: War Begins

Mrs. Spruance and Mrs. Bogart described Spruance's emotional reaction to the Pearl Harbor attack. Spruance's activities at sea are from letters from Long and W. M. McCormick to the author. *Halsey* describes the initial actions of Task Force 8. Spruance recalled his reactions to the first month of war in a letter to Forrestel. *Morison III* describes the American strategy in the early part of the war. Spruance's planning considerations for the Wotje raid are especially well summarized in his post-action report to Halsey dated 5 February 1942, *NWC mf*. Long and *Halsey* also described the Wotje planning.

Chapter 8: The Marshalls Raid

The Wotje raid narrative is from Spruance's post-action report, supplemented with personal observations in the Long and McCormick letters. *Halsey* describes the withdrawal and the return to Pearl Harbor. Spruance's emotional malaise afterwards is described in a letter from Oliver to the author.

Chapter 9: More Raids

Oliver described Spruance's behavior during and after the Wake raid in a letter to the author. Details of the Wake attack are from various post-action reports in *NWC mf,* from *Halsey* and Long, and in a letter from Spruance to Forrestel. Spruance's bravery in battle has been described by many people: Long, McCormick, Oliver, and members of his Fifth Fleet staff. Mrs. Spruance and Mrs. Bogart confirmed his fatalism. Spruance's personal feelings on bravery were described in a letter to Potter and in a letter from G. M. Slonim (Spruance's Japanese language officer) to Forrestel. (The author suspects that Spruance valued his schnauzers because of their fearlessness and fighting spirit.)

Spruance became critical of the raids, especially the Doolittle Tokyo raid, because they did not have military value. His feelings were expressed in a Spruance letter to Forrestel and in a conversation with Oliver by the author.

Chapter 10: Midway Preliminaries

Halsey's physical distress and his determination to pass command to Spruance were recounted by William H. Buracker (operations officer to Halsey and Spruance) during an interview by the author. Spruance's personal activities are in letters from Oliver to the author and from Spruance to Forrestel.

The assessment of Browning is primarily from Buracker; letters from former Halsey staff officers H. D. Moulton and W. H. Ashford; a letter to the author from Admiral Walter F. Boone; the oral history of Admiral J. J. Clark; and from the memorandum of a conversation between Fleet Admiral King and his biographer, Walter M. Whitehill.

Chapter 11: The Battle of Midway

The author, with few exceptions, did not refer to the numerous secondary published sources on the Battle of Midway. The emphasis of this chapter concerned the activities of Spruance and his staff on *Enterprise,* a subject that has not been adequately treated heretofore. Thus the author relied largely upon unpublished primary sources.

Spruance's version of the battle was first expressed in a personal letter to Nimitz dated 8 June 1942. He sent an amplifying report to Nimitz on 16 June 1942. Copies of both letters are in the NHC.

Another extensive summary is contained in a Spruance letter to

Another extensive summary is contained in a Spruance letter to Forrestel dated 14 December 1962, and he sent Forrestel several supplementary letters, as well. Newsmen frequently interviewed the admiral on major anniversaries of the battle, and his published comments generally corroborate his written reports. Spruance enjoyed talking about the battle with anyone who was interested, but Walter Lord was apparently the only other person (other than reporters) who ever took notes, which he generously made available to the author.

Midway Study is an excellent record of the battle based upon hundreds of messages, reports, logs, and orders, which would have been impossible for the author to assemble and analyze in the time available. The author did, however, refer extensively to the war diaries and battle reports of the *Enterprise* and *Hornet,* contained in *NWC mf,* because these two ships were most directly involved with Spruance and the staff. Although Spruance later said that the *Hornet* report was not historically accurate, it nevertheless contained a personal narrative by the *Hornet* operations officer that clearly revealed how the Spruance staff performed in the eyes of those on adjacent ships.

Barde was another important source, for it is scholarly, well-documented, and extensively researched. It contains considerable material, particularly personal accounts of the battle, which has never been mentioned in the better-known published versions. A copy has been retained in the Naval War College Library, thanks to the cooperation of Doctor Barde.

Robert J. Oliver, Spruance's flag lieutenant, provided the comprehensive view of Spruance and the staff at Midway. His firsthand accounts were always fascinating and often startling, for they frequently conflicted with the commonly accepted versions of the activities on the flag bridge. The author was initially skeptical and exhaustively checked every facet of Oliver's narrative. He unequivocally concluded that Oliver had been extremely accurate and scrupulously objective throughout, both in his letters and in his conversations with the author. The former flag lieutenant's version of the battle has never before been published, because no other Midway author has ever interviewed him.

The reasoning behind Spruance's decision to launch at 0700 on June fourth has been inaccurately recorded in previous published works. Nearly all have stated that Spruance intended to close to 100 miles and launch at 0900, but that Browning convinced him to launch "early" at

0700 in order to catch the enemy carriers recovering from their first strike. *The source of this version has never been disclosed in any of the published works on Midway,* and for this reason alone its credibility is questionable.

What, then, has Spruance said about his decision to launch at 0700? "I wanted to hit the Japanese carriers as early as possible with all the air strength we had available for this purpose," he wrote Forrestel. Once he knew where the enemy was, "I speeded up to 25 knots and made preparations to launch aircraft when we got within striking distance." Striking distance was generally regarded at 150 to 175 miles. Nowhere has Spruance suggested in writing that he intended to close to 100 miles, only to change his mind because of Browning.

Spruance once explained Browning's role in determining launch time in a 1966 interview with Walter Lord, who was gathering material for *Incredible Victory.* "There was no argument or discussion about when to launch," Lord recorded immediately after the interview. "Spruance not for holding out longer. He wanted planes to go as soon as possible and told Browning to attend to it. Up to Browning to decide the exact time—that was his business—but Spruance all for anything he decided, as long as it was as soon as possible. The key to everything was *surprise* . . . to hit the Japs before they discovered the U.S. forces. This meant hit them the earliest possible moment we were within range. It became all the more important when we monitored the Jap call for a second strike."

In all fairness to Walter Lord, it must be noted that his version of the 0700 decision in *Incredible Victory* does not correspond to his written notes of the interview. The author asked him why. For the record, excerpts of his reply are quoted below.

"As for your question," wrote Lord in June 1973, "I didn't mean to imply that Spruance 'intended' to launch at 0900 when I said that this was 'originally his own inclination.' I was trying to connote something less strong than intention, or even taking any firm position on the matter.

"Seven years is a long time, but as I recall our conversation, Spruance did say that he had originally leaned towards a 0900 launching, but as soon as Miles Browning came up with 0700, he went right along with it. His main point was that there was absolutely no argument or discussion about it as indicated by Morison, Tuleja, Forrestel, and most of the other writers on Midway."

Lord also mentioned in his letter that former staff officer Bromfield

Nichol had written him that "Spruance suggested that launching be delayed until we could run in closer . . ." and that "the Admiral had the good judgment to take the advice of others." The author regards Nichol's account as being inconsistent with the overwhelming evidence.

In summary, it is clear that Spruance indeed intended to launch at the earliest possible moment. In that Spruance told Browning to "launch the attack" shortly after 0600 (as reported by Oliver), it is not logical that Spruance would then decide to wait *three hours* (until 0900) and take the unacceptable risk of the Japanese hitting him first.

One may ask why Spruance never denied the erroneous published accounts. The reason is simple: Spruance avoided controversies. He had many serious problems with Browning and the rest of Halsey's staff, which he would never reveal or discuss. He preferred praise to criticism. He was content to let history record that he was in command of the two American carriers, that he made the final decisions, and that the Americans won the Battle of Midway.

The accurate reconstruction of what was said on the radio during the interval between the 0700 launch and McClusky's attack is difficult to ascertain. All the participants were under extreme tension, and voice radios worked erratically. Nervous listeners may have heard only parts of messages, or the words may have been distorted in transmission. Some messages were transmitted and never heard, or if heard, never acknowledged. Thus beginneth the "fog of war."

It seems certain that Gray made the two transmissions about low fuel and sighting the enemy. (*Midway Study,* page 128; *Morison IV,* page 122; and *Hornet* battle report.) Morison seems to have good sources in stating that Browning shouted, "Attack," and that McClusky responded (*Morison IV,* page 122). In a letter to the author in November 1971, Buracker told of the sense of relief when they heard McClusky's "tallyho," although no other authoritative source contains any record of receiving McClusky's report. But Spruance and the staff certainly must have heard McClusky's radioed directions to his other aircraft, assigning targets.

There were published reports that Lieutenant Commander John C. Waldron, the heroic skipper of Torpedo Squadron 8, had sighted the Japanese force but was low on fuel and had requested permission to return and refuel before attacking. The story goes that Spruance denied this permission and ordered the suicidal attack, thereby establishing

Spruance's cold, ruthless character. This story is wholly without foundation, for there is no evidence that Waldron made any such request.

A number of other significant events have been addressed in the text that were not emphasized—and in some cases not mentioned—in earlier published works. The difficulties with Point Option on 4 June were first brought up in a letter from Admiral Boone to the author. Boone had been aboard *Enterprise* as her prospective executive officer. "It was generally understood," he wrote in late 1971, "that Browning was responsible for a grave error in judgment in setting the course and speed of 'Point Option' for the air operations on 4 June. As a result, the task group was many miles east of Point Option when our planes returned from their strikes far to the northwest. Quite a number of pilots ran out of fuel in trying to locate their parent carriers and had to make water landings. The loss of so many planes in this manner must have shaken Admiral Spruance considerably. . . ."

The *Hornet* battle report and *Midway Study* revealed the details of the Point Option fiasco.

The uncoordinated second launch on the afternoon of 4 June was reconstructed from the *Hornet* battle report and *Midway Study*. It became clear to the author that the Halsey staff had not been equal to the task. This evaluation will be hotly disputed, but the circumstantial evidence is overwhelming.

Throughout the war, Halsey's staff reflected his personality and style of leadership. Halsey was a poor administrator and a sloppy planner. He made war boldly and aggressively, but all too often on impulse. His subordinate commanders rarely knew what to expect or what was expected of them until the last moment. It followed that Halsey needed a chief of staff who could exert a stabilizing influence and could translate Halsey's imaginative schemes into orderly plans. Browning could not provide this need. Buracker told the author that Browning drove the staff to utter distraction by his irascible behavior. When Oliver came aboard *Enterprise* just before the battle, he found that Halsey's files and administrative procedures were in chaos. Thus it is reasonable to assume that the staff, poorly led and poorly organized by Browning, was the principal cause for the foul-up of Point Option in the morning and the confused signals and haphazard second launch in the afternoon.

Browning's decline began in the Battle of Midway. He later was fired as Halsey's chief of staff when it became apparent he could not handle the demands of the South Pacific theater (after Halsey had replaced Ghormley). He eventually got command of a new carrier; he failed and was soon replaced.

One might ask whether Spruance was responsible for the confusion on the fourth. The answer is possibly but not probably. By nature he remained aloof from the execution of the detailed plans, once he had made his major decisions. The responsibility for implementing a naval commander's decision has traditionally rested with the chief of staff and the staff officers. Buracker has stated time and again that Spruance left all details of task force operations to the staff. Initially Spruance had reason to believe the staff was competent to do their duty. He did not want to do their work for them. When they stumbled and fell, he could only grit his teeth and hope for the best.

The Browning-McClusky argument on the afternoon of 5 June (about bomb loads and launch times) was first mentioned by Oliver. McClusky confirmed the incident in a letter to the author, and it was further substantiated by *Barde,* who quoted letters from McClusky and the staff intelligence officer, Marine Colonel Julian P. Brown.

The inimical relationship between Spruance and Browning is from both Buracker and Oliver.

Chapter 12: Chief of Staff

Spruance's duties and routine as chief of staff are largely contained in letters to his wife, in the 1956 *Paris-Match* interview, in letters from former Nimitz staff officers to the author, and in letters from Spruance to Potter. The March 1943 conference with the JCS in Washington is extracted from the minutes of the meeting. Spruance's participation in planning for the Gilberts-Marshalls campaign is contained in his letter to Isely.

Chapter 13: Planning for the Gilberts

The activities of the staff are derived from the Moore oral history and from interviews with Barber and Forrestel. The background for substituting Makin for Nauru is contained in a Spruance letter to the Director of Naval History and in *Smith.* Moore's oral history describes the heated exchange between Nimitz and King that Moore had provoked.

The debates on the use of carriers came from many sources: a letter from Spruance to all flag officers dated 29 October 1943 and his

Gilberts Operation Order (*NWC mf*); the *Match* interview; a Spruance letter to Forrestel; the author's conversation with Admiral Radford; and *Dyer*. Several naval writers have quoted extensively from the Towers diary for their version of the debate. The author's judgment is that the diary does not accurately reflect the real issues between Spruance and the aviators. For example, it time and again put words in Spruance's mouth that Spruance would never have said. The only conclusion that one can confidently draw from the diary is that Spruance and Towers frequently argued.

The comparison between the operation orders of Spruance and Halsey was derived from a letter to the author from Admiral Boone, from conversations with Admirals Radford and T. H. Robbins, Jr., and from Potter's article, "Command Personality," *U.S. Naval Institute Proceedings,* January 1969.

The question of logistical support has perhaps been too briefly addressed in the text. The author does not intend to slight its importance. For a thorough treatment of the subject, the reader is referred to Chapter VI of *Morison VII*. One of the greatest logistics practitioners of the Pacific was Commodore Worrall R. (Nick) Carter; his experiences are recorded in *Beans, Bullets, and Black Oil* (Washington: Government Printing Office, 1953).

Chapter 14: The Gilberts

The primary sources were the Fifth Fleet War Diary (*NWC mf*), the Moore oral history, and the author's interview with Barber. Other sources included the Harry W. Hill oral history, letters from Barber to his parents, and letters from Hill and Turner to Spruance in the NHC. Spruance's feelings about the enemy are from Moore, Mrs. Spruance, and Mrs. Bogart.

The Navy has no official history of World War II; Samuel Eliot Morison is the author of the "unofficial" history and addresses the Gilberts in *Morison VII*. The Marine Corps official history of the Gilberts campaign is contained in *Shaw*. The Army official history is in *Crowl and Love*. The Army historians on page 126 commented upon Holland Smith's criticism of the 27th Infantry Division's performance on Makin. "Considering the size of the atoll," they wrote, "the nature of the enemy's defenses, and the great superiority of force enjoyed by the attacking troops, [Smith's] criticism seems justified. It is all the more so when to the cost of tardiness is added the loss of a valuable escort aircraft carrier [*Liscome Bay*] with more than half the hands aboard."

Chapter 15: Planning for the Marshalls

The controversy over the selection of objectives is contained in *Dyer;* the *Match* interview; a letter from Spruance to Isely; the Moore oral history; Potter's article "Command Personality"; and the memorandum of a 1961 conversation between Admiral Nimitz and Rear Admiral H. E. Eccles of the Naval War College. The Fifth Fleet War Diary for December 1943 reflected the planning tempo.

Spruance's theories on amphibious warfare were expressed in the Admiral's 1948 address before the Amphibious Warfare School at Quantico. The Army's land warfare tactics were discussed in *Morison VII,* page 298, and the Moore oral history. Spruance's dislike of the methodical Army tactics on Makin are revealed in the *Match* interview. His opinion of Air Force bombing tactics is most cogently expressed in a 1950 letter to Isely.

The arguments between Spruance and Towers, concerning carrier warfare tactics, continued during the planning for the Marshalls. Clark Reynolds, in his book *The Fast Carriers,* pages 123–124, cites Towers's diary to assert that Spruance believed that the carriers were in danger of attack from the Japanese fleet at Truk, and that Spruance "feared the loss or damage to his carriers if they were committed too early in the operation." Clark also uses the diary to claim that Spruance was equally reluctant to release the fast battleships for shore fire bombardment, because he was "fearful that they would be needed to defend the carriers against enemy air or surface-ship attacks."

The Towers diary is, one suspects, self-serving nonsense. The facts are these. Spruance did not fear any attack from the Japanese fleet at Truk. (Spruance to Isely, 3 July 1949; and Spruance's Marshalls Operation Order.) Spruance demanded that the carriers attack the Marshalls air bases well in advance of the amphibious forces and to maintain continuous air cover thereafter. (Spruance to Director of Naval History, 25 April 1966.) Indeed, the CINCPAC staff, with Towers calling the shots, was reluctant to provide that continuous air cover. (Spruance to Director of Marine Corps History, 10 September 1962; and Spruance to Potter, 4 January 1959). Furthermore Spruance always *had* wanted the fast battleships to bombard the airfields (Spruance to Director of Naval History, 25

April 1966; and Spruance to Rear Admiral E. G. Small, 8 January 1944, NHC); he needed no urging from Towers in this respect.

Chapter 16: The Marshalls

The Fifth Fleet War Diary, Moore's oral history, and the author's interview with Barber provided most of the data for this chapter. Spruance's letters to Margaret are obvious sources in every chapter and will not be repeated in subsequent chapter notes.

For further details on the Marshalls campaign, the reader is referred to *Morison VII, Shaw,* and *Crowl and Love.*

Chapter 17: Marianas Preliminaries

This chapter is largely based upon the Fifth Fleet War Diary and the Moore oral history. The best source for the background to the Marianas planning is *King,* pages 532–537, and *Crowl,* Chapter I. Mrs. Spruance and Mrs. Bogart described the admiral's vacation in Monrovia.

Chapter 18: Battle of the Philippine Sea

The Fifth Fleet War Diary and the Moore oral history reflected the battle as seen by Spruance and the staff at the time. Spruance's practice of trying to think like his enemy was described in conversations between the author and Barber, and in a letter from the admiral's son-in-law to the author. Another view by a staff member is expressed in G. M. Slonim's article, "A Flagship View of Command Decision," *U.S. Naval Institute Proceedings,* April 1958.

Spruance wrote about the battle in letters too numerous to mention, beginning with his official report to Nimitz dated 4 July 1944. All subsequent letters say essentially the same thing. He also discussed the battle in the *Match* interview.

Mitscher's official report of the battle (*NWC mf*) expressed his side of the story, as well as several details omitted in the Fifth Fleet War Diary.

A popular topic of debate concerns the origin of the order to turn on the lights on the night of 20 June. Admiral Arleigh A. Burke (former chief of staff to Mitscher) wrote the author that Mitscher authorized the lights before the attack was launched, and that Spruance did not object. The *Indianapolis* OOD told the author he distinctly remembers hearing Spruance's voice on the TBS after dark ordering Mitscher to "turn on the lights." (Interview with R. K. Joslin, 5 February 1972.) Rear Admiral J. J. (Jocko) Clark, commanding a carrier task group within Task Force 58, claims (page 173 of his book *Carrier Admiral*) that he turned on his lights on his own initiative and that the remainder of Task Force 58 followed his example.

For those readers desiring to read further about this battle, the author suggests Chapters XIV through XVI of *Morison VIII*.

Chapter 19: The Marianas Campaign

The Fifth Fleet War Diary and the Moore oral history were again the primary sources.

A number of books have addressed the Smith-Smith controversy: *Crowl*, Chapter X; *Shaw*, pages 317–319; *Smith*, pages 171–180; and *Dyer*, pages 925–930. The Moore oral history was used by the author, as well. An Army historian told the author that he was shocked that Turner had ignored Moore's pleas not to chastise General Richardson. In the Army, said the historian, the word of the chief of staff is law, and no one would dare to disobey. Even though the chief of staff may be junior, he speaks for the commander. The historian therefore felt that Moore should have ordered, not asked, Turner to lay off Richardson.

The relationship between Spruance, Turner, and Moore was obviously different. The three were friends of long years' standing—rank and position were meaningless. Turner did as he pleased, whether Moore approved or not.

The showdown with Turner over the selection of the Tinian landing beaches was recounted in Hill's oral history.

For additional details on the Marianas campaign, the reader is referred to *Crowl*, *Shaw*, and *Morison VIII*.

Chapter 20:
Planning for Okinawa and Iwo Jima

Spruance's reasoning for advocating the seizure of Iwo Jima and Okinawa is contained in his address before the Royal United Service Institution in London, 30 October 1946, and in letters to Isely and Forrestel. The San Francisco meeting which deleted Formosa is described in the *Match* interview, in a Spruance letter to Forrestel, and in *Appleman*. Mrs. Spruance and Mrs. Bogart recalled the admiral's social activities in the United States during this period.

The author could no longer use Moore's oral history for Spruance's daily activities, for Moore had been relieved and had returned to the States. As substitutes the author used conversations with Barber and Forrestel; Spruance's letters to his wife and to Carl Moore; a letter from Cy Huie to the author; and a letter from Davis to Forrestel.

The debate over the length of the prelanding bombardment on Iwo Jima is described in *Dyer, Smith, Garand,* and in Spruance's letters to Isely. Spruance's unhappiness with the Air Force bombing of Iwo Jima is from a letter to Isely. See also *Morison XIV,* pages 10–13.

The strategic bombing of Japanese aircraft production plants is discussed in a 30 November 1944 letter from Spruance to Admiral Hoover, and a 1950 letter from Spruance to Isely. The Air Force problems with the B-29 bombers over Japan are from *Craven,* pages 553–568, and *LeMay,* pages 342–347.

Chapter 21: Iwo Jima

Spruance's meeting with LeMay is from the *Match* interview and a Spruance letter to Forrestel. The "press conference" is described in Spruance's letters to his wife and to Carl Moore. Turner's illness is mentioned by *Dyer* and in the Hill oral history.

The Tokyo raids are extracted from official reports by Spruance and Mitscher, supplemented by the *Match* interview, letters to Margaret, and a letter from Barber to his parents.

The Iwo Jima assault is based largely upon the Fifth Fleet War Diary, supplemented with letters to Margaret.

Spruance's soliloquy on personal publicity is contained in a letter to Forrestel from a close friend who was with Spruance aboard *Indianapolis.* He has asked to remain anonymous.

The Air Force decision to begin fire raids against Japan is covered in *Craven,* pages 608–627, and in *LeMay,* pages 347–354. Spruance's justification for seizing Iwo Jima for use as a B-29 base is expressed in a 1963 letter to Forrestel.

For additional details on the Iwo Jima assault, the reader is referred to *Morison XIV* and *Garand.*

Chapter 22: Okinawa

The primary sources were the Fifth Fleet War Diary and the *Match* interview. Barber and Huie described the kamikaze attacks on *Indianapolis* and *New Mexico.* Barber provided many details of the daily activities of the staff.

The relations between the Navy and the Air Force in efforts to attenuate the kamikaze threat are from *Craven*, pages 632–635; *LeMay*, pages 370–372; and *Halsey*, page 253.

Additional details on the Okinawa campaign are contained in *Morison XIV*, *Appleman*, and *Frank*.

Chapter 23: Victory and Occupation

Spruance's reasoning for invading China and bypassing Japan is from a 1964 letter to Forrestel and from the *Match* interview. The activities of Spruance and the staff on Guam are from the Barber interview and a letter from Huie to the author. Spruance's reaction to the news that the war was over is described in a letter from Edward Spruance to Forrestel.

Spruance's admiration of MacArthur and his later support for MacArthur's policy in the Korean War is contained in a 1964 letter to Forrestel.

The occupation of Japan is covered in the Fifth Fleet War Diary, conversations with Barber, in a letter from Huie to the author, and in Spruance's letters to Margaret.

Chapter 24: President, Naval War College

The archives of the Naval War College were the primary source of research material. Spruance's views on communism and the Soviet Union are contained in his letter to Professor Vincent Davis, formerly of the Naval War College. Spruance's theories on the intellect of naval officers are expressed in his letters to Potter.

Spruance's concepts on future wars are revealed in *HASC* and in a 1947 address before the National War College.

The Navy Department's treatment of Spruance as he approached retirement is from an interview with John Nicholas Brown.

Mrs. Spruance and Mrs. Bogart recounted the admiral's personal life during this period.

Chapter 25: Ambassador to the Philippines

The logical place to seek research material for this chapter was the files of the State Department. The author therefore asked for permission to read these files. The Department replied that the approximate volume of the 1953–1955 correspondence between the Department and the Philippine Embassy is sixty cubic feet. These and all Department files from approximately 1947 on are not open for unofficial research.

The Department asked the author if he could limit his area of interest by identifying specific subject categories. This procedure would allow the Department's research specialists to identify appropriate documents which then would be perused by the Department's "substantive people" to determine whether the documents could be released to the author. Given these restrictions, the author decided to limit the scope of this chapter to the 1953 Philippine national elections.

The Department subsequently located 190 documents pertaining to the elections, but only 97 were made available to the author. The remaining 93 have been withheld. The material released to the author is difficult to evaluate because it is incomplete. It gives only a very limited picture of the total correspondence that passed between Washington and Manila on this subject. None of these selected documents imply any deviation from the Dulles policy statement of 14 March 1953. Nevertheless, the degree of the Department's involvement in the elections cannot be ascertained until all the pertinent documents are made available to the public.

The search for other information began with *Snow,* an excellent work that drew upon all unclassified sources available through 1967. It provided a summary and an analysis of the election campaign that was invaluable, and Mr. Snow kindly loaned his thesis to the author. A copy has been retained in the Author's Collection. *Abueva* provided a recent assessment of Magsaysay that was published after Snow's paper.

The only published accounts of the CIA activities in the Philippines (that the author is aware of) are contained in *Lansdale,* Chapters 8 and 9, which is limited to the work of Lansdale alone; and in Halberstam's *The Best and the Brightest,* which describes many of Lansdale's CIA exploits. The author interviewed both General Lovett and General Lansdale, and they provided additional information on the role of the CIA during the 1953 elections. They also confirmed that Spruance was well informed of the Philippine CIA operations.

Ambassador Lacy discussed the role of the embassy during the elections in an interview with the author. General Cannon recalled the tense atmosphere of the election campaign and the deployment of his Military Advisory Group on election day.

Spruance's personal assessments of the political, economic, and social situation in the Philippines are contained in letters to Mrs. Bogart, Arthur Sproul, and Bessie Hiss. Spruance explained his primary role during the elections in several 1964 letters to Forrestel, which emphasized the activities of Lansdale; his own close, personal relationship with Magsaysay; and his own determination to ensure free and honest elections. A 4 September 1964 letter to Forrestel was especially revealing.

"I am not surprised," he wrote, " that the Far Eastern people in the State Department do not wish to have made public what went on in the Philippines during the 1953 election out there. I think most of the Filipinos had a pretty good idea of what went on to ensure an honest election that year, but the Embassy did everything possible to leave no fingerprints about. In fact, I am surprised that anything that would have compromised us ever went in the mails to the State Department. I had made a quick trip to Washington shortly before the election, had seen the President, Secretary Dulles, Assistant Secretary Walter Robertson, and Allen Dulles, all of whom were generally familiar with the situation out there. [The White House appointment book noted that Spruance met with the President for 15 minutes on the morning of 14 October 1953. The subject was the Philippine political campaign.] I know that President Quirino knew what was going on, but he could not pin anything on us, although he tried to do so."

Spruance made another revealing statement in an April 1967 letter to Snow. "Personally," he wrote, "I have always been rather proud of the way things were handled in that 1953 election."

There is no question that Spruance was admired and respected by the career Foreign Service officers on the embassy staff. "Ambassador Spruance, a quiet person by nature," wrote one associate to Forrestel, "listened, absorbed, and then formed his own independent, sound judgments. His decisions, calmly and carefully considered, but definite in purpose, reminded me of a steam roller pursuing a determined, inexorable course. His quietness is deceptive. He is a deep thinker, a meticulous planner, and a person of unusual intuition and perception. The absence of bombast in a person of his achievements is one of his greatest attributes."

The same associate then described Spruance's influence in the Japanese-Philippine Peace Treaty. "His frank open manner and sincerity quickly warmed the Philippine people," he wrote. "During his early days in Manila ratification of the Japanese Peace Treaty became a matter of urgent business. John Foster Dulles, who was a chief negotiator of the treaty, had toured the Far East earlier without eliciting much enthusiasm in favor of ratification of the treaty. Feelings against the Japanese in the

Philippines at that time were probably more bitter than those in any of the other areas occupied by the Japanese forces. The lot of the Filipinos, who were regarded by the Japanese as 'puppets' of the United States, was a particularly severe one. In the face of this bitterness, and with the hope of encouraging approval of the treaty by the Philippine Senate, Ambassador Spruance invited each Philippine Senator singly and in turn to have breakfast with him at his residence. He quietly and with great logic pointed out to each Senator wherein lay his own and his country's best interests, leaving personal animosities and feelings aside. The Ambassador's sincerity and evident honesty were more persuasive than all the blandishments of flag waving could ever have been. Some of the Senators left the breakfast table convinced. Others promised carefully to reflect on the Ambassador's views. Few were opposed, but when the treaty finally came before the Philippine Senate for ratification, opposition to it had been greatly reduced by the efforts of Ambassador Spruance and the treaty was soon ratified. In working diligently for his own Government he never lost sight of the aspirations of the Philippine people, and the Senators with whom he talked could not help but realize it."

Still another embassy officer wrote this letter to Forrestel. "You ask if his appointment was acceptable to the regular Foreign Service personnel," he wrote. "I once heard a rather high ranking Foreign Service Officer (never attached to the Manila Embassy) refer to him as one of the finest men he had ever known but the world's worst diplomat. With that I would emphatically disagree, and I believe the great majority of the officers who served with him would feel the same way. For while they might fidget about his unconcern about protocol and the niceties of diplomatic double talk, they knew he was highly respected by the Filipinos and that he would always give the most careful attention to anything his staff suggested. Then too, their affection for him was such that they would have always supported him, right or wrong. I believe firmly that in the long run an Ambassador's most valuable assets will be his sincerity and understanding plus the ability, without fanfare, to convince the people of the country to which he is accredited that he believes it be his first and primary task to protect the interests of his own country. The Filipinos have had long and intimate contact with Americans, and they respect men like that. They can spot a phony a mile away. Over a period of forty years I saw a lot of well known Americans come and go, and it was always my impression that the Filipinos were faintly suspicious of people who courted popularity by excessive flattery. It was always men like Leonard Wood, Stimson and Spruance who were held in high respect even when the people did not always agree with them.

"On the little things the Admiral's simplicity of manner was his outstanding trait. He absolutely refused to allow the service attaches to put on their dress uniforms and accompany him as aides. He said he was not an Admiral then and was not supposed to have an aide. If the elevator was not available, and generally even when it was, he went up the two flights of stairs to his office two steps at a time while younger men with jaws dropping waited for the elevator. One thing I always chuckled about was his hatred for public speaking. I am sure that on the rare occasions when we were able to talk him into making a speech he approached it with far more nervousness than he ever did the Japanese fleet."

Chapter 26: The Final Years

This chapter is based almost entirely upon conversations with Mrs. Spruance and Mrs. Bogart.

INDEX

ABOUT THE EDITOR

JOHN B. LUNDSTROM is a naval historian and author of two books: *The First South Pacific Campaign: Pacific Fleet Strategy December 1941–June 1942* (Annapolis, 1976), and *The First Team: Pacific Naval Air Combat from Pearl Harbor to Midway* (Annapolis, 1984). He is currently working on the sequel to *The First Team*, which will cover carrier fighter operations in the Guadalcanal campaign. He holds B.A. and M.A. degrees in history from the University of Wisconsin-Milwaukee and is working towards his Ph.D. at the University of Wisconsin-Madison. He is an assistant curator of history at the Milwaukee Public Museum.

CLASSICS OF NAVAL LITERATURE

JACK SWEETMAN, SERIES EDITOR